# GROWTH, EMPLOYMENT AND INFLATION

John Cornwall, 1997.
Source: Findlay Muir, Dalhousie University

# Growth, Employment and Inflation

## Essays in Honour of John Cornwall

Edited by

## Mark Setterfield
*Associate Professor of Economics*
*Trinity College*
*Hartford*
*Connecticut*

First published in Great Britain 1999 by
**MACMILLAN PRESS LTD**
Houndmills, Basingstoke, Hampshire RG21 6XS and London
Companies and representatives throughout the world

A catalogue record for this book is available from the British Library.

ISBN 0–333–71794–5

First published in the United States of America 1999 by
**ST. MARTIN'S PRESS, INC.,**
Scholarly and Reference Division,
175 Fifth Avenue, New York, N.Y. 10010

ISBN 0–312–22013–8

Library of Congress Cataloging-in-Publication Data
Growth, employment and inflation : essays in honour of John Cornwall
/ edited by Mark Setterfield.
p.   cm.
Includes bibliographical references and index.
ISBN 0–312–22013–8 (cloth)
1. Economic development.   2. Capitalism.   3. Inflation (Finance)–
–Econometric models.   4. Unemployment—Effect of inflation on–
–Econometric models.   5. Economic history—1990–   I. Cornwall,
John.   II. Setterfield, Mark, 1967–   .
HD82.G755   1999
338.9—dc21                                                98–43273
                                                              CIP

This book is printed on paper suitable for recycling and made from fully managed and
sustained forest sources.

10   9   8   7   6   5   4   3   2   1
08   07   06   05   04   03   02   01   00   99

Printed and bound in Great Britain by
Antony Rowe Ltd, Chippenham, Wiltshire

# Contents

# List of Tables

# List of Figures

# Notes on the Contributors

**Philip Arestis** is Professor of Economics at the University of East London, England, having previously taught at the Universities of Surrey, Cambridge and Greenwich. He is joint editor of the *International Papers in Political Economy*, has served on the editorial boards of a number of journals and has been an elected member of the Council of the Royal Economic Society. Arestis has authored, co-authored, edited or co-edited numerous books, including *Post-Keynesian Monetary Economics: New Approaches to Financial Modelling* (as editor; 1988), *The Post-Keynesian Approach to Economics: An Alternative Analysis of Economic Theory and Policy* (1992) and *Money, Pricing, Distribution and Economic Integration* (1997). He has also published widely in journals and books in the fields of post-Keynesian economics, macroeconomics, monetary economics and applied econometrics.

**Villy Bergström** is editor-in-chief of the Swedish daily newspaper *Dala-Demokraten*, having formerly been a Ford Foundation visiting scholar at Stanford University, and Lecturer and Associate Professor at Uppsala University. He is responsible for establishing the Trade Union Institute for Economic Research (FIEF), an academic research institute owned by the LO, the Swedish blue collar trade union confederation. His most recent book is *Government and Growth* (as editor; 1997), part of the FIEF Studies in Labour Markets and Economic Policy series.

**Iris Biefang-Frisancho Mariscal** is Senior Lecturer in Economics at the University of East London, England, having previously been affiliated with the University of Münster. She has published in a variety of scholarly journals and books, including the *Journal of Post Keynesian Economics*, *Weltwirtschaftliches Archiv*, *Empirica*, *Applied Economics* and the *British Review of Economic Issues*, contributing to the fields of applied econometrics, macroeconomics, monetary economics and wage and unemployment determination.

**David Colander** is the Christian A. Johnson Distinguished Professor of Economics at Middlebury College, Middlebury, Vermont, USA, having previously taught at Columbia University, Vassar College and the University of Miami. He has authored, co-authored, or edited over 30 books and over 80 articles on a wide range of topics. These include *Principles of Economics* (1998), *History of Economic Thought* (with Harry Landreth; 1994), *Why Aren't Economists as Important as Garbagemen?* (1991), and *MAP: A Market Anti-Inflation Plan* (with Abba Lerner; 1980). His books have been, or are being, translated into a number of different languages, including Bulgarian, Polish, Italian, and Spanish. Colander has served on the boards of numerous economics societies and has been President of the Eastern Economic Association and the History of Economic Thought Society. He is currently on the editorial boards of the *Journal of the History of Economic Thought*, *Journal of Economic Education*, *Eastern Economic Journal*, and *Journal of Economic Perspectives*.

**Wendy Cornwall** is Professor of Economics at Mount Saint Vincent University, Halifax, Canada, and Adjunct Professor at Dalhousie University, Halifax, Canada. Before this, she held an appointment in the Economics Department at Dalhousie University. Her publications include *Economic Recovery for Canada: A Policy Framework* (with John Cornwall; 1984) and *A Model of the Canadian Financial Flow Matrix* (with J.A. Brox; 1989). She has published a variety of articles on the flow of funds, applied econometrics and economic growth, both in scholarly journals and in books. She is currently writing a book with John Cornwall for Cambridge University Press, entitled *Modelling Capitalist Development*.

**Rod Cross** is Professor of Economics at the International Centre for Macroeconomic Modelling, Department of Economics, University of Strathclyde, Glasgow, Scotland. His current research interests include the modelling of economic systems with hysteresis, and transition strategies for central Europe. In recent years, he has served on the HM Treasury Academic Panel and as a consultant to the Polish National Bank. He is the editor of *The Natural Rate of Unemployment: Reflections on 25 Years of the Hypothesis* (1995) and has published in such journals as the *Economic Journal, Journal of Political Economy, Scandinavian Journal of Economics* and *Review of Economics and Statistics*.

**Jan Fagerberg** is Professor of Economics at the University of Oslo, Norway, having previously been affiliated with the University of Aalborg, the Ministry of Finance and the Norwegian Institute for Foreign Affairs. His specific research interest is the impact of technology on trade and growth, and he has published extensively in books and major journals, including the *Economic Journal, Cambridge Journal of Economics* and *Journal of Economic Literature*. Fagerberg has served as a consultant to both the OECD and the European Union.

**John Foster** is Professor of Macroeconomics at the University of Queensland, Australia, having previously held positions at the Universities of Manchester, Glasgow, British Columbia and Adelaide. He has published a number of books on theoretical and applied evolutionary economics, including

*Evolutionary Macroeconomics* (1987), *Mixed Economics in Europe* (edited with Wolfgang Blaas, 1992) and *Economics and Thermodynamics* (edited with Peter Burley, 1994), and is responsible for developing a new statistical modelling methodology suitable for application to evolutionary environments. He has published in a variety of general and specialist journals, such as the *Economic Journal, Cambridge Journal of Economics, Journal of Evolutionary Economics* and *Structural Change and Economic Dynamics*.

**Geoff Harcourt** is Emeritus Reader in the History of Economic Theory at the University of Cambridge, England, Emeritus Fellow of Jesus College, Cambridge, England, and Professor Emeritus at the University of Adelaide, Australia. He has published many articles in learned journals and has authored or co-authored, edited or co-edited seventeen books, including *Some Cambridge Controversies in the Theory of Capital* (1972), five volumes of selected essays, and *A 'Second Edition' of The General Theory*, 2 vols (edited with P.A. Riach; 1997).

**Shaun Hargreaves Heap** is a Senior Lecturer in the School of Economic and Social Studies, University of East Anglia, Norwich, England. His research is in macroeconomics (with a focus on hysteresis and the effects of minimum wages) and in topics at the interface between philosophy and economics (particularly the concept of rationality). His publications include *Rationality in Economics* (1989), *The New Keynesian Macroeconomics* (1992), *Game Theory: A Critical Introduction* (with Y. Varoufakis; 1995) and articles in the *Economic Journal, Journal of Post Keynesian Economics* and *Kyklos*. He has recently started research on the economics of the media.

**Geoff Hodgson** is a Research Professor at the University of Hertfordshire Business School, Hertford, England and was formerly a Reader in Institutional and Evolutionary Economics at the University of Cambridge. His books include *Economics and Institutions* (1988), *After Marx and Sraffa* (1991), *Economics and Evolution* (1993) and *Economics and Utopia* (1998). Academic journals in which he has published include the *Journal of Economic Literature, Economic Journal, Journal of Economic Behavior and Organization*, and *Cambridge Journal of Economics*. A recent survey of academic opinion in Japan, carried out by the *Diamond Business Weekly*, ranked him as one of the top 23 economists of all time.

**John McCombie** is Fellow in Economics at Downing College, Cambridge, England, and a member of the Department of Land Economy at the University of Cambridge, England, having previously held positions at the University of Hull and Melbourne University. His research interests include the study of growth disparities between advanced countries, economic growth and the balance-of-payments constraint, Kaldorian growth models, the economics of Keynes, criticisms of the aggregate production function, and economic methodology. He has published in such journals as the *Economic Journal*, *Journal of Post Keynesian Economics*, *Oxford Economic Papers*, *The Manchester School* and *Urban Studies*, and is the author, with A.P. Thirlwall, of *Economic Growth and the Balance-of-Payments Constraint* (1994).

**Mehdi Monadjemi** is a Senior Lecturer in the School of Economics, University of New South Wales, Sydney, Australia. He has published in a variety of scholarly journals, including the *Economic Record*, *Australian Economic Papers*, *Applied Economics*, *Journal of Macroeconomics*, *Journal of International Money and Finance*, *International Economic Journal* and *International Review of Financial Analysis*.

**Basil Moore** is Professor of Economics at Wesleyan University, Middletown, CT, USA, and at the University of Stellenbosch, Stellenbosch, South Africa. He is the author of *An Introduction to the Theory of Finance: Assetholder Behavior Under Uncertainty* (1968), *An Introduction to Modern Economic Theory* (1973) and *Horizontalists and Verticalists: The Macroeconomics of Credit Money* (1988). He has published more than 100 articles in such journals as the *American Economic Review*, *Economic Journal*, *Journal of Finance*, *Canadian Journal of Economics*, *Economica*, *Cambridge Journal of Economics*, *Journal of Post Keynesian Economics*, *Scottish Journal of Political Economy*, *Eastern Economic Journal*, *Asian Economic Journal* and *South African Journal of Economics*.

**Pascal Petit** is Director of Research in Economy for the CNRS and is situated at CEPREMAP in Paris, France, a research institute affiliated with the French Commissariat du Plan. His research focuses on the issues of structural change, productivity gains and economic growth within the OECD. He has published various books and articles dealing with the nature and consequences of contemporary technical change and the effects of the service sector on the dynamics of economic growth, including *Slow Growth and the Service Economy* (1986), *The Economics of Industrial Modernization* (with Cristiano Antonelli and Gabriel Tahar; 1992) and, as editor, *L'economie de l'information* (1998).

**Steven Pressman** is Professor of Economics and Finance at Monmouth University, West Long Branch, New Jersey, USA. He is the North American Editor of the *Review of Political Economy* and Associate Editor of the *Eastern Economic Journal*. He has published over 50 articles and has written or edited seven books. His most recent books are *Economics and Its Discontents* (edited with Richard P.F. Holt; 1998), the *Encyclopedia of Political Economy* (edited with Phil O'Hara and Marc Lavoie; 1998) and *50 Major Economists* (1999).

**Kurt Rothschild** is Emeritus Professor of Economics at the University of Linz, Austria, having previously held positions at the Austrian Institute of Economic Research and the University of Glasgow. He is the holder of honorary degrees from the University of Aachen (1987), the University of Augsburg (1990), the University of Bremen (1995) and the University of Leicester (1995). He has written or edited numerous books, including *The Theory of Wages* (1954), *Power in Economics* (as editor, 1971) and *Ethics and Economic Theory* (1993), and has published articles in a variety of learned journals, including the *American Economic Review*, *Journal of Political Economy*, *Economic Journal*, *Kyklos* and *Weltwirtschaftliches Archiv*.

**Mark Setterfield** is Associate Professor of Economics at Trinity College, Hartford, Connecticut, USA. His principal research interests are macroeconomic dynamics and, in particular, theories and applications of path dependency in macroeconomics. He is the author of *Rapid Growth and Relative Decline: Modelling Macroeconomic Dynamics with Hysteresis* (1997) and has published in such journals as the *Cambridge Journal of Economics*, *European Economic Review*, *Journal of Post Keynesian Economics* and *The Manchester School*.

**Peter Skott** is Associate Professor of Economics at the University of Aarhus, Denmark. He is the author of *Conflict and Effective Demand in Economic Growth* (1989) and has published in a variety of journals, including the *International Economic Review*, *Economic Journal*, *Cambridge Journal of Economics*, *Oxford Economic Papers* and *Journal of Post Keynesian Economics*.

**Douglas Strachan** is Lecturer in Economics and Adviser of Studies at Strathclyde Business School, University of Strathclyde, Glasgow, Scotland. His research interests range from industrial economics and corporate finance to the economics of development and transition. He has held international placements and consultancies in Ghana, Ethiopia, Poland and Albania and his most recent publications can be found in *Kyklos* and the *Journal of Economic Studies*.

**Bart Verspagen** is Professor of the Economics of Technological Change in the Faculty of Technology Management, Eindhoven University of Technology, and at MERIT, Maastricht University, both in the Netherlands. His work focuses on the relationship between international trade, technological change and economic growth. He is an editor of *Structural Change and Economic Dynamics*, and has published in journals such as *Weltwirtschaftliches Archiv*, *Regional Studies*, *Technological Forecasting and Social Change* and the *Journal of Evolutionary Economics*.

# 1 Introduction

## Mark Setterfield

This volume of essays is a tribute to someone who has made numerous important contributions to macroeconomics over the past forty years, and who takes economics seriously. A life-long Keynesian and a tireless advocate of the importance of demand in the determination of both short- and long-run macroeconomic outcomes, John Cornwall, in his work, provides novel and illuminating discussions of a pantheon of economic issues. His contributions to growth theory include pioneering accounts (which are all too often unheralded as such) of the impact of technology transfers on relative growth rates, whilst there is no clearer and more forceful advocate of the need for permanent incomes policies in the pursuit of full employment with stable inflation. Neither can Cornwall's contributions to economic methodology be overlooked. Woven into his accounts of growth, inflation and unemployment outcomes are important discussions of the significance of institutions in determining these outcomes, and of the concomitant importance of building economic models in a manner that takes institutions into account. Discussions of the redundancy of traditional long-run equilibrium constructs and the promise of concepts of path dependency combine with the substance of his applied economics in an equally seamless fashion.

But contributing to economics does not necessarily involve taking economics seriously. The latter requires explicit recognition of the social significance of economics and what this implies about the appropriate pursuit of the discipline. In an age in which economics graduate students profess to attach little importance to knowledge of the economy and in which large parts of the discipline as a whole seem to be devolving into an intellectual game played according to internally defined rules,[1] it is refreshing to encounter in John Cornwall an economist who openly embraces the social significance of economics and whose work is explicitly motivated by a desire to change human society for the better or, to put it plainly, a desire to 'do some good'. It is this attitude, combined with the significance of his contributions, that has earned him such widespread appreciation and respect amongst his peers.

The essays that follow are organized into three main sections, pursuing themes related to economic methodology, economic growth and the political economy of unemployment and inflation respectively. The volume begins, however, with an intellectual biography of the honouree, courtesy of Geoff Harcourt and Mehdi Monadjemi. Written by two self-confessed admiring friends of John Cornwall, this essay functions on a variety of levels, providing

1

the reader with insights into the nature and importance of Cornwall's work, the strength and clarity of his 'pre-analytic vision' and resulting conception of how and why economics should be done, and the way in which he has guided and influenced his research students.

The six essays that follow this biography pursue broadly methodological themes. The chapters by Rod Cross and Douglas Strachan, Basil Moore and Mark Setterfield all address the issue of path dependence, which has played an ever increasing role as an organizing concept in John Cornwall's thinking over the past twenty-five years. Cross and Strachan begin by noting the growing free market triumphalism that has succeeded the retreat of welfarism and the collapse of communism over the past two decades, identifying financier George Soros as an important critic of this trend. Soros identifies current *laissez-faire* euphoria with a marked retreat from the Popperian notion that all knowledge is fallible. For Soros, economic knowledge is necessarily fallible because of reflexivity – the tendency of the economy to begin to behave in ways that imitate the manner in which it is described as behaving by economic analysts. Reflexivity implies that the economy is socially constituted and that its workings are, as a result, pliable and subject to redefinition. This creates an environment of fundamental uncertainty for decision-makers, in which the assuredness of absolute (that is, infallible) knowledge is necessarily absent. Because it is precisely such absolute knowledge that forms the basis of neoclassical equilibrium theory, Soros rejects the latter as a description of capitalism. As Cross and Strachan point out, this clears the ground for a reconstruction of economic theory using organizing concepts such as bounded rationality, complexity and hysteresis that are more faithful to the evolutionary, path-dependent dynamics of actually existing capitalism.

Basil Moore begins by distinguishing the complex from the merely complicated, on the basis that complex (unlike complicated) systems can never be understood simply as the sum of their individual parts. Moore goes on to discuss the applicability of the 'new science' of complexity to economics, placing particular emphasis on the self-organizing properties of complex systems – that is, their propensity to produce macroscopic emergent properties from the aggregate interactions of microscopic units – and the transformatory, evolutionary nature of this self-organization, which defies explanation/ description in terms of 'laws of motion'. Characteristics of actual economies are then shown to be akin to the characteristics of complex systems. The implications of this for economics are far-reaching. If the economy is an evolving complex system, thinking about its behaviour over time necessitates the abandonment of traditional, determinate long-run equilibrium models and the reductionist 'microfoundations' project.

The chapter by Mark Setterfield surveys John Cornwall's main contributions since his 1972 book *Growth and Stability in a Mature Economy*, with a view to illuminating the evolution of Cornwall's macrodynamic methodology over the past twenty-five years. Three macrodynamic models central to the corpus of Cornwall's work are identified. It is suggested that the central feature of the evolution of Cornwall's macrodynamic method is that it has moved ever further away from conventional equilibrium analysis towards an increasingly explicit emphasis on path dependence. The chapter goes on to demonstrate that studying the evolution of John Cornwall's macrodynamic methodology yields important insights for current researchers into how to go about modelling macrodynamics in path-dependent terms.

In addition to its increasingly explicit emphasis on path dependence, Cornwall's work also displays a keen awareness of the importance of institutions in determining macroeconomic outcomes and of the affinity between institutionalism and Keynesian macroeconomics, owing to the organic vision of economic relations that is common to both. This latter theme is central to Geoff Hodgson's chapter, which argues that Post-Keynesianism and institutionalism possess a shared vision of the economy characterized by anti-reductionism and a view of macroeconomics as a relatively autonomous subject. Moreover, it is suggested that, from a perspective informed by the history of economic thought, institutionalism deserves more credit for the ideas central to what eventually became known as the Keynesian revolution. Hence the notion of systemic emergent properties that cannot be accounted for by studying the parts of a system in isolation – the *raison d'être* of macroeconomics and, as also noted in Moore's essay, an idea that involves outright rejection of reductionism – is traced to C. Lloyd Morgan's influence on Thorsten Veblen. Furthermore, the notion of macroeconomics as a relatively autonomous inquiry is implicit in the work of Wesley Mitchell, whose pioneering contributions to national income accounting are based on a belief in the viability of studying 'mass phenomena' without first beginning with a theory of individual behaviour. Hodgson concludes that forging closer ties between Post-Keynesianism and contemporary institutionalism may provide a fruitful basis for continuing the revolution in economic thinking begun in the early part of the twentieth century, so much of which has since been badly distorted, forgotten or ignored.

The two remaining chapters in this first section are both, in large measure, assessments of the state of economics as a discipline. Both draw attention to the narrowness of the subject matter and methodology of contemporary economics, which provides a fitting if ultimately rather unfortunate (for the discipline) contrast with the scope of John Cornwall's work and his commitment to a socially relevant economics. Villy Bergström identifies a triumph of technique over substance in contemporary economic research. The key characteristic of the latter is its emphasis on the principle of optimization at the expense of social relevance. Bergström associates this emphasis with the broader socialization processes that mould economists before they enter the profession. Furthermore, he remarks on its capacity for replication due to the increasingly internal (to the discipline) criteria by which economists judge themselves. His conclusion is that few contemporary economists can usefully be called 'social scientists' and that the structure of the discipline offers little hope that this will soon change.

Kurt Rothschild touches on similar themes in his examination of the recent emergence of the term 'deregulation' as a catchword in economic policy-making circles. He argues that the only non-ideological basis for advocating general deregulation is that variant of general equilibrium analysis which conceives an economic 'state of nature' consisting of a system of markets capable of generating Pareto optimal outcomes. For Rothschild, this is a wholly inadequate framework, failing as it does to recognize that actually existing economies emerged from and are thus constituted by a mixture of economic and non-economic forces, both public and private. There is, then, no 'pure market' 'state of nature' and, as such, economic theorists need to be more like Bergström's 'social scientists' – actively embracing aspects of sociology, history and political science – if they are to form a proper appreciation of the issues surrounding deregulation. Rothschild identifies two partial but failed attempts to provide such an interdisciplinary theory of (de)regulation, but concludes by reaffirming the importance of economists' involvement in the deregulation debate if the latter is not to degenerate into a morass of subjective catchwords.

The second group of essays is devoted to themes related to economic growth. Few who are familiar with Post-Keynesian macrodynamics will fail to recognize the importance of John Cornwall's contributions to the economics of growth, especially in *Growth and Stability in a Mature Economy* (1972) and *Modern Capitalism: Its Growth and Transformation* (1977).[2] An outstanding feature of these works is their multisector approach to the analysis of growth, something that provides the point of departure for the first two chapters in this second section. Jan Fagerberg and Bart Verspagen begin by revisiting two of the key hypotheses in *Modern Capitalism* – the notion that the manufacturing sector acts as an engine of growth, and the idea that growth is influenced by the transfer of labour resources between more and less dynamic sectors of the economy. The question they address is whether or not these hypotheses are still relevant in the modern capitalism of the past twenty-five years. Fagerberg and Verspagen's tests of the engine of growth hypothesis reveal strong support for this hypothesis in newly industrializing and some less developed economies. No support for the hypothesis is found in advanced capitalist economies. This latter result emerges only after the exclusion of three outliers (including Japan) from the sample of advanced capitalist economies, however, leading the authors to suggest that the engine of growth hypothesis may explain some of the difference in growth rates between these outliers and the rest of the advanced capitalist group. Meanwhile, Fagerberg and Verspagen's results support the existence of a link between economy-wide growth and the transfer of labour between sectors. A particularly strong relationship emerges between increases in the employment share of the electrical machinery industry and overall productivity growth.

Contrary to the approach adopted by Post-Keynesians such as John Cornwall, who incorporate multisector analysis into a demand-led vision of long-run growth, recent neoclassical incursions into the analysis of multi-sector growth have adopted an explicitly supply-oriented approach. As John McCombie remarks, sectoral differences within the economy matter in neoclassical theory because of the possibility that certain sectors of the economy are characterized by higher marginal productivities of capital and/or labour, produce goods that complement productive activity in other sectors, or set technological and organizational standards that are imitated by other sectors. Empirical results appear to confirm that a variety of sectors – including the export and government sectors – do, indeed, play this 'lead sector' role in the determination of economy-wide growth rates. However, McCombie shows that the empirical models estimated in the neoclassical literature cannot support the interpretations that are imposed upon them, because of the relationships between these models and certain accounting identities. These relationships render alleged 'tests' of the neoclassical lead sector hypothesis infallible and therefore ultimately quite spurious. McCombie concludes that the neoclassical approach can therefore shed no light on the importance of sectoral differences for national growth rates.

Kaldor's model of cumulative causation has had an important influence on the direction and substance of John Cornwall's work on growth, and so it is fitting that this model should play a central role in the next two chapters. Pascal Petit's focus is the relationship between integration and convergence in per capita incomes within the European Union (EU) and, in particular, the extent to which more of the former is conducive to the latter. Studying this question within the framework of a Kaldorian model of cumulative causation enables Petit to revisit the tension between catch-up and divergence in the capitalist growth process explored in *Modern Capitalism*. It is shown that, in a Kaldorian model, the possibility of convergence is ultimately related to relative wage and profit dynamics on one hand, and relative technological trends on the other. As a result, if the effects of integration are uniform across countries, then integration has no direct effect on convergence. However, it may have indirect and country-specific effects on wage and profit dynamics which, under certain circumstances, favour convergence. Petit argues that these conditions prevailed during the initial phase of EU integration during the 1960s.

However, the author goes on to suggest that since the early 1970s, the EU has entered a new phase of (slower) growth accompanied by changes in the nature of integration and in the form of competition, with non-price competition supplanting the cost-based variety. It is shown that incorporating this new competition into the demand side of the Kaldorian growth model adds to the forces of divergence within this model. Furthermore, it is suggested that further integration within the EU since 1973 has enhanced the impact of this new source of divergence. Petit suggests that this may significantly affect the EU's chances of success, to the extent that a necessary condition for the latter is the reduction of current disparities in per capita incomes amongst member states.

Peter Skott examines Kaldor's model of cumulative, divergent growth based on increasing returns and sectoral differences in light of another of Kaldor's celebrated contributions to the economics of growth – the empirical regularities known as 'Kaldor's Laws'. Two formal models of divergent growth along Kaldorian lines are discussed. The argument that emerges is that the connection between these models and the growth laws is tenuous at best. In particular, this is because estimations of Kaldor's Laws treat the growth of manufacturing output as exogenous to the rate of growth of manufacturing productivity. But, as Skott points out, a positive feedback from manufacturing productivity growth to manufacturing output growth is essential for cumulative causation, the mechanism on which Kaldorian models of divergent growth are based. Skott concludes that debate over the empirical validity of Kaldor's Laws provides few clues as to the validity of Kaldor's underlying theoretical vision of the long-run growth process.

The final chapter in this section, by Shaun Hargreaves Heap, is centred upon the claim that in a world of decentralized, strategic decision-making, shared beliefs in non-instrumental norms that dictate 'right', 'proper' or 'just' behaviour in certain general, recurring circumstances can act as co-ordinating devices that result in Pareto superior outcomes as compared with the results of situations in which shared beliefs do not exist and purely instrumental decision-making rules are followed. According to Hargreaves Heap, these shared beliefs constitute 'social capital', something which serves to reduce conflict, litigiousness and so on at the point of production and in the process of exchange. Social capital will be beneficial to growth if it facilitates uninterrupted production, smooth technological change and so forth. It also bears obvious comparison to the sort of institutional structures which, in John Cornwall's theory of inflation dynamics, attenuate the inflationary bias emanating from unregulated distributional conflict at the point of production, thus enhancing 'macroeconomic efficiency' by reducing the need to rely on high unemployment as a disciplinary anti-inflation tool. Hargreaves Heap suggests that an important channel through which these shared beliefs about non-instrumental norms arise is discussion about aspects of popular culture, such as television shows or sporting events. This suggests that importance attaches to what television shows portray and the extent to which they are commonly experienced, since both will influence discussion in a straightforward fashion. Hargreaves Heap thus argues against the current trend towards increasing the play of 'market forces' in the provision of popular culture, through mechanisms such as pay-per-view television. These mechanisms ignore the social costs arising from the diminished construction of welfare-enhancing shared beliefs in non-instrumental norms that is associated with their erosion of common experience.

The final section of the book brings together five essays that discuss various theoretical and empirical aspects of the political economy of unemployment and inflation. Since the late 1970s, many of John Cornwall's major contributions to macroeconomics have placed central emphasis on the relationship between aggregate demand-constrained employment outcomes and inflationary pressures emanating from conflict over the appropriate distribution of income between capital and labour. His central concerns have been the tendency of policy-makers to use the former to 'solve' the latter by creating high unemployment regimes inimical to the bargaining power of workers, and the need for institutional solutions to an inflation problem that is essentially institutional in nature. Each of the chapters in this final section takes this vision as its point of departure.

The first three chapters, by John Foster, Steven Pressman and David Colander, are theoretical in nature. The focus of Foster's chapter is the rise in unemployment and the concomitant increase in the degree of income inequality in the OECD economies over the past twenty-five years. He deplores the retreat of economic theory from the historical/evolutionary vision of Marshall and Keynes into the static/mechanical metaphors of contemporary neoclassicism, championing Schumpeter as an adherent of the former approach. For Foster, an advantage of Schumpeter's work is its explicit focus on the long-run. Hence, whereas investment appears as a single expenditure category in Keynes's short-run theory, Schumpeter delineates between different types of investment depending on their intended impact on the structure of the firm. Foster postulates that these different types of investment have different effects on unemployment, growth and distributional outcomes, and that current high unemployment/high inequality outcomes are the result of an evolutionary change in the structure of investment since the Second World War, away from research directed at product and process innovation and towards the introduction of cost-cutting methods of production.

David Colander revisits the issue of wage and price (in)flexibility and the existence of Keynesian unemployment equilibria. Colander takes a Post-Walrasian view of inflexible wages and prices, in which the latter form wage–price 'regimes' that help to coordinate economic activity by contributing to the institutional macrofoundations of microeconomic behaviour. From this Post-Walrasian perspective, perfectly flexible wages and prices – the *sine qua non* of conventional Walrasian economics – would only help to undermine the institutional 'operating system' within which economic activity is framed, resulting in inferior macroeconomic outcomes as compared to a regime of wage and price inflexibility. A clear result of the chapter, then, and a source of affinity with Keynesian economics, is that the benefits of wage and price flexibility are model-specific and, as such, may not exist at all in the real world.

As with Colander, Steven Pressman's concern is with the fundamental nature of macroeconomics and macroeconomic outcomes. This time, however, the author critiques the Post-Keynesian view that money is essential to the explanation of unemployment, arguing instead that central importance attaches to features of the production process. By examining a series of hypothetical economies, Pressman shows that involuntary unemployment is unlikely to emerge in a self-employment economy but is likely in a wage labour economy – regardless of whether trade involves the use of credit or commodity money, or is based purely on barter. He therefore concludes that the money-using feature of modern capitalist economies is not the ultimate cause of unemployment in these economies, which is, instead, their relations of production (specifically, the existence of wage labour). Pressman does argue, however, that money *exacerbates* the problem of unemployment, so that Post-Keynesian policies designed to reduce unemployment in actual, money-using economies remain valid.

The two remaining chapters, by Philip Arestis and Iris Biefang-Frisancho Mariscal, and Wendy Cornwall, are empirically oriented discussions of the high unemployment that has been witnessed over the past twenty-five years. Arestis and Biefang-Frisancho Mariscal focus specifically on unemployment in the UK and Germany. Despite the current fashion for supply-side explanations of European unemployment based on real wages that are too high and/or the absence of appropriate incentives to work, they emphasize the role of aggregate demand – and, in particular, investment spending – in explaining persistent high unemployment in the UK and Germany. The notion is that high unemployment can be associated with capital shortages. Restrictive aggregate demand policies designed to curb distributional conflict and hence wage and price inflation lead to capital-scrapping, but this capital is not automatically replaced once restrictive aggregate demand policies are abandoned. The result is that unemployment remains high unless some other inducement to increase investment is introduced. Arestis and Biefang-Frisancho Mariscal present preliminary empirical evidence suggesting that this is a plausible explanation of persistent high unemployment in both the UK and Germany, with both countries seemingly stuck in a 'low-level equilibrium' characterized by low rates of investment, normal rates of capacity utilization and high unemployment over the past twenty-five years. The authors conclude with a call for monetary and fiscal polices conducive to increasing the rates of capital formation in both countries.

It is fitting that the final essay in the volume is authored by Wendy Cornwall, whose collaborations with John over the past fifteen or so years have produced some of the central contributions to the applied economics of growth, inflation and unemployment that are associated with the Cornwall name. She contends that, contra the received wisdom of vertical Phillips curve analysis, in which unemployment is a purely economic problem based on an equilibrium defined in terms of supply-side variables, aggregate demand influences unemployment and does so in a way that is vitally conditioned by an economy's institutional framework. The latter is seen as being of particular significance in determining both the position of the unemployment/inflation trade-off and the socio-political preferences of a society, reflecting its willingness to trade off higher unemployment for lower inflation. This gives rise to a model of optimal unemployment based on the societal maximization of preferences for different combinations of unemployment/inflation rates, subject to the constraint imposed by the Phillips curve. Given the institutional determinants of both the social preference mapping and the Phillips curve, what emerges is a testable model in which unemployment is a function of various institutional variables. Estimation of this model provides clear support for the hypothesis that institutions, which condition macroeconomic outcomes through their influence on the optimal combination of unemployment and inflation rates, play a central role in the determination of unemployment outcomes in the OECD economies.

### Notes

1. See Klamer and Colander (1990) on the first point and Bergström's essay in this volume on the second.
2. Although, as Harcourt and Monadjemi remind us in their biography, some of the central themes of these volumes were taking shape in the 1950s and 1960s and are evident in Cornwall's earlier research papers.

### Reference

Klamer, A. and D. Colander (1990) *The Making of an Economist*, Boulder, CO, Westview Press

# 2 The Vital Contributions of John Cornwall to Economic Theory and Policy: A Tribute from Two Admiring Friends on the Occasion of His 70th Birthday

Geoff Harcourt and Mehdi Monadjemi

## INTRODUCTION

G.H. first met John Cornwall in 1963 and M.M. was his doctoral student at Southern Illinois University from 1970 to 1972. John and G.H. were both on leave from their respective universities (Tufts and Adelaide) in Cambridge during the latter's most exciting decade of the postwar years. Ken Arrow and Bob Solow were both spending a year there, Solow to give the Alfred Marshall Lectures on two mythical creatures, 'Joan' and 'Nicky' (with only one of the real creatures, Joan, able to attend, as Nicky was in Australia). Frank Hahn and Robin Matthews were writing Hahn and Matthews (1964) and Piero Sraffa's (1960) book had only recently been published. The 'Secret Seminar' was in full flight and the members of the Faculty of Economics and Politics (which included the Department of Applied Economics) read almost like a *Who's Who* in modern economics, young and old. John and G.H. saw a great deal of each other; G.H. found John to be the nearest to an Australian an American was ever likely to be! They had endless discussions on economics and other matters. John wrote a comment (entitled 'Wham') on the first draft of Hahn and Matthews's survey of growth theory, and advised G.H. on the two-sector model which he was then developing (Harcourt, 1965), introducing him to the term 'recursive' to describe the method used in it.

M.M. met John at Southern Illinois University in Carbondale in 1970 as a graduate student in a seminar course in advanced macroeconomics. The course was offered in the autumn of 1970, its purpose being to generate ideas for graduate students to pursue in their doctoral dissertations. A dozen students enrolled, all enthusiastic to gain inspiration from the professor of economics newly appointed from Tufts University. Given his distinguished background – Cornwall had been a student of James Duesenberry's and he had published several articles in prestigious economic journals, such as the *American Economic Review*, the *Quarterly Journal of Economics* and the *Review of Economics and Statistics* – we felt proud to be his students. John based the course on monetary transmission mechanisms, with particular emphasis placed on the countercyclical behaviour of housing in the United States. His approach was likely a result of his working at that time on Cornwall (1972), or else his observation of the two severe downturns in housing construction in the United States in 1966 and 1969. He introduced us to many leading articles in the area of housing cycles, although it became clear that no previous study had emphasized disintermediation as a prime cause of housing downturns, as did John (see Cornwall, 1972).

Because I was so impressed by John's teaching and research leadership in the seminar course, I enthusiastically enrolled in another of his courses (on economic dynamics and growth) in the winter of 1971. So many students had become aware of Cornwall's reputation by then that the class was three times larger than the previous one. Almost all of the economics graduate students participated. John directed us towards many leading articles in growth theory including Harrod (1959) and Domar (1947), where for full employment of labour and capital to be maintained, output must grow at the warranted rate which, in turn, must equal the natural rate of growth. He also introduced us to several articles by Robert Solow, including Solow (1956, 1957, 1970), and also Denison's (1964) embodied technological growth model. During the semester, he referred to his conversations with Solow and discussed the neglected role of demand in neoclassical growth theories. This objection is still relevant and is still apparent in John's recent writings on growth (see Cornwall, 1970; Cornwall and Cornwall, 1994).

The remainder of this chapter is organized as follows. Cornwall's major intellectual contributions to M.M.'s economic thinking are discussed in the penultimate section, following G.H.'s discussion of John's contributions to economic theory and policy.

## CORNWALL'S GROWTH SCHEMA

When John came to Cambridge in the autumn of 1963, he had more in common with the first generation of Keynesians – Austin and Joan Robinson, Richard Kahn, Nicky Kaldor, Dick Goodwin – than with the more neoclassical (though also Keynesian) economists either encamped or visiting – James

Meade, Robin Matthews, Frank Hahn of the locals, Ken Arrow and Bob Solow of the visitors. He had just published his lead article in the *QJE*, 'Three paths to full employment growth' (1963), and was reading Alexander Lamfalussy's *Investment and Growth in Mature Economies* (1961). The seeds of the first of his six (to date) great books were being planted (see Cornwall, 1972, 1977, 1983, 1990, 1994; Cornwall and Maclean, 1984).

In those days, Cornwall was an optimistic and enthusiastic Keynesian as far as his theoretical structures were concerned. (Another great influence was his PhD supervisor at Harvard, James Duesenberry, especially the approach which Duesenberry took to growth and cycle theory. To John, Duesenberry 'was the first economist [he] had known who understood the need for economic theory to have explanatory power' (Cornwall, 1992, p. 98)). He was also vitally interested in the long-term historical episodes of modern capitalist economies, the formation of institutions and their role in the political economy of societies. His politics were left-wing by any standards and remarkably so by those of the USA – he and Arrow were doves on the Vietnam War, for example, whilst the need for conscious intervention by the state in economic life was never a stumbling block for John, either then or now. He was (and remains) a vigorous democrat who hated injustice and underprivilege and who wished to see them eliminated, especially if they arose from needless malfunctionings of the economic system.

John was keenly interested in but also most critical of growth theory, both Keynesian and neoclassical alike. His starting point was a profound critique of Harrod's basic approach, which implied that the warranted and natural rates of growth, $g_w$ and $g_n$ respectively, could be analysed as though their values were independent of each other – as though the factors responsible for one were entirely, or at least overwhelmingly, separate from those responsible for the other. John regarded this as an incorrect extension of the Marshallian distinction between demand and supply and of the factors responsible for them to the analysis of the economy as a whole. How can it be argued that $g_n$ is independent of $g_w$ (and vice versa)? For surely the potential rate of growth of the economy due to the growth of the labour force and of its efficiency due to technical advances (neutral or biased) cannot be regarded as independent of the demand factors subsumed in $g_w$? The rate of growth of potential productivity is directly dependent on the rate at which new things are embodied by investment in the stock of capital goods (and, now increasingly, in the stock of human capital as well). That is to say, it is dependent on effective demand and the rate of accumulation, the latter either being equal to $g_w$, or related to it in the sense that the ways in which rates of actual accumulation move depend upon their relationships (and those of planned accumulation) to $g_w$ itself.

So growth in a Keynesian setting has to be seen at the very least as the outcome of the interrelationships of the supply and demand factors underlying

$g_w$ and $g_n$, taking into account the considerable overlap involved, especially in the direction $g_w \rightarrow g_n$, though Cornwall initially stressed the relative strength of $g_n \rightarrow g_w$ in a system of some mutual determination. Hence $g_n$ itself can affect expectations and therefore whether or not actual growth equals $g_w$. John's approach to the theory of growth was always to proceed from this basic foundation, one which leads immediately to path-dependent processes and the notion of cyclical growth (in the sense of Goodwin) rather than to steady-state growth (separate from the cycle) in the sense of the Keynesians, or the pure neoclassicals or even the neoclassical Keynesians, such as Meade, Solow and Swan.[1]

Another of John's criticisms of conventional growth theory concerned its neglect in any but the most mechanical sense of technical progress. Repeatedly we find him arguing that in the real world, technical advances and demand changes leading to the need for large structural changes in economies are so rapid that models which concentrate on the properties of the ultimate steady-state equilibria on which the model economies converge (if they do) have little relevance. This is because the calendar time required for this convergence process is so much greater than the calendar time necessary for changes in technical knowledge (and their application) and in tastes and demand to occur. The latter are often induced through advertising and other devices. John was also critical of the almost universal use of perfectly competitive microeconomic market structures in growth theory. These points of view made him, on the one hand, as critical of Joan Robinson's and Richard Kahn's Golden Age analysis as of the Solow/Swan model and, on the other, partial to Kaldor who, while he thought of steady growth as a 'stylized fact', was nevertheless always impatient to have his models apply directly to real world situations. John's approach rejected the strategy of Joan Robinson, Kahn and also Pasinetti of going through the preliminary stage of Golden Age analysis in order to get various key relationships clear and concepts defined in the simplest but also the most abstract setting.

## PHASES OF CAPITALISM

With this theoretical approach, John set about interpreting the various phases of the history of capitalism, using the OECD countries as his laboratory and extending and modifying his basic models as postwar capitalism moved through its 'Golden Age' – the 'long boom', as the Marxists called it – to the unstable 'stagflation' era and now to the most recent phase of relative stagnation (when compared to the mostly remarkable performances of economies during the 'long boom') and inflation rates near or at the 'Golden Age' values. At each stage, Cornwall has identified both the strengths and weaknesses of the economy, distinguishing between transient characteristics and those likely to last. He has also identified the presence of contradictions, whether inherent in the workings of the systems themselves, or resulting from faulty diagnosis by policy-makers or the deliberate designs of the dominant classes in society. John has always robustly, even brutally, called spades spades!

In recent years, Cornwall has become increasingly gloomy about the possibility of implementing sensible and enlightened policies in the advanced capitalist economies whether they act alone or together (which he now sees as necessary if not sufficient if these economies are to overcome their individual and collective problems). The problem is not so much one of diagnosis, though this is a serious problem in its own right, but lack of political courage, wisdom and goodwill in political decision-making centres. John remains faithful to Keynes – to his economic analysis, views on the educational role of economists, and on the role of the state and its public servants, whose motivation may be summed up in Harrod's (1951, pp. 183, 192–3) phrase, 'the presuppositions of Harvey Road'. This last referred to the class of intelligent, well-trained and disinterested persons who analysed situations, gave advice, and were driven by a desire to make their societies more rational, fair and humane rather than to maximize their incomes or status (though the latter often occurred if they were good at their jobs).

Having made coherent and explicit the sources of the strengths and weaknesses of the years of the 'long boom', John turned to the subsequent phases. There he identified at least two major factors at work: first, the increasing dominance of the Keynesians by the monetarists, and then, the new classical macroeconomists, that is to say, the return to dominance of those whom Keynes dubbed the classical economists in the provision of explanation and policy. In particular, this implied a resurgence of the view that a capitalist economy is strongly self-regulating provided only that competitive institutions rule in all its markets and activities – and especially in its labour markets. Large domestic monopolies or oligopolies are but the powerless price-takers of the competitive model when set in the world scene, according to Milton Friedman who, at the same time, would cheerfully smash a labour union whenever he saw one.

Second, John identified as a major issue the implementation of the recommendations of the McCracken Report (1977), the authors of which were mostly pragmatic Keynesians who were turning their attention to the emergence of inflationary pressures. The latter were associated with the profound sociological changes that had taken place over the course of the 'long boom', whereby the balance of political, social and economic power had moved progressively from capital to labour (with the leaders of labour itself becoming the most articulate, educated and confident set in history); the breakdown of the Bretton Woods institutions and 'rules of the game'; the financing of the war in Vietnam in the USA as though the US economy were a peacetime one; and the first oil shock.

Cornwall singled out for detailed criticism the McCracken strategy of a short sharp shock to the system – read: quickly create high levels of unemployment – to rid it once and for all of inflationary expectations, coupled with the belief that the system would then move back to the full employment trend rate of growth of the Golden Age with (early) Golden Age rates of inflation. John could not accept this analysis because he felt that it lacked a proper understanding of the behaviour of the labour market and of the behaviour of business people in general. He attributed much of the successful performance in the early to middle years of the 'long boom' to the behaviour of labour itself. In many of the OECD economies, labour voluntarily imposed self-restraint on money-wage increases. This allowed notions of 'fairness' with regard to increases in real wages and patterns of wage relativities to be met by the underlying growth in productivity, redistributions through taxes and expenditure in the public sector, and full employment itself. (Not all OECD countries were so blessed: John distinguishes two main models, the one described above which he calls 'a social bargain strategy' (Cornwall, 1997, p. 400), the other 'a market power strategy' (Cornwall, 1997, p. 399). In the latter, wage settlements are the outcome of a collective bargaining process in which little account is taken of common interest or national goals.)

John also believed that the relatively fixed exchange rate regimes operating in the years of the 'long boom' and especially the controls on capital movements kept speculation in check and allowed any deficits in the balance of payments, themselves not alarmingly large in those countries which experienced them, to be addressed without resort to unduly drastic retrenchment policies.

## INSTITUTIONAL CHANGE AND ECONOMIC BREAKDOWN

The happy conjunction of events and results that characterized the 'Golden Age' unravelled during the next twenty years or so. Well-established norms were ruptured towards the end of the period, labour generally became more militant and strove for maximum gains from the money-wage bargain regardless of the systemic outcome, and disillusionment with 'big government' became increasingly widespread both within and between countries. John analyses what he dubs the systemic 'inflationary bias' which emerged as the 'Golden Age' progressed. This is associated with real wage resistance and the 'fair' pattern of wage relativities, neither of which would be surrendered in the event of an exogenous shock to the system – oil price rises, for example, or secular changes in the terms of trade which necessitate real income adjustments. He feels that attempts to rid the economy of its inflationary tendencies by contracting demand are doomed to failure because whatever short-term success they may have will not be maintained. This is partly (but importantly) because contraction has a negative impact on the rate of accumulation which in turn affects the rate of growth of productivity. When the upturn, either natural or policy-induced, occurs, there is not a high enough rate of growth of productivity to meet the renewed money-wage demands without the resurgence of inflation, especially as wage-earners aim at increases in real wages which embody a catch-up element. Cornwall, like Marx and Keynes, appreciates that the processes at work in capitalism often imply basic contradictions, that the measures taken to get labour and its costs under control (the euphemism is flexible labour markets) adversely affect the 'animal spirits' and so the desire of capitalists to invest. Those in the real world, as opposed to the mathematical models of it, know that reviving 'animal spirits' after a policy-induced shock is an incredibly difficult task to perform quickly, or even at all. This is especially so when financial capital dominates industrial and commercial capital, so that the rewards for risk-taking appear, and often are, much greater and more obvious in the former's sphere than in the latter's. As a result, long-term real investment projects associated with much-needed structural change are increasingly neglected, not least because the brightest (if not necessarily the best) are attracted to the huge rewards from finance capital.

These destabilizing elements have been reinforced by other institutional changes, especially the floating of exchange rates and the deregulation of financial markets, together with the huge technical advances which have tended to make at least the financial aspects of the operations of capitalism 'one-world capitalism'. Devaluations are likely to be ineffective, partly because of real wage resistance, partly because of the huge rise in the proportions of total foreign exchange transactions accounted for by speculative transactions. This leads to one-way speculative-induced movements of currencies which greatly affect the domestic cost of living (through increases in the prices of imports, importables and exportables) in the countries concerned. John may be inclined to revise this generalization a little following the recent British experience. In autumn 1992 the UK was forced to leave the European Exchange Rate Mechanism and, as a consequence, experienced the devaluation which many British Keynesians were advocating. The then Tory government ridiculed their suggestion until it was forced upon them. They then attributed the beneficial results of the devaluation, including the absence of the offsetting reactions which John had predicted, to their own coherent, explicit policy wisdom.[2]

Increasingly, John has been adopting a hysteresis analysis of labour markets, combined with a critique of the usefulness of the concept of the natural rate/ NAIRU. He rejects the first variant because he does not accept that the world may be thought of as a competitive Walrasian general equilibrium system in the way in which that fine Marshallian scholar, Milton Friedman, first defined the natural rate, so that the latter was a resting place without any involuntary unemployment present. John is, of course, willing to concede that in any situation-specific episode, there could be a level of statistical unemployment (or indeed levels) at which the forces making for accelerating price rises would be offset by those making prices go in the other direction, resulting in a sustainable constant rate of change of prices.[3] However, he is not willing to admit that such a position has any optimum or necessarily desirable properties – much less, that it would be free of undesirable, unacceptable levels of involuntary unemployment and worsening distributions of income and property. He also criticizes those who come some way to meet him by admitting that not all unemployment at the NAIRU is voluntary, only to claim that, nevertheless, it is all classical, associated with 'too high' real wages rather than a lack of effective demand. Indeed, he believes that real wages can never be too high because they are set in the product market (except in the unlikely case where the labour force is governed by one big monopoly union).

## FINANCIAL DISINTERMEDIATION AND THE HOUSING CYCLE

My main encounter with John Cornwall was when he agreed to be my dissertation supervisor. It was an honour to be able to write a dissertation under his supervision. The problem of choosing an appropriate topic was quickly resolved when John suggested an empirical study of postwar housing cycles in the United States, using quarterly flow of funds data. He stressed the use of quarterly data because annual data are incapable of showing the turning points of households' portfolio substitution and mortgage flows during short cycles. John strongly supported the idea of housing-led recovery, a view that is now dominant in industrial countries with developed financial sectors.

Many studies in the 1960s (such as Albert, 1962; Guttentag, 1961; Maisel, 1963; Sparks, 1967) attempted to provide theoretical explanations for the postwar housing cycles in the United States. John's explanation departed from these studies, however, by taking account of 'the portfolio adjustments undertaken by the household sector in response to changes in different yield differentials' (Cornwall, 1972, p. 185) and emphasizing the supply of funds and the process of disintermediation as a primary cause of housing cycles (Cornwall, 1972, pp. 173–201). He argued that most of the liabilities of thrift institutions (TIs) (savings and loan associations and mutual savings banks) are held by households. Furthermore, during the 1960s and 1970s, 75 per cent of total residential mortgage flows were, on average, accounted for by TIs. Naturally, any significant change in the liabilities of TIs would produce a substantial change in total mortgage flows and residential construction expenditure. John stressed the process of 'disintermediation' as a major cause of downturns in the housing market. In fact the word 'disintermediation' was introduced in the financial literature during the so-called credit crunch of 1966, when all of the financial intermediaries in the United States experienced an unusual loss of deposits to the capital market. The main cause of disintermediation is a rise in the rates on capital market instruments relative to the rates paid by financial intermediaries on their deposits. This change in the yield differential provides an incentive for households and other depositors at financial intermediaries to reduce or withdraw their funds and place them directly on the market. In the 1960s, the widening of the yield spread between securities and deposits was mainly due to the inflexibility of the rates paid on deposits. This rigidity was in turn due to the long-term nature of the assets held by the intermediaries which caused a slow turnover of their portfolio. At a time when market rates were rising, if these institutions had attempted to increase their deposits and match the increase with an increase in rates on their assets, the higher rates on deposits would have applied to all deposits, whereas the higher rates on assets applied only to newly acquired assets, which were a fraction of total deposits.

At the time, mortgage rates in the United States were fixed for the life of the mortgage. During tight money periods, the yield spread between capital market instruments and deposits widened and the flow of deposits into financial intermediaries declined. This process of disintermediation in turn affects mortgage lending and expenditure on housing. The most severe bout of disintermediation occurred during the unusually tight money period of 1966, when all financial intermediaries experienced a drastic loss of deposits to the capital market. This development forced financial intermediaries to reduce their mortgage lending and was soon followed by a sharp decline in residential construction expenditures. Similar and equally severe developments occurred during 1969. In short, John argued that 'thrift institutions are an important source of construction loans to tract builders. If the flow of funds into these thrift institutions is cut back, as it would be in a process of disintermediation, mortgage lending and housing must be affected, unless other lenders make up for the cutback in mortgage lending by thrift institutions' (Cornwall, 1972, p. 116).

The title of my dissertation, which involved a theoretical and empirical analysis of housing cycles in the United States during the postwar period, was 'Savings Deposits, Residential Mortgage Credit, and Housing Starts'. Guided by John, the theoretical part of the study emphasized household portfolio adjustments and the consequent effects of these adjustments on mortgage flows and housing expenditure. The empirical analysis employed quarterly flow of funds data, which was relatively new at the time, building an econometric model for TIs' savings deposits and mortgage flows. John also suggested that the dynamic properties of the model would shed some light on the countercyclical behaviour of residential construction during the postwar period.

Most of the studies from the 1960s that attempt to explain the countercyclical behaviour of housing assume that the demand for commercial credit is sensitive to changes in aggregate economic activities, but relatively insensitive to the cost of funds, whereas the demand for mortgage credit is sensitive to the terms of credit but relatively stable with respect to changes in economic activities. Moreover, lenders have a high cross-elasticity of demand for mortgages with respect to bond yields. Based on these assumptions, changes in aggregate economic activities create forces which cause mortgage flows and residential construction to move countercyclically. John remarked on the need to provide some form of analytical explanation for the countercyclical behaviour of housing. Figure 2.1, an extract from my dissertation, summarizes my response to his suggestion.

In Figure 2.1, *DM* and *SM* are the demand for and supply of residential mortgage funds and $Or_0$ and *OA* are the initial equilibrium mortgage rate and quantity of mortgage funds, respectively. *DF* and *SF* are the demand for and supply of non-housing funds and $O'r_0'$ and $O'A'$ are the initial equilibrium bond yield and quantity of funds respectively. As aggregate economic activity increases, *DF* shifts to the right more than *DM*, hence bond yields rise relative to mortgage rates, that is, $r_0'r_1' > r_0r_1$. Given lenders' high cross-elasticity of

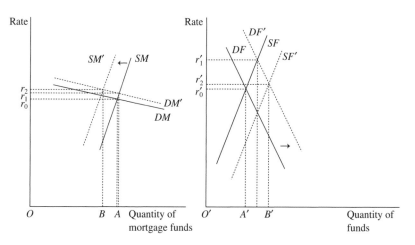

*Figure 2.1* The market for residential mortgage and non-housing funds

demand for mortgages with respect to bond yields, they shift from mortgages to bonds, hence $SF$ shifts to $SF'$ and $SM$ shifts to $SM'$, and the supply of mortgage credit declines. This causes the mortgage rate to rise to $Or_2$ and with a highly elastic demand for mortgage funds, the quantity of mortgages demanded falls, $OB < OA$. On the other hand, the equilibrium quantity of non-housing funds expands, that is, $O'B' > O'A'$. When economic activity decreases, the opposite movements take place and the equilibrium quantity of mortgage funds demanded and supplied increases.

Cornwall (1972, pp. 117–18) argues that 'during the boom, as the demand for loanable funds begins to outstrip the supply, interest rates, especially those on primary securities, begin to rise absolutely and relative to rates paid on fixed-price near monies. This induces the non-financial domestic holders of funds to bypass financial intermediaries, and to place them directly in the capital markets.' Anderson (1964) shows that in the tight money periods of 1953, 1957 and 1959, the inflow of deposits into the Boston mutual savings banks were at their lowest levels, whilst outflows in the form of withdrawals were at their highest levels. A similar type of development was experienced by savings and loan associations when, from 1960 to 1968, their inflow of deposits declined by 1.8 per cent.

My supervisor wanted to see an econometric study of housing cycles emphasizing changes in the flow of funds as a source of instability in the housing market. Sparks (1967) comes close to adopting this approach. His study places heavy emphasis on the mortgage market and the flow of savings deposits at the financial intermediaries. Sparks's regression results may be criticized, however, for estimating the supply of mortgage credit without using a mortgage rate in the equation. It is difficult to interpret Sparks's regression as a supply function, because it is neither a reduced form model nor a true supply function which should include a mortgage rate. Sparks's study can also be criticized for using annual data. John encouraged me to use quarterly data to explain households' responses to changes in capital market conditions and the effect of such changes on mortgage lending. The response of savings deposits to changes in the market rate of interest is so quick that low-frequency data may fail to indicate these responses.

The main object of my dissertation was to develop an econometric model capable of testing the hypothesis proposed in Cornwall (1972), that fluctuations in residential construction are largely explained by changes in the flow of funds at thrift institutions. The model consisted of an equation for changes in household holdings of savings deposits at the TIs, and a simultaneous equation model for the mortgage market consisting of a demand and a supply function. The statistical results, based on quarterly data from 1953 to 1970, produced a statistically significant coefficient for the yield spread between the savings rate and the corporate bond rate in the equation for savings deposits. Furthermore, simulation experiments indicated that changes in interest rates lead to changes in mortgage flows and housing cycles ahead of cycles in economic activity, and in particular that changes in the yield differential between TIs' deposit rates and corporate bond rates in recession and boom periods are consistent with the countercyclical behaviour of mortgage flows at thrift institutions. In short, my dissertation showed that the salient role played by TIs in conjunction with the inflexibility of savings deposit rates account for the countercyclicality of the housing market – precisely the view that is maintained in Cornwall (1972).

It is interesting that widespread bankruptcy among major mortgage lenders during the early 1980s has been attributed to the substantial disintermediation that occurred during this period. From 1980 to 1986 about 600 out of 4000 TIs failed (Brumhaugh, Carron and Litan, 1989). Brumhaugh and Carron (1987) blame regulatory constraints and the inability of TIs to adapt to rising interest rates for the crises of 1980s, drawing renewed attention to a point first emphasized in Cornwall (1972). It seems that John's perceptive conjectures during the 1960s and 1970s were all too amply confirmed by the experience of the 1980s.

## CONCLUSION

John has always had a fiercely independent mind; he was scornful of the mainstream equilibrium economics which dominated the courses when he first became an economist.[4] As he reveals in his fascinating autobiography in Arestis and Sawyer (1992), he approached economics by reading widely in the originals of his own and other disciplines, ultimately developing an approach that has embraced the dynamic analysis of growth and distribution, historical knowledge and an awareness of how institutions form, change and affect economic processes. To read his books – again, as an independent free spirit, he has resisted the fashionable cringe to the natural scientists' approach of only publishing articles – and see his views evolve as concrete situations change is both a privilege and an inspiration to his friends and admirers, ourselves amongst them. So happy 70th birthday, John, and here's to many more birthdays, appropriately interspersed with your enlightening and courageous writings.

**Notes**

1. It is significant that Solow (1994, p. 379) has recently stated his agreement with this view (even though those who followed his initial lead have usually missed the point entirely).
2. In a comment on a draft of this chapter John wrote: 'What I maintained in the 1990 and 1994 books was that devaluations *accompanied by AD policies aimed at*

*achieving full employment* would fail, because the devaluations would be offset by speculation and real wage resistance. The 1992 devaluation worked because, unlike Mitterand's efforts in the early 1980s, it was not accompanied by strong stimulative AD policies.' (Emphasis in original)

3.     Indeed, he stresses that many such positions may exist at any given point in time. This claim is important because it makes Cornwall's long-run Phillips curve (LRPC) negatively sloping, not vertical. All of the points along this negatively-sloping LRPC involve stable inflation, with the realized outcome depending on aggregate demand and the policies that affect it. The entire structure is then subject to hysteresis effects, as movements along the LRPC can also result in shifts in the position of the LRPC itself.

4.     John suggests that his response was based on measured argument rather than scorn, but we think he combined both!

## References

Albert, W.W. (1962) 'Business cycles, residential construction cycles, and the mortgage market', *Journal of Political Economy*, 70, 263–81

Anderson, P. (1964) 'Mutual savings banks and tight money,' *New England Business Review*, January, 10–11

Arestis, P. and M. Sawyer (eds) (1992) *A Biographical Dictionary of Dissenting Economists*, Aldershot, Edward Elgar

Brumhaugh Jr, D. and A. Carron (1987) 'Thrift industry crises: causes and solutions', *Brookings Papers on Economic Activity*, 2, 349–455

Brumhaugh Jr., D., A. Carron and R. Litan (1989) 'Cleaning up the depository institution mess', *Brookings Papers on Economic Activity*, 1, 243–83

Cornwall, J. (1963) 'Three paths to full employment growth', *Quarterly Journal of Economics*, 77, 1–25

Cornwall, J. (1970) 'The role of demand and investment in long-term growth', *Quarterly Journal of Economics*, 84, 48–69

Cornwall, J. (1972) *Growth and Stability in a Mature Economy*, London, Martin Robertson

Cornwall, J. (1977) *Modern Capitalism: Its Growth and Transformation*, London, Martin Robertson

Cornwall, J. (1983) *The Conditions for Economic Recovery: A Post-Keynesian Analysis*, London, Martin Robertson

Cornwall, J. (1990) *The Theory of Economic Breakdown: An Institutional–Analytical Approach*, Oxford, Basil Blackwell

Cornwall, J. (1992) 'John Cornwall', in P. Arestis and M. Sawyer (eds)

Cornwall, J. (1994) *Economic Breakdown and Recovery: Theory and Policy*, Armonk, NY, M.E. Sharpe

Cornwall, J. (1997) 'Notes on the trade cycle and social philosophy in a post-Keynesian world', in G.C. Harcourt and P.A. Riach (eds)

Cornwall, J. and W. Cornwall (1994) 'Growth theory and economic structure', *Economica*, 61, 237–51

Cornwall, J. and W. Maclean (1984) *Economic Recovery for Canada*, Toronto, James Lorimer

Denison, E.F. (1964) 'The unimportance of the embodied question', *American Economic Review*, 54, 90–4

Domar, E.D. (1947) 'Expansion and employment', *American Economic Review*, 37, 34–5

Guttentag, J. (1961) 'The short cycle in residential construction, 1946–59', *American Economic Review*, 51, 275–98

Hahn, F.H. and R.C.O. Matthews (1964) 'The theory of economic growth: a survey', *Economic Journal*, 74, 779–902

Harcourt, G.C. (1965) 'A two-sector model of the distribution of income and the level of employment in the short run', *Economic Record*, 41, 103–17

Harcourt, G.C. and P.A. Riach (eds) (1997) *A 'Second Edition' of The General Theory*, 2 vols, London, Routledge

Harrod, R.F. (1951) *The Life of John Maynard Keynes*, London, Macmillan

Harrod, R.F. (1959) 'Domar and dynamic economics', *Economic Journal*, 69, 451–64

Lamfalussy, A. (1961) *Investment and Growth in Mature Economies*, New York, Macmillan

McCracken, P., G. Carli and H. Giersch (1977) *Towards Full Employment and Price Stability*, Paris, OECD

Maisel, S.J. (1963) 'A theory of fluctuations in residential construction starts', *American Economic Review*, 53, 359–83

Monadjemi, M. (1972) 'Savings deposits, residential mortgage credit, and housing starts', unpublished PhD dissertation, Department of Economics, Southern Illinois University

Pasinetti, L.L. and R.M. Solow (eds) (1994) *Economic Growth and the Structure of Long-Term Development*, London, Macmillan

Solow, R.M. (1956) 'A contribution to the theory of economic growth', *Quarterly Journal of Economics*, 70, 65–94

Solow, R.M. (1957) 'Technical change and the aggregate production function', *Review of Economics and Statistics*, 39, 312–20

Solow, R.M. (1970) *Growth Theory*, Oxford, Oxford University Press

Solow, R.M. (1994) 'Concluding comments', in L.L. Pasinetti and R.M. Solow (eds)

Sparks, G.R. (1967) 'An econometric analysis of the role of financial intermediaries in postwar residential building cycles', *Determinants of Investment Behavior*, New York, National Bureau of Economic Research

Sraffa, P. (1960) *Production of Commodities by Means of Commodities. Prelude to a Critique of Economic Theory*, Cambridge, Cambridge University Press

# Part I

# Reflections on the Methodology and Practice of Economics

# 3 Soros on 'Free Market' Equilibria

Rod Cross and Douglas Strachan

During the 1990s, the ideology of the 'free market' has come to dominate much of the world. As far as individual behaviour is concerned the nostrum is that the largely untrammelled pursuit of self-interest is most conducive to the common economic good, and at the aggregate level the prescription is for a minimalist or 'nightwatchman' state as far as intervention in markets is concerned.

The collapse of the communist regimes in Central and Eastern Europe has had much to do with this mood of 'free market' triumphalism. Decades of central planning had left the former communist countries with dilapidated economies so, *post hoc ergo propter hoc*, the only viable solution was seen as embarking on a transition to 'free market' economies. Further along the spectrum, social market economies in Western Europe are diagnosed as having high unemployment rates because of the lack of flexibility in their labour markets, so the cure is seen to be the dismantling of barriers to labour market flexibility (OECD, 1994). Deviant behaviour can be checked by IMF surveillance:

> the economics profession has not discovered the magic formula that assures rapid and steady economic growth, low inflation, financial stability, and social progress . . . however, based on experience across many countries, a consensus has emerged about the broad guidelines for policies that serve these goals . . . achieving high rates of sustainable economic growth depends primarily on private-sector activities . . . market-orientated economic systems with high levels of competition are generally more efficient in allocating resources to meet consumer needs and to support worthwhile investment and growth. (Mussa, 1997, pp. 28–9)

Given the strong claims that have been made with regard to the efficacy of 'free market' systems of resource allocation, it is worth reexamining some of the foundations on which the argument is based. Critics of *laissez-faire* in the nineteenth century tended to focus on how market forms of exchange subverted established norms of social exchange: 'never, on this earth, was the relation of man to man long carried on by Cash-payment alone . . . if, at any

27

time, a philosophy of *Laissez-Faire*, Competition and Supply-and-Demand, start up as the exponent of human relations, expect that it will end soon' (Carlyle, 1874, p. 235). A prime concern for Engels and Marx was the alienation arising from labour being treated as a commodity. Rather than socialist revolutions, however, the more advanced capitalist countries experienced *laissez-faire* modified by the growth of trade unions and by the establishment of welfare state provision for those at the bottom of the heap.

Towards the end of the twentieth century, however, the wheel turned towards emasculation of trade union powers and the dismantling of many welfare state provisions, particularly in large tracts of Western Europe deemed to have become sclerotic because of reduced exposure to market disciplines. From the 1940s to the 1970s many states accepted responsibility for maintaining a sufficient level of aggregate demand to ensure 'full' employment. Since then this commitment has largely been replaced by a commitment to achieve low rates of inflation, with the deregulated market-place being assigned the role of determining the 'natural' level of real economic activity. It is this 'free market' system that is presented to the transition economies in Central and Eastern Europe and elsewhere as the only viable recipe for economic success.

The task in the present essay is to discuss the warnings of the dangers of placing too much faith in 'free markets' that have, ironically enough, been expressed by a market operator *par excellence*, the financier George Soros:

> although I have made a fortune in the financial markets, I now fear that the untrammeled intensification of *laissez-faire* capitalism and the spread of market values into all areas of life is endangering our open and democratic society . . . the main enemy of the open society, I believe, is no longer the communist but the capitalist threat. (Soros, 1997, p. 45)

At the heart of the Soros caveats regarding 'free market' ideology is his view that the underpinning provided by the neoclassical analysis of demand, supply and market equilibria is fundamentally flawed. The obvious retort is 'so what?', given that many practitioners view economic analysis as being out of touch with the 'real' world, without bothering to propose alternative analytical constructs that would be relevant to actual economic behaviour. What makes Soros interesting is that he does indicate how economic analysis needs to be reconstructed, and that his proposals are based on a reasonably clear understanding of the philosophy of scientific knowledge.

The next section discusses the epistemological basis for the Soros critique of 'free market' nostrums. In the following section we focus on the Soros critique of neoclassical equilibrium analysis and ask how economic analysis can be reformulated to accommodate the Soros objections. The final section concludes.

SOROS ON EPISTEMOLOGY

Soros left his native Hungary in 1947 and took an economics degree at LSE in the early 1950s (see Soros (1995) and Slater (1996) for, respectively, autobiographical and biographical details). At LSE he was exposed to the ideas of his intellectual amuensis, Karl Popper. The influence of Popper's *Open Society and its Enemies* resulted in an initially unpublished treatise, *The Burden of Consciousness*, completed in 1962, which 'was very much a regurgitation of his [Popper's] ideas' (Soros, 1995, p. 33). The other main influence was Popper's account of the logic of scientific knowledge. Soros accepted Popper's account of the fallible, conjectural nature of scientific knowledge, but objected to the idea that the methods appropriate in the natural sciences could be applied in the social, including economic, sphere:

> Karl Popper has proposed the doctrine of the unity of science: the same methods and criteria apply in the study of both natural and social phenomena ... I consider the doctrine misguided ... there is a fundamental difference between the two pursuits: the subject matter of the social sciences is reflexive in character, and reflexivity destroys the separation between statement and fact which has made the critical process so effective in the natural sciences ... the very expression 'social science' is a false metaphor; it would seem more appropriate to describe the study of social phenomena as alchemy, because the phenomena can be moulded to the will of the experimenter in a way that natural substances cannot. (Soros, 1995, p. 269)

**Openness and values**

One basic way that 'free market' nostrums could pose a threat to open societies is if those proposing such ideas claim to know the truth, or have a monopoly of knowledge as to the most efficacious way to organize economic systems. This would be inconsistent with the recognition of the fallibility of knowledge about the external world that characterizes open societies. Knowledge is encapsulated in hypotheses that cannot be demonstrated to be true, because the logic of *modus ponens* applies only to purely axiomatic constructs. Instead only the logic of *modus tollens* can be applied, which means that hypotheses are conjectures whose implications are subject to refutation.

The question is then one of how tolerant societies in the 1990s are of alternatives to the ideology of *laissez-faire*. As far as the main political parties are concerned, in countries such as the USA, the UK, France and Germany, it is difficult to identify major differences in the degree of commitment to 'free markets' within each country, and international organizations such as the IMF and World Bank discourage deviations from the 'free market' approach. The governing party may change, but *plus ça change* as far as economic policies are concerned.

The obvious retort is that from the 1940s to the 1970s doctrines of state intervention in the market-place and Keynesian commitments to full employment held sway in the countries in question, and were common ground between the main political parties. The societies in question were then open enough to allow the resurrection of *laissez-faire* doctrines, so is there any good reason to fear that interventionist doctrines will not be able to resurface as and when the fallibilities of the *laissez-faire* approach become manifest? Election campaigns now seem to be dominated by clashes between marketing strategies rather than policies or ideas, but are the media concerned not open to the transmission of other than the 'free market' message?

The problem for Soros is that 'economic theory takes values as given', yet

> market values served to undermine traditional values . . . as the market mechanism has extended its sway, the fiction that people act on the basis of a given set of nonmarket values has become progressively more difficult to maintain . . . advertising, marketing, even packaging, aim at shaping people's preferences rather than, as *laissez-faire* theory holds, merely responding to them . . . unsure of what they stand for, people increasingly rely on money as the criterion of value . . . people deserve respect and admiration because they are rich – what used to be a medium of exchange has usurped the place of fundamental values, reversing the relationship postulated by economic theory . . . what used to be professions have turned into businesses . . . the cult of success has replaced a belief in principles . . . society has lost its anchor. (Soros, 1997, pp. 51–2)

### Fallibility and imperfect knowledge

In the Soros critique a further threat to the open society arises from the neoclassical postulates about economic behaviour that often underlie the case for *laissez-faire*. The basic problem is that the postulates assume that economic agents have 'perfect' knowledge of the environment in which they operate. Take a modern, rational expectations, formulation of the neoclassical maximization hypothesis: each agent maximizes an objective function subject to some perceived constraints; and the constraints perceived by the agents in the system are mutually consistent. This is a strong assumption: 'the decisions of one person form parts of the constraints upon others, so that consistency, at least implicitly, requires people to be forming beliefs about others' decisions, about their decision processes and even about their beliefs' (Sargent, 1993, p. 6).

If the rational expectations hypothesis were true, it would be possible for agents to know the equilibrium probability distributions for the events about which they form expectations. This clashes with the basic Popper–Soros premise that knowledge is fallible. Economists themselves do not know what such distributions are, and are obliged to use econometric and other techniques to estimate probability distributions and 'laws' of motion. The resulting inferences are fallible and fragile, as is apparent from the disagreements amongst economists: 'rational expectations models impute *more* knowledge to the agents within the model (who use the *equilibrium* probability distributions in evaluating their Euler equations) than is possessed by an econometrician, who faces estimation and inference problems that the agents in the model have somehow solved' (Sargent, 1993, p. 3; emphasis in original). Hence the rational expectations hypothesis is implausible because it attributes knowledge to economic agents that even economists or econometricians do not, and could not, have. Thus neoclassical economic analysis, according to Soros, is dangerous in that it fails to take as its point of departure 'the imperfect understanding of the participants (recognition of which is the basis of the concept of the open society) and the indeterminacy of the process in which they participate' (Soros, 1997, p. 50).

**Reflexivity**

The key to the Soros account of the difference between the physical sciences and social sciences such as economics is that in the latter the economic agents who are trying to acquire knowledge of their economic environment are also participants whose behaviour affects the economic environment they are trying to understand. The obvious objection is that observations in the physical sciences are also theory-dependent, with, say, observations of subatomic particles being at least in part generated by hypotheses speculating that such particles exist. The Soros reply is that 'Heisenberg's famous uncertainty principle implies that the act of observation may interfere with the behaviour of quantum particles . . . but it is the observation that creates the effect, not the uncertainty principle itself . . . in the social sphere, theories have the capacity to alter the subject matter to which they relate' (Soros, 1997, p. 50). As far as perceptions of the world are concerned, it is not clear that the Soros distinction holds: different theories in the physical sciences do lead to different perceptions of the subject matter, and can form the basis for different interventions, in the form of, say, 'splitting the atom', that change the underlying subject matter.

The self-referential aspects of hypotheses underlie the Soros notion of reflexivity: 'on the one hand, reality is reflected in people's thinking – I call this the cognitive function; on the other hand reality is affected by people's decisions – I call this the participating function – these events have a different structure from the events studied by natural science – they need to be thought about differently . . . I call these events reflexive' (Soros, 1995, p. 14). Soros argues that the presence of reflexivity means that knowledge of economic behaviour is inherently more fraught with uncertainty than knowledge in the physical sciences. Presumably this is because all agents in economic systems are 'scientists' in the sense that they formulate conjectures about their economic environment, and change the economic environment when acting on the basis of their conjectures. But part of their economic environment is the conjectures made by other economic agents, so the agents are involved in guessing games such as those invoked in Keynes's beauty contest analogy (Keynes, 1936, p. 156). So the actual economic outcomes about which economic conjectures are formed rest in part on a bootstrap involving a potentially infinite regress of conjectures about conjectures. In the event of a particular agent's conjecture being wrong it will be difficult or impossible to disentangle whether the blame lies with incorrect understanding of 'fundamentals', or with incorrect guesses as to the conjectures other agents have used as the basis for their actions.

As discussed in the next section of this chapter, the presence of reflexivity, according to Soros, invalidates the neoclassical conception of equilibrium, or of how market prices are determined:

> In the absence of equilibrium, the contention that free markets lead to the optimum allocation of resources loses its justification . . . the supposedly scientific theory that has been used to validate it turns out to be an axiomatic structure whose conclusions are contained in its assumptions and are not necessarily supported by the empirical evidence . . . the resemblance to Marxism, which also claimed scientific status for its tenets, is too close for comfort . . . I do not mean to imply that economic theory has deliberately distorted reality for political purposes . . . but in trying to imitate the accomplishments (and win for itself the prestige) of natural science, economic theory attempted the impossible. (Soros, 1997, p. 50)

Neoclassical economists drew their metaphors about the workings of economic systems from Newtonian mechanics or conservative fields of force (see Mirowski, 1989). According to Soros, the presence of reflexivity in economic behaviour implies that it is more appropriate to draw metaphors from Newton's writing on alchemy: 'the alchemists made a big mistake trying to turn base metals into gold by incantation . . . with chemical elements alchemy doesn't work . . . but it does work in the financial markets, because incantations can influence the decisions of the people who shape the course of events' (Soros, 1995, p. 221).

## ALCHEMY AND EQUILIBRIUM ANALYSIS

In neoclassical equilibrium analysis the positions of supply and demand curves are independent of each other in the sense that they are pinned down, respectively, by conditions of production and preferences that are taken to be given independently of each other. This assumption, according to Soros, is invalid because of the presence of reflexivity:

> the condition that supply and demand are independently given cannot be reconciled with reality, at least as far as the financial markets are concerned – and financial markets play a crucial role in the allocation of resources . . . buyers and sellers in financial markets seek to discount a future that depends on their own decisions . . . the shape of the supply and demand curves cannot be taken as given because both of them incorporate expectations about events that are shaped by those expectations . . . there is a two-way feedback mechanism between market participants' thinking and the situation they think about – 'reflexivity' . . . instead of tending towards equilibrium, prices continue to fluctuate relative to the expectations of buyers and sellers . . . there are prolonged periods when prices are moving away from any theoretical equilibrium . . . even if they eventually show a tendency to return, the equilibrium is not the same as it would have been without the intervening period. (Soros, 1997, pp. 49–50)

Taken at face value, this suggests that in economic systems 'everything depends on everything else', where the 'everything else' includes agents' heterogeneous perceptions of the world and of the perceptions of other agents. How then can economic systems be analysed? The apparent nihilism of this position, most evident in *The Alchemy of Finance* (1987, 1994), is partly dispelled by the sharper distinction between *near-equilibrium* and *far-from-equilibrium* conditions drawn in Soros (1995). In *near-equilibrium* conditions, 'the discrepancy between thinking and reality is not very large and there are forces at play that tend to bring them close together, partly because people can learn from experience, and partly because people can actually change social conditions according to their desires' (Soros, 1995, p. 69). In such situations rules of thumb, such as Keynes's convention 'that the existing state of affairs will continue indefinitely', are compatible with 'a considerable measure of continuity and stability in our affairs' even though 'philosophically speaking, [they] cannot be uniquely correct, since our existing knowledge does not provide a sufficient basis for a mathematical calculation' (Keynes, 1937, p. 152).

The Soros *far-from-equilibrium* conditions arise because, as in Keynes, market valuations are established as 'the outcome of the mass psychology of a large number of ignorant individuals' and because there are 'no strong roots of conviction to hold it steady' (Keynes, 1936, p. 154). In Soros, 'the prevailing bias and the prevailing trend reinforce each other until the gap between them becomes so wide that it brings a catastrophic collapse' (Soros, 1995, p. 70). Economic agents can have only fallible knowledge of their economic environment, but are obliged to use such hunches as guides to action. Thus instead of being driven by perfect knowledge of probability distributions covering market equilibria:

> participants cannot confine their thinking to facts . . . they must take into account the thinking of all participants including themselves . . . instead of a correspondence, there is almost always a discrepancy between participants' perceptions and the actual state of affairs and a divergence between the participants' intentions and the actual outcome . . . misconceptions and mistakes play the same role in human affairs as mutation does in biology. (Soros, 1995, p. 68)

In this world perceptional or expectational errors do not lead to temporary deviations from fixed-point or fixed-path equilibria, as in the neoclassical world, but instead are endogenous sources of change in the basic structure of economic systems.

**Bounded rationality**

The question, then, is one of how economic analysis can be constructed to deal with fallible knowledge and reflexivity. An obvious first step is to drop the strong rationality assumptions embodied in the rational expectations hypothesis, and focus instead on the behavioural context of decisions, as in Herbert Simon's notion of bounded rationality. This involves populating economic models with agents who use heterogeneous heuristic devices as decision rules, and postulating how these decision rules are updated or revised in the light of experience. Instead of assuming, as in the rational expectations hypothesis, that agents have worked out how the complex system in which they participate behaves, the way the system itself behaves is the outcome of the heuristic devices used by the agents.

An example of this approach is provided in Sargent (1993), where boundedly rational models 'expel rational agents from our model environments and replace them with "artificially intelligent" agents who behave like econometricians . . . these "econometricians" theorise, estimate and adapt in attempting to learn about probability distributions which under rational expectations, they already know' (Sargent, 1993, p. 3). Drawing an analogy between economic agents and econometricians appears absurd until it is recognized that the procedures available to econometricians to revise their specifications in response to refutations are 'typically informal, diverse and implicit' (Sargent, 1993, p. 22). As Duhem pointed out, there may be good reason to revise a theory in a particular way in the event of its implications being refuted, but 'these reasons of good sense do not impose themselves with the same implacable rigor that the reasons of logic do . . . there is something vague and uncertain about them . . . they do not reveal themselves at the same time and with the same degree of clarity to all minds . . . hence the possibility of lengthy quarrels' (Duhem, 1954, p. 217). The use of the analogy between economic agents and econometricians also serves to embed the Soros self-referential notion of reflexivity: 'such a system can contain intriguing self-referential loops, especially from the standpoint of macroeconomic advisers, who confront the prospect that they are participants in the system they are modelling, at least if they believe that their advice is likely to be convincing' (Sargent, 1993, p. 23). Soros himself doubts whether it is feasible to close the self-referential loops in such a system (Soros, 1995, p. 220), though he clearly has not been reduced to a state of puzzled indecision by the potentially infinite regress of self-referential loops.

## Complexity

In many sciences the traditional emphasis has been the reductionist one of attempting to discover successively finer-grain explanations of phenomena. In economics this trait has been mirrored by the insistence that macro models have micro foundations. During recent decades this emphasis has been countered by an interest in models of complexity, wherein the problem is to explain how complex systems can arise from basic elements that are taken to be irreducible or given (see Anderson, Arrow and Pines, 1988). This is the approach recommended by Soros:

> it is high time to liberate social phenomena from the straitjacket of natural science, especially as natural science itself is undergoing a radical change . . . analytical science is superseded in certain fields by the study of complexity . . . the analytical sciences are confined to closed systems . . . that is why they can produce determinate results . . . the science of complexity studies open, evolutionary systems . . . it does not expect to produce deterministic predications, or explanations . . . all it seeks to do is to build models or run simulations – this has been made possible by the development of computer technology – or produce vague, philosophic generalisations without the predictive power of Popper's model. (Soros, 1995, p. 220)

An application of this approach to financial markets is provided in Brock and Hommes (1996). The model is populated with agents who use different heuristic devices in the form of different trading rules: some extrapolate current trends – the 'trend is your friend'; others bet against the trend, believing that what goes up must come down; some traders use 'fundamental' economic forces to second-guess market prices; and yet others see market prices as reflecting the weights of the different trading rules adopted by other traders. The traders in such a system are then postulated to modify or change their beliefs in light of how the initial rules perform in terms of generating trading profits, which act as 'fitness' functions. Thus trading rules, and hence market prices, evolve according as to whether the trading rules adopted by particular agents allow them to survive in the market-place (see Arthur, Holland, Le Baron, Palmer and Taylor, 1994). In this set-up economic agents and their hypotheses or decision rules evolve in tandem: 'just as species, to survive and reproduce, must prove themselves by competing and being adapted within an environment created by other species, in this world hypotheses, to be accurate and therefore acted upon, must prove themselves by competing and being adapted within an environment created by other agents' hypotheses' (Arthur, 1994, p. 408).

### Hysteresis

Neoclassical economic analysis was based in metaphors drawn from Newtonian mechanics:

> scarcely a writer on economics omits to make some comparison between economics and mechanics . . . one speaks of a 'rough correspondence' between the play of 'economic forces' and mechanical equilibrium . . . another compares uniformity of prices to the level-seeking of water . . . another (Jevons) compares his law of exchange to that of the lever . . . another (Edgeworth) figures his economic 'system' as that of connected lakes of various levels . . . in fact the economist borrows much of his vocabulary from mechanics . . . instances are: equilibrium, stability, elasticity, expansion, inflation, contraction, flow, force, pressure, resistance. (Fisher, 1892/1925, p. 24)

This borrowing was not merely pedagogic in nature, but also served to import the classical principles of *conservation*, *symmetry* and *reversibility* (see Feynman, 1992) into the analysis of economic systems. These principles in turn mean that standard economic analysis assumes that economic systems are *homeostatic* or self-adjusting, in that disturbances that move economic systems away from equilibria are followed by a reversion to the initial equilibria once the disturbances abate (see Arrow, 1988).

In the Soros *near-equilibrium* conditions this *homeostatic* analysis may offer a tolerable approximation. But in his *far-from-equilibrium* conditions reflexive behaviour is not consistent with a return to the *status quo ante* once disturbances abate: 'there are prolonged periods when prices are moving away from any theoretical equilibrium . . . even if they eventually show a tendency to return, the equilibria is not the same as it would have been without the intervening period' (Soros, 1997, pp. 49–50).

In arguing that economic systems are not homeostatic, Soros has intellectual forebears of some stature. Marshall argued that

> the theory of stable equilibrium . . . does not diverge from the actual facts of life so far as to prevent its giving a fairly trustworthy picture . . . it is only when pushed to its more remote and intricate logical consequences . . . that it slips away from the conditions of real life . . . if the normal production of a commodity increases and afterwards again diminishes to its old amount, the demand price and the supply price are not likely to return, as the pure theory assumes that they will, to their old positions for that amount. (Marshall, 1890, pp. 425–6)

Marshall then proceeds to point out that temporary disturbances are likely to be accompanied by the acquisition of different preferences, on the demand side, and by changes in the cost of production, on the supply side. Thus, once the disturbances abate, the legacy will be new equilibria occasioned by the induced changes in conditions of demand or production, rather than a return to the *status quo ante*. At a more aggregate level, Keynes answered his own question, 'is the economic system self-adjusting?', in the negative: economic systems would not return to some unchanged 'full employment' equilibrium after deflationary shocks such as those experienced by the UK during the years immediately preceding the return to gold in 1925 (Keynes, 1934).

If economic equilibria are not deemed to be *homeostatic*, the question arises of how *heterostatic* equilibria can be analysed. Once obvious route involves changing the metaphor from Newtonian mechanics to *hysteresis* in fields of force (see Cross (1993) for the lineage of this metaphor). Two necessary conditions for hysteresis are *heterogeneity* in the elements that make up the system, and *non-linear* responses to disturbances. The Soros world is populated with agents having heterogeneous hypotheses or decision rules with which they interact reflexively, so the first *heterogeneity* condition is present. To introduce the second condition of *non-linear* responses all that needs to be invoked is the presence of fixed costs of agents adjusting their behaviour, so imparting increasing returns to adjustment processes. Given that most economic adjustments occur discontinuously, in large doses, this is not an implausible assumption. Firms, for example, usually face fixed, sunk costs of investment or market entry which cannot be fully recouped should the investment project be abandoned or the firm exit the market (Dixit and Pindyck, 1994). This makes it plausible to postulate two-way switching rules: the economic environment $E$ faced by an agent has to reach some upper switching value $H$ to induce the agent to adjust behaviour upwards, and has to reach some lower value $L$ in order to induce the agent to switch downwards.

If the Soros view of the world is reconstructed in such a way the implication is hysteresis (see Krasnosel'skii and Pokrovskii (1989) for the general mathematical analysis). Such systems display remanence, in that the application and removal of a disturbance will not be followed by a return to the *status quo ante*. This can be seen intuitively by considering an agent initially faced by an economic environment $E_1$, with $L < E_1 < H$. If the environment 'improves', raising $E$ to some $E_2 \geq H$ the agent will go ahead with a particular decision. But if the economic environment then 'deteriorates' back to $E_1$ the agent will not reverse the initial decision to go ahead, but will remain active: the initial decision would only be reversed if the environment deteriorated to some $E \leq L$.

The second key property of such systems with *hysteresis* is one of *selective memory*: each new extremum value of the disturbances experienced shapes a new equilibrium for the system, but only the *non-dominated extremum values* of the disturbances are retained within the memory bank. The intuition behind this property is that each agent, at a particular point in time, is characterized by some $(H, L)$ combination of switching values, but heterogeneity means that the switching values differ between agents. This means that each extremum value of disturbances to the environment $E$ changes the partition between agents who have adjusted their behaviour in response to the disturbance, and those who have not. Over time the partition is a palimpsest on which the relative sizes of successive disturbances is written. Thus a major expansionary disturbance will wipe the memory of lesser disturbances from the system's memory, and contractionary disturbances that are more severe than previously experienced will have similar effects in the opposite direction. In this framework the hypotheses or switching rules of agents can be allowed to interact reflexively with the environment, with the hypotheses or switching rules of agents interacting with the disturbances experienced to shape the successive equilibria that emerge (see Amable, Henry, Lordon and Topol (1995) and Cross (1994, 1995) for economic applications of this framework). Thus economic equilibria and the hypotheses or switching rules of agents co-evolve in response to the disturbances experienced.

## IMPLICATIONS

The theme of this essay has been that Soros not only provides a critique of standard equilibrium analysis in economics but also makes constructive suggestions as to how economic analysis might be reformulated.

Perhaps the most fundamental criticism of standard economic analysis raised by Soros is that it endows economic agents with knowledge, in the form of probability distributions governing market equilibria, that they could not have. Even if economics were a 'science', economic agents would at best be able to make only fallible conjectures about their economic environment.

Economists and econometricians themselves do not, and could not, have the knowledge that standard analysis bestows on economic agents. The obvious way forward, then, is to 'dumb down' economic agents to the level of economists. Such agents/economists have different hypotheses about their economic environment, often disagree with each other, and have only informal means of revising their hypotheses in the light of experience.

For Soros, however, economics is not a science because of the self-referential nature of economic hypotheses. If a particular hypothesis is promising at least some agents are likely to use it as a basis for action. Thus hypotheses in economics are reflexive in the sense that they are capable of changing the world that is their subject matter. Incantations can work, so economics is more akin to alchemy than science. The nagging doubt here is that this holistic argument, in which thought, objects of thought and human intervention interact, could, if pushed to extremes, also cloak the physical sciences in alchemy.

Such doubts aside, the Soros critique provides a useful antidote to the overstatement of the case for 'free markets' provided by standard economic analysis. The confidence with which the 'free market' ideology is touted rests uneasily with the common perception of economics as being a disputatious, all-too-fallible pursuit. The discipline of economics is actually a broad church in which alternative views of the way economic behaviour is conducted, and of the way economic systems work, continue to be debated. It is useful that Soros has reminded the general public of this state of affairs. Let the debate about how economic behaviour is coordinated and about the appropriate degree of intervention in markets remain open.

## References

Amable, B., J. Henry, F. Lordon and R. Topol (1995) 'Hysteresis revisited: a methodological approach', in R. Cross (ed.) *The Natural Rate of Unemployment: Reflection on 25 Years of the Hypothesis*, Cambridge, Cambridge University Press

Anderson, P.W., K.J. Arrow and D. Pines (eds) (1988) *The Economy as an Evolving Complex System*, Redwood City, CA, Addison-Wesley

Arrow, K.J. (1988) 'Workshop on the economy as an evolving complex system', in P.W. Anderson, K.J. Arrow and D. Pines (eds)

Arthur, W.B. (1994) 'Inductive reasoning and bounded rationality', *American Economic Review*, 84, 406–11

Arthur, W.B., J.H. Holland, B. Le Baron, R. Palmer and P. Taylor (1994) 'An artificial stock market', mimeo, Santa Fe Institute

Brock, W.A. and C.H. Hommes (1996) 'Models of complexity in economics and finance', mimeo, University of Wisconsin

Carlyle, T. (1874) *Past and Present*, London, Chapman & Hall

Cross, R. (1993) 'On the foundations of hysteresis in economic systems', *Economics and Philosophy*, 9, 53–74

Cross, R. (1994) 'The macroeconomic consequences of discontinuous adjustment: selective memory of non-dominated extrema', *Scottish Journal of Political Economy*, 41, 212–21

Cross, R. (1995) 'Is the natural rate hypothesis consistent with hysteresis?', in R. Cross (ed.) *The Natural Rate of Unemployment: Reflections on 25 Years of the Hypothesis*, Cambridge, Cambridge University Press

Dixit, A. and R. Pindyck (1994) *Investment under Uncertainty*, Princeton, NJ, Princeton University Press

Duhem, P. (1914, translated 1954) *The Aim and Structure of Physical Theory*, Princeton, NJ, Princeton University Press

Feynman, R. (1992) *The Character of Physical Law*, London, Penguin Books

Fisher, I. (1892/1925) *Mathematical Investigations in the Theory of Value and Prices*, New Haven, CT, Yale University Press

Keynes, J.M. (1934) 'Poverty in plenty: is the economic system self-adjusting?', *The Listener*, 21 November

Keynes, J.M. (1936) *The General Theory of Employment, Interest and Money*, London, Macmillan

Keynes, J.M. (1937) 'The general theory of employment', *Quarterly Journal of Economics*, 51, 209–23

Krasnosel'skii, M.A. and A.V. Pokrovskii (1989) *Systems with Hysteresis*, Berlin, Springer-Verlag

Marshall, A. (1890) *The Principles of Economics*, 1st edn, London, Macmillan

Mirowski, P. (1989) *More Heat Than Light*, Cambridge, Cambridge University Press

Mussa, M. (1997) 'IMF surveillance', *American Economic Review*, 87, 28–31

OECD (1994) *Jobs Study*, Paris, OECD

Sargent, T. (1993) *Bounded Rationality in Macroeconomics*, New York, Oxford University Press

Slater, R. (1996) *Soros: The Life, the Times and Trading Secrets of the World's Greatest Investor*, Chicago, IL, Richard D. Irwin

Soros, G. (1987, 1994) *The Alchemy of Finance*, New York, John Wiley & Sons

Soros, G. (1995) *Soros on Soros: Staying Ahead of the Curve*, New York, John Wiley & Sons

Soros, G. (1997) 'The capitalist threat', *The Atlantic Monthly*, February, 45–58

# 4 Economics and Complexity[1]

## Basil Moore

John Cornwall has for some time been interested in a methodology which incorporates the path dependence of macroeconomic phenomena. It is now increasingly accepted that most economic time series are accurately characterized as possessing a unit root. This implies that they do not follow any deterministic trend path, and that any 'trends' found are time-dependent. Shocks are permanent in their effects, so that the system does not return to its original trend path.

These features are consistent with the newly emerging science of complexity. The purpose of this essay is to provide an outline of this new approach.[2]

## DEFINING COMPLEXITY

Understanding what is going on around us is accomplished by building 'models' and comparing them with observations. At each moment in time our sensory systems scan our surroundings in the world about us; our brain registers and compares the observations with respect to images already formed, and eventually reaches a preliminary conclusion. One of the basic steps in this model-building procedure is the extensive use of analogies, metaphors and archetypes (McCloskey, 1985, 1990).

We live in a world of astonishing biological complexity. Molecules interact with molecules to form cells. Cells interact with cells to form organisms, and organisms interact with organisms to form ecosystems, societies and economies. Nevertheless, 'complexity' is a controversial notion. Although contemporary economies are readily described as complex, reactions to 'complexity' as an analytical framework diverge sharply.

It is helpful first to distinguish between 'complicated' and 'complex'. If a system can be given a complete description in terms of its individual constituents, and so analysed by the method of reductionism, like computers, software programs, or jumbo jets, it is merely complicated.[3]

In contrast, a complex system is one in which the constituents of the system, and the interaction between the system and its environment, are of such a nature that the system as a whole cannot be fully understood solely by analysing its components. The behavioural relationships among its components are not fixed, but shift and change over time. Complex systems have novel features such as self-organization and 'emergent properties'. (Life itself is perhaps the

41

greatest emergent property.) Complex systems are associated with life: living organisms of all kinds (in particular the human brain) and all their products: languages, cultures, social systems – and economies (Kaufman, 1995; Dawkins, 1986).

Complex phenomena by definition cannot be described realistically in terms of any simple model. The notion of 'incompressibility' is fruitful. Complex systems cannot be reduced to a simpler model of their 'basic' components. This is not because the system is not constituted by them, but because the relational information, which as stated is not given, gets lost in the process of reduction (Gell-Mann, 1994).

Complex systems can only be modelled with complex resources. With the astonishing increase in the capacities of the computer, our technology to simulate may become more powerful than our ability to understand. It may eventually be possible to model a complex system. But to describe a complex system one has, in a certain sense, to repeat the system. If the models must be as complex as the systems they model, it is difficult to see how they can result in any significant simplification of our understanding of the system (Pagels, 1982, 1988; Gould, 1989).

Modelling techniques utilizing powerful computers may at some future date eventually allow us to simulate the behaviour of complex systems, without necessarily enabling us to completely understand them. Since complexity results from the interaction between the components of a system, complexity is manifested at the level of the system itself. There is neither something at a level below (a fundamental cause), nor at a level above (a metadescription) that is capable of capturing the essence of complexity (Dupré, 1993).

The past few centuries of science have been predominately reductionist, breaking complex systems into simpler parts, and these parts in turn into ever simpler parts. In many areas in science the reductionist programme has been spectacularly successful and fruitful, and will certainly continue to be so. But it has raised a substantial difficulty. It is now recognized that complex systems exhibit 'emergent properties', which cannot be explained by examining the individual parts (Cilliers, 1997).[4]

Traditionally, it was generally assumed that random behaviour was due to the extreme complexity of a system. Chaos theory has now revealed that random behaviour in non-linear systems need not involve an enormous number of degrees of freedom. The underlying structure of chaotic systems may be very simple, and governed only by a small number of degrees of freedom. It appears there may be substantial commonality among systems with such behaviour.

For chaotic dynamics, nearby trajectories separate at an exponential rate. Linear systems would then tend to infinity, since for linear systems, orbits that are locally unstable are also globally unstable. But for non-linear systems this is not the case. Local instability coexists with bounded motion. Nearby trajectories may separate exponentially, but eventually be folded back together, and so contained within a bounded region. This is the property of 'hidden attractors'.

Chaos is inherently non-linear. Conventional linear statistical measures, such as correlation functions, are quite inadequate to describe it. A chaotic process can be completely uncorrelated over short periods of time, and yet also be completely deterministic. The property of linear correlation does not provide us with the proper information to accurately characterize chaotic behaviour. Other statistical descriptions, based on non-linear statistical averages such as entropy and Lyapunov exponents, are then more appropriate (Arthur, 1994).

Chaotic systems are characterized by sensitive dependence on initial conditions. But our world is bounded by uncertainty. Any empirical measurement has only a finite precision. Initial conditions can never be precisely determined. Reality inevitably contains unknown factors that we cannot hope to take into account. As a result, any law, no matter how sophisticated or dynamical, can only represent an approximation (Waldrop, 1992).

Chaotic processes may be modelled as the outcome of deterministic dynamical systems. However it is never possible to infer the structure of the system from observing its chaotic and apparently random behaviour. It seems safe to assume that the complexity we observe in the real world reflects an open and non-deterministic system, even though this step must strictly speaking be accepted as an act of faith. If there were a deterministic generating process 'out there', we could never identify it. The belief that the complexity we observe is the product of a deterministic chaotic system strains credulity. Life is not like a movie. To affirm our humanity, we must assume that our future is not predestined, but rather created by our present choices and behaviour.

Most complex phenomena change continuously over time. Ordinarily our empirical measurements reduce time observations to a stream of discrete symbols. In statistical mechanics this is called 'coarse graining'. Changing the level of coarse graining may be regarded as analogous to changing the resolution of our instruments (Pagels, 1988).

Complex systems are constituted by intricate sets of non-linear relationships and feedback loops. Only selected aspects of the system can be analysed at a point in time, so that any analysis of a complex system is necessarily partial, and as a result always distorted. A complex system may be viewed as one where 'there are more possibilities than can be actualized' (Luhmann, 1985, p. 25).

The general attributes of complex, dynamic, self-organizing systems may be summarized as follows (Cilliers, 1997):

1. The system's macroscopic behaviour emerges from microscopic interactions. The individual components operate on local information. 'Simple' local interactions result in 'complex' macroscopic behaviour.

2. The structure of the system is the result of interaction between the system and its environment. It is not the result of *a priori* design. The structure of the system continually adapts dynamically to changes in the environment, even when the changes are not regular.

3. Self-organization is not guided or determined by specific goals. It is difficult to talk about the 'function' of complex systems. They are the result of evolutionary processes whereby the system will not survive if it cannot adapt to new circumstances. Self-organization is only possible if the system can remember and forget. Information stored and not used simply fades away. Self-organization involves higher-order non-linear processes. They cannot be described linearly.

4. Self-organizing systems increase in complexity over time. They 'learn' from experience, and 'remember' previously encountered situations. This increase in complexity implies a local reversal of entropy. Nevertheless they remain bound by the finite constraints of the physical world. They eventually become saturated, and they 'age' over time.

5. A reductionist discourse is inadequate when describing emergent system properties. Microscopic units do not 'know' about their macroscopic effects. Yet these effects do not involve anything besides these microscopic units.

The study of complex dynamic systems has thus uncovered a fundamental flaw in the time-honoured and successful analytical method of reductionism. A complex system is constituted not merely by the sum of its components, but also by the relationships among its components. By 'cutting up' the system, reductionism necessarily destroys what it seeks to understand (Cilliers, 1997).

## THE SELF-ORGANIZING, EVOLUTIONARY NATURE OF COMPLEXITY

The notion of the structure of a dynamic system pertains to the mechanism developed by complex systems to receive, encode, transform and store information, and to react to such information by producing some form of output. The internal structure evolves through a process of self-organization, a complex interaction between the environment, the present state of the system and the history of the system. Self-organization is an 'emergent property' of complex systems. It enables them to develop adaptively in order to cope with or manipulate their environment.

Economic systems are clearly self-organizing. Their structure changes in response to a number of factors, for example, technological change, environmental change, or changes in aggregate demand. The interaction of these factors is too complex to allow the construction of a dynamical system.

However, intervention in an economic system's internal structure is possible, through changes in selected prices and quantities: interest rates, exchange rates, tax rates, public expenditures, property rights. Some short-run ordinal effects of these interventions may be predictable. But over the long run, detailed prediction is impossible. The spontaneous adjustment of the economic system involves the complex interaction of too many uncontrollable factors. Long-run analysis of complex systems is necessarily primarily speculative and conjectural. The system's long-run behaviour is too complex to be successfully modelled. This insight largely puts 'paid' to all long-run deterministic economic modelling.

The self-organization of complex systems may be described as the emergence of macroscopic behaviour through the activity of microscopic units responding solely to local information. For a self-organizing structure to emerge, a number of general preconditions must be present (Cilliers, 1997):

1. The system must consist of a large number of relatively undifferentiated micro units.
2. The strengths of the interconnections must change as a result of local information. (These changes may be self-maintaining (positive feedback), and may cause the system to move towards a more differentiated state.)
3. There must be competition among the micro units for limited resources. (Boundaries, limits and constraints are a precondition for structure.)
4. There must be cooperation among some units. (Mutual reinforcement is also a precondition for structure.)
5. Interactions among units must be non-linear. (Small changes are able to have large effects.)
6. Symmetry-breaking must be achievable spontaneously, due to non-linearities.
7. Entrainment must occur, so that some patterns catch others in their wake. (Resonance increases the order in the system.)
8. The memory of the system must be stored in distributed fashion. (Traces of information are distributed over many units.)
9. There must be self-organized criticality – minor events can start a chain reaction. (The mechanism that leads to major events is the same that leads to minor events. Complex systems tend to organize themselves toward the critical point where events have the widest possible range of effects. The system tends to balance itself between order and chaos, so that it can change its state with the least amount of effort.)
10. Self-organization must be dynamic. (The structure of the system is continuously transformed through the interaction of contingent external and internal factors.)

As a result of complex patterns of interaction, system behaviour cannot be explained solely in terms of its atomistic components, despite the fact that the system does not consist of anything else but the basic components and their interactions. Complex characteristics 'emerge' through the process of interaction within the system. Hence:

> Modeling aggregation requires us to transcend the level of the individual cells. In dealing with systems of large numbers of components, we must make recourse to 'holistic concepts', that refer to the behavior of the system as a whole. These system properties may not ultimately be definable in terms of the states of individuals. Yet this fact does not make them fictions. They are causally efficacious (hence real) and have definite causal relationships with other system variables, and even to the states of the individuals. (Garfinkel, 1987, pp. 202–3)

In classical reductionism, the behaviour of holistic entities can ultimately be explained by reference to the nature of their constituents, because the entities 'are just' collections of lower-level objects with their interactions. Although it may be true in some sense that systems 'are just' collections of their elements, it does not follow that a complex system's behaviour can be understood by examining the responses of its component parts, together with a theory of their interconnections.

The analysis of complex systems must avoid the temptation of trying to find 'master keys'. Due to the mechanisms by which complex systems structure themselves, any single principle can necessarily provide only an inadequate and partial insight. The analyst must be sensitive to complex and self-organizing interactions, and appreciate the play of patterns that perpetually transform the system itself and even the environment in which it operates.

No complex system, whether biological or social, can be understood without considering its history. Two similar systems, placed in identical conditions, may respond in vastly different ways if they have different histories. The history of a system is not merely important in understanding its behaviour. It co-determines the very structure of the system.

The evolutionary history of a system is not present in such a way that it can be deconstructed. The effects of the history of the system are important for its behaviour. But history itself is continuously transformed through a self-organizing process in the system. Only the traces of history remain, distributed through the system. These traces do not correspond to facts, ideas or symbols that can be recalled from a filing cabinet. They are rather patterns of information, 'smeared' over many units, stored in a distributed fashion, and continually altered by experience. For example severe recessions change the stock of human capital embodied in those workers who find themselves unemployed for long periods. They also change the expectations and so behaviour of investors and asset-holders concerning 'normal' levels of future interest rates on securities, and price/earnings ratios on common stocks.

A self-organizing system may be viewed as suspended between active and passive modes. It reacts to the state of the environment, and simultaneously transforms itself as a result, often affecting its environment in turn. The distinction between active and passive, causal and caused, itself comes under pressure. Self-organization is a self-transforming process, so that the system acts upon itself. A meta-level description can be constructed. But only 'snapshots' of the system, as it exists at a given moment, are possible. The temporal complexities produced by the reflexive nature of self-organizing systems cannot be represented in the metadescription (Cilliers, 1997).

These notions have important implications for the way we should think about economic systems. The classical definition of stability states that small causes produce small effects. But in a critically organized complex system, this is no longer the case. By classical considerations, complex systems would be called unstable. But as far as complex systems are concerned, classical stability (equilibrium) amounts to stagnation, and even death.

The classical definition of instability as used by Poincaré was probabilistic. Unstable events are defined as events that have no observable cause. They are chance events, as opposed to deterministic ones. In complex systems, however, unpredictable behaviour is not the result of chance. It is 'caused' by the complex interaction of a number of system factors.

Complexity is not to be confused with randomness. But it also may not be describable in first-order logical terms. 'I find no alternative but to accept multiple, formally incompatible descriptions as a satisfactory explanation of many types of biological events . . . a theory based on chance events, including those of quantum theory . . . serves only as an escape from classical determinism: it is not a theory of self-organization' (Pattee, 1987, pp. 329–30).

If a system is too rigid – that is, characterized by too much central control – it will not be able to cope with unpredictable changes. On the other hand, it will also be disastrous if the system tries to adjust itself to every superficial change, since such changes may easily be reversed without notice. Being able to discriminate between changes that should be followed and changes that should be resisted is vital to the survival of the system.

To be able to predict accurately the behaviour of a system is the classic criterion for a successful theory. But complex systems cannot be fully described by means of classical theory. Predicting their future behaviour in detail is not possible. The output of the system follows the 'history' of the system, which itself depends on its previous output taken as input. Contingency is central to system behaviour. The system's development is determined by its mechanisms, but cannot be predicted in advance. No reliable rule or pattern emerges in the output itself.

The mapping of the major constraints pertaining to a system, combined with some knowledge of its history and environment, permits very short-run local predictions to be attempted, though never with certainty. Accurate long-run predictions generally cannot be made. Economists must eventually learn how to live within these limitations, and put all long-run deterministic equilibrium models behind them.

## QUANTIFYING COMPLEXITY

As previously stated, traditional reductionist approaches to complexity are inherently flawed. A complex system cannot be 'reduced' to a simpler one, unless it was not really complex to begin with. The 'true nature' of the system cannot be revealed in terms of a small number of logical principles. Any realistic model of a complex system has to 'conserve' its complexity. The model has to be as complex as the system it models.

In many areas of science, both theoretical and applied, natural and behavioural, there is growing discontent with determinate analytical methods and descriptions. One of the first responses to this unease was a rapid growth in statistical approaches. However, most statistical models do not imply a break with deterministic methods. Statistics as presently used remains a tool in the process of uncovering the 'true' mechanisms of the phenomena being investigated. The heavy price paid, of averaging out the complex internal detail, is usually glossed over.

Ever since Kepler's insistence that 'to measure is to know', analysis in terms of loosely ordered relationships, rather than in terms of deterministic laws, has been foreign to the quantitative descriptions and calculations deemed necessary for science. Nevertheless many phenomena, especially in the life and behavioural sciences, but also in physics and mathematics, cannot be properly understood in terms of deterministic, rule-based, statistical processes. For example, quantum mechanical descriptions of subatomic processes are solely relational. On a more macroscopic level, it is relations that determine the nature of matter. The significance of each atom is determined not by its basic nature, but as the result of a large number of relationships between itself and other atoms (Cilliers, 1997).

One of the first successful attempts to deal with complexity in science was the development of thermodynamics in the second half of the nineteenth century. 'This response was expressed in terms of the dissipation of energy, the forgetting of initial conditions, the evolution toward disorder. Classical dynamics, the science of eternal, reversible trajectories, was alien to the problems facing the 19th century, which was dominated by the concept of evolution' (Prigogine and Stengers, 1984, p. 129).

In classical mechanics, time is reversible, and so not part of the equation. In thermodynamics, in contrast, time plays a vital role. This is perhaps best expressed in the second law of thermodynamics. This states that over time, the entropy of a system can only increase. The concept of entropy is a complex one. Entropy can be seen as a measure of the 'disorder' in a system. As a system transforms energy, less and less of it remains in a usable form, and the 'disorder' in the system increases.

By replacing 'energy' with 'information' in the equations of thermodynamics, Shannon (1948) was able to show that the amount of information in a message is equal to its 'entropy'. The more disorderly a message, the higher is its information content. Consider a message consisting of a string of digits that is being transmitted to you one at a time. For example, if the string consists of 'fours' only, you will notice this quickly at the receiving end. The next digit is so predictable, it will carry no new information whatsoever. Although the message is highly structured, its information content is very low.

The less able the receiver is to predict the next digit in the sequence, the higher is the information content of the message. A message high in information content is one low in predictable structure, and therefore high in 'entropy'.

There is, however, one major problematic implication of all this. If information equals entropy, then the message with the highest information content would be one that is completely random. Randomness must be defined not in terms of unpredictability, but in terms of 'incompressibility'. 'A series of numbers is random if the smallest algorithm capable of specifying it to a computer has about the same number of bits of information as the series itself' (Chaitlin, 1975, p. 48).

Talking only about series of numbers may seem a little superficial. But any formalism can be expressed as a series of numbers via the Godel numbering system (Cilliers, 1997). Randomness is no longer understood in terms of unpredictability, but in terms of the denseness with which the information is packed. This provides an interesting definition of complexity: 'The complexity of a series is equal to the size of the minimal program necessary to produce that series' (Chaitlin, 1975, p. 49).

To prove that a sequence is not random is easy. One only has to find a program that is shorter. To prove that a sequence is random, you have to prove that no shorter program exists. Such a proof cannot be found. Randomness is falsifiable, but never verifiable.

We appear now at last to have arrived at a truism: complexity is complex. A complex system cannot be reduced to a simple one if it was not simple (or merely complicated) to begin with. Truly complex problems can only be approached with complex resources.

This realization offers a reinterpretation of the anti-reductionist position. A complex system cannot be reduced to a collection of its basic constituents, not because the system is not constituted by them, but because too much of the relational information gets lost in the process. Strict quantification of complexity does not seem to be feasible. The notion of incompressibility is central. When dealing with complexity, there are no short cuts without peril.

MODELLING COMPLEXITY

A complex system must grapple with changing environments. To cope with the open demands on it, the system must have two capabilities:

(i)  it must be able to store information concerning the environment for future use; and
(ii) it must be able to adapt its structure when necessary.

The first of these is the process of representation, the second the process of self-organization.

Any complete model of a complex system must possess these capabilities. The processes of representation and self-organization must be given some kind of formal description in order to be simulated by the model. The relationships between the elements of the system change under the influences of both the external environment and the history of the system. Since the system has to cope with unpredictable changes in the environment, it must be 'plastic'. The processes of representation and self-organization must both be modelled mathematically.

Models are required to describe, understand, predict and possibly affect the behaviour of complex systems. To be effective, these models have to produce results. At this point there are immediately problems. How are such models to be tested and evaluated? If the complex systems they attempt to simulate are by nature non-deterministic, models cannot lead to better quantitative predictions or forecasts. The main requirement of our models must shift away from having to be correct, towards their offering greater richness in understanding. The shift from prediction to understanding implies that model evaluation in terms of performance may have to be abandoned.

Once we have a better understanding of the dynamics of complexity, we can start looking for similarities and differences between different complex systems. We may thereby develop a clearer understanding of the strengths and limitations of different models. Models of complexity can only become successful once we begin to understand more about the nature of complexity.

Interdisciplinary approaches can open up new avenues for research. Consider two possible ways of modelling complex systems: rule-based systems and connectionist systems.

Over the past-half century, the search for artificial intelligence (AI) has provided a focal point for research on complexity. The astonishing growth in the capacities of digital and quantum-mechanical computers created expectations that it would be possible to construct computers capable of behaving intelligently, for example, solving maths problems or playing chess.

Symbolic rule-based systems have constituted the classical approach to the modelling of complexity. The behaviour of a complex system is reduced to a set of rules that describe the system on an abstract level. Symbols must be used to represent important concepts, so that the unnecessary detail of implementation can be ignored. Each symbol represents a specific concept, known as local representation. The set of rules is governed by a system of centralized control, known as the metarules of the system. This central system decides which of the production rules become active at each stage of the computation. If the central control fails, the entire system falls.

Researchers differ on many points of detail, as well as on the scope and power of rule-based systems. There is a split between supporters of strong AI, who claim that formal systems can eventually provide an adequate model for all aspects of human intelligence, and supporters of weak AI, who see formal systems merely as a powerful tool. But rule-based systems remain the paradigm.

However, the important hallmarks of intelligence, perception, imagination, intuition, movement and use of language have unfortunately proved to be complex beyond all previous estimation. In these respects, no AI computing device has capabilities even remotely close to those of human beings. As a result, expectations of AI have recently been severely deflated, although there have been a number of useful by-products of this research.

In contrast, connectionist systems such as neural networks approach the problem from an entirely different viewpoint. They attempt to simulate the physiological workings of the human brain. The human brain has always held a special place in studies of complexity, because of its own structural complexity and because of the mind–body problem: 'I think, therefore I am'.

From a strictly functional point of view, the brain, that three-pound 'computer made of meat', consists of nothing more than a huge network of richly connected neurons. Each neuron can be seen as a simple processor, which calculates the sum of all its inputs. Should the sum exceed a certain threshold, it generates an output, which in turn becomes the input to all the neurons connected to it. Each connection is mediated by a synapse, which causes the incoming signal either to excite or inhibit the target neuron, and so determines the strength of the influence. The connection strength between two neurons increases proportionally to how often it is used.

At the level of the individual neuron, no complex behaviour is discernible. But the system is capable of performing specific, highly complex tasks. Complex behaviour emerges from the interaction between many simple processes which respond in non-linear fashion to local information. Recently, connectionist systems such as neural networks have been constructed which are able to 'learn' simple tasks.

## CHARACTERISTICS OF COMPLEX SYSTEMS

In light of the preceding reflections, the following list offers a brief description of ten key characteristics of complex systems (Cilliers, 1997):

1. Complex systems consist of an indefinitely large number of individual elements. (As a result, conventional means of description (for example, any finite system of equations) cannot lead to any *complete* understanding of the system.)
2. In order to constitute a complex system, these individual elements have to *interact*. (Since a complex system changes over time, this interaction must be *dynamic*.)
3. The interaction must be *fairly rich*, so that any element in the system influences, and is influenced by, many other ones. (The behaviour of the system is not determined by the exact number of interactions associated with specific elements. If there are enough elements in the system, some of which are redundant, a set of sparsely connected elements can perform the same function as one richly connected element.)
4. The interactions are local and non-linear: small causes have large effects, and vice versa. (*Non-linearity* is a precondition for complexity.)
5. The interactions have a fairly *short range*, that is, information is received primarily from immediate neighbours. (This does not preclude wide-ranging influence, but the influence gets mediated (enhanced, suppressed) along the way.)
6. There are loops in the interactions, so that the effects of any action can feed back on itself, positively (enhancing) or negatively (inhibiting). Both kinds are necessary. (The technical term for this aspect of a complex system is *recurrency*.)
7. Complex systems are *open*, that is, they interact with their environment. It is often difficult to define the border of a complex system. (The scope of the system is influenced by the purpose of the description of the system. It is influenced by the position of the observer.)
8. Complex systems operate under conditions *far from equilibrium*. (There must be a continual flow of energy to maintain the system and ensure its survival.)
9. Complex systems have *histories*. (They evolve through time, and their past is co-responsible for their present behaviour.)
10. Each element in the system is ignorant of the behaviour of the system as a whole, and responds solely to the local information available to it. (Complexity is the result of a rich interaction of simple elements that respond only to the limited information each of them are presented with. Complexity emerges as a result of the patterns of *interactions* between the elements.)

Consider how each of the above characteristics are manifest in the economy of a single country:

1. There are a large number of individual economic agents, usually many millions.
2. Economic agents interact by buying and selling, borrowing and lending, taking and giving goods and services, and by creating and extinguishing means of payment. These relationships are continually changing.
3. Each economic agent interacts with a large number of other agents. Some agents are more active than others. Individual agents differ widely in the amount of purchasing power that they control.
4. Economic agents interact principally with others in their near vicinity (economically not spatially), that is, in markets where transactions are highly specialized.
5. The interaction among agents is non-linear. Behaviour depends critically on agents' expectations of the future behaviour of the system. Investments may produce large positive or negative returns *ex post*. As the future becomes present, expectations are either confirmed or disappointed.
6. Expectations are frequently contagious and self-fulfilling. For example, *ex ante* expectations of an expansion of future activity lead to increased deficit spending, which generate an increase in the money supply, money income, nominal aggregate demand, and higher *ex post* returns on investment projects. Expectations of future events are formed both extrapolatively and regressively by different agents.
7. Economies are open and continuously influenced by changes in technology, factor supplies, political developments and international relationships.
8. Economies are driven by the dynamics of aggregate demand and aggregate supply changes. They never stand still. Expectations of future events are continuously changing over time.
9. Economies are greatly influenced by their histories. In the very short run, their behaviour is largely predetermined. Today's wages and prices, like today's capital stock and technology, depend primarily on yesterday's. Similarly most expectations ordinarily change fairly slowly. But sudden sharp changes in the collective consensus of an economy's future prospects sometimes occur. Agents' expectations of the unknowable future state of the economy are largely based on social conventions, which can be fragile and unstable.
10. Each agent belongs to more than a single cluster of agents, such as family, business, occupation, residential area, political party, and recreational activity and occupies a different rank and status in the hierarchy of each cluster. Economic agents do not know what other agents are thinking or doing either in the present or in the future. Yet many of their decisions

(investment expenditures in particular) are based directly on their expectations of the future behaviour of other agents.

In this light, it is certainly strange that when it comes to descriptions of the functioning of the economy (an obviously relational structure), there is such strong adherence among economists to the desirability of reductionist micro representation and deterministic models. One of the reasons must surely be that economics, like all other behavioural sciences, has inherited its methodology from a classical analytical tradition which, at its core, is deeply deterministic.

## CONCLUSIONS

*Dynamical systems* is the term given to the modelling of systems that change over time. Dynamical systems are systems that exhibit complex behaviour, but for which there is some hope that the underlying structure is simple, in the sense of being governed by a small number of degrees of freedom.[5]

In all non-linear systems, uncertainties are amplified exponentially as the time horizon expands. At least in the case of the behavioural sciences, it is impossible to quantify and measure all of the degrees of freedom involved. The necessary model is far too big to run on any computer. The interactions are so complicated and so poorly understood that it is not possible to model them with mathematical precision. We are reminded that the hallmark of a complex system is that its essence cannot be captured by any simpler model.

Social systems are so complex that only ordinal behavioural properties, that is, greater or less, can ordinarily be derived. At present it is not possible to simulate the behaviour of such systems by building a formal dynamical system. We must abstract, and be content to build *dynamical models*, describing the behaviour of only a few selected variables, and not the entire system itself. Dynamical models do not attempt to model the entire complex system. Instead they confine their analysis to only a few selected variables. Their defining characteristic is that they explicitly contain time, as either a discrete or continuous variable.

The key characteristic of dynamical models is that they attempt to analyse the temporal flow *processes* of the selected variables, not their equilibrium states. Equilibrium (the concept of an unchanging steady state) becomes useless as an analytical tool for the study of complex systems. Complex systems are never in equilibrium.

Based on its observed past and present behaviour, the goal is to develop a model to simulate and understand the system. To this end, theorizing must abstract some of the key variables and properties of the observed phenomena and attempt to formulate them into a dynamical model. Because of the nature of complexity, even our best (most successful) models will never be able to predict accurately and consistently even the system's future ordinal behaviour, except perhaps, if we are very lucky, over the very short run. But I hope they will increase our understanding of the system's temporal dynamics. In this manner, they will assist us in formulating policy measures to change system behaviour in desirable ways.

## Notes

1. This chapter is heavily dependent on Cilliers (1997).
2. The essay is also the opening chapter of a forthcoming book, entitled *Macroeconomics for a Complex World*.
3. As someone, presumably a Frenchman, has said, 'A snowflake is complicated, but a mayonnaise is complex.'
4. The battle over the appropriateness of reductionism is being fought over all disciplines. In a chapter in his biography entitled 'The Molecular Wars', the evolutionary biologist Edward Wilson (1994) describes the grim determination with which molecular biologists have fought to extirpate non-molecular research in biology. This professional hostility is but 'the latest in a long history of frequent and deep-seated disagreement among scientists, pitting so-called reductionists, who seek explanations at the cellular, molecular or atomic level – against scientists interested in higher levels of organization. The battle alternatively pits so-called "hard scientists", working in fields where controlled repeated laboratory experiments are feasible, against so-called "soft scientists", who are dependent on other methodologies' (Diamond, 1995). Diamond continues, 'It ought to be obvious that both reductionist understanding and higher level understanding are essential, and that it is pointless to berate scientists for failing to do controlled experiments on subjects for which controlled experiments would be immoral, illegal, or impossible . . . Unfortunately in their belief that only reductionist experimental approaches qualify as true science, many molecular biologists continue to try to strangle evolutionary biology, ecology, and related fields. The strangulation takes the form of vigorously opposing academic appointments and research funds for evolutionary biologists' (p. 18). Wilson reports Nobel Laureate James Watson's response to his proposal that Harvard appoint even one ecologist: 'Anyone who would hire an ecologist is out of his mind.' The situation is broadly parallel in economics between the mainstream and Post-Keynesians.
5. See Jen (1990, Introduction).

## References

Arthur, B. (1994) *Increasing Returns and Path Dependence in the Economy*, Ann Arbor, University of Michigan Press

Chaitlin, G.L.J. (1975) 'Randomness and mathematical proof', *Scientific American*, 232, 47–52

Cilliers, P. (1997) *Complexity and Post Modernism*, London, Routledge

Dawkins, R. (1986) *The Blind Watchmaker*, London, Longman

Diamond, J. (1995) '*Naturalist*, by Edward Wilson', *New York Review of Books*, 12 January, 16–19

Dupré, J. (1993) *The Disorder of Things*, Boston, MA, Harvard University Press

Garfinkel, A. (1987) 'The slime mold dictyostelium as a model of self-organization in social systems', in F.E. Yates (ed.) *Self-Organizing Systems: The Emergence of Order*, New York, Plenum Press

Gell-Mann, M. (1994) *The Quark and the Jaguar*, London, Little, Brown

Gould, S.J. (1989) *Wonderful Life: The Burgess Shale and the Nature of History*, New York, Norton

Jan, E. (ed.) (1990) *Lectures in Complex Systems*, Redwood City, CA, Addison-Wesley

Kaufman, S. (1995) *At Home in the Universe*, Oxford, Oxford University Press

Luhmann, N.A. (1985) *A Sociological Theory of Law*, London, Routledge

McCloskey, D. (1985) *The Rhetoric of Economics*, Madison, University of Wisconsin Press

McCloskey, D. (1990) *If You're So Smart*, IL, Chicago, University of Chicago Press

Pagels, H. (1982) *The Cosmic Code: Quantum Physics as the Language of Nature*, New York, Simon & Schuster

Pagels, H. (1988) *The Dreams of Reason: The Computer and the Rise of the Sciences of Complexity*, New York, Simon & Schuster

Pattee, H.H. (1987) 'Instabilities and information in biological self-organization', in F.E. Yates (ed.) *Self-Organizing Systems: The Emergence of Order*, New York, Plenum Press

Prigogine, I. and I. Stengers (1984) *Order Out of Chaos, Man's New Dialogue with Nature*, London, Heinemann

Shannon, C.E. (1948) 'A mathematical theory of communication', *Bell Systems Technology Journal*, 27, 379–423

Waldrop, M.M (1992) *Complexity: The Emerging Science at the Edge of Order and Chaos*, New York, Simon & Schuster

Wilson, E. (1994) *Naturalist*, Washington, DC, Island Press

# 5 Modelling a Path-Dependent Economy: Lessons from John Cornwall's Macrodynamics

Mark Setterfield[1]

## INTRODUCTION

Dynamics are an innate feature of Keynes's and Post-Keynesian economics. So much is obvious from the pages of *The General Theory* itself, and was only made more apparent by the rush of early Keynesians to extend Keynes's theory into the long run.[2] Keynes and the Post-Keynesians conceive capitalism as a monetary production economy, wherein nominal contracts and monetary exchange link the activities of buying inputs, producing output and realizing profits from the sale of output – activities that are separated temporally. A capitalist economy functions, then, in historical time. Decisions and actions in the present take place in the context of an immutable past and an as yet unmade (and hence fundamentally uncertain) future. Great importance attaches to the sequential nature of economic activity and the concomitant tendency of economic systems to evolve over time as a result of their concrete historical functioning.

In light of all this, it is hardly surprising to find that the work of an eminent Post-Keynesian such as John Cornwall has been largely concerned with issues of economic dynamics and, in particular, macrodynamics. As Cornwall's own account of his early progress in economics testifies:

> I developed a keen interest in the process of transformation of capitalist societies and the forces generating social and economic change, an interest that I have retained throughout my career. (Cornwall, 1992, p. 97)

This is not to say, of course, that John Cornwall's work only explores one theme. Rather, the point is that his various contributions – be they on the notion of technology transfers and catch-up processes in long-run growth, the idea of a hierarchy of goods which causes structural change in consumers' expenditure patterns, or the role of institutions in determining short-run macroeconomic outcomes – have all been either innately dynamic, or else have been developed in the service of a broader vision of macrodynamics and structural change. Furthermore, it would be equally inappropriate to infer that John Cornwall has always 'sounded the same tune' with regard to issues of macrodynamics. First, and most obviously, his work includes investigations of both quantity and price dynamics – that is, both growth and inflation processes. Second, the breadth of John Cornwall's macrodynamic vision has permitted him to explore – sometimes simultaneously – the issues of expansion, macroeconomic fluctuations and structural change. This contrasts with the narrower conception of macrodynamics in neoclassical economics, in which the chief preoccupation has traditionally been – and largely remains – the determination of steady-state outcomes. Third, the nature of John Cornwall's *methodology* for studying macrodynamics has, fittingly, evolved over time, moving ever further away from equilibrium analysis towards an increasingly explicit emphasis on history or path dependence. This development mirrors the postwar trajectory of Nicholas Kaldor, one of his chief influences, and its importance is evident in the tenor of Cornwall's (1991) appraisal of his own work. Here, equilibrium economics is berated for its conception of outcomes as being predetermined inevitabilities based on exogenous data and ahistorical convergence processes (p. 101), the author having previously summarized the importance of his early–1980s work on inflation thus:

> I was now able to see more clearly how important was the role of hysteresis or path dependence in the development process of economies and how important the need to formalize this role explicitly. (Cornwall, 1992, p. 100)

Cornwall's methodological evolution therefore provides an useful perspective for a review of his contributions to macrodynamics. The propriety of this perspective is enhanced by the important lessons it yields with regard to the process, practicalities and potential insights of model-building in a manner that avoids reliance on long-run equilibrium and instead seeks greater consistency with the evolutionary properties of historical time.

The remainder of this chapter proceeds as follows. The next section discusses three models central to the corpus of John Cornwall's macro-dynamics. These are the growth models from *Growth and Stability in a Mature Economy* (Cornwall, 1972) and *Modern Capitalism* (Cornwall, 1977), and the model of inflation and unemployment outcomes in *The Theory of Economic Breakdown* and *Economic Breakdown and Recovery* (Cornwall, 1990, 1994).[3] The chief purpose of discussing these models is to highlight the ongoing methodological evolution that they display. The following section then discusses the lessons that can be learned from Cornwall's macrodynamic methodology and finally, the last section offers some conclusions.

## THREE MACRODYNAMIC MODELS

### From equilibrium to cumulative causation: the Growth and Stability and Modern Capitalism models

As intimated earlier, Cornwall's macrodynamic vision exceeds the confines of the 'history versus equilibrium' debate. Several features of his growth analysis in *Modern Capitalism* and *Growth and Stability in a Mature Economy* merit attention. First, growth is conceived as a transformatory process, involving structural change in the composition of output and employment, partly in response to changes in consumer spending that occur as an economy progresses through the commodity hierarchy.[4] Second, demand influences long-run growth outcomes. Growth is not simply explained by the expansion of potential output on the supply side, as in both the original and more recent vintages of neoclassical growth theory. Third, technology transfers between regions at different levels of development can impact on regional growth through the 'catch-up' mechanism. Fourth, capital is treated as heterogeneous and 'lumpy'. Increasing returns to scale are possible as rising output facilitates the adoption of more capital-intensive techniques of production, characterized by greater indivisibilities of capital, from amongst a discrete choice of techniques. Indivisibilities coupled with the limited *ex ante* and *ex post* substitutability of capital and labour compound the impact of fundamental uncertainty about the magnitude of future product demand on firms' investment decisions. Finally, pricing and distribution are explained in non-marginalist terms. Both the rate of profit and the value of the real wage are *ex post* phenomena, contingent upon the target-return pricing strategies of firms and the level of aggregate demand (Cornwall, 1972, p. 75).

The Growth and Stability model involves a process of 'joint interaction', in which supply influences demand and vice versa, as 'supply adjusts to demand through changes in productivity and factor supplies' (Cornwall, 1972, p. 56). The initial model comprises the following equations:

$$r_{yt} = r_{xt} \tag{5.1}$$

$$r_{xt} = \gamma_0 + \gamma_1 r_{yt-1} \tag{5.2}$$

where $r_y$ denotes the rate of growth of demand, $r_x$ denotes the rate of growth of maximum output (supply) and $t$ subscripts denote time periods. Equation (5.1) is the long-run rate of growth derived from a flexible accelerator model which exhibits damped oscillations about an exogenously given trend rate of growth of maximum output, $r_x$ (Cornwall, 1972, pp. 56–7). Equation (5.2) makes $r_x$ endogenous to the past rate of growth of demand (and hence actual output) for reasons that will be discussed in more detail below.

Substituting equation (5.2) into equation (5.1), we arrive at:

$$r_{yt} = \gamma_0 + \gamma_1 r_{yt-1} \tag{5.3}$$

Denoting initial growth conditions as $r_{y0}$, equation (5.3) can be rewritten as:

$$r_{yt} = \gamma'_1 r_{y0} + \gamma_0 \sum_{i=1}^{t} \gamma'^{i-1}_1 \tag{5.4}$$

from which it follows that

$$\lim_{t \to \infty} r_{yt} = r^*_y = \frac{\gamma_0}{1 - \gamma_1} = r^*_x$$

given $0 < \gamma_1 < 1$ and equation (5.1). We therefore have a model of endogenous growth, in which the long-run growth rate is a determinate, steady-state equilibrium, defined and reached independently of the path taken towards it.

The model of joint interaction, then, is a conventional, path-independent equilibrium model. The author is clearly aware of this limitation, judging by his comments on the model (Cornwall, 1972, p. 59) and his subsequent development of what turns out to be a nascent model of path-dependent growth outcomes. In order to understand how the model of joint interaction is transformed in this manner, we must examine more closely the economics of equation (5.2) above, according to which demand influences potential output.

Cornwall (1972) makes two basic arguments concerning the influence of demand on supply. First, the rate of growth of demand has an indirect influence on productivity growth as the composition of consumer demand changes with the growth of disposable income. The movement of consumers through the commodity hierarchy pulls resources into new industries with unexploited scale economies and hence higher-than-average productivity growth rates, thus enhancing aggregate productivity growth.[5] Second, demand growth directly affects productivity growth by influencing firms' discrete choices between techniques of production embodying indivisible capital and localized technological progress. Assume that there are a limited number of techniques of production, and that it is possible to reap economies of scale by fully utilizing more capital-intensive techniques. Assume further that there is limited *ex post* substitutability between capital and labour, and that indivisibilities in the capital stock increase with the capital-intensiveness of the technique. Then rapid demand growth will foster expectations amongst firms that they will be able to fully utilize indivisible, capital-intensive techniques. This will encourage adoption of these techniques, resulting in the realization of productivity-enhancing economies of scale.

One feature of the supply side that purportedly enhances this mechanism is the localized nature of technical progress. The understanding that technical progress can only be realized by accumulating and 'learning by using' specific types of capital assets, and that technical progress does not accrue in a disembodied form that benefits all techniques of production equally, will provide a fillip to firms as they plan their investment decisions in the hope of maintaining or enhancing their competitiveness (Cornwall, 1972, pp. 63–4). However, and for our purposes, quite significantly, this does not rule out the possibility of there existing complementarities between elements of a heterogeneous capital stock. This idea, derived from Lachman (1947), has, of course, recently resurfaced in the context of neoclassical endogenous growth theory in the guise of spillover effects (see, for example, Grossman and Helpman, 1991).[6] Its significance for our purposes is that the notion of complementarities is used to justify the assumption that, for certain values of $r_y$, the elasticity of potential output with respect to demand is equal to one – or in other words, $r_{xt} = r_{yt-1}$. Thus instead of equation (5.2), we can now write:

$$r_{xt} = \gamma_0 + \gamma_1 r_{yt-1} \;\forall\; r_y < r_{y1}$$
$$r_{xt} = r_{yt-1} \;\forall\; r_{y1} \leq r_y \leq r_{y2}$$
$$r_{xt} = \gamma'_0 + \gamma_1 r_{yt-1} \;\forall\; r_y > r_{y2} \tag{5.2a}$$

where $\gamma'_0 > \gamma_0 > 0$. The influence of demand on supply now involves discontinuities at the critical growth rates $r_{y1}$ and $r_{y2}$.[7] Of critical significance in this extended model of joint interaction is the region between $r_{y1}$ and $r_{y2}$ where $r_{xt} = r_{yt-1}$. Focusing exclusively on this region, we can write:

$$r_{yt} = r_{xt} \tag{5.1}$$
$$r_{xt} = r_{yt-1} \tag{5.2a}$$

This creates multiple equilibria where $r_{xt} = r_{yt} = r_{yt-1}$ between $r_{y1}$ and $r_{y2}$, giving rise to a form of path dependence in which the long-run growth rate is determined by initial growth conditions. Hence given (5.2a), equation (5.4) becomes:

$$r_{yt} = r_{y0} \tag{5.4a}$$

from which it is obvious that

$$\lim_{t \to \infty} r_{yt} = r_y^* = r_{y0} = r_x^*$$

Notice that what this implies is a growth process in which initial growth outcomes are purely self-reinforcing. In other words, we have essentially arrived at a model of cumulative causation, thus anticipating a central result of *Modern Capitalism*.[8]

There are some important differences between the Modern Capitalism and Growth and Stability models. First, in *Modern Capitalism*, exports join investment spending as a key source of aggregate demand.[9] Second, the influence of supply on demand changes. Instead of the rate of growth of potential output determining the trend rate of growth of demand as in the Growth and Stability model, the rate of growth of productivity (and hence potential output) now indirectly influences export demand via its effects on the ratio of domestic to foreign prices. Finally, *Modern Capitalism* incorporates explicit discussion of potential supply-side impediments to the continuance of a virtuous circle of cumulative causation. These include inelasticity in the supply of labour to industry, and the inability of firms to transform production processes and the composition of their output in order to keep abreast of technological change and the progress of consumers through the commodity hierarchy. These latter concerns raise issues connected with entrepreneurship and the state of social relations between capital and labour at the point of production.

However, the key similarity between *Modern Capitalism* and the extended model of joint interaction in *Growth and Stability in a Mature Economy* is that both characterize growth as a process of cumulative causation, in which initial conditions propagate subsequent self-reinforcing growth outcomes. Hence in *Modern Capitalism*:

> An initial competitive advantage generates relatively rapid rates of growth of exports, output and productivity for a country, which feed back to reinforce the initial advantage. (Cornwall, 1977, pp. 166–7)

However, and perhaps rather ironically, neither account focuses explicitly on the path dependence of the growth process and the fundamental difference between path-dependent and determinate equilibrium growth outcomes, such as that derived from equations (5.1) and (5.2) above. As Cornwall (1992, pp. 99–100) himself admits, explicit recognition of the importance of path dependence was only to emerge in his subsequent work. Furthermore, accompanying this increasingly explicit focus on path dependence in later work is an important qualitative change in Cornwall's conception of path-dependent processes. This is easily understood in terms of the changing focus of Cornwall's macrodynamics after 1977, from explaining a sustained period of stable dynamic outcomes (the postwar Golden Age, 1945–73) to explaining the transition from one macroeconomic regime (the Golden Age) to another (the post–1973 era). This new focus requires an emphasis on historical *change* rather than the historical *continuity* that is ultimately embodied in the self-reinforcing dynamics of cumulative causation. This leads us to the model of hysteresis developed in *Economic Breakdown and Recovery*.

## From cumulative causation to hysteresis: the Economic Breakdown model

In *Economic Breakdown and Recovery*, attention is turned from growth to unemployment and inflation outcomes.[10] Unemployment is explained as a result of deficient aggregate demand for goods and services in product markets. Inflation, meanwhile, is conceived as primarily a cost-push phenomenon. A key source of inflationary pressure is the conflict over income shares that arises between capitalists and workers struggling for 'fair' wages. This conflict is, of course, influenced by the economic discipline of unemployment, over which policy-makers have some control owing to their ability to manipulate aggregate demand through monetary and fiscal policies. However, equally important is the role that institutions play in the wage- and price-setting process. Wages and prices are innately institutional, owing to the role played by conventions (such as the notion of fair wages and target-return price mark-ups) in their determination. Furthermore, conflict between labour and capital over the value of the real wage is mediated by the institutions of the industrial relations system. These latter institutions and their propensity to evolve over time in response to macroeconomic outcomes play a vital role in the Economic Breakdown model.

Consider, then, the following (simplified) wage- and price-setting equations:

$$\dot{w}_t = \alpha + \beta \dot{p}_t^e - \gamma U_t \tag{5.5}$$

$$\dot{p}_t = \dot{w}_t - \dot{q} \tag{5.6}$$

where $w$ denotes the nominal wage, $p$ is the price level and $p^e$ the expected price level, $U$ is the rate of unemployment and $q$ denotes labour productivity. A dot above a variable denotes the proportional rate of growth of that variable and $t$ subscripts denote time periods. Equation (5.6) is derived from a standard mark-up pricing equation in which prices are set as a fixed mark-up over the average actual cost of labour. Equation (5.5) posits that nominal wage growth is a function of the market power of labour (which varies indirectly with $U$) and inflationary expectations, as workers struggle to achieve and maintain a target real wage. Note that the coefficients of the wage inflation equation are properly conceived as being institutionally determined – they tell us about the state of the industrial relations system and, in particular, the degree of coordination between labour and capital with respect to wage and price setting. This applies equally to the coefficient $\beta$, which measures the ability of workers to index their nominal wages to anticipated changes in prices.[11] Note that this ability will be, in general, incomplete – that is, we expect to observe $\beta < 1$. This does not mean that workers are irrational. No doubt they would like to have $\beta = 1$, but this does not mean that they can achieve this objective in practice.[12]

Substituting (5.5) into (5.6), we arrive at:

$$\dot{p}_t = \alpha - \dot{q} + \beta \dot{p}_t^e - \gamma U_t \tag{5.7}$$

Consider now a situation of expectational equilibrium, where $\dot{p}_t = \dot{p}_t^e = \dot{p}^*$. We can solve (5.7) for this equilibrium rate of inflation as follows:

$$\dot{p}^* = \frac{1}{1 - \beta} \cdot [\alpha - \dot{q} - \gamma U_t] \tag{5.8}$$

Suppose that the exact value of $\dot{p}^*$ is set by the inflation target of the policy authorities. Then we can solve (5.8) for the unique equilibrium rate of unemployment:

$$U^* = \frac{1}{\gamma} \cdot [\alpha - \dot{q} - (1 - \beta)\dot{p}^*] \tag{5.9}$$

Now suppose that we begin an era during which $U^*$ is relatively low. However, suppose that the institutionally determined coefficients $\alpha$, $\beta$ and $\gamma$ are sensitive to the cumulative experience of low unemployment. For example, material security may, in the context of the contested terrain of a capitalist economy, breed new demands on the part of the labour movement (Cornwall, 1994, pp. 188–9). If we now observe a breakdown of consensual industrial relations practices – a major institutional change – the inflation–unemployment relationship in (5.7) will deteriorate. Suppose, for simplicity, that this is reflected in an increase in $\alpha$, *ceteris paribus*. Then for any rate of unemployment, we will now observe a higher equilibrium rate of inflation in equation (5.8). Alternatively, suppose that the policy authorities maintain their inflation target. This means that instead of tolerating higher inflation in (5.8), the policy authorities will allow equilibrium unemployment to rise in equation (5.9), as they pursue deflationary policies designed to restore inflation to its target level.

What the model sketched above suggests is that policies designed to maintain full employment and which succeed in bringing about full-employment outcomes may eventually result in institutional changes which constrain the subsequent ability of policy authorities to pursue full-employment policies. What follows is the austerity of deflationary macroeconomic policies and a concomitant deterioration in macroeconomic performance as measured by increasing misery indices.[13] This suggests a path-dependent, joint interaction of policies, macroeconomic performance and institutions explaining the endogenous breakdown of the postwar Golden Age and the subsequent characteristics of the post-1973 era.

Two important observations arise from further consideration of this model. The first concerns its rather bleak prognosis of the future. Given the breakdown of Golden Age institutions and the low inflation policy preferences of policy authorities, an era of mass high unemployment is inevitable (Cornwall, 1994, pp. 197–210). Indeed, deflationary macroeconomic policies may exacerbate the problems at hand, if they are seen as unfair by labour and if this, in turn, fosters a 'get even' mentality which causes a further deterioration of the inflation–unemployment relationship (Cornwall, 1991, 1994, pp. 207–8).[14]

It is certainly true that we have yet to see whether or not the relatively low rates of inflation (compared to the 1970s) achieved during the 1980s and 1990s can be maintained if the OECD economies return to 1950s/60s unemployment rates – mainly because policy authorities have little intention of allowing this to happen, having redefined full employment at ever higher rates of unemployment. However, the Economic Breakdown prognosis may be complicated by other path-dependent institutional responses to the end of the Golden Age. In particular, the response to economic breakdown has been *corporate* as well as public, and *legal* as well as macroeconomic. Hence in some countries (for example, the UK and the USA) the state has coupled deflationary macroeconomic policies with changes in labour laws designed to undermine the bargaining position of workers at any level of employment. Furthermore, 'corporate restructuring' has accompanied the state reaction to the end of the Golden Age. Particularly important – especially in the UK and the USA – has been the growth of non-standard work practices such as contracting out and part-time and temporary work.[15] This has resulted in an increasingly dualistic form of labour market segmentation – that is, the creation of polarized 'good' and 'bad' jobs. Furthermore, at any given level of unemployment (as measured by the conventional 'head count' method), we now observe the phenomena of *hours*-constrained (rather than *jobs*-constrained) involuntary part-time and temporary workers (Blank, 1990).[16] The bargaining position of these and other part-time and temporary workers is weak, because of their relatively high rates of turnover and lack of union representation. Meanwhile, the growth of secondary employment undermines the bargaining power of primary sector workers, whose 'outside option' at any level of unemployment deteriorates owing to the increased prospect of involuntary part-time or temporary work.[17] These factors may actually *improve* the inflation–unemployment relationship in equation (5.7), although not in a manner that is necessarily desirable from an equity point of view. 'Zapping labour' is arguably less desirable than improving the inflation–unemployment relationship through a consensual approach based on a second generation of centrally coordinated incomes policies. Furthermore, note that to some extent the corporate restructuring mechanism outlined above creates only an illusory improvement in the inflation–unemployment relationship. This is because of the measurement issues that are raised by workers who are hours- rather than jobs-constrained, but who are nevertheless counted as employed rather than unemployed under the conventional statistical definitions of these terms. Rather than thinking of the 'inequality prognosis' discussed above as an alternative to John Cornwall's Economic Breakdown prognosis, then, we may find ourselves in the worst of all worlds, experiencing some measure of *both* outcomes simultaneously.

A second observation arises from further consideration of the Economic Breakdown model, one that is more closely allied to the central methodological theme of this chapter. This concerns the explicit discussion in the Economic Breakdown model of the path-dependent nature of macrodynamics, coupled with the more subtle conception of this path dependence as compared with the Growth and Stability and Modern Capitalism models (see, for example, Cornwall, 1994, pp. 23–5). Macroeconomic evolution is conceived as a recursive process in which policies affect performance which affects institutions, only for the latter to affect subsequent policy options and actions, and so on. Moreover, this recursive interaction is not simply self-reinforcing. Rather, it is more appropriately conceived as being hysteretic – feedback may be discontinuous and negative rather than, as in a process of cumulative causation, continuous and purely positive. Indeed, Cornwall ultimately shows how we may observe both positive and negative feedbacks within the same causal chain. Hence the feedback of macroeconomic outcomes on to institutions may initially be neutral or even positive, as desirable outcomes reinforce the sociopolitical basis of the institutions on which they are founded. However, successive periods of neutral or positive feedback may eventually give rise to negative feedback, in response to *cumulative* effects of the recursive interaction of policy, performance and institutions (Cornwall, 1994, p. 24). These cumulative effects, which gestate over long periods but impact abruptly on the economy, can be associated with discontinuities and structural change – factors that are now taken to be the hallmark of hysteresis in social systems (Cross, 1993; Amable *et al.*, 1995; Setterfield, 1998). By this point, then, Cornwall's methodological journey is complete. The Growth and Stability, Modern Capitalism and Economic Breakdown models are all models of joint interaction – all are concerned with the way that realized economic outcomes feed back on to the so-called 'data' of conventional equilibrium analysis. This central principle of feedback or joint interaction gives rise to increasingly sophisticated models of path dependence, as Cornwall's treatment of macrodynamics progresses from determinate equilibrium constructs through cumulative causation to evolutionary models based on hysteresis.

## LESSONS FOR CURRENT RESEARCH

It only remains to draw attention to the lessons for current research that arise from consideration of John Cornwall's macrodynamics. First, it is evident from

Cornwall's work that there is no unique or truly general theory of evolutionary, path-dependent economies. Instead, the task that faces researchers is to apply the most appropriate path-dependent organizing concept to the analysis of different economic phenomena. This requires the explicit adoption of a 'horses for courses' approach to doing economic theory.

Second, the Economic Breakdown model is suggestive of the close link between institutions and path dependence. Institutions create conditional closure in an otherwise open, historical economic environment, the conditionality stemming from the fact that institutions themselves are not 'given' but instead evolve over time. Nevertheless, taking institutions as exogenous in the short run (despite their long-run endogeneity) facilitates the construction of fully articulated *conditional* model economies by economic theorists. Such models are necessarily intermediate (as opposed to 'pure') theories of how the economy operates, grounded in *both* abstract analytics *and* the stylized facts of actually observed institutional regularities. Cornwall's Economic Breakdown model exemplifies the possibilities of this approach.

Third, models such as that presented in *Economic Breakdown and Recovery* characterize economic evolution as an endogenous indeterminate process, in which it is possible to specify the recursive causal relations that exist between economic variables, but not in the deterministic manner necessary to facilitate their use for *a priori* prediction of evolving future outcomes. In the context of these models, then, the economist's traditional concern with prediction must be substantially downplayed.[18] Note, however, that models of endogenous–indeterminate evolution are capable of *ex post* explanation – they suggest that economists can and should seek to understand the causal relations operative in capitalism by studying its history, because evolutionary change is ultimately explained by processes at work within the economic system itself. This provides a fitting contrast with determinate equilibrium models, which seek to 'explain' change by appealing to exogenous shocks. In fact, such models are incapable of even *ex post* explanation of change, there being, by definition, no means of 'explaining' extraneous, random disturbances.[19]

Finally, it is worth drawing attention to the important role that discontinuities play in Cornwall's macrodynamics. Discontinuities are important in *Growth and Stability in a Mature Economy*, entering into the capital theory and the structural equations of the extended model of joint interaction therein.[20] They also play a critical role in explaining the abrupt transition between macroeconomic regimes in the Economic Breakdown model and in this model, discontinuities are central to the form of the path dependence that arises from the joint interaction of policy, macroeconomic performance and institutions. As intimated earlier, this emphasis on discontinuities in macroeconomics and especially their role in generating path dependence clearly anticipates current work that attaches importance to non-linearities in explaining path-dependent macroeconomic outcomes (see, for example, Cross, 1993; Amable *et al.*, 1995; Setterfield, 1998).

## CONCLUSION

This chapter traces the development of John Cornwall's macrodynamics since the publication of *Growth and Stability in a Mature Economy* in 1972. The purpose has been to show how Cornwall's macrodynamic method moves ever further away from the conventional equilibrium framework towards increasingly sophisticated models of path dependence. Hence the model of joint interaction in *Growth and Stability in a Mature Economy* gives rise to a nascent model of cumulative causation which is developed more explicitly in *Modern Capitalism*. Finally, a model of hysteresis is developed in *Economic Breakdown and Recovery* to explain the transition between different macroeconomic regimes, each of which contains different stable (and even self-reinforcing) policy, performance and institutional features.

John Cornwall's macrodynamic models demonstrate how to go about doing useful macroeconomic theorizing couched in path-dependent terms. The richness of his analysis is such that it embodies a number of important methodological lessons that both heterodox macroeconomists and practitioners of the current orthodoxy alike would do well to contemplate.

**Notes**

1.    I would like to thank John Cornwall and Geoff Harcourt for their comments on an earlier version of this chapter. The usual disclaimer applies.
2.    Harrod (1939) is a notable example, although his sympathy with Keynes's theory should not obscure the fact that Harrod's efforts to model the fundamentals of economic dynamics pre-date *The General Theory* (see, for example, Asimakopulos, 1991, pp. 138–9).
3.    This focus omits numerous earlier contributions to macrodynamics published in the form of journal articles, concentrating instead on what Cornwall himself identifies as his mature scholarly output (see Cornwall, 1992, pp. 98–9).
4.    Differences in productivity growth rates between sectors also influence changes in the composition of employment. See, for example, Sundrum (1990) and Cornwall and Cornwall (1994a, 1994b).
5.    This argument is, of course, compromised if low productivity growth service industries come to dominate the commodity hierarchy. See Sundrum (1990) and Cornwall and Cornwall (1994a).
6.    Indeed, Cornwall's discussion of 'Frankel's modifier' results in his development of what would now be termed an 'AK' model of endogenous growth. See, for example, Rebelo (1991).

7. The elasticity of potential output with respect to demand is less that one for $r_y < r_{y1}$ and $r_y > r_{y2}$. The latter case is explained by limits to the exploitation of increasing returns and intersectoral resource transfers. The former case results from the presence of high and/or rising unemployment when $r_y$ is low relative to $r_x$, which is held to discourage firms from switching to capital-intensive techniques of production and reduce the receptiveness of labour to innovations involving the introduction of these techniques. See Cornwall (1972, p. 67).

8. Cumulative causation is not formally equivalent to a conventional situation of multiple equilibria, because in systems which display cumulative causation, the set of long-run or final outcomes may not be well-defined *ex ante*; indeed, it may be inappropriate to speak of 'final' outcomes in such systems. However, cumulative causation shares with models of multiple equilibria the important characteristic of sensitivity to initial conditions.

9. This innovation, first apparent in Cornwall (1976), has remained a feature of Cornwall's subsequent growth models. See, for example, Cornwall and Cornwall (1994b).

10. Some of the ideas in this book are reiterated in recent papers such as Cornwall (1997) and Cornwall and Cornwall (1997a).

11. $\beta$ is properly construed as depending on $U$ as well as labour market institutions. See, for example, Palley (1997).

12. Notice also that as long as mark-ups remain fixed, the rate of growth of real wages derived from equation (5.6) is constant (equal to the given rate of growth of productivity) regardless of the rate of inflation and the level of unemployment. Hence no one is 'fooled' when changes in unemployment and/or inflation occur. See Cornwall (1994, p. 62).

13. A misery index is the sum of the unemployment and inflation rates. If equilibrium unemployment rises at any given target level of inflation, then the value of the misery index will clearly rise.

14. Depressed demand conditions may also adversely affect the inflation–unemployment relationship by lowering the trend rate of productivity growth via the Verdoorn Law.

15. The growth of contracting out and part-time and temporary work are not necessarily independent trends, of course.

16. See also Bregger and Haugen (1995) for measures of the extent of this problem.

17. This may help to explain why many full-time workers are *over*employed – working more hours than desired – even as other workers are involuntarily underemployed. See Stewart and Swaffield (1997).

18. Although forecasting the evolutionary process itself is not possible due to its structural indeterminacy, as long as the forces of structural change are relatively slow – as they appear to be in the case of institutional change – then there remains the possibility of *conditional* prediction. This is based on the *ceteris paribus* assumption that current institutions will persist over the forecast horizon. See Cornwall and Cornwall (1997b, pp. 377–8).

19. There is no way of predicting such disturbances – so of course, determinate equilibrium models cannot *predict* change either.

20. Discontinuities do not enter crucially into the path dependence of the Growth and Stability model, however.

## References

Amable, B., J. Henry, F. Lordon and R. Topol (1995) in R. Cross (ed.) *The Natural Rate of Unemployment: Reflections on 25 Years of the Hypothesis*, Cambridge, Cambridge University Press

Asimakopulos, A. (1991) *Keynes's General Theory and Accumulation*, Cambridge, Cambridge University Press

Blank, R. (1990) 'Are part-time jobs bad jobs?', in G. Burtless (ed.) *A Future of Lousy Jobs?* Washington, DC, Brookings

Bregger, J.E. and S.E. Haugen (1995) 'BLS introduces new range of alternative unemployment measures', *Monthly Labor Review*, 118, 19–26

Cornwall, J. (1972) *Growth and Stability in a Mature Economy*, London, Martin Robertson

Cornwall, J. (1976) 'Diffusion, convergence and Kaldor's laws', *Economic Journal*, 86, 307–14

Cornwall, J. (1977) *Modern Capitalism: Its Growth and Transformation*, London, Martin Robertson

Cornwall, J. (1990) *The Theory of Economic Breakdown*: *An Institutional-Analytical Approach*, Oxford, Basil Blackwell

Cornwall, J. (1991) 'Prospects for unemployment in the 1990s with hysteresis', in J. Cornwall (ed.) *The Capitalist Economies: Prospects for the 1990s*, Aldershot, Edward Elgar

Cornwall, J. (1992) 'John Cornwall', in P. Arestis and M. Sawyer (eds) *A Biographical Dictionary of Dissenting Economists*, Aldershot, Edward Elgar

Cornwall, J. (1994) *Economic Breakdown and Recovery: Theory and Policy*, Armonk, NY, M.E. Sharpe

Cornwall, J. (1997) 'Notes on the trade cycle and social philosophy in a Post-Keynesian world', in G.C. Harcourt and P.A. Riach (eds) *A 'Second Edition' of The General Theory*, Vol. 1, London, Routledge

Cornwall, J. and W. Cornwall (1994a) 'Growth theory and economic structure', *Economica*, 61, 237–51

Cornwall, J. and W. Cornwall (1994b) 'Structural change and productivity in the OECD', in P. Davidson and J.A. Kregel (eds) *Employment, Growth and Finance*: Economic Realty and Economic Growth, Aldershot, Edward Elgar

Cornwall, J. and W. Cornwall (1997a) 'The unemployment problem and the legacy of Keynes', *Journal of Post Keynesian Economics*, 19, 525–42

Cornwall, J. and W. Cornwall (1997b) 'Unemployment prospects for modern capitalism', in P. Arestis *et al.* (eds) *Markets, Unemployment and Policy: Essays in Honour of Geoff Harcourt*, Vol. 2, London, Routledge

Cross, R. (1993) 'On the foundations of hysteresis in economic systems', *Economics and Philosophy*, 9, 53–74

Grossman, G.M. and E. Helpman (1991) *Innovation and Growth in the Global Economy*, Cambridge, MA, MIT Press

Harrod, R. (1939) 'An essay in dynamic theory', *Economic Journal*, 49, 14–33

Lachman, L. (1947) 'Complementary and substitution in the theory of capital', *Economica*, 14, 108–19

Palley, T. (1997) 'Does inflation grease the wheels of adjustment? New evidence from the U.S. economy', *International Review of Applied Economics*, 11, 387–98

Rebelo, S. (1991) 'Long run policy analysis and long-run growth', *Journal of Political Economy*, 99, 500–21

Setterfield, M.A. (1998) 'Adjustment asymmetries and hysteresis in simple dynamic models', *The Manchester School*, 66, 283–301

Stewart, M.B. and J.K. Swaffield (1997) 'Constraints on the desired hours of work of British men', *Economic Journal*, 107, 520–35

Sundrum, R.M. (1990) *Economic Growth in Theory and Practice*, London, Macmillan

# 6 Post-Keynesianism and Institutionalism: Another Look at the Link

## Geoff Hodgson

The work of John Cornwall has been widely described as both Post-Keynesian and institutionalist. Such designations are both appropriate because, as well as developing Post-Keynesian ideas, Cornwall makes frequent reference to the role of institutions and to institutionalism. Furthermore, he makes particularly extensive use of the work of Nicholas Kaldor, who was one of the Post-Keynesians closest to institutionalist tradition. For instance, Kaldor's mentor Allyn Young was an admirer of Veblen, and Kaldor explicitly and repeatedly acknowledged the influence of the institutionalist Gunnar Myrdal.

In 1989, I published an essay on the 'missing link' between institutionalism and Post-Keynesianism (Hodgson, 1989). In it, I argued that an institutionalist research programme has something to offer as a behavioural and micro-economic foundation for Post-Keynesian macroeconomics. I remain convinced of this view, and support for it can be found in, for example, Cornwall (1972), which makes several references to Duesenberry's (1949) book on the consumption function. Duesenberry's work was profoundly influenced by Thorstein Veblen's (1919) conception of the role of habit in economic life.

Here, I wish to supplement this argument by taking a historical approach to the links between institutionalism and Keynesianism. It will be argued that the links may not simply be established on the basis of a shared understanding of human agency, but also on a shared rejection of reductionism and a shared assertion of the relative autonomy of macroeconomics.

Before Keynes, macroeconomics was an underdeveloped mode of analysis. Karl Marx is one of the few precursors, with his focus on the formation and flow of monetary and labour time aggregates in *Capital*. The links and similarities between Marx and Keynes have been widely explored, notably by Robinson (1942). However, the conceptual and empirical contribution of American institutionalism to the emergence of macroeconomics is generally underestimated. This essay outlines the contribution of Thorstein Veblen, Wesley Mitchell, other earlier institutionalists and allied thinkers to the Keynesian theoretical revolution. It is argued that with institutionalism as a midwife, Keynesian macroeconomics was born.

PHILOSOPHY: THE PROBLEM OF REDUCTIONISM

Economists educated in the Post-Keynesian age will take it for granted that macroeconomics constitutes a viable and partially autonomous level of analysis. It is widely assumed that aggregate functions and relations are appropriate theoretical means for understanding the behaviour of the economy as a whole. The Chicago counter-revolution against Keynes – in the 1960s and thereafter – centred on this very issue, by insisting that all such aggregates had to be placed upon the 'sound microfoundations' of individual, utility-maximizing behaviour. The attack emanating earlier from Hayek (1931) and the Austrian school was even more radical, by denying the validity of any such aggregate functions.

What is partly at stake here is what is known in philosophy as the problem of reductionism. Reductionism can be defined as the idea that all aspects of a complex phenomenon must be explained in terms of one level, or type of unit. According to this view there are no autonomous levels of analysis other than this elemental foundation, and no such thing as emergent properties upon which different levels of analysis can be based.[1] Reductionism is still conspicuous in social science today and typically appears as methodological individualism. This is defined as 'the doctrine that all social phenomena (their structure and their change) are in principle explicable only in terms of individuals – their properties, goals, and beliefs' (Elster, 1982, p. 453). It is thus alleged that explanations of socioeconomic phenomena must be reduced to properties of constituent individuals and relations between them. Such methodological notions have been prominent in the postwar attack on the economics of Keynes.

However, there are two serious problems involved in this reductionist attack. First, complete reductionism is both impossible and a philosophically dogmatic diversion. Even moderately complex systems defy complete analytical reduction. Consider the relatively 'simple' case of the three-body problem in mechanics. While this problem has been solved for two bodies, the differential equations that result from applying these laws to three bodies are so complicated that a general solution has not been found. Instead, partial solutions have been achieved by resorting to approximations or constraints of various kinds, such the assumption that one body has negligible mass (Stewart, 1989, pp. 66–72). Hence mathematical solutions cannot be found to configurations of this very first level of complexity, involving just three bodies. Similar problems of intractability arise from the Schrödinger equations for subatomic particles. Even more severe problems of mathematical reduction are also common in biology (Wimsatt, 1980).

Chaos theorists have shown that in non-linear systems, tiny changes in crucial parameters can lead to dramatic consequences. The result is not simply to make prediction difficult or impossible; there are serious implications for the notion of reductive explanation in science. We cannot with absolute confidence associate a given outcome with a given set of initial conditions, because we can never be sure that the computations traced out from those initial conditions are precise enough, and that the initial conditions themselves have been defined with sufficient precision. Hence in chaos theory, the very notion of explaining a phenomenon by reference to a system and its initial conditions is challenged. Chaos theory 'brings a new challenge to the reductionist view that a system can be understood by breaking it down and studying each piece' (Crutchfield *et al.*, 1986, p. 48). With chaos theory, not only is the common obsession with precise prediction confounded; the whole atomistic tradition in science of attempting to reduce each phenomenon to its component parts is placed into question.

What it is important to stress is that the process of analysis cannot be extended to the most elementary subatomic particles presently known to science, or even to individuals in economics or genes in biology. Complete reductionism would be hopeless and interminable. As Karl Popper has declared: 'I do not think that there are any examples of a successful reduction' to elemental units in science (Popper and Eccles, 1977, p. 18). Reduction is necessary to some extent, but it can never be complete.

It should be pointed out at the outset that the general idea of a reduction to parts is not being overturned here. Some degree of reduction to elemental units is inevitable. Even measurement is an act of reduction. Science cannot proceed without some dissection and some analysis of parts. What is widely contested is the possibility of complete analytical reduction. The acknowledged failure of the microfoundations project in economics should not go unnoticed (Kirman, 1989; Rizvi, 1994).

These problems are omnipresent in economics, and not simply because abundant complexities and non-linearities are found therein. For example, if individual agents are profoundly affected by their circumstances, as well as circumstances being affected by agents, then the analytical reduction proposed in methodological individualism, of socioeconomic phenomena to the preferences and purposes of individuals, can never provide a complete explanation (Hodgson, 1988).

Another serious problem in methodological individualism, and in the version of reductionism at the forefront of the Keynesian counter-revolution, is that it is internally inconsistent by its own canons. If analytical reduction to parts or lower levels is required, then why stop with the individual? If we can reduce explanations to individual terms why not further reduce them to genes or other biological characteristics? The inconsistency here has been pointed out by Wilson and Sober (1989). The same arguments concerning explanatory reduction from social groups to individuals apply equally to explanatory reduction from individual to gene.

Only the hard-core 'Chicago' reductionists have an answer to this challenge in its own terms. Since the rise of sociobiology in the 1970s, Gary Becker

(1976), Jack Hirshleifer (1977, 1978) and Gordon Tullock (1979) have argued that the postulates of neoclassical economics – including the presumed ubiquity of scarcity and competition – apply equally to biology. They hence use this presumption as an argument for 'economic imperialism': the idea that the 'economic' concepts of maximization and equilibrium should apply to other sciences. However, this does not, in fact, mean the conquest of other sciences by economics, but the dissolution of economics into biology. By their own reductionist arguments, they are forced to reduce economics to biological terms. Even if these principles have some resemblance to neoclassical economics, biology must be the prior substratum of any economic system: it is primary and more basic. Instead of 'economic imperialism', the Chicago gambit means the end of economics as a science.

This sets the scene for our historical excursion. In Western social science in the latter decades of the nineteenth century, it was widely believed that social phenomena should be reduced analytically to biological terms. In social science in the 1870–1920 period, reductionism was prominent and typically took a biological form. In the writings of Albert Schäffle from Germany, Herbert Spencer from England and William Graham Sumner from America, attempts were made to explain the behaviour of individuals and groups in terms of their alleged biological characteristics. Even if culture and institutions changed, according to these writers, social evolution occurred only in so far as the biological characteristics of human beings were altered. It was in this context that Thorstein Veblen prepared an intellectual revolution that was to have lasting ramifications for social science.

## BIOLOGY AND SOCIAL SCIENCE: VEBLEN, WHITEHEAD AND KEYNES

Veblen was steeped in these biological ideas. He first read Spencer in the 1870s when he was a student at Carleton College (Dorfman, 1934, p. 30). During the 1880s, and especially during his years at Yale University, Veblen also came under the influence of Sumner (Dorfman, 1934, pp. 43–6). Like many others, Veblen was absorbed by Spencer's and Sumner's ideas of socioeconomic evolution (Edgell and Tilman, 1989; Eff, 1989). Spencer and Sumner were both Lamarckians. The Lamarckian principle of acquired characteristics meant to some degree that acquired habits and other characteristics could be passed on *biologically* through genetic inheritance to the next generation. In the Lamarckian scheme a relatively rapid evolution of the human organism was thus presumed to be possible.

During the 1890s, Veblen was also absorbed with problems of theoretical Marxism. Although sympathetic to socialism, in a review of Max Lorenz's *Die Marxistische Socialdemokratie*, Veblen (1897) noted that its author

(Lorenz, 1896, p. 50) had found a crucial defect in Marxian theory. This criticism of Marxism recurs forcefully in later works (Veblen, 1919, pp. 313–4, 416, 441–2). Following Lorenz, Veblen rightly argued that the mere class position of an individual as a wage labourer or a capitalist tells us very little about the specific conceptions or habits of thought, and thereby the likely actions, of the individuals involved. Individual interests, whatever they are, do not necessarily lead to accordant individual actions. As Veblen (1919, p. 442) pointed out, and as sophisticated Marxists such as Antonio Gramsci later emphasized, the members of the working class could perceive their own salvation just as much in terms of patriotism or nationalism as in socialist revolution. The class position of an agent – exploiter or exploited – does not imply that that person will be impelled towards any particular view of reality or any particular pattern of action.

This argument has a number of ramifications, both theoretical and political. The theoretical issue that is relevant here is the alleged failure of Marxism to provide an adequate analysis of the relationship between actor and structure, of the relationship between the individual and the socioeconomic whole. Instead, Marx assumes that individuals are largely bearers of social forces. There is no adequate psychology or theory of human agency.

Unlike Marx, Veblen conceived of the individual in *both* biological and socioeconomic terms. Humans are biotic as well as social beings, so their biology should not be ignored. In contrast to both Marxism and neoclassical economics, a viable social science must be linked with biology. However, at the same time, he opposed the reductionist notions of Spencer and Sumner that socioeconomic phenomena should be reduced *exclusively* to biological terms.

Veblen thus begins to argue for a level of analysis that has some degree of autonomy from the level of the individual organism, but is at the same time linked conceptually with it. Today we are used to social sciences insisting on their separation from biology. However, this is more a phenomenon of the years from the First World War to the 1960s, and not so much before or since (Degler, 1991). When Veblen was writing in the 1890s, biology and social science were linked. His innovation involved a complex manoeuvre: on the one hand, to maintain links between biology and the social science, and on the other, to assert the autonomy of the latter from the former.

A crucial influence in this respect came in 1896. According to Dorfman (1934, p. 139), in 1896 the zoologist and philosopher C. Lloyd Morgan delivered a lecture at the University of Chicago, key points of which were later published in his book *Habit and Instinct* (1896).[2] Morgan was Professor of Geology and Zoology at University College, Bristol, in England. Arguably, Morgan's presence in Chicago provided a keystone in the architecture of Veblen's theory of socioeconomic evolution. Although it was some years later that Veblen first referred to Morgan, it was with definite approval, showing that Veblen was familiar with Morgan's 1896 book (Veblen, 1914, p. 30n).

In opposition to Spencer and other Lamarckians, Morgan contended that acquired habits are not passed on by genetic inheritance. This Darwinian stance created an apparent paradox: despite tremendous advances in civilization and technology in the past few millennia, in *biotic and genetic terms* humankind had evolved only to a very slight degree. Genetically, humans had changed very little in the centuries that had witnessed enormous advances in science, technology and civilization. To nineteenth-century intellectuals infused with ideas of biological determination, how could such a mismatch be explained? In contrast, Lamarckian thinking denied this genetic conservatism and thus escaped the problem, by insisting on the possibility that newly acquired habits and other characteristics could readily be passed on genetically from generation to generation. Lamarckians thus saw the development of civilization as paralleled by the rapid development of the human genotype or organism. Lamarckism permitted a reductionist explanation of socioeconomic development in biological terms, as exemplified in Spencer's work.

Rejecting Lamarckism, Morgan then asked: if human beings had evolved only slightly in genetic terms, then *what* had evolved in the last millennium or so of human society? In this period, human achievements have been transformed beyond measure. His answer to the puzzle was that 'evolution *has been transferred from the organism to the environment* . . . In social evolution on this view, the increment is by storage in the social environment to which each new generation adapts itself, with no increased native power of adaptation' (Morgan, 1896, p. 340; emphasis in original).

In opposition to Lamarckism, Morgan's Darwinian understanding of evolution led him to promote the idea of an *emergent level* of socioeconomic evolution that was not explicable exclusively in terms of the biological characteristics of the individuals involved. Evolution occurred at this emergent level as well, and without any necessary change in human biotic characteristics. Accordingly, the crucial concepts of emergence and emergent properties were liberated by the Darwinian insistence of a barrier between acquired habit and biotic inheritance. The biological and the social spheres became partially autonomous, but linked, levels of analysis. In later works the philosophical concept of emergence was developed by Morgan and others influenced by him. Indeed, he was a pioneer of the modern philosophical concept of emergence (Morgan, 1927, 1933). In fact it was he who coined the term. For this reason he is remembered by modern philosophers of biology such as Mayr (1985). His work also influenced Whitehead (1926, p. xxiii) among others.

However, Morgan did not make the objects and mechanisms of socio-economic evolution clear. He did not specify what the social 'environment' consisted of. He did not identify the units of selection, the sources of variation and the nature of the selective process. He simply indicated the possibility of 'storage in the social environment' through the written record, in social traditions, technology and art. This was, nevertheless, a highly significant point.

Morgan's conception of 'environmental' evolution implied that, despite change, some degree of inertia and continuity in environmental conditions was necessary, so that appropriate ontogenetic development could occur. In short, the means of preservation of information were necessary for learning. It was left to Veblen to make the crucial next step: institutions rather than individuals became the objects of selection in socioeconomic evolution.

Morgan's argument directed attention to the phenomenon of socio-economic evolution, and gave it a degree of autonomy from the question of biological inheritance. With Morgan's intervention, the scene was set for Veblen's intellectual revolution: the concept of the evolution and selection of institutions, as emergent entities in the socioeconomic sphere. It is thus perhaps no accident that shortly after Morgan's visit to Chicago the idea of an evolutionary process of selection of institutions began to appear in Veblen's work, most notably and extensively in his 1899 classic *The Theory of the Leisure Class*.

This may at first sight seem an obscure development in late 1890s philosophy and social theory, of little interest to a single-minded, hard-headed macroeconomist. However, the concept of emergent properties, and its implicit transplantation into economics, were both necessary for macro-economics to become established. Without the concept of emergent properties in economics, there is no reason why macroeconomic phenomena should not be analysed simply in microeconomic terms: there is no need f or a relatively autonomous level of analysis above the microeconomic. The existence of emergent properties at the macroeconomic level makes a relatively autonomous macroeconomics possible.

Although Veblen implicitly adopted the notion of emergent properties in economics for the first time, there is no evidence that Veblen was a significant influence on Keynes. However, strong parallels between Veblen's (1904) analysis of the business system and Keynes's theory of employment have been noted. Rutledge Vining (1939, pp. 692–3) has argued that: 'Much of Keynes's theory of employment can be dug from Veblen's intuitions.' Nevertheless, Keynes remained silent on Veblen's legacy. Veblen was given some recognition by the leading Post-Keynesian Joan Robinson (1975, p. vii; 1979, pp. 37–40, 94–5, 116) who belatedly stumbled upon Veblen's concept of capital and deployed it in the capital theory debates. She (Robinson, 1979, p. 95) then concluded that Veblen was 'the most original economist born and bred in the USA'.

In regard to the philosophical question of different, but linked, levels of analysis, a much more obvious influence on Keynes was Alfred North Whitehead. Keynes came under the influence of Whitehead in Cambridge in the first decade of the twentieth century, before Whitehead's transfer to London in 1910 and his emigration to the United States in 1924. As well as his ventures into logic and mathematics, Whitehead promoted an organicist philosophy. Institutionalist writers such as Allan Gruchy (1948) have noted the organicist thinking in Keynes's *General Theory*, and it is reasonable to suggest that Whitehead is partly responsible for this feature (Winslow, 1986, 1989).[3]

In an organicist ontology, relations between entities are internal rather than external, and the essential characteristics of any element are outcomes of relations with other entities. This relates to the central question in social theory as to whether or not structure may be represented simply as the property of the interactions between given individuals. Organicism denies that individuals may be treated as elemental or immutable building blocks of analysis. Just as society cannot exist without individuals, the individual does not exist prior to the social reality. Individuals both constitute, and are constituted by, society. We often hear the truism that society is composed of individuals. The organicist does not deny this, but insists that individuality is itself a social phenomenon.

Related to Whitehead's ontology is his notion of reality as being composed of linked, hierarchical levels. Whitehead (1926, p. 203) wrote: 'In so far as there are internal relations, everything must depend upon everything else. But if this be the case, we cannot know about anything till we equally well know everything else.' Whitehead's solution to this problem was to propose a nested hierarchy of sets of internal relations. Each layer in this hierarchy relates to a particular set of characteristics, thus defining the units at any given level. The hierarchy has the feature that the layers relating to wider and more general phenomena are more stable than the narrower and more specific ones. Such a hierarchy within an overall system allows for the possibility of theoretical abstraction, disregarding certain aspects of the phenomena at hand, to focus on the main causal linkages.

In short, in his postulate of a nested hierarchy, Whitehead provides the philosophical basis for an economics consisting of linked, but partially autonomous, microeconomic and macroeconomic levels. Whatever the precise influence of Whitehead on Keynes, this ontological standpoint is consistent with Keynes's own standpoint in the *General Theory*.[4] Furthermore, the idea of a nested hierarchy of internal relations, where causal processes are analysed at a number of distinct but connected levels, each encompassing different causal factors and time periods, is central to the Post-Keynesian analyses of Cornwall (1990), Kregel (1976) and others, even if the explicit connection with Whitehead is not made.

## STATISTICS: KEYNES AND MITCHELL

Another important link between institutionalism and the development of Keynesianism was the innovation of national income accounting, in which the work of the American institutionalist Wesley Mitchell played a vital part. Being traditionally linked with organicist or holistic views, institutionalism thereby developed and sanctioned the conceptualization and measurement of economic aggregates. The theoretical and empirical work involved here was of major importance in the development of twentieth-century economics.

Mitchell was the third in the founding generation of American institutionalists, and, additionally, one of the fathers of modern macroeconomics. Mitchell's work is notable for its implicit anti-reductionist thrust and its consequent contribution to the development of Keynesianism. Mitchell (1937, p. 26) argued that economists need not begin with a theory of individual behaviour but with the statistical observation of 'mass phenomena'. Mitchell and his colleagues in the National Bureau for Economic Research in the 1920s and 1930s played a vital role in the development of national income accounting, suggesting that aggregate, macroeconomic phenomena have an ontological and empirical legitimacy.

This was an important incursion against reductionism in economics. It created space for the construction of Keynesianism, but the counter-attack from reductionism has been persistent up to the present day. Notably, in defending Mitchell's approach against the reductionist and neoclassical criticisms of Koopmans (1947), Vining (1949, p. 79) argued that phenomena such as 'trade fluctuations' were not merely aggregates 'of the economizing units of traditional theoretical economics'. Furthermore, 'we need not take for granted that the behaviour and functioning of this entity can be exhaustively explained in terms of the motivated behaviour of individuals who are particles within the whole'. This is a classic rejection of reductionism, in terms of the existence of emergent properties that cannot be completely explained in terms of the constituent parts.

For Keynesianism, Mitchell's anti-reductionist thrust was crucial. Being traditionally linked with organicist or holistic views, institutionalism developed and sanctioned the conceptualization and measurement of economic aggregates. Through the development of national income accounting the work of Mitchell and his colleagues influenced and inspired the macroeconomics of Keynes (Mirowski, 1989, p. 307). With the innovatory macroeconomic concepts in Keynes's *General Theory*, the legitimacy of dealing with aggregates was established. Crucial theoretical developments in early postwar Keynesian economics, such as Duesenberry's (1949) 'habit persistence' theory of the consumption function, were influenced by institutionalists such as Veblen.

It was left to a nagging minority to complain that neoclassical microeconomics was incompatible with much of Keynesian macroeconomic theory. In particular, standard Walrasian general equilibrium analysis predicted a full employment equilibrium, whereas textbook Keynesianism did not. Keynesians accepted the possibility of such an involuntary surplus of labour, thereby conflicting with Robbins's (1932) very definition of the subject in terms of 'scarce means'.

Paradoxically, however, the rise of Keynesian economics undermined American institutionalism. The paradox exists because American institutionalists embraced the Keynesian revolution. In policy terms, the rise of Keynesianism coincided with a drift of Anglo-American opinion towards state intervention and planning, and in the 1930s American institutionalists were active in the inspiration, development and promotion of President Franklin Roosevelt's New Deal (Barber, 1994; Stoneman, 1979; Wunderlin, 1992). Sympathetic economists such as William Jaffé and Richard Ely perceived parallels between the works of Veblen and Keynes, and their joint consummation in Roosevelt's policies (Tilman, 1992, pp. 111–12). On the theoretical side, institutionalism formed its own synthesis with Keynesianism, giving less emphasiz to mathematical modelling and interpreting Keynes in terms of an organicist ontology (Dillard, 1948; Gruchy, 1948).

We now turn to the reasons why the 'Keynesian' revolution ultimately undermined American institutionalism.

## MATHEMATICS: FROM KEYNES TO KEYNESIANISM

The crisis in American institutionalism came to a head in the Great Crash of 1929. The personal recollections of Myrdal are particularly apposite. When he came to the USA at the end of the 1920s, institutional economics was still seen by many as the 'wind of the future'. However, at that time Myrdal was 'utterly critical' of this orientation in economics and was himself at the 'theoretical' stage of his own development. He 'even had something to do with the initiation of the Econometric Society, which was planned as a defense organization against the advancing institutionalists' (Myrdal, 1972, p. 6). Myrdal goes on to explain a key event in the decline of the popularity of institutionalism in the United States:

> What I believe nipped it in the bud was the world-wide economic depression. Faced with this great calamity, we economists of the 'theoretical' school, accustomed to reason in terms of simplified macro-models, felt we were on the top of the situation, while the institutionalists were left in a muddle. It was at this stage that economists in the stream of the Keynesian revolution adjusted their theoretical models to the needs of the time, which gave victory much more broadly to our 'theoretical' approach. (Myrdal, 1972, p. 7)

It seems that the institutionalists, while emphasizing the complexity of economic phenomena and the need for careful empirical research, were out-theorized by the mathematical Keynesians. This group of young and mathematically-minded converts to Keynesianism, led by Paul Samuelson and others, developed what now seem in retrospect to be extraordinarily simple macroeconomic models. The attraction of this approach was partly its technocratic lure, and partly because it proposed very simple apparent solutions to the urgent problem of the day. It appeared that the problem of unemployment could be alleviated simply by increasing a variable called $G$. The 'solution' was plain and transparent, dressed up in mathematical and 'scientific' garb, and given all the reverence customarily accorded to such presentations in a highly technocratic culture.[5] Notably, without referring to Myrdal, Ross (1991) corroborates the argument:

> Institutionalism as a movement . . . fell victim to the Great Depression and its Keynesian remedy. For self-proclaimed experts in historical change, their inability to come to any better understanding of the Depression than their neoclassical colleagues was a considerable deficit. Mitchell in particular, who predicted like everyone else that the downturn would right itself within a year or two, was driven deeper into his program of empirical research by this proof of ignorance. Whether a more powerful and genuinely historical institutional economics would have done better is impossible to say. Like the left–liberal economists generally, the institutionalists were drawn into the Keynesian revision of neoclassicism. (Ross, 1991, p. 419)

Frank Knight, who regarded himself as an institutionalist – albeit a maverick one – and who was in the strategic location of Chicago in the 1930s, came to a similar verdict. He asserted that institutionalism was 'largely drowned by discussion of the depression, or perhaps boom and depression, and especially by the literature of the Keynesian revolution' (Knight, 1952, p. 45).

Of course, the rising 'Keynesianism' of the 1930s was different in several key respects from the economics of Keynes. Key contributions in the 1930s and 1940s, notably from Alvin Hansen, John Hicks, Paul Samuelson and Jan Tinbergen, helped to transform Keynesian ideas and make them mathematically tractable. As noted by Benjamin Ward (1972) and Terence Hutchison (1992), this became as much a 'formalistic revolution' as a Keynesian one.[6] The evidence suggests, however, that Keynes himself was at best sceptical of econometrics and mathematical modelling in economics. What did emerge in the 1930s were the foundations of the neoclassical–Keynesian synthesis, based on key developments in neoclassical microeconomics and a mechanistic system of macroeconomic modelling with some Keynesian affinities. Keynes's own views on mathematical modelling are clear in a letter to Roy Harrod of 16 July 1938: 'In economics . . . to convert a model into a quantitative formula is to destroy its usefulness as an instrument of thought' (Keynes, 1973, p. 299).

Of course, the 'Post-Keynesianism' of John Cornwall, Paul Davidson, Alfred Eichner, Hyman Minsky and George Shackle has much more to do with the economics of Keynes than with the 'Keynesian' synthesis of the postwar era. American institutionalism had strong creative links with the former, but was partly destroyed by the latter.[7]


## IN CONCLUSION

It has been shown above that American institutionalists played an important theoretical and empirical part in laying the foundations of the Keynesian revolution. What were Keynes's own personal links with the earlier institutionalists? Although Keynes did not acknowledge Veblen, he had a profound respect for the American institutionalist John Commons. On 26 April 1927 Keynes wrote to Commons: 'Judging from limited evidence and at great distance, there seems to be no other economist with whose general way of thinking I find myself in such genuine accord' (Commons, 1982). However, Keynes was much less clear about the details of this agreement.

However, the philosophical and theoretical links are much more subtle and extensive that the limited Keynes–Commons correspondence would suggest. In this present chapter it is argued that the institutionalists provided much of the philosophy and statistical methodology for Keynesianism. In particular, Veblen implicitly embraced the notion of emergent properties. Influenced by this, and contrary to methodological individualism, Mitchell established the legitimacy and practicality of macroeconomic aggregates. This important incursion against reductionism in economics created space for, and openness to, Keynes's ideas.

A theoretical justification for the relatively autonomous status of macro-economics has been elaborated elsewhere (Hodgson, 1993, pp. 261–5). Remarkably, after the failure of the microfoundations project, such notions are back on the agenda today. Sciences dealing with complex phenomena have rediscovered the concept of an emergent property. In recent years much work has been done – in Santa Fe and elsewhere – with complex, non-linear computer systems, attempting to simulate the emergence of order and other 'higher-level' properties. Reviewing the modelling of such 'artificial worlds', David Lane (1993, p. 90) writes that a main thrust 'is to discover whether (and under what conditions) histories exhibit interesting *emergent properties*' (emphasis in original). His extensive review of the literature in the area suggests that there are many examples of artificial worlds displaying such attributes.

The literature on complex systems and emergent properties lends support to the 'old' institutionalist idea that the economy can and must be analysed at different levels. There is a valid and sustainable distinction between the 'micro' and the 'macro', without reducing the former to the latter, or vice versa. The concept of an institution provides a key conceptual bridge between the two levels of analysis. The concept of an institution connects the microeconomic world of individual action, of habit and choice, with the macroeconomic sphere of seemingly detached and impersonal structures. While analyses at each level must remain consistent with each other, the macroeconomic level has distinctive and emergent properties of its own.

Such alternative approaches do not always lend themselves to formal modelling. Complexity itself imposes limits on mathematical modelling and formal theory. This should not mean, however, that institutionalists become mere data-gatherers. No understanding or explanation is possible without theory. Contrary to some past and present exponents of the 'old' institutionalism, theory does not arise by mere induction from data. All empirical analysis presupposes a set of concepts and an implicit or explicit theory. Even if a theory makes little or no use of mathematics it is still required to be rigorous. Complaints about the inadequacy of mainstream theory are not enough. Now the urgent task is to build something new.

### Notes

1. An emergent property has recently been defined by Lane (1993, p. 91) as a feature of a complex system that: (a) can be described in terms of macro- or aggregate-level concepts, without reference to the attributes of specific micro-level entities; (b) persists for time periods significantly greater than those required for describing the underlying micro-interactions; and (c) is not explicable entirely in terms of the micro-properties of elemental components of the system.

2. Lloyd Morgan should not be confused with Lewis Henry Morgan, the famous nineteenth-century anthropologist who greatly influenced both Veblen and Frederick Engels.

3. However, Bateman (1989) and Davis (1989) argue that Keynes's adoption of organicism was highly limited.

4. Since Keynes, Whitehead has had little influence on economics, reflecting the resurgence of the mechanistic and atomistic view in the postwar period. An explicit exception, however, is the work of Georgescu-Roegen (1971), particularly in regard to such concepts as purpose and time. With his idea of the hierarchic ordering of the real world, Whitehead also had a strong personal influence on pioneering systems theorists such as Miller (1978).

5. Ironically, this reigning view ignored the fact that any practical implementation of a policy to increase government expenditure depended precisely on a detailed knowledge of the workings of government, financial and other *institutions*. For their concern with such details the institutionalists were much maligned by the mathematical technocrats. Their expert knowledge in this area, however, partly explains the fact that they were in government bodies at the forefront of the implementation of the semi-Keynesian economic policies of the Roosevelt era.

6.  For an interesting analysis of the contemporary rhetoric and attitudes to mathematics of the formalistic pioneers Samuelson and Harrod, see Klamer (1995).
7.  It should noted, however, that Post-Keynesians have not yet paid sufficient attention to the theory of the state and of public policy. Keynes's own excessive faith in the powers of economists to persuade influential public figures has been well-criticized. I have argued elsewhere that it is in this area, as well as the related theoretical question of human agency, that Post-Keynesians still have much to learn from institutionalists (Hodgson, 1988, ch. 10).

## References

Barber, W.J. (1994) 'The divergent fates of two strands of "institutionalist" doctrine during the new deal years', *History of Political Economy*, 26, 569–87

Bateman, B.W. (1989) '"Human logic" and Keynes's economics: a comment', *Eastern Economic Journal*, 15, 63–7

Becker, G.S. (1976) *The Economic Approach to Human Behaviour*, Chicago, University of Chicago Press

Commons, J.R. (1982) *John R. Commons Papers*, State Historical Society of Wisconsin

Cornwall, J. (1972) *Growth and Stability in a Mature Economy*, New York, John Wiley and Sons

Cornwall, J. (1990) *The Theory of Economic Breakdown: An Institutional–Analytical Approach*, Oxford, Basil Blackwell

Crutchfield, J.P., P. James, J. Farmer, J. Doyne and N.H. Packard (1986) 'Chaos', *Scientific American*, 255, 38–49

Davis, J.B. (1989) 'Keynes on atomism and organicism', *Economic Journal*, 99, 1159–72

Degler, C.N. (1991) *In Search of Human Nature: The Decline and Revival of Darwinism in American Social Thought*, Oxford, Oxford University Press

Dillard, D. (1948) *The Economics of John Maynard Keynes: The Theory of a Monetary Economy*, London, Crosby Lockwood

Dorfman, J. (1934) *Thorstein Veblen and His America*, New York, Viking Press. Reprinted 1961, New York, Augustus Kelley

Duesenberry, J.S. (1949) *Income, Saving and the Theory of Consumer Behavior*, Cambridge, MA, Harvard University Press

Edgell, S. and R. Tilman (1989) 'The intellectual antecedents of Thorstein Veblen: a reappraisal', *Journal of Economic Issues*, 23, 1003–26

Eff, E. Anton (1989) 'History of thought as ceremonial genealogy: the neglected influence of Herbert Spencer on Thorstein Veblen', *Journal of Economic Issues*, 23, 689–716

Elster, J. (1982) 'Marxism, functionalism and game theory', *Theory and Society*, 11, 453–82

Georgescu-Roegen, N. (1971) *The Entropy Law and the Economic Process*, Cambridge, MA, Harvard University Press

Gruchy, A.G. (1948) 'The philosophical basis of the new Keynesian economics', *International Journal of Ethics*, 58, 235–44

Hayek, F.A. (1931) *Prices and Production*, London, Routledge & Kegan Paul

Hirschleifer, J. (1977) 'Economics from a biological viewpoint,' *Journal of Law and Economics*, 20, 1–52

Hirschleifer, J. (1978) 'Competition, cooperation and conflict in economics and biology,' *American Economic Review*, 68, 238–43

Hodgson, G.M. (1988) *Economics and Institutions: A Manifesto for a Modern Institutional Economics*, Cambridge, Polity Press and Philadelphia, University of Pennsylvania Press

Hodgson, G.M. (1989) 'Post-Keynesianism and institutionalism: the missing link', in J. Pheby (ed.) *New Directions in Post-Keynesian Economics*, Aldershot, Edward Elgar. Reprinted in G.M. Hodgson (1991) *After Marx and Sraffa: Essays in Political Economy*, London, Macmillan

Hodgson, G.M. (1993) *Economics and Evolution: Bringing Life Back Into Economics*, Cambridge, Polity Press and Ann Arbor, and University of Michigan Press

Hutchison, T.W. (1992) *Changing Aims in Economics*, Oxford, Basil Blackwell

Keynes, J.M. (1936) *The General Theory of Employment, Interest and Money*, London, Macmillan

Keynes, J.M. (1973) *The Collected Writings of John Maynard Keynes, Vol. XIV, 'The General Theory and After: Defence and Development'*, London, Macmillan

Kirman, A.P. (1989) 'The intrinsic limits of modern economic theory: the emperor has no clothes', *Economic Journal (Conference Papers)*, 99, 126–39

Klamer, A. (1995) 'The concept of modernism in economics: Samuelson, Keynes and Harrod', in S.C. Dow and J. Hillard (eds) *Keynes, Knowledge and Uncertainty*, Aldershot, Edward Elgar

Knight, F.H. (1952) 'Institutionalism and empiricism in economics', *American Economic Review (Papers and Proceedings)*, 42, 45–55

Koopmans, T.C. (1947) 'Measurement without theory', *Review of Economics and Statistics*, 29, 161–72

Kregel, J.A. (1976) 'Economic methodology in the face of uncertainty', *Economic Journal*, 86, 209–25

Lane, D.A. (1993) 'Artificial worlds and economics' parts I and II, *Journal of Evolutionary Economics*, 3, 89–107, and 3, 177–97

Lorenz, M. (1896) *Die Marxistische Socialdemokratie*, Leipzig, George M. Wigand

Mayr, E. (1985) 'How biology differs from the physical sciences', in D.J. Depew and B.H. Weber (eds) *Evolution at a Crossroads: The New Biology and the New Philosophy of Science*, Cambridge, MA, MIT Press

Miller, J.G. (1978) *Living Systems*, New York, McGraw-Hill

Mirowski, P. (1989) *More Heat Than Light*, Cambridge, Cambridge University Press

Mitchell, W.C. (1937) *The Backward Art of Spending Money and Other Essays*, New York, McGraw-Hill

Morgan, C.L. (1896) *Habit and Instinct*, London, Edward Arnold

Morgan, C.L. (1927) *Emergent Evolution*, 2nd edn (1st edn 1923), London, Williams & Norgate

Morgan, C.L. (1933) *The Emergence of Novelty*, London, Williams & Norgate

Myrdal, G. (1972) *Against the Stream: Critical Essays in Economics*, New York, Pantheon Books

Popper, K.R. and J.C. Eccles (1977) *The Self and Its Brain*, Berlin, Springer International

Rizvi, S.A.T. (1994) 'The microfoundations project in general equilibrium theory', *Cambridge Journal of Economics*, 18, 357–77

Robbins, L. (1932) *An Essay on the Nature and Significance of Economic Science*, 1st edn, London, Macmillan

Robinson, J. (1942) *An Essay on Marxian Economics*, London, Macmillan

Robinson, J. (1975) *Collected Economic Papers – Volume Three*, 2nd edn, Oxford, Basil Blackwell

Robinson, J. (1979) *Collected Economic Papers – Volume Five*, Oxford, Basil Blackwell

Ross, D. (1991) *The Origins of American Social Science*, Cambridge, Cambridge University Press

Stewart, I. (1989) *Does God Play Dice? The Mathematics of Chaos*, Oxford, Basil Blackwell

Stoneman, W. (1979) *A History of the Economic Analysis of the Great Depression*, New York, Garland

Tilman, R. (1992) *Thorstein Veblen and His Critics, 1891–1963: Conservative, Liberal, and Radical*, Princeton, NJ, Princeton University Press

Tullock, G. (1979) 'Sociobiology and economics', *Atlantic Economic Journal*, September, 1–10

Veblen, T.B. (1897) 'Review of Max Lorenz, *Die Marxistische Socialdemokratie*', *Journal of Political Economy*, 6, 136–7

Veblen, T.B. (1899) *The Theory of the Leisure Class: An Economic Study in the Evolution of Institutions*, New York, Macmillan

Veblen, T.B. (1904) *The Theory of Business Enterprise*, New York, A.M. Kelly

Veblen, T.B. (1914) *The Instinct of Workmanship, and the State of the Industrial Arts*, New York, Augustus Kelley. Reprinted 1990 with a new introduction by M.G. Murphey and a 1964 introductory note by J. Dorfman, New Brunswick, NJ, Transaction Books

Veblen, T.B. (1919) *The Place of Science in Modern Civilization and Other Essays*, New York, Huebsch. Reprinted 1990 with a new introduction by W.J. Samuels, New Brunswick, NJ, Transaction Books

Vining, R. (1939) 'Suggestions of Keynes in the writings of Veblen', *Journal of Political Economy*, 47, 692–704

Vining, R. (1949) 'Methodological issues in quantitative economics', *Review of Economics and Statistics*, 31, 77–86

Ward, B. (1972) *What's Wrong With Economics?*, London, Macmillan

Whitehead, A.N. (1926) *Science and the Modern World*, Cambridge, Cambridge University Press

Wilson, D.S. and E. Sober (1989) 'Reviving the superorganism', *Journal of Theoretical Biology*, 136, 337–56

Wimsatt, W.C. (1980) 'Reductionist research strategies and their biases in the units of selection controversy', in T. Nickles (ed.) *Scientific Discovery, Volume II, Historical and Scientific Case Studies*, Dordrecht, Holland, Reidel. Reprinted in E. Sober (ed.) (1984) *Conceptual Issues in Evolutionary Biology: An Anthology*, Cambridge, MA, MIT Press

Winslow, E.A. (1986) '"Human logic" and Keynes's economics', *Eastern Economic Journal*, 12, 413–30

Winslow, E.A. (1989) 'Organic interdependence, uncertainty and economic analysis', *Economic Journal*, 99, 1173–82

Wunderlin Jr, C.E., (1992) *Visions of a New Industrial Order: Social Science and Labor Theory in America's Progressive Era*, New York, Columbia University Press

# 7 Are Economists Social Scientists?

## Villy Bergström

The strength of economics, as well as its weakness, is its hard theoretical core. The theoretical core of economics is basically a theory of self-interest. Mainstream economic theory uses as its main instrument the principle of maximization. Individuals or households are assumed to maximize their 'utility', while firms are assumed to maximize their profit or the value of the firm in the portfolios of its owners.

It is quite clear that many things can contribute to an individual's utility. For instance, an individual can put a high value on an even distribution of society's income. He or she may ascribe a high value to the abolition of poverty in society. These values could easily be contained in the utility function of an individual or a household. Furthermore, the maximization principle is dependent on a number of axioms that express the rationality of individuals and firms. But the principle of maximization always means that self-interest or egoism is the starting point of economic theory.

That the above propositions are true is well-illustrated by the extension of economic theory to the analysis of politics and bureaucracies by the branch of economics called 'public choice' theory. Bureaucrats are assumed to maximize the amount of resources they control and their number of subordinates. Politicians are assumed to maximize electoral support. The conservative ideal of the unselfish, impartial civil servant as well as the idealistic politician are absent from the theory of public choice. Self-interest purportedly governs public service and politics.

The strength of using the maximization principle as the unifying principle of economic theory is that the theoretical development of economics is cumulative. Brick after brick is added to the construction of economic theory, each brick methodologically consistent with the last. Challenges to the dominant paradigm are seldom effective. If a new paradigm is introduced, it usually incorporates the principle of maximization. The theoretical core exerts a strong discipline against loose speculation.[1]

But there is a drawback. The strong rule of economics that all economic theory should be based on the principle of maximization by individuals or firms can lead to a loss of empirical relevance. Theoretical precision is, however, often valued higher than relevance. For example, macroeconomic theory originally led a parallel existence beside the microeconomic theory of individuals, households and firms. The so-called behavioural relations of macroeconomic theory, relations that describe the actions of groups of individuals, households and firms, were seldom based on utility maximization.

Nowadays, however, there is a strong tendency to consider only macroeconomic relations that are derived from microeconomic maximization. This is illustrated by modern Keynesian macroeconomic theory, developed by American, French and British economists, which builds upon price rigidities and rationing (see, for example, Barro and Grossman, 1971; Hey, 1981; Benassy, 1982, 1986). This formulation of Keynesian economics has not gained acceptance in the USA, however, because the central feature of the new theory, price rigidities, is not explained by utility or profit maximization by individuals or firms. By using established microeconomic theory, it can be argued that all agents in the economy would gain from the flexibility of wages and prices. Therefore, a theory based on fixed prices is not commonly accepted. There have been different attempts at formalizing a theory of rigid prices, for instance, those based on cost minimization coupled with the idea that price changes are costly. But these attempts are not regarded as being sufficiently general to form the basis of a general theory of unemployment.[2]

Despite the relevance of new Keynesian theory, new classical macroeconomics dominates both scientific and political debate in the OECD countries. One reason is that this theory is based on microeconomic utility and profit maximization. This theoretical feature explains the dominance of new classical macroeconomic theory within the economics profession. It also underpins the so-called norm-based economic policy in the European Union and in Sweden. New classical macroeconomic theory and its associated supply-side economics has succeeded effective demand management in the discussion of policy issues concerning the unemployment problem in Europe.

Keynesian theory is not fully based on utility and profit maximization. This is why it is perceived by economists and among policy-makers as being weak – with dire consequences for unemployment in the industrialized world. Although Keynesian theory is primarily an economic theory of the short run, it can make an important contribution to the explanation of the persistent unemployment that has been plaguing Europe for a couple of decades now: overall demand has been held down by central banks and by restrictive fiscal policies in order to avoid a revival of inflation. This is especially true for Europe in the mid-1990s. In a trough, all countries of the European Union (EU) tried to fulfil the conditions for membership of the planned European Monetary Union (EMU). Taxes were raised and government expenditures were cut to meet the rules set up by the Maastricht Treaty. This represented a pro-cyclical 'Keynesian policy', contributing to mass unemployment in Europe.

The argument for this policy has been that only persistently low inflation can lead to fast, sustainable growth and long-run full employment. But this assertion is still only a hypothesis. Furthermore, even if the hypothesis is correct, it is an altogether different question as to whether or not a country can move from high inflation to low inflation and preserve low unemployment. The policy hypothesis described above is based upon the fact that it is possible to observe, at any point in time, some countries with high inflation and low unemployment and others with both low inflation and low unemployment. But these countries may differ in their institutional set-up, their historical experiences and their labour market traditions. It may be the case that a country like Sweden, that has had full employment for forty years and, during the past two decades, an inflation rate of 7–9 per cent per year, may need a couple of decades before it will be possible to combine full employment with low inflation. If so, the question is whether or not it is worthwhile to change regime. Resources will be lost and welfare destroyed if mass unemployment exists for, say, twenty years before a new regime is established (Ball, 1993). Many European countries (including, among the Nordic countries, Denmark) started austerity policies fifteen years ago. Mass unemployment still lingers in these countries, despite low inflation.

## SCIENCE AND POLITICS

The famous Swedish political scientist Herbert Tingsten defined political ideologies as systems of values combined with a conception of the world. If this definition is reasonable and useful, it is easily recognized that there must be a close connection between a person's belonging to a scientific school and his or her political ideology. The scientific school that a researcher adheres to must be strongly influenced by his or her conception of the world.

Are people well-informed and rational in their behaviour so that their actions and choices are consistent rather than logically contradictory? Are wages and prices reasonably flexible over time horizons that are not too long? Answers to these (vague) questions are important for understanding which scientific school an economist belongs to.

An economist who answers 'yes' to these questions probably belongs to a different school of thought than the economist who thinks that prices and wages are sticky and do not vary much in the short run in response to differences between supply and demand. One's membership of a scientific school and adherence to a particular ideology is also influenced by what one believes about the set of information available to individuals and households, and what one thinks of their capacity to absorb information and interpret it. Another decisive belief concerns production technologies. Are they very flexible in the short run, so that substitution between factors of production occurs easily, or are they inflexible and limited to fixed proportions?

In sum, if one regards ideologies as Tingsten does – that is, as combining certain values with a view of the world – it follows that ideologies and scientific schools overlap. The scientific school that a person belongs to is determined by the same conception of the world that his or her political ideology is based upon. What I have tried to describe here concerning the connection between science and politics or between ideological adherence and membership of certain schools of thought in economics is amply illustrated by the Dutch economist Arjo Klamer in his interviews with famous economists (Klamer, 1984). One group among the interviewees belongs to the Keynesian school of thought. The older economists among the Keynesians are Robert Solow, James Tobin and Franco Modigliani. Allan Blinder is a generation younger. The reason why these people started to study economics and what maintained their interest was concern with social problems. Solow, Tobin and Modigliani witnessed the Great Depression. They studied economics because they wanted to understand how societies could deteriorate to the point of mass poverty and unemployment, despite the fact that there were overwhelming social needs to be met. Allan Blinder is too young to have witnessed the Great Depression. He grew up in a liberal (in the American sense) Jewish home in a suburb of New York. And, as such, his concern was with unemployment and poverty rather than inflation.

Another group of economists, with advanced theoretical and technical skills – people like Robert Lucas and Thomas Sargent – are mainly interested in theoretical problems internal to the science of economics, problems mostly formulated by the use of powerful mathematics. Issues of formalization rather than social problems triggered their interest in economics. For example, Robert Lucas was studying history when he discovered the mathematical methods used in economic research. He found these methods so interesting that he changed subject from history to economics.[3] When Klamer asked Lucas if he saw any ethical problems with the capitalist social order, Lucas's answer was: 'Well, sure. Governments involve social injustice.'

Lucas is very strict in demanding that macroeconomic theory must be based on microeconomic optimization. In Klamer's book, he describes how macroeconomics has developed step by step from so-called behaviouristic relations, without sound theoretical underpinning, to theories based on microeconomic optimization. The consumption function is now based on optimization thanks to formulations introduced by, among others, Franco Modigliani. Dale Jorgenson tried to base the investment function on similar principles and James Tobin did the same with the money demand function. Lucas's own contribution is the last step in this development, basing expectations about the future on optimization in the form of so-called 'rational expectations'.

The two schools discussed here represent, roughly, European social democracy and social liberalism on the one hand, and conservatism and new liberalism on the other. The point is, political and scientific beliefs are clearly formed by experiences. The older economists were impressed by the Great Depression. The younger economists often find the experience of the older ones irrelevant in their own, more contemporary, context. They are often more concerned with the inflation-prone societies of the postwar industrial world, whose ills they associate with regulation, trade unions and attempts at stabilization policies – all things that hamper the free functioning of markets.

The experiences that stimulate different researchers to begin studying economics lie behind the conception of the world that forms both their choice of scientific school and their political beliefs. It is, therefore, difficult to believe in value-free science, certainly as an instrument for social engineering, when scientific results are applied to social problems. Gunnar Myrdal held the view that social scientists should always declare the values on which economic judgements are based. Often, science and politics merge in social debate. When listening to advice given by an economist, one should always take into account the political ideology that the economist subscribes to.

John Cornwall, to whom this book is a tribute, is a good example of an economist whose interest in economics was triggered by social problems rather than mathematical intricacies. Early in his career he met European scholars who introduced him to the works of Marx, Weber, Tawney and Keynes. This was after a certain disappointment with his experience of the teaching of economic theory in the USA and the UK. All of Cornwall's books are based on a concern for society and its development. He knows economic theory well and is able to combine economics with historical and institutional techniques to study the transformation of capitalism over time. Moreover, Cornwall's work explicitly recognizes the importance of economic and political power – factors that are quite absent from neoclassical economic theory.

## 'INTERNAL SCIENCE' OR SOCIAL SCIENCE?

Since ancient times, scientific development has involved specialization. The starting point of science was philosophy. During the centuries following the classical period, subjects such as natural science, history and linguistics emerged as special subjects, separate from philosophy. Later, there was a split into different disciplines within the natural sciences and within these, further divisions developed, such as the division of astronomy and atomic physics from general physics, the division of inorganic and organic chemistry from chemistry, and so on.

Such specialization also occurs in economics. The principle of maximization leads to ever stronger logic, more powerful mathematics and, to the extent that there is empirical research, ever more refined methods of statistics and econometrics. But as the scientific development of economics progresses, so internal criteria for judging good and important scientific achievements become increasingly important relative to the criterion of social relevance.[4] In Sweden today, there are professors of economics who have not written their doctoral dissertation in economics but in mathematics. Due to the way that economics has developed, these people can be very successful as economists even without a background in social science. There are papers written on game theory and other branches of mathematical economics where not even the problems that the papers deal with are comprehensible to other economists working on similar problems in adjacent areas. Fifty years ago, it was possible for a good economist to have an overview of the whole subject of economics. Today very few economists, if any, have such an overview.

The international reward system in economics, to which Sweden belongs, takes account only of papers published in internationally renowned, peer-reviewed, scientific journals. To be able to write papers that are acceptable to such journals, one has to be technically able and capable of using advanced mathematical and/or statistical methods. Committees that, in Sweden, are responsible for selecting people for chairs in economics may consist of only non-Swedish speaking economists. As such, papers or books written in Swedish cannot be taken into account in the selection process.

Only participation in this 'war of publication' can lead to a position at a good university. Because of this, a strong driving force for economists today is the set of internal scientific criteria by which economists judge themselves, rather than the social relevance of their work. Modern economists are often ideological innocents who have a weak interest in and knowledge of the societies in which they live.

There are, of course, exceptions to all this. The greatest of economists, those who break new paths for the subject or open up new fields of research for generations of followers, usually have a great feeling for relevance, an overview of vast parts of the subject, and deep insights into institutional and empirical aspects of the societies in which they live. But the majority of researchers are much more limited. Because it is so difficult to reach the frontiers of scientific research, which makes publication in scientific journals possible, economists tend to be narrowly focused. They are often highly specialized in a narrow field of the discipline.

As early as twenty-five years ago, when I was a visiting scholar at Stanford University in California, it struck me that it was often difficult to have a conversation with colleagues outside their own field of research. I was among people who specialized in investment theory and empirical research, people who estimated production functions and investment functions. When, during lunch breaks, I tried to discuss, for instance, the 'European snake' for exchange rate stabilization (a policy problem in Europe at that time), the conversation died and silence broke out.

I have seen this tendency in medicine in Sweden. When my leg was operated on, I found that the operating professor's interest in my body was limited to a few inches above and below the area of the operation. When I was plagued by problems after the operation, I had to consult a general practitioner for help.

The heads of clinics at Swedish hospitals are professors of medicine. Once, after an operation, I met the head of the clinic where I was hospitalized. He was visibly disoriented and uncertain in front of the patients. The personnel of the clinic evidently saw his weekly round among the patients as necessary, but ultimately irrelevant for the care of the patients. This professor had no doubt done important research and had reached the top of his specialized field. Furthermore, the results of his research will probably reach general practitioners who are capable of combining new research results with experience, intuition and insights acquired by lengthy and meaningful contact with their patients. But he was neither a good doctor nor a good head of his clinic.

Developments similar to the one I have just described in medicine are also apparent in economics. One should not always expect prominent professors of economics to have anything interesting to say about social problems, or about economic policy. One can be a professor of economics and continue to be uninterested in social matters. On the other hand, one might be very engaged in some field of mathematics or mathematical statistics with applications in a certain field of economic research. If the results of such research are of importance, they will be recognized by practical economists – people who can read economic journals, pick up on theoretical and empirical results and combine these results with their experience of social developments and social policy. This seldom happens quickly, however. It often takes several years, during which time new results are confirmed after critical discussions among scholars and tests on different data sets, until the new results are accepted and become useful. Furthermore, much research in economics is motivated mostly by the internal competition for jobs and is of little relevance outside the economics profession itself. This becomes a self-perpetuating process once theoreticians come to dominate the profession, as people tend to favour their own kind. Is a great deal of irrelevance a price worth paying in order to produce a few shining stars who combine technical skills with relevance and a deep knowledge of social institutions? I, for one, think that the reward system in economics is disadvantageously biased in favour of theoretical skills at the expense of relevance.

It seems, then, that we are likely to get the same division among economists as there is between doctors and researchers in medical science. Among economists, the equivalents of practising doctors are the economists found in banks, government agencies, trade unions and employers' organizations. These economists are tied to certain interests. They undertake practical investigations and very specific pieces of analysis. The values they subscribe to are often quite clear, as they are employed by institutions whose aim it is to promote certain values and ends.

There are, of course, many purely academic economists who pursue successful careers at universities and who, at the same time, are social scientists with profound knowledge of social institutions, politics and social structures. They are consequently able to define and explore scientific problems with great relevance to their societies. However, their value systems are often not at all clear. Furthermore, with the present system of academic rewards and in view of the kind of research that pays in the competition for academic positions, the group of academic economists who are also social scientists will surely diminish in the future. As a rule, more and more academic economists, those with the highest levels of scientific competence, will be narrow specialists. Many of these people will not be social scientists. It will not matter to them whether they analyse, for instance, the trajectory of a rocket or that of the capital stock as a problem of dynamic optimization. They have little to say about society and they are not very interested in social matters, except in so far as they can be formally analysed within the special field of economics to which they contribute.

In sum, certain fields of specialized research in economics seem to have very little relevance for the societies in which we live. This is because research is driven by internal scientific problems. In all likelihood, this development is unavoidable. Specialization has been going on as long as scientific research has been undertaken by humans. But universities should be aware of the risks involved in supporting too much research driven by internal scientific criteria and too little by the yardstick of social relevance.

## CONCLUSIONS

My proposition concerning the close connection between politics and science, between a person's political stance and his or her belonging to a specific scientific school, is well-illustrated by current economic and social debate in Europe. The dominant group of Swedish economists want to solve the urgent social problem of mass unemployment by microeconomic reforms: deregulation of the labour market, less powerful unions, and more flexible relative wages that can easily be adjusted to reflect productivity differences between branches of industry and between different jobs and employees. They recommend lower replacement ratios in unemployment insurance, so that unemployed persons will accept lower wages and so that unions will give up previously agreed-upon wage levels and minimum wages. The aim is to promote wage flexibility and physical mobility. According to most Swedish economists, unemployment will decline as a result. These economists belong to the dominant school of thought that is called new classical macroeconomics. They stress supply-side economics rather than demand management.

Economists of this school of thought believe in the capacity of individuals to solve problems by themselves. They are sceptical of collective action and they want to diminish the role of the state in the economy as well as the role of unions, institutions that uphold wage levels, and workplace and labour market regulations. This school of thought is closely connected, intellectually, to conservative political parties in Europe and, in the USA, to the Republican party.

Another school of thought is the Keynesian school, including the new Keynesians. Economists of this school see the present mass unemployment in Europe as a result of austerity programmes used to fight inflation. Economic policy – monetary policy and fiscal policy taken together – does not permit European economies to grow by more than just about 2.5 per cent per year. This is approximately the rate of growth of output generated by productivity growth and the growth of labour supply. By refusing to allow demand to grow faster, it is impossible to reduce unemployment. This conclusion is no more than a simple application of Okun's Law.[5]

Unemployment has been downplayed as a policy priority in favour of price stability. European countries have abandoned their commitment to full employment, some following the first oil crisis in 1973–74, some after the second oil crisis in 1979–80. Sweden continued to pursue a policy of full employment in the 1980s until, at the beginning of the 1990s, price stability succeeded full employment as the first priority of economic policy.

Most Keynesians view unemployment as a macroeconomic problem that can be remedied by macroeconomic policy, that is, by stimulating demand by means of monetary and fiscal policies. This may no longer be true for a single country, especially not for a small open economy, as long as the new economic liberalism permits free capital movement. But unemployment could certainly be remedied at a European level by concerted policy action initiated, say, by the EU.

In Keynesian theory, the state has an important role to play. It should stabilize demand and capacity utilization to keep unemployment and inflation low and stimulate economic growth. This school of thought is closely connected to social democracy in Europe and to the political view of trade unions. In the USA, part of the Democratic party (Democrats of the Roosevelt, Johnson and Kennedy type) is close to the spirit of European social democracy.

This does not mean that Keynesians completely deny the importance of the deregulation and supply-side economics recommended by new classical macroeconomics. But they do see such reforms as being of secondary importance in comparison to demand management policies designed to stabilize capacity utilization and unemployment. Only when the latter problems are taken care of does deregulation become important.

It should be clear by now that there are no value-free opinions about economic policy. This does not, of course, mean that one should blame economists for the fact that their policy opinions are presented as scientific truths by interest groups who happen to share the same values. For example, the views held by supply-side economists are widely cited by employers' organizations, federations of industry and conservative politicians. The policy prescriptions of supply-side economists are put forward as scientific truths, despite the fact that they are sometimes based on rather loose speculations combined with political values, as was illustrated above with reference to the problem of unemployment. Similarly, trade unions and labour parties often refer to Keynesian economists in order to give scientific status to their policy recommendations. This manipulation of science is evident from the pattern of invitations to conferences organized by interest groups such as unions and employers' organizations. At least in Sweden, it is still the case that economists expressing opposing views are often invited to these conferences. The saving grace of an open society is that adversaries are prepared to listen to each other's arguments.

Are economists social scientists then? Not universally, although some of them are. Two decades ago I met with Gunnar Myrdal in California, to have dinner with him and a visiting professor at Stanford, Brinley Thomas from Great Britain. Myrdal asked Thomas, who had been a student of his back in the 1930s, what I was doing at Stanford. Thomas replied that I was at Stanford to learn mathematical economics and econometrics. Myrdal retorted: 'You will be locked up in your offices and nobody will take an interest in what you are doing!', although the venerable old social scientist then stressed that he himself had used mathematics as a young scholar.

However, the number of economists who, like Myrdal, *are* social scientists is at risk of diminishing because of the reward system that is commonly used when people are chosen for academic positions. The writing of scientific papers is necessary for success in a university position. It is part of a screening process, much like the study of ancient Greek and Latin in the European gymnasiums.

Some economic research has already developed into a kind of a syntax or applied logic, quite detached from social relevance. Summers (1991) suggests that, when evaluating a contribution to research, the economics profession should pay less attention to the methods used to make the argument. Instead, he argues, we should ask whether or not interesting facts are reported – facts that affect our view of how the economy operates. And yet:

> All too often researchers, referees and editors fail to ask these scientific questions. Instead, they ask the same questions that jugglers' audiences ask – Have virtuosity and skill been demonstrated? Was something difficult done? Often these questions can be answered favorably even where no substantive contribution is made. It is much easier to demonstrate technical virtuosity than to make a contribution to knowledge. Unfortunately it is also much less useful. (Summers, 1991, p. 146)

On a more positive note, it seems that the American university system is more open to different branches of research and different methods than the European universities are. Universities in the USA are often very large and an economics department can offer positions to theoreticians, econometricians, historians, labour economists, financial economists, policy-oriented scholars and teachers who do good work as advisers and tutors. Quality is upheld in the American system by the fact that universities in the USA compete for grants, students and academic rank in the minds of the public.

This system is impossible in Sweden, however, because of the selection process for positions at universities. When a position is open, experts are called in to choose between applicants. Scientific skill is ranked, and the most skilful applicant gets the position, regardless of whether the department would have profited more from the choice of a person slightly less skilled but with a different orientation. (It should be recognized that this formal process can be circumvented by various means, for instance, by the choice of scrutinizing experts.)

Perhaps the American system should be introduced for professions – such as most natural sciences and, among the social sciences, economics – that have adopted international norms for their research. The formal system now used in countries such as Sweden risks making economics an uninteresting playground for narrow technicians. Sometimes I ask myself how taxpayers would react if they understood what goes on within the economics departments of Swedish universities. Perhaps we should all accustom ourselves to asking the same question.

**Notes**

1.   There is one exception to this tendency to base economic theory on the maximization principle, this being a relatively new branch of empirical economics that goes completely against the maximization principle and is almost theory-less. Instead of using microeconomic optimization as the foundation of hypotheses and tests, data are investigated to 'see what they reveal'. Theory only plays a role as a guide to the selection of variables that may be part of a long-run relationship. This is the so-called VAR-model, VAR being an acronym used in econometrics to stand for vector autoregression. The VAR-model and similar approaches to empirical economics start from very general hypotheses and narrow down the general formulations to more specific ones, but the method is only loosely connected to economic theory of any kind.
2.   See the two volumes of Mankiw and Romer (1991).
3.   This claim is taken from an interview with Lucas, connected with his receiving the Nobel Prize, in the Swedish daily newspaper *Dagens Nyheter*, 10 December 1995 (Örn, 1995).
4.   See, for example, Summers (1991).
5.   On this see Dornbusch (1994).

## References

Ball, L. (1993) 'How costly is disinflation? Historical evidence', *Business Review*, Federal Reserve Bank of Philadelphia, November–December

Barro, R.J. and H.I. Grossman (1971) 'A general disequilibrium model of income and employment', *American Economic Review*, 61, 82–93

Benassy, J.P. (1982) *The Economics of Market Disequilibrium*, New York, Academic Press

Benassy, J.P. (1986) *Macroeconomics: An Introduction to the Non-Walrasian Approach*, New York, Academic Press

Dornbusch, R. (1994) 'Is there a role for demand policy?', *Swedish Economic Policy Review*, 1, 153–77

Hey, J.D. (1981) *Economics in Disequilibrium*, Oxford, Martin Robertson

Klamer, A. (1984) *The New Classical Macroeconomics: Conversations with New Classical Economists and Their Opponents*, Brighton, Wheatsheaf

Mankiw, N.G. and D. Romer (1991) *New Keynesian Economics, Volume 1, Imperfect Competition and Sticky Prices, Volume 2, Coordination Failures and Real Rigidities*, Cambridge, MA, MIT Press

Örn, G. (1995) 'Lucas förklarar bluffen', *Dagens Nyheter*, 10 December

Summers, L.H. (1991) 'The scientific illusion in empirical macroeconomics', *Scandinavian Journal of Economics*, 93, 129–48

# 8 Deregulation: The Anatomy of a Catchword

## Kurt Rothschild

The question of the desirability and extent of state intervention in market processes is a recurrent theme almost as old as economic theorizing itself. Starting with the confrontation between the *laissez-faire* ideology emanating from Manchester and its sceptical opponents in the less developed nations (List in Germany, Carey in the United States), the question resurfaces in the never-ending free trade–protectionism debate, the battle between Chicago/Freiburg liberals and Keynesian interventionists, and so on and so forth. With the wave of conservatism that began in the early 1970s, there has been a noticeable shift in these seesaw discussions in favour of market-oriented policies, with 'deregulation' and 'privatization' emerging as popular catchwords. My aim is to look a bit more critically at the recent battle-cry for deregulation.

I want to begin on a somewhat polemical note. Can one imagine a book or a symposium entitled, or based on the demand for, 'Deregulation of Traffic' or 'Deregulation of Temperature'? The terms sound odd. On the other hand, it is perfectly reasonable to talk about 'Regulation of Traffic' or 'Regulation of Temperature'. Yet *'De*regulation of Markets or of the Economy' has become an extremely acceptable theme in economic theory and in policy discussions. Why is this so? Why is it not sufficient to talk about 'Regulation of the Economy'?

When we start to talk about the regulation of traffic or temperature, we make no initial assumption about the appropriate *direction* of the regulatory action. We assume that the traffic needs some direction and that the temperature should reach a certain level. Proposals for regulation can then call for either more or fewer traffic lights, or measures for a higher or lower temperature. In the same way, there is no reason why we should not be able to cover *all* questions of state intervention in the economy with the old and obvious term 'regulation of economic activity'. Why is a special, additional term 'deregulation' necessary? The term 'deregulation' could be defended by perceiving it as being analogous to 'deflation', but 'deflation' is a complement to 'inflation', which has a clear directional (upward) meaning, so that deflation denotes a movement in the opposite direction. Regulation, on the other hand, does not signify a movement but a *state*, which can be fixed at either a higher or lower level. Furthermore, inflation and deflation refer to a unique indicator (the price level), while regulation – used as a general term – covers a combination of very different subjects and policies.

So what explains the use of the special term 'deregulation' when 'regulation' seems to be all that is needed? Two different explanations may be offered. The first is more fundamental in the sense that it is closely connected with differences in basic economic paradigms and the different policies they imply. Obviously, deregulation is a meaningful term when we begin with the concept of a fully functioning system of free markets. This justifies the assertion that any intervention whatsoever will involve the danger of disturbing the workings of a delicate, complex system. Seen from this perspective, deregulation has a clear and unique meaning: it aims ultimately at the removal of all regulations (with perhaps a few exceptions) – that is, a complete *laissez-faire*.

It is clear that such a perspective can arise fairly easily on a theoretical plane if one remains consistently (and not too critically) within the confines of theories which take their lead from general equilibrium models. Since models of this sort show that competitive markets with flexible prices have an endogenous tendency to achieve Pareto optimal outcomes, it is more or less logical to reject regulation *on principle*. Exceptions can only be granted when the market is unable to function properly, that is, in the 'classical' cases of market failure – natural monopolies, external effects, public goods – and cases of serious information barriers. Economists' extensive interest in public goods follows from the general idea that firm rules have to be sought whenever regulation can be justified, if it has to be used at all.

Two remarks are in place with regard to this model-oriented deregulation postulate. The first is of a general nature and deals with normative issues. Even accepting the theoretical basis of competitive equilibrium theory, it does not follow that unremitting deregulation is the optimal policy. This would only be the case if allocative efficiency and Pareto optimality are accepted as the only valid goals of society. This is a particularly attractive strategy for economists because economic efficiency is a 'value' close to their heart, as it probably should be.

But we must then keep in mind that *recommendations* for deregulation are based on purely *economic* value judgements, while in practice, regulations do not aim exclusively at allocative efficiency but are also concerned with other targets, such as income distribution, social constellations and so on. When certain economists argue that one should first achieve an efficient result via a free market process, leaving the consideration of other targets to *ex post* adjustments, they overlook the fact that political processes are also subject to various mechanisms and constraints and cannot be used *ad libitum*. Regulative interventions into market processes – 'market disturbances' from the perspective of an equilibrium standpoint – might be the only way to achieve some results, which could not be obtained through *ex post* action. Without an appropriate political theory it would be difficult to estimate the final outcome of a sequential economic–political process; hence acceptance of a crude deregulation rule favours the one-dimensional value judgement of economists concerning allocative efficiency. In so far as economists plead for making economics a truly positive science free from normative elements, they should, it would seem, abstain from recommending more or less regulation, instead restricting themselves to analysis of the factual relationships between regulation and economic targets and the probable consequences of regulatory change.

Even more important than these normative issues, however, is the questionable theoretical background on which arguments for deregulation are based. The issue is whether or not theoretical general equilibrium models present us with an appropriate standard when it comes to judging real world situations. Only if this is the case can a *general* deregulation rule be regarded as a plausible recommendation. The question is not, of course, whether or not the neoclassical model 'corresponds' to reality. It does not and it cannot, because all theories must by necessity offer a highly abstract picture of reality if we want to reduce the complexity of the real world and make it more amenable for scientific analysis. A theoretical conception of traffic flow problems need not be useless merely because it assumes that all roads are straight. Abstraction is essential; what one has to find are adequate and relevant abstractions.

The problem with general equilibrium-type models is not their high level of abstraction: it is the fact that such models are not particularly suited to act as standards for judging regulation problems. The birth of free market models originated from the general spread of a market economy more than two hundred years ago, when the question first arose as to whether or not it is possible for an economy based on a division of labour and the individual decisions of millions of people to create viable results and, if so, what these results look like. To tackle such difficult questions it was necessary to concentrate on a few problem-relevant assumptions – a simple decision rule, competition, price flexibility – and to neglect a host of other features – economic and political ones – which were not absolutely essential for the problem under observation. The results of this research strategy were and are impressive. It is possible to show the plausibility and characteristics of a purely individualistic market equilibrium, and the ensuing development of this approach has led to an ever deeper understanding of the 'pure mechanics' of market processes.

But parallel to this growing theoretical refinement in the analysis of the functioning of a 'perfect' market economy, we witnessed the development of a real market economy which, from the very start, differed quite considerably from the free market model and was always characterized by a mixture of economic and non-economic elements. As a result of the constant interplay between markets and politics, between market forces, institutions, and conflicting interests, economies in all countries developed into mixed constructs with more or less competition, more or less government intervention and so on. Speculative theories of economic systems, particularly the German *Ordnungstheorien* of the Freiburg school, introduced a sharp dichotomy between a pure market economy on the one hand and a fully planned economy on the other, although neither of the two can be regarded as a suitable characterization of the types of mixed economies that are the *only* economies we encounter in reality. The 'pure' market model, which presents a useful abstraction for the analysis of market mechanisms, is not a sufficient basis for judging the possibilities and consequences of market-intervention combinations in a world which already functions in a market-intervention environment. Unfortunately, we have no satisfactory *general* model that could be properly applied to such an environment, although some useful approaches and partial analyses exist. Moreover, since history and institutions contribute to the shaping and functioning of mixed economies, we can hardly hope for general and rigid theories in this field that could ever reach the standards of general equilibrium theories, whose 'pure' markets remain untainted by such 'disturbing' factors.

In view of these circumstances, one must reach the conclusion that a purely economic point of view cannot provide a firm theoretical basis for producing a catalogue of regulation rules, let alone for the postulate of general deregulation. The remarks of the well-known liberal Swiss economist Walter Adolf Jöhr – made more than forty years ago at an International Economic Association Conference on Regulation – are still valid today: 'The extreme adherents of *laissez-faire*', he said,

> deny the possibility of any regulation of the competitive mechanism. Others admit the possibility of regulation, but maintain that it can only make things worse, as it would mean a mixture of planning and competition – these being considered to be mutually exclusive solutions of the same problem. But this question cannot be answered in the abstract. The answer must result from an analysis of the different methods of regulations. (Jöhr, 1954, p. 342)

So far, I have talked about deregulation as an absolute and general postulate, which turns out to be either meaningless and/or of dubious merit. But there can be a more restrictive and more realistic interpretation of the term 'deregulation' which marks it off from 'regulation'. Calling for deregulation can mean that one recommends a general reduction of the *existing* level of regulation. This has been an important position in the heated deregulation debates of recent decades and is, without doubt, a meaningful proposal that can be discussed in realistic terms. Since in mixed economies interventions play an important role and can be either 'good' or 'bad', considering their extent and usefulness is not only meaningful but highly desirable. But when it comes to critical examination of existing interventions, it turns out that the catchword 'deregulation' is far too crude to offer any practical guidance. While, for instance, a demand for deflation has a clear one-dimensional goal, that is, a decrease in the price index, deregulation refers to a multidimensional world of diverse regulations using different methods and aiming at different targets. A situation where *all* these regulations should be cut down without exception seems highly unrealistic, unless we return to the dogmatic belief in *laissez-faire* discussed earlier.

Thus even if there exists a feeling or a consensus that, on the whole, there has been too much regulation and/or regulation of an inappropriate kind, this can only mean that the spectrum of regulations should be scrutinized with abolitions here and modifications there; it cannot mean the application of a one-dimensional deregulation strategy covering anything and everything. 'Deregulation' is not much help as a policy target in a complex world of regulations, interests, and dynamic changes. 'Reregulation' would be a far better term, pointing as it does to the *permanent* need for continuing consideration of the justification for, and need for reform in, regulatory systems in an environment of constant change.

One of the principle causes of the emphasis laid on deregulation in policy debates is the special interests of lobby groups who occupy strong market positions and who fear that their decision processes will be hampered by government interventions. A general anti-regulation ideology is favoured in order to block interventions *in principle*. This standpoint, however, seldom prevents the same groups and persons from asking for and accepting interventions which further their own interests. The long history of combining the preaching of free trade in principle with demands for protectionism in practice offers a good example of such tendencies.

Although up to this point my arguments against 'deregulation' as a *general* policy target have been quite forthright, this does not mean that the discussions that have evolved around this catchword are quite without value. Whatever their motives and theoretical bases, the claim associated with protagonists of the deregulation debate, that problems of regulation are important and that their role in the macroeconomic process should receive more attention, deserves full support. The development of a theory of regulation – an old demand of George Stigler's – together with more empirical research and closer interdisciplinary ties with political science, sociology and history could provide a firmer basis for debates about the pros and cons of particular acts of regulation or deregulation. Such a broad theoretical background does not yet exist. Certain theories and empirical results have emerged, but much of this work is controversial and requires further research. Certain aspects of the regulation–deregulation problem can be discussed, however, in light of the work done so far, and it is to this task that I now turn.

When one tries to approach the subject of regulation in a systematic way, difficulties arise immediately in the act of trying to formulate an exact definition of the phenomenon. Definitions have their use, but *quarrels* about definitions are usually unproductive, despite their popularity. In view of the generality and brevity of my observations we do not need to delve into the question of a 'proper' definition. But it is worth noting that while the 17-volume *International Encyclopedia of the Social Sciences* of 1968 contains an article referring to 'Regulation of Industry', there is no mention whatsoever of 'Deregulation'. The more recent *New Palgrave Dictionary of Economics* does contain an article entitled 'Regulation and Deregulation', but here, regulation is described rather than defined. 'Regulation', we are told, 'particularly in the United States, consists of governmental actions to control price, sales and production decisions of firms in an avowed effort to prevent private decision-making that would take inadequate account of the "public" interest' (vol. 4, p. 128).

The vagueness of definitions of 'regulation' is a consequence of the many facets of the phenomenon and, in particular, the fuzziness of the lines drawn between different acts of government and the differences between regulatory institutions and practices in various countries. This vagueness is certainly unsatisfactory, but need not detain us here, since the core of the regulation problem is sufficiently compact as to permit us to use the term 'regulation' without fear of being misunderstood.

As mentioned earlier, there does not exist any traditional and well-founded theoretical body which could be called 'The Theory of Regulation'. But there are several approaches that are relevant for assessing general questions of regulation and the current trend towards deregulation in particular. These approaches are sometimes divided into two groups: normative and positive theories of regulation. This distinction is not entirely satisfactory, since – as we shall see – representatives of the positive theory make substantial normative judgements. Nevertheless, we shall discuss these two types of theory in turn. Both depart from the extreme *laissez-faire* position, in so far as they admit that market failures and other disturbances occur and can provide reasons for regulatory action. Where they differ is in regard to their attitude towards the effectiveness and the desirable extent of regulation, these differences following largely from their diverging views regarding the nature of government behaviour. This latter issue is an important source of many weaknesses and uncertainties in all regulatory theories.

Let me now turn to normative types of regulation/deregulation theories. The normative theories have a long tradition going back, in particular, to the American institutionalists, German historical economists and to German theories of *Gemeinwirtschaft* (public economy). They also found, of course, an important place in Pigou's classic *Economics of Welfare*. These contributions were motivated both by economic considerations regarding classical market failures (like monopolies and externalities) and a social concern about inequalities and injustices arising from normal market processes. Reforms and regulations were recommended from a societal point of view, and the government and other public bodies were expected to carry these out in a spirit of serving the general interest. The existence of conflicts of interest, of failures and inefficiencies in government actions and so on were not overlooked, but on the whole the political complex consisting of the parliamentary system, government and bureaucracy was seen as a 'benevolent' system working for the common good. These approaches probably tend to look upon the activities of governments and bureaucrats rather too naively, and to underestimate the influence of power, political and economic lobbies, and so forth. On the other hand, it would be wrong to overlook the fact that elections, traditions, social motivations and so on are at work, and that these provide a framework within which the promotion of public welfare can and does occur. An important question is, of course, how much weight is attached to the claims of general social welfare, as opposed to those of special interests. This question is one of the main dividing lines between the normative theories and their positive counterparts, to which we now turn.

Positive theories of regulation are a more recent development and have an obvious affinity to both the 'New Political Economy' and the 'Economic Theory of Politics', with their roots in the work of Schumpeter and Downs. While the normative theories tended to draw too friendly a picture of benevolent and disinterested governments and bureaucracies working for the social good, we find the positive school in critical opposition to this view, moving right to the other extreme in its behavioural assumptions. The *Homo politicus* is modelled entirely along the lines of *Homo oeconomicus*, as an individual whose actions can be fully deduced from an individualistic utility-maximizing strategy. Since one of the aims of politicians is – so the theory goes – to be reelected, their interventions in the economic process will be fully subordinated to this aim. This will promote interventionist actions which favour the special interests of comparatively small and influential groups, such as firms, regions or professions. The reason for this is that interventions of this sort can bring considerable advantages to the groups concerned, while the 'costs' of such actions are spread over the totality of consumers who – as individuals – hardly feel the burden of single regulatory acts. Lobbies can, therefore, exert considerable pressure for 'favourable' regulations without meeting any particular counter-pressure from the large and unorganized body of consumers, and politicians will give in to these pressures in the hope of winning the support of influential groups in forthcoming elections and throughout their subsequent careers. Rent-seeking by various groups, that is, attempts to obtain monopolistic advantages of one sort or another, become – in this perspective – an important, if not the most important, factor in the regulation process, whose general working cannot, therefore, be regarded as an instrument for improving the market mechanism or for the promotion of social well-being.

The positive theory of regulation, particularly as initiated by Stigler and others a quarter of a century ago, deserves our attention for two reasons: it is the dominant approach in today's mainstream economics, and it constitutes an important theoretical argument for current policies of deregulation, obtaining a normative character in the process. The modern positive theory of regulation – like the New Political Economy on which it is based – quickly commanded the attention and adherence of economists because it adopts the traditional analytical style and formal structures of neoclassical theory. It is thus able to produce elegant models which make economists feel at home. The positive theories of politics and regulation discuss politico-economic problems with the same formal consistency and rigour that characterize neoclassical economic models, while traditional political science and normative regulation theories can handle these problems only in a less generalized and less formalized manner, with frequent references to historical and institutional peculiarities.

But the formal elegance of neoclassical theory, which has its problems even when one deals with purely economic matters, demands a high price when applied to the analysis of real world politics and policy-making. This is particularly serious when one deals with patterns of political decision-making. While a narrowly defined utility maximization principle (going beyond mere tautology) can perhaps be accepted as a useful provisional basis for analysis of the choices of *Homo oeconomicus*, it is definitely too meagre, if not altogether misleading, when it comes to the study of the more complex motivations of *Homo politicus*, which cannot simply be subsumed under the goal of vote maximization or something of that sort. Stigler's claim that: 'There is, in fact, only one general theory of human behaviour and that is the utility-maximizing theory' (Stigler, 1975, p. 137) is – if it is anything other than pure tautology – an untenable assertion and indeed one that must look rather outlandish to most people outside the economics profession.

Steven Rhoads, a prominent political scientist, whose book *The Economist's View of the World* is full of praise for the methods and perspectives of economic theorists, nevertheless complains that economists seem to be unable to pay sufficient attention to various non-selfish motives like conscience and ideology, feelings of responsibility and duty, an urge for efficiency and so on. This neglect, he argues, introduces a bias into their theories when it comes to politico-economic matters. 'Through their training economists learn that they and their discipline can be more powerful if money and self-interest matter even more than they first thought' (Rhoads, 1985, pp. 162–3). Of course, the theory of purely self-interested behaviour and utility-maximizing can survive as a *formal* theory if the terms 'interest' and 'utility' are defined so comprehensively that all the afore-mentioned motives are included. But then the theory becomes so spongy that falsification becomes impossible.

We are thus faced with the fact that neither the normative nor the positive theories of regulation provide an entirely satisfactory representation of the real situation. The complicated web of political and economic activities is not just ruled by benevolent and well-informed public bodies that are fully dedicated to the common good. It is equally inappropriate, however, to think that public interventions are always made in the service of some sinister special interest. Important as the positive theory of regulation is as an antidote to the naivety of some normative theories, it certainly cannot claim to provide, by itself, a sufficiently comprehensive picture of regulatory activity.

In a complex situation where interests, motives and theoretical viewpoints of all sorts intermingle in an effort to mould interventions in what is already a mixed economy, we cannot expect to obtain simple theories of regulation that permit us to derive generally valid prescriptions for regulatory actions under all circumstances. I think one has to agree with the Swiss economist Bruno Frey when he suggests (in a discussion of competition policy) that: 'On the basis of theoretical research alone we are not even able to specify in which *direction* competition policy should proceed' (Frey, 1981, p. 108; emphasis in original). In such a situation, simplistic demands for deregulation do not constitute meaningful policy advice.

Some hope for offering practical advice might be found in cost–benefit analyses of concrete regulation or deregulation projects. Though not exactly presenting a proper theory, the methods developed by economists in this field could, it seems, offer a more 'rational' basis for regulatory decision-making. However, as useful and desirable as cost–benefit calculations can be, they cannot completely determine the regulatory decision. Too many of the items included in the calculus of costs and benefits must be estimated with the aid of speculations that have no firm basis. In particular, when we have to deal with important matters where 'big' things (like life, health, education and so on) are involved, the choices of the items to be considered and their valuation are far from being objective facts. They are, instead, subject to precisely the play of motives and interests that cost–benefit analysis seeks to avoid in its quest for objectivity.

What, then, is the result of these considerations? Certainly not the defeatist conclusion that since nothing definite is known, economists should remain silent. On the contrary, I believe that economic expertise can make important contributions to policy debates concerning regulation. But it is important to ensure that the economist does not become the prisoner of an ill-suited model, and that he or she is continuously conscious of the complex power and interest relationships that are at work and of the limitations of our theoretical knowledge. As long as he or she is not wedded to an extreme *laissez-faire* philosophy, the economist can always make an important contribution to policy debates about regulation. Above all, discussion of regulation, deregulation or reregulation should never be reduced to the level of emotionally biased catchwords.

## References

Frey, B.S. (1981) *Theorie demokratischer Wirtschaftspolitik*, München, Vahlen-Verlag

Jöhr, W.A. (1954) 'Regulation of competition', in E.H. Chamberlin (ed.) *Monopoly and Competition and Their Regulation*, London, Macmillan

Rhoads, S.E. (1985) *The Economist's View of the World*, Cambridge, Cambridge University Press

Stigler, G.J. (1975) *The Citizen and the State: Essays on Regulation*, Chicago, IL, University of Chicago Press

# Part II

# Economic Growth in Theory and Practice

# 9 'Modern Capitalism' in the 1970s and 1980s

Jan Fagerberg and Bart Verspagen

## INTRODUCTION

The past decade has witnessed important changes in how economic growth is conceived by the economic profession. The traditional neoclassical model (Solow, 1956), based on the ideas of perfect competition, decreasing returns and exogenous technology (a global public good), has had to give way to more realistic approaches emphasizing among other things innovation (through R&D investments or learning in private firms), scale economics and market power.[1] This change of perspective was clearly anticipated by John Cornwall in his path-breaking study, *Modern Capitalism* (1977). Here he suggests a model of economic growth in which technological progress is endogenized, that is, an 'endogenous growth model' to use a more recent term. Manufacturing, Cornwall argues, plays an important role in this context, because it is the locus of technological progress, whether in the form of learning by doing (scale economics) or as the result of search activities by entrepreneurs. Hence his main focus is on what shapes growth in manufacturing (since this is considered to be the main source of overall growth).

A central issue in the recent discussions on economic growth is the so-called 'convergence controversy'. Do poor countries catch up with the rich ones and if so, why? Under the standard assumptions,[2] the traditional neoclassical model predicts that due to decreasing returns to capital accumulation, convergence in GDP per capita will more or less automatically occur.[3] This – as might be expected – was not Cornwall's position. He argued that although the existence of technology gaps between rich and poor countries does imply a potential for technological catch-up through imitation, the realization of this potential requires a lot of extra effort (and, in particular, investment). Hence, according to Cornwall's view, convergence is conditional on investment and other necessary supporting factors. He was probably the first to present empirical tests for what since has been dubbed 'conditional convergence', and to discuss the implications of this notion for long-run differences in growth between countries.

As Cornwall himself was the first to recognize, his theoretical perspective was richer than his modelling efforts or subsequent empirical work. For

113

instance, he pointed out that the prospects for growth were not the same across all manufacturing industries and that, indeed, some of them might be more important than others in fostering technological progress and hence growth. However, in his model and empirical tests he focused on manufacturing as a whole. His empirical work, mainly based on data for the 1950s and 1960s, gave some support to the idea of manufacturing as an 'engine of growth', as well as to his emphasis on investment-embodied catch-up as an important source of growth in manufacturing. In this chapter we return to these and related questions for a larger group of countries and a more recent time period. We ask: is there any evidence that manufacturing is an 'engine of growth' in this later period, and are all manufacturing industries equally conducive to growth? What does this more recent evidence have to say about the impact on growth of investment in physical capital compared to the impact of other supporting factors such as, for instance, education and R&D? Finally we raise the issue of what all this tells us about the working of contemporary 'modern capitalism' as compared to that of the 1950s and 1960s.

## MANUFACTURING – AN 'ENGINE OF GROWTH'?

One of the most crucial hypotheses in *Modern Capitalism* is that of the manufacturing sector as the engine of economy-wide growth. Cornwall points to two main arguments for this.

First, the manufacturing sector displays dynamic economies of scale through so-called 'learning by doing' (Young, 1928; Kaldor, 1966, 1967). When production expands, the scope for learning and productivity increases becomes larger. Hence, the rate of growth of productivity in manufacturing will depend positively on the rate of growth of output in manufacturing (the Kaldor–Verdoorn Law).[4]

The second line of argument concerns the special role of the manufacturing sector in enhancing productivity growth through its linkages with the non-manufacturing sectors. Cornwall argues that the manufacturing sector is characterized by strong backward linkages, that is, increased final demand for manufacturing output will induce increased demand in many sectors 'further down the line'.[5] In other words, increased output in manufacturing, due to increased final demand, does not only lead to increased productivity in the manufacturing sector (the Kaldor–Verdoorn Law), but also to increased output and, perhaps, productivity in the sectors further down the line. In addition to these backward linkages, Cornwall emphasizes that the manu-facturing sector also has many forward linkages, through its role as a supplier of capital goods (and the new technologies that these goods embody). In fact, he considers capital goods from the manufacturing sector to be the main carriers of new technology (Cornwall, 1977, p. 135). Moreover, although 'learning by doing' may be an important source of productivity growth in non-manufacturing industries as well, it is argued that the realization of this 'learning potential' will in many cases require capital goods supplied by the manufacturing sector.

Cornwall's model of economic growth can be summarized in two equations as follows (1977, p. 139):

$$\hat{Q} = c_1 + a_1 \hat{Q}_m \tag{9.1}$$

$$\hat{Q}_m = c_2 + a_2 \hat{Q} + dq_r + e(I/Q)_m \tag{9.2}$$

In these equations, $Q$ is output, $q_r$ is GDP per capita relative to the technology leader (the USA), $I/Q$ is investment as a fraction of output, $c$, $a$, $b$, $d$ and $e$ are parameters and the subscript $m$ indicates the manufacturing sector. Equation (9.1) states that manufacturing is the engine of growth, hence the parameter $a_1$ is expected to be positive, and larger than the share of manufacturing in GDP. Equation (9.2) introduces a feedback from overall demand growth on manufacturing production, hence $a_2$ is expected to be positive. In addition it allows for catching up by industrial latecomers (hence $d$ is expected to be negative). The inclusion of the investment share ($e$ positive) reflects Cornwall's emphasis on investment as a necessary supporting factor for successful catch-up.

Cornwall does not estimate equation (9.1), but refers to OLS estimates by Kaldor (1966), Cripps and Tarling (1973) and the UN (1970). Based on data for developed market economies in the 1950s and 1960s, these studies estimate $a_1$ to be about 0.6, more than twice the share of manufacturing in GDP. Hence, the evidence from these studies seems to support the hypothesis of manufacturing as an engine of growth. However, in Cornwall's model, both GDP growth and growth of manufacturing output are endogenous variables, and in that case equation (9.1) should have been estimated by a method other than OLS. Indeed, the OLS estimate of 0.6 may be seriously biased.

Looking at the model in equations (9.1) and (9.2) from a simultaneous equation perspective, one must conclude that the second equation is not identified. It does not satisfy the order condition, which says that the equation must exclude at least $N-1$ exogenous variables, where $N$ is the number of equations in the model (in this case 2). Hence, it cannot be estimated by any estimation technique.[6] The first equation, however, is over-identified, and may be estimated by a single equation technique that takes the simultaneous equation bias into account, such as, for instance, the instrumental variables/two-stage least squares method (2SLS).

The analysis here will proceed by using such a procedure to estimate equation (9.1) for a large sample of countries. The sample includes 67 countries: 19 developed countries (including Japan), 6 countries from East Asia and the Pacific (excluding Japan), 18 countries in Latin America and the

Caribbean, 17 sub-Saharan African countries, and seven other countries (among which two oil exporters). We thus have a rather heterogeneous set of countries. The dependent variable is the growth rate of GDP in real terms over 1973–89 (taken from the Penn World Tables,[7] version 5.5). The independent variable is the growth rate of manufacturing value added (in fixed prices) for the same period, taken from World Development Indicators (World Bank).[8] However, for some of the developed countries, no data on manufacturing growth were available in World Development Indicators. For these countries data were taken from the STAN database (OECD). Both growth rates are average annual compound growth rates over the period specified.

To estimate the equation with the chosen (instrumental variable) technique, we need a number of exogenous variables (or instruments). The chosen variables are in most cases well-known from previous econometric work in this area: *initial GDP per capita* (in log form, taken from the Penn World Tables), *investments in physical capital* as a share of GDP (mean value over 1973–89, also from the Penn World Tables),[9] *education* (enrolment of the relevant age group in secondary education, from the World Development Indicators) and *inflation* (yearly average increase in the CPI 1973–89, taken from the World Development Indicators). Finally, and less conventionally, we include a variable for *technology investment*[10] as proxied by patents (taken out in the USA over the 1975–85 period per head of the population of the country in question, as recorded by the US Patent and Trademark Office).[11]

A well-known problem in estimations using cross-country data sets is the possible bias from inclusion of outliers, that is, countries with patterns that deviate from the other countries in the sample. If such countries are included, we may be lead to conclusions that in fact are not valid for the majority of the countries in our sample. We therefore adopt a procedure which identifies and excludes such outliers.[12]

The results of the instrumental variable/2SLS estimations are given in Table 9.1. The results for OLS are also provided for reference.[13] Estimates are reported for the three country groupings and for the sample as a whole. The three country groupings are the developed *market economies*, comparable to Cornwall's sample (though larger), the industrializing countries of *East Asia and Latin America* and a group of *other countries* (low-income), most of which are from sub-Saharan Africa.

In general, the results obtained by the instrumental variable/2SLS method are not very different from those obtained by OLS.[14] Hence, simultaneity bias does not seem to be an important problem here. This might indicate that the feedback from overall growth on manufacturing output is not so important after all, that is, that manufacturing growth is important for overall growth, but not the other way around.

For the sample as a whole there appears to be a significant positive relationship between manufacturing growth and GDP growth, with coefficient

*Table 9.1* Estimation results for Cornwall's 'manufacturing as an engine of growth' equation, OLS and 2SLS, various countries, 1973–90

| Eq. num | Est. method | Sample (n) | Manufacturing growth | Constant | Adj. $R^2$ |
|---|---|---|---|---|---|
| 1 | OLS | Market economies (17) | 0.104 (0.70) | 0.024 (11.55***) | 0.00 |
| 2 | 2SLS | Market economies (14) | 0.083 (0.21) | 0.024 (6.01***) | 0.00 |
| 3 | OLS | East Asia, Latin America (22) | 0.721 (12.36***) | 0.008 (3.20***) | 0.88 |
| 4 | 2SLS | East Asia, Latin America (17) | 0.829 (8.45***) | 0.006 (1.82*) | 0.83 |
| 5 | OLS | Other countries (22) | 0.371 (4.47***) | 0.014 (3.00***) | 0.47 |
| 6 | 2SLS | Other countries (15) | 0.827 (2.86***) | –0.005 (0.35) | 0.40 |
| 7 | OLS | All countries, no dummies (61) | 0.514 (10.54***) | 0.014 (7.49***) | 0.65 |
| 8 | 2SLS | All countries, no dummies (49) | 0.488 (5.98***) | 0.016 (5.62***) | 0.49 |
| 9 | OLS | All countries, dummies (61) | 0.473 (8.45***) | Continent dummies | 0.69 |
| 10 | 2SLS | All countries, dummies (45) | 0.719 (4.54***) | Continent dummies | 0.57 |

*Note*:
Values between brackets are absolute *t*-statistics. One, two and three asterisks denote significance at the 10%, 5% and 1% level, respectively, in a 2-tailed *t*-test.

estimates close to the 0.6 estimate cited by Cornwall, and significantly larger than the share of manufacturing in GDP at the 5 per cent level. This might be interpreted as supporting the idea of manufacturing as an engine of growth. But from inspecting the estimates for the three sub-samples it becomes clear that this result is very much dependent on the inclusion of countries other than the developed market economies. For the East Asia–Latin America group as well as the 'other countries', we find a highly significant and positive relationship between the two variables. However, for the developed countries the evidence is less clear. Initially, a significant and positive relationship was found for the developed market economies, but this result turned out to depend heavily on the inclusion of three outliers (Italy, Japan and Finland). When these countries were excluded, we found no evidence of a relationship between the growth of GDP and manufacturing growth.[15] Thus, although manufacturing may explain some of the difference in growth between the three outlier countries and the remaining developed countries in the sample, it clearly does not explain the differences in growth performance among the latter.

In summary, the results in this section indicate that for most developed market economies, manufacturing no longer plays the important role it was found to play in the 1950s and 1960s. This is in sharp contradiction to Cornwall's theory in *Modern Capitalism*, which posits that such a relationship should exist, particularly for developed countries.[16] However, Cornwall's argument on the relevance of manufacturing seems to hold good for a number of fast-growing 'newly industrializing countries' (NICs) as well as for some developing countries.

## GROWTH AND TRANSFORMATION

In *Modern Capitalism*, Cornwall depicts growth as a process of qualitative change (transformation), with large and persistent differences in factor returns between dynamic and less dynamic activities. Hence, he points out, the economic success – or lack of such – of a country will to a large extent depend on its 'flexibility', that is, its ability to devote (transfer) resources to new and promising activities. As discussed in the previous section he attaches a lot of importance to the performance in manufacturing which he saw as the centre of technological progress in the economy. Within manufacturing, he especially emphasizes the importance of the chemical, electronic and machine tools industries, both as conduits of technological progress and suppliers of new and improved products and processes to the entire economy (1977, p. 135). These three industries, he notes, totally dominate 'the technology sector' of the economy. This raises the question of the relationship between the industries that make up what he terms 'the technology sector' and other manufacturing activities. To put it bluntly: are all parts of manufacturing equally conducive to growth?

As mentioned in the introduction, Cornwall also emphasizes the potential for catch-up in productivity through imitation for countries behind the world technology frontier. However, he is at pain to stress that this catch-up is far from a free ride. Among the supporting factors, he especially emphasizes the supply of skills (workers and entrepreneurs), materials and capital equipment (1977, p. 111). In his modelling efforts and subsequent empirical work, however, he confines attention to investment as a share of value added which, together with the potential for imitation (proxied by GDP per capita), is assumed to determine the growth of manufacturing output. Note that this relationship can be seen as a reduced form of the model discussed in the previous section (1977, p. 139).

In this section we will return to the relationship between growth, catch-up and structural change discussed by Cornwall, taking into account the possible impact on growth of structural changes within manufacturing, as well as that of other 'conditioning' factors, to use a more recent term. To do so, we need data that are less aggregated than those used earlier. UNIDO publishes data on manufacturing value added and employment for a large number of countries at different levels of development, and it seems natural to try to use these data here. The data cover both three- and four-digit ISIC, but the coverage of the latter is too restricted in terms of countries and time-span for our purposes. Since the relationship between productivity growth and structural change is of a long-term nature, a sufficiently long time-span is necessary. After examining the data, the years 1973 and 1990 were chosen, since this allows more countries to be included than any other combination of years spanning roughly two decades. The desire to include other conditioning factors, such as investments in education, physical capital and R&D, also limits the number of countries that can be included in the analysis. Furthermore, the analysis is confined to market economies (broadly defined). The final data set consists of forty countries from all parts of the world: Africa, America, Asia, Europe and Oceania. With the exception of the first, the data set appears quite representative (due to data problems only three African countries could be included).

The dependent variable in our analysis is the growth rate of labour productivity (not production). Labour productivity is defined as value added divided by employment measured at current prices and converted to US dollars by the exchange rate (as supplied by UNIDO). The entries for 1990 are deflated to constant 1973 dollars by dividing by an index reflecting the growth in US producer prices over the period. Hence, productivity growth as defined here reflects changes in the quantities of the products that a country produces, changes in the relative prices of these products and changes in the exchange rate. The use of current exchange rates introduces a possible bias, to the extent that the exchange rates of any country in 1973 and/or 1990 were seriously over- or undervalued. However, one should expect any such effect, although important from a short-run perspective, to be small over the longer run.

The hypothesis that we wish to test is that it matters for a country whether it puts its resources into expanding areas or chooses to concentrate its efforts on activities where prospects for growth are bleak. This hypothesis – obvious as it may seem – is not trivial since, as noted by Cornwall, it is often disputed by neoclassical economists. We define growth industries as the upper third of the distribution of the industries in our sample, ranked in terms of their productivity growth rates. The top-ranking growth industry during this period was electrical machinery (including electronics, arguably the technologically most progressive industry in recent decades). We therefore divide the growth industries into two groups, electrical machinery (ISIC 383) and high-growth (ISIC 351, 352, 341, 385, 382, 342, 313) and, for each country, calculate the change in the share of the manufacturing labour force that goes to these two groups. The assumption, then, is that if structural change does not matter for growth, then the changes in these shares should not be correlated with growth, at least not significantly so.

However, we have to take into account that structural change within the manufacturing sector is not the only factor that affects the growth of manufacturing productivity. If there are other omitted variables, and these tend to be correlated with our measures of structural change, we may get a biased estimate. To control for this, we include a number of variables that relate to the country as a whole and which may be thought of as characteristics of 'the national system of innovation', or the pool of factors available at the national level for manufacturing (and other sectors of the economy). Among the variables included are those emphasized by Cornwall: initial productivity (in manufacturing) and the ratio of investment to GDP. In addition, we include some of the variables fashioned in recent econometric work on growth such as primary and secondary education (share of age group enrolled) and export orientation/openness (exports as a share of GDP). In contrast to most analyses in this area, we also control for the effort devoted to innovation (R&D as a share of GDP), since this may be a source of growth in its own right. All of these variables are measured mid-period (1980 or closest available year).[17]

Table 9.2 contains estimation results for the growth of manufacturing productivity as a function of the increase in the employment shares of *high-growth* and *electrical machinery* industries and the other variables mentioned above. As in the previous section, we adopt a procedure that identifies and excludes outliers. This reduces the number of countries by between two and five depending on the specification.

Equations (1) and (4) report the results with only the two structural variables and a constant term (not reported) included, with and without continent dummies, respectively.[18] The latter may be thought of as a rough test of the impact of other non-identified factors that happen to be correlated geographically. Equations (2) and (5) repeat these regressions with education, investment and initial productivity, all in log form, included as conditioning factors, that is, we test to what extent structural change matters when the effects of other growth-inducing factors have been accounted for. The results are very clear. High productivity growth and increases in the share of resources devoted to the electrical machinery industry go hand in hand. A 1 per cent increase in the employment share of the electrical machinery industry implies about 0.5 per cent higher overall growth of manufacturing productivity. Increasing the share of employment going to other high-growth industries matters much less, though. The inclusion of other conditioning factors does not change these results to a significant extent, but the explanatory power of the model increases. Among the additional factors, education (especially secondary) is the most important.[19] Neither the share of investments in GDP nor the initial level of productivity seems to matter much for growth. The

*Table 9.2* Structural change and productivity growth

|  | 1 | 2 | 3 | 4 | 5 | 6 | 7 | 8 |
|---|---|---|---|---|---|---|---|---|
| High growth | 0.29 | 0.11 | 0.15 | 0.20 | 0.08 | 0.17 | 0.07 | 0.19 |
|  | (1.73)* | (0.62) | (0.79) | (1.17) | (0.59) | (1.07) | (0.34) | (1.59) |
| Electrical machinery | 0.47 | 0.57 | 0.52 | 0.46 | 0.41 | 0.49 | 0.57 | 0.48 |
|  | (1.94)* | (2.98)*** | (2.91)*** | (2.26)** | (2.38)** | (2.79)*** | (3.01)*** | (2.69)*** |
| Primary education |  | 3.51 | 3.11 |  | 2.85 | 4.21 | 5.67 | 6.79 |
|  |  | (0.96) | (0.79) |  | (0.82) | (1.34) | (1.31) | (1.34) |
| Secondary education |  | 2.36 | 2.10 |  | 1.07 | 2.42 |  |  |
|  |  | (1.99)* | (1.50) |  | (0.87) | (1.91)* |  |  |
| Investment |  | −1.33 |  |  |  |  |  |  |
|  |  | (0.69) |  |  |  |  |  |  |
| Initial productivity |  | −0.58 | −0.52 |  | −0.42 | −0.54 | −0.60 | −0.76 |
|  |  | (0.86) | (0.73) |  | (0.58) | (0.69) | (0.67) | (0.98) |
| Export share |  |  |  |  |  | −0.46 |  |  |
|  |  |  |  |  |  | (0.62) |  |  |
| R&D |  |  |  |  |  |  | 1.03 | 0.74 |
|  |  |  |  |  |  |  | (1.49) | (1.20) |
| Interaction R&D – electrical machinery |  |  |  |  |  |  | 0.01 | 0.23 |
|  |  |  |  |  |  |  | (0.04) | (1.22) |
| Continent dummies | No | No | No | Yes | Yes | Yes | No | Yes |
| $R^2$ ($\bar{R}^2$) | 0.16 | 0.48 | 0.42 | 0.50 | 0.61 | 0.52 | 0.48 | 0.64 |
|  | (0.11) | (0.37) | (0.32) | (0.41) | (0.48) | (0.42) | (0.34) | (0.49) |
| N | 35 | 35 | 34 | 34 | 34 | 35 | 29 | 32 |

*Note*:
Estimated with OLS. Absolute *t*-statistics in brackets under coefficients. One, two and three asterisks denote significance at the 10%, 5% and 1% level, respectively, in a two-tailed test. $R^2$ in brackets is adjusted for degrees of freedom.

same holds – surprisingly perhaps – for 'openness' as reflected in exports as a share of GDP (equation (6)).[20]

The two last equations in the table ((7) and (8)) take into account investments in R&D (measured as a share of GDP), which recent theorizing in this area would suggest as being important (see, for example, Romer, 1990). This leads to a reduction in the number of countries included. Doubts may also be raised about the quality and comparability of the R&D data. Anyway, for this sample of countries, secondary education and R&D are so closely correlated that only one of them can be retained. When R&D is chosen, the coefficient is positive as expected, but not significantly different from zero at the 10 per cent level.[21] We also include an interaction variable, reflecting the hypothesis that the effects of R&D investment on growth are larger if undertaken in conjunction with an expansion of the electrical machinery industry. This hypothesis, however, receives only very moderate support.

The results from this section give ample support to Cornwall's argument regarding the importance of flexibility, or the ability to transfer resources to technologically progressive areas, for productivity growth. Hence, transformation clearly matters for growth. However, Cornwall's emphasis on investment in physical capital in this context is not justified for the period under study here. Rather, the recipe for high growth of manufacturing productivity seems to be a combination of flexibility (targeting the right industries) and investments in skills.

## QUO VADIS MODERN CAPITALISM?

Cornwall built his analysis of modern capitalism on a combination of two strands of thought: the Schumpeter–Svennilson view of capitalist development as a process of qualitative change driven by innovation and diffusion of technology, and the Kaldorian idea of static and dynamic economies of scale in manufacturing as the driving force behind economic progress in the industrialized world. Combining these (and other) insights into a coherent perspective on modern economic growth was an important achievement in itself. He also provided convincing evidence from a group of industrialized countries in the 1950s and 1960s that supported his interpretation of the events.

What we have done in this chapter is to update and extend his empirical analysis using a larger sample of countries and more recent data. We have found that the Schumpeter–Svennilson perspective of growth as a process of qualitative (and structural) change, and the emphasis on the importance of skills and flexibility, has a lot to commend it. On the second set of ideas the evidence is more ambiguous. At least for many of the technologically and economically most advanced countries, manufacturing does not seem to be the 'engine of growth' assumed by Kaldor and Cornwall. Rather, it is for countries in the process of industrialization (NICs) that manufacturing seems to matter most. This may have to do with the role of the manufacturing sector in acquiring foreign technology and generating learning and skills, in combination with forward and backward linkages, as argued by Cornwall in the case of the developed countries. However, it may also have to do with another issue discussed extensively by Cornwall (1977, ch. IV): the existence of persistent differences in productivity levels (and growth) between sectors ('the dual economy'), and the role of the manufacturing growth in speeding up the transfer of labour from low- to high-productivity activities (from agriculture to manufacturing, for instance).

The differences in findings between the studies cited by Cornwall and the present study may also reflect a change in the way 'modern capitalism' works. Arguably, the first decades after the Second World War constituted a period during which the diffusion of scale-intensive technology, from the USA to Europe and Japan, and learning from the use of these technologies, played a large role (Abramovitz, 1994). However, the role as 'engine of growth' has relocated to electronics and other industries characterized by a strong science base and heavy investments in R&D. Our results indicate that there is a strong, positive and very robust correlation between a country's performance in these new growth industries and the rate of growth of manufacturing productivity. This may indicate that there are strong positive spillovers from these kinds of activities, and that these spillovers, to some extent at least, are nationally embedded. However, there are reasons to believe that the technologies that emerge from the new growth industries (especially electronics), and the learning that follows, are equally (or even more) relevant in many service industries. This is, of course, consistent with the finding of this chapter that in most advanced countries, the distinction between manufacturing and services has lost much of its economic significance.

## Notes

1. For overviews see Verspagen (1992) and Fagerberg (1994).
2. These include among other things a common technology, equally available to all countries (a global public good), identical saving rates (or more generally that the incentives to save are the same) and identical rates of labour force growth. See Fagerberg (1994) for an extended discussion.
3. If saving behaviour and labour force growth differ across countries, countries will still converge towards the same *rate of growth* of GDP per capita (given by exogenous technological progress), but the *levels* of GDP per capita in long-run equilibrium will differ. Hence, only countries that share the same characteristics (in terms of saving behaviour and labour force growth) will converge towards the

same level of GDP per capita. This is often called 'conditional convergence' (Barro and Sala-i-Martin, 1995).

4.  There is an extensive literature on this topic, both theoretical and empirical, which it is beyond the scope of this chapter to summarize (see, for example, McCombie and Thirlwall, 1994).

5.  An empirical approach to the study of such linkages is the so-called triangulation of input–output matrices (Cornwall, 1977, pp. 130–5). This procedure takes an input–output table and rearranges the order of the sectors (rows and columns) of the table such that (in the 'ideal' case) a sector only supplies to sectors listed above it, and only purchases from sectors listed below it. Hence, sectors ranked at the top tend to purchase large quantities from other sectors (further below) and supply mostly to final demand, while sectors ranked at the bottom tend to supply mostly to other sectors (instead of final demand), only being dependent on a limited number of other sectors for their inputs. Cornwall argues that work based on this methodology shows that manufacturing is a sector with strong backward linkages: it supplies a relatively large part of its output to final demand, and purchases large quantities of inputs from other sectors.

6.  Cornwall solved the identification problem by estimating only the reduced form of the model, which is adequate for testing the overall explanatory power of the model. However, when one wants to test the role of manufacturing as an engine of growth separately from the other elements of the theory, this approach is not sufficient, because in general one can not calculate a parameter estimate for $a_1$ from the reduced form.

7.  We use the RGDP variable, that is, real GDP in international prices using a Laspayeres price index.

8.  Version on CD-ROM, 1997.

9.  Due to data availability we use economy-wide investment as a share of GDP instead of investment in manufacturing as a share of manufacturing output.

10. See Fagerberg (1987, 1988) for discussion of different indicators of technology gaps and technology investment, and an analysis of the impact of technology gaps and technology investment on growth.

11. As with most of the literature in this area we use patents taken out in the USA, because this provides us with more consistent and economically relevant data than data drawn from a variety of different national sources.

12. This method identifies outliers by calculating the so-called hat-matrix, $X(X^TX)^{-1}X^T$, where $X$ is the matrix of independent variables. Observations with entries larger than $2k/n$, where $k$ is the number of independent variables, and $n$ the number of observations in the regression, were excluded. See Belsley *et al.* (1980).

13. Note that the 2SLS estimates generally have fewer observations, due to missing values for some of the instrumental variables.

14. The 2SLS estimates are higher than the ones obtained by OLS in three cases, and in two cases it is the other way around. However, in no case are the 2SLS estimates significantly different from those obtained by OLS at a 5 per cent level of significance.

15. It is possible that the engine of growth equations as estimated here suffer from a bias due to omitted variables. Manufacturing may indeed be an important factor

explaining growth in other sectors, but there may be other factors explaining economy-wide growth, or growth in non-manufacturing sectors, which should have been taken into account when estimating the relationship. For instance, one might argue (see, for example, Cornwall, 1977, p. 133) that some of the factors explaining growth in manufacturing also explain economy-wide growth, that is, one may include some of the instrumental variables in our 2SLS procedure as exogenous variables in equation (1). We tested various equations from this perspective, but always found that the results reported above are robust to the inclusion of other possible explanatory factors. These results are available from the authors on request.

16. More recently, Cornwall has argued that above a certain threshold level of development, the importance of manufacturing for growth should be expected to decrease, since the rise in income per capita encourages a shift in demand from manufacturing products towards services (see Cornwall and Cornwall, 1994a, 1994b). While this may be true, it does not explain the finding of no correlation at all between growth of GDP and growth of manufacturing for a cross-section of developed countries.

17. The industry data (productivity and employment shares) are from UNIDO, investment and exports as shares of GDP and education from the World Development Report (World Bank, various editions), and R&D data are from OECD and UNESCO. In a few cases these data were supplemented with data from national sources.

18. Oceania (Australia and New Zealand) is included in Asia in this study.

19. In most cases, the countries that were identified as outliers (and hence excluded) were poor countries with low educational standards. In the initial estimations (with these countries included) education (especially primary education) had somewhat more impact.

20. We also estimated a version more akin to Cornwall's reduced form, that is, with only initial productivity ($Y_{73}$) and investment ($INV$) as exogenous variables, and growth of labour productivity ($G$) as the endogenous variable. This model turned out to have very little explanatory power. The result was (absolute *t*-values in brackets):

$$G = 0.75Y_{73} + 3.19INV$$
$$\quad (1.32) \qquad (1.77)$$

$$R^2(\overline{R}^2) = 0.11(0.06)$$

21. In the initial estimation (before exclusion of outliers) the impact of R&D was found to be both larger and significant (at the 1 per cent level).

## References

Abramovitz, M.A. (1994) 'The origins of the postwar catch-up and convergence boom', in J. Fagerberg *et al.* (eds) *The Dynamics of Technology, Trade and Growth*, Aldershot, Edward Elgar

Barro, R. and X. Sala-i-Martin (1995) *The Theory of Economic Growth*, Cambridge, MA, MIT Press

Belsley, D.A., E. Kuh and R.E. Welsch (1980) *Regression Diagnostics: Identifying Influential Data and Sources of Collinearity*, New York, John Wiley & Sons

Cornwall, J. (1977) *Modern Capitalism: Its Growth and Transformation*, London, Martin Robertson

Cornwall, J. and W. Cornwall (1994a) 'Structural change and productivity in the OECD', in P. Davidson and J.A. Kregel (eds) *Employment, Growth and Finance: Economic Reality and Economic Growth*, Aldershot, Edward Elgar

Cornwall, J. and W. Cornwall (1994b) 'Growth theory and economic structure', *Economica*, 61, 237–51

Cripps, F. and R. Tarling (1973) *Growth in Advanced Capitalist Economics 1950–1970*, Cambridge, Cambridge University Press

Fagerberg, J. (1987) 'A technology gap approach to why growth rates differ', *Research Policy*, 16, 87–99

Fagerberg, J. (1988) 'Why growth rates differ', in G. Dosi *et al.* (eds) *Technical Change and Economic Theory*, London, Pinter

Fagerberg, J. (1994) 'Technology and international differences in growth rates', *Journal of Economic Literature*, 32, 1147–75

Kaldor, N. (1966) *Causes of the Slow Rate of Economic Growth of the United Kingdom*, Cambridge, Cambridge University Press

Kaldor, N. (1967) *Strategic Factors in Economic Development*, Ithaca, NY, Cornell University Press

McCombie, J.S.L. and A.P. Thirlwall (1994) *Economic Growth and the Balance-of-Payments Constraint*, London, Macmillan

Romer, P.M. (1990) 'Endogenous technological change', *Journal of Political Economy*, 98, 1002–37

Solow, R.M. (1956) 'A contribution to the theory of economic growth', *Quarterly Journal of Economics*, 70, 65–94

United Nations (1970) *Economic Survey of Europe 1969, Part 1*, New York, United Nations

Verspagen, B. (1992) 'Endogenous innovation in neo-classical models: a survey', *Journal of Macroeconomics*, 14, 631–62

Young, A. (1928) 'Increasing returns and economic progress', *Economic Journal*, 38, 527–42

# 10 A Problem with the Empirical Neoclassical Analysis of Multisector Growth

John McCombie

## INTRODUCTION

One of John Cornwall's major contributions to our understanding of the economic growth process is to remind us that even the postwar growth of the advanced countries cannot be understood without reference to the massive structural change that has occurred, and continues to occur, in these economies.[1] This was brilliantly set out, *inter alia*, in his 1977 book, *Modern Capitalism*. This work showed the limitations of trying to analyse economic growth in terms of the aggregate one-sector Solow–Swan model, where (steady-state) economic growth is determined by the exogenous growth of the labour force and the rate of technical progress. Cornwall's careful marshalling of the evidence showed conclusively that the growth of the labour supply was endogenous, not exogenous. Moreover, his estimations of the Verdoorn Law showed that technical change was largely induced by output growth – that is, determined *endogenously*, thus anticipating the results of the 'new growth theory'. Factors affecting the demand for a country's output cannot be ignored in any understanding of disparities in economic growth.

Like Kaldor, Cornwall argued that growth could only be properly understood by considering the role played by the different sectors of the economy in the growth process. This includes the impact of agriculture in supplying labour to the other sectors, especially in continental Europe where, in the early postwar period, there was much disguised agricultural unemployment. This intersectoral transfer of labour ensured that there was a relatively elastic supply of labour to manufacturing (which for much of the early postwar period was the 'engine of growth'). It also directly contributed to an increase in overall productivity as workers moved from a low-productivity sector (agriculture) to a high-productivity sector (manufacturing).

One of the criticisms of the one-sector neoclassical growth model that Cornwall (like Kaldor, 1966) implicitly highlights is that it abstracts from the

127

importance of structural change and the differing role of the various sectors in explaining economic development.

In a seminal article, 'On Exports and Economic Growth', published in the *Journal of Development Economics* in 1983, Gershon Feder attempted to develop a two-sector model. He extended the neoclassical production function approach explicitly to allow for a dual economy (exports and the 'rest of the economy') in the less developed countries (LDCs). This approach was later extended by others to include additional sectors, including defence expenditure and government services, and the model was also applied to the advanced countries.

The purpose of this chapter is somewhat nihilistic. It extends and develops an argument first noted by Sheehey (1991). It is shown that these models are deeply flawed and cannot support the interpretation placed upon them.

## THE NEOCLASSICAL APPROACH TO THE DUALISTIC ECONOMY

Feder started from the observation that there is often a close correlation between the growth of GDP and exports, which he interpreted as the latter causing the former. One explanation of this relationship is that it represents the effect of the balance of payments constraint working through the Hicks super-multiplier (McCombie and Thirlwall, 1994).

However, Feder proposed a supply-side, rather than a demand-oriented, explanation, and one which is quite independent of the existence of a balance of payments constraint. His approach dichotomizes the economy into the export sector and the rest of the economy. The basic premise is that the LDCs are essentially in disequilibrium, with the marginal products of capital and labour being higher in the export sector than elsewhere in the economy. This is because it is held that the export sector is more advanced and commercialized than the rest of the economy and so factor inputs are used there more efficiently. Consequently, as the export sector expands and factors are transferred to it from the rest of the economy, so there will be a gain in both output and total factor productivity. The loss in production in the rest of the economy as a unit of a factor of production is withdrawn from this sector is more than offset by the gain in output obtained by using this resource in the export sector. Moreover, the export sector itself will also raise productivity in the rest of the economy by providing a gateway for modernizing techniques and attitudes that will raise the level of efficiency outside the export sector.

Consequently, the growth of the export sector exerts a positive externality on the rest of the economy. It is an externality since the effect is not reflected in market prices. Feder specified a model (discussed below) to test these effects and estimated this using cross-country data for a number of LDCs. On the basis of these regression results, Feder (1983, p. 71) reaches the important conclusion that 'the success of economies which adopt export-oriented policies is due, at least partially, to the fact that such policies bring the economy closer to an optimal allocation of resources. The estimates show that there are, on average, substantial differences in marginal factor productivities between export and non-export sectors.'

It was quickly realized that this methodology could be adapted putatively to test the role of other key sectors in the economic growth process. Most notably, Ram's (1986) influential study considered the impact of the growth of government expenditure, rather than exports, on economic growth in both advanced and less developed countries. While he extended the approach to include time-series regression analysis, the basic framework remained that of Feder.

Ram's study attracted a great deal of attention because the conclusions he drew from the regression results were at variance with the orthodox view of the detrimental impact of government expenditure on economic growth. The conventional wisdom is that government goods and services are inherently inefficiently produced and 'crowd out' private sector investment and that high tax rates reduce incentives and distort the price mechanism, thereby further reducing the growth rate. Therefore, at first glance, it was perhaps surprising that Ram should find that the growth of government expenditure had a positive externality effect on the growth of GDP and, furthermore, that the marginal factor productivities were higher in the government, as opposed to private, sector.[2] 'The main result [of this study] is that it is difficult not to conclude that government size has a positive effect on economic performance and growth, and the conclusion appears to apply in a vast majority of settings considered. Even more interesting seems to be the nearly equally pervasive indication of a positive externality effect on government size on the rest of the economy' (Ram, 1986).

While this approach has not been without its critics (see, for example, Carr, 1989; Rao, 1989), it has given rise to a number of other studies along similar methodological lines (Biswas and Ram, 1985; Ram, 1987; Grossman, 1988, 1990; Kohli and Singh, 1989; Alexander, 1990, 1994). However, as noted above, it will be shown that the whole approach is misconceived and cannot shed any light whatsoever on the issue of the importance of the determinants of economic growth. The reason for this is the presence of two underlying accounting identities on which the model is implicitly based.

## FEDER'S MODEL

It is useful to begin by outlining Feder's model. In the simplest version, the economy is divided into two sectors and the output of each sector is denoted by $Q_1$ and $Q_2$. Production in the latter sector is assumed to have an externality effect on the output of the former, for the reasons set out above. It is assumed that each sector may be represented by a well-behaved production function of the form:

$$Q_1 = F(L_1, K_1, Q_2) \tag{10.1}$$

and

$$Q_2 = G(L_2, K_2) \tag{10.2}$$

(For expositional ease, technical change is ignored for the moment.)

As we have noted, in the two pioneering studies, the sectors were taken as either non-exports and exports (Feder, 1983) or the private sector and government services (expenditure) (Ram, 1986). Ram (1986) merely applies Feder's model using government expenditure in place of exports. Of course, if both exports and government services are thought to play an important role in economic growth, there is nothing to stop a three-sector model from being specified where, for example, $Q_3$ has an externality effect on $Q_2$ and both have an externality effect on $Q_1$:

$$Q_1 = F(L_1, K_1, Q_2, Q_3) \tag{10.3}$$

$$Q_2 = G(L_2, K_2, Q_3) \tag{10.4}$$

$$Q_3 = H(L_3, K_3) \tag{10.5}$$

Alexander (1994) extends the Feder model in this fashion, using equations (10.3) to (10.5), where $Q_2$ and $Q_3$ are exports and government services. The model can be generalized to include any number of sectors (subject only to having sufficient degrees of freedom). A sector that has also been commonly included is defence (Biswas and Ram, 1985; Alexander, 1990). However, one can think of a number of other sectors, such as manufacturing, as suitable candidates.

Apart from the externality effect, we have noted that the effect of differing marginal productivities between the various sectors may also have a positive effect on growth if the sectors with the highest productivity growth rates are the fastest growing sectors. Confining our attention to the two-sector model, Feder (and Ram) assume that the marginal productivities of capital and labour differ between sectors by the same amount (although there is no *a priori* reason to believe that this is necessarily the case), that is:

$$G_K = (1 + \delta)F_K \tag{10.6}$$

$$G_L = (1 + \delta)F_L \tag{10.7}$$

where $\delta > 0$.

Consequently, the marginal productivities of labour and capital in the second sector (which, it will be recalled, is either exports or government services) each exceed those of the rest of the economy by the same proportion. This is a limitation of the analysis, especially when cross-country data are used, because it implies that this proportion is the same for every country, no matter what its level of development. Feder, consequently, regards the estimate of $\delta$, derived from the reduced form of the model (discussed below) merely as some average value for the LDCs. Equations (10.6) and (10.7) suggest that if $\delta > 0$, there is a misallocation of resources with too little capital and labour being devoted to exports. A further implicit assumption is that the productivity differential decreases until it is extinguished as the share of $Q_2$ relative to $Q_1$ increases, otherwise it would be optimal to have all the resources concentrated in the second sector.

A problem immediately arose because data limitations meant that it was not possible to estimate specific functional forms for equations (10.1) and (10.2) separately. There were no statistics available for capital and labour at the required sectoral levels. Nevertheless, Feder circumvented this difficulty by specifying a reduced form equation for the model that only requires data on output, employment and capital (investment) for the whole economy and output data for the other sectors. To achieve this, equations (10.1) and (10.2) are differentiated with respect to time. Using the identities $Q \equiv Q_1 + Q_2$ (where $\dot{Q} = dQ/dt$, etc.); $dK/dt \equiv \dot{K}_1 + \dot{K}_2$; and $dL/dt \equiv \dot{L}_1 + \dot{L}_2$, together with the assumption that $F_L = \mu Q/L$, the following equation is obtained for the growth of total output:

$$\dot{Q}/Q = \mu \dot{L}/L + F_K I/Q + [\delta/(1+\delta) + F_{Q_2}](\dot{Q}_2/Q_2)(Q_2/Q) \tag{10.8}$$

where $I/Q$ is the gross investment–output ratio; $F_K$ is $\partial F/\partial K$, the marginal product of capital in Sector One; and $F_{Q_2}$ is $\partial F/\partial Q_2$.

It is still not possible to obtain separate estimates of $\delta$ and $F_{Q_2}$ from equation (10.8). Feder consequently derives an alternative specification that enables this to be accomplished by assuming that exports ($Q_2$) affect the production of the rest of the economy with a constant elasticity, $\gamma$, that is, $Q_1 = Q_2^\gamma f(L_1, K_1)$. In this case, the growth of total output is given by:

$$\dot{Q}/Q = \mu \dot{L}/L + F_K I/Q + [\delta/(1+\delta) - \gamma](\dot{Q}_2/Q_2)(Q_2/Q) + \gamma(\dot{Q}_2/Q_2) \tag{10.9}$$

Thus, from equation (10.9) it is possible to derive estimates of the marginal productivities differential ($\delta$) and the externality elasticity ($\gamma$).

While Feder considers this to be a plausible specification, further consideration suggests that this is not in fact the case, since it suggests that exports are a *sine qua non* for non-export production. If $Q_2 = 0$ it follows that $Q_1 = 0$. While the externality effect may be important for increasing the level of output in the rest of the economy, it is not realistic to postulate that *no* production could take place in a closed economy. Moreover, none of the reasons cited above, which Feder suggests are responsible for the externality, imply that export production is indispensable for production in the rest of the economy.

A further problem is the possibility of severe multicollinearity between $(\dot{Q}_2/Q_2)(Q_2/Q)$ (or equivalently $\dot{Q}_2/Q$) and $\dot{Q}_2/Q_2$. If $Q_2$ is a constant fraction of $Q$, then there will be perfect multicollinearity and it will not be possible to obtain precise estimates of the coefficients of $(\dot{Q}_2/Q_2)(Q_2/Q)$ and $(\dot{Q}_2/Q_2)$ and hence of $\delta$ and $\gamma$. While it is unlikely that the share of exports in total output will be exactly the same for all countries, the possibility of problems posed by multicollinearity nevertheless remains.

Finally, Feder points out that if $\delta/(1+\delta) = \gamma$ (which would be a remarkable coincidence), the model reduces to:[3]

$$\dot{Q}/Q = \mu\dot{L}/L + F_K I/Q + \gamma(\dot{Q}_2/Q_2) \tag{10.10}$$

To summarize, there are three specifications of the model which can be estimated, namely:

$$\dot{Q}/Q = b_0 + b_1\dot{L}/L + b_2 I/Q + b_3(\dot{Q}_2/Q_2)(Q_2/Q) \tag{10.11}$$

$$\dot{Q}/Q = b_0 + b_1\dot{L}/L + b_2 I/Q + b_3(\dot{Q}_2/Q_2)(Q_2/Q) + b_4(\dot{Q}_2/Q_2) \tag{10.12}$$

$$\dot{Q}/Q = b_0 + b_1\dot{L}/L + b_2 I/Q + b_4(\dot{Q}_2/Q_2) \tag{10.13}$$

where $b_0$ is a constant and supposedly captures the rate of exogenous technical progress.

In Table 10.1, we reproduce a selection of the more important results from Feder's and Ram's studies, together with some results from a comment on Ram by Rao (1989). However, before discussing these results, it is necessary to mention briefly some criticisms common to all of the studies.

First, there is the poor quality of the data which inevitably have large measurement errors, especially for the LDCs. Capital input, for example, is proxied by the gross investment–output ratio. Under normal neoclassical assumptions, there should be a deduction for scrapping (if we assume a one hoss shay) or for depreciation (if we assume economic loss and physical wear and tear occurs over the life of the asset). The use of the gross investment–output ratio as the correct measure of the growth of capital input has been advocated by Scott (1989), but this is a very controversial proposition.[4] None of the studies provides an explicit justification for the use of the gross investment ratio along these lines, and presumably it is used simply *faute de mieux*.

Second, the growth of total population is used as a proxy for the growth of labour input and it is unnecessary to emphasize just how crude this procedure is, especially for the LDCs where disguised unemployment is likely to be widespread and to differ markedly between countries.

*Table 10.1*  Selected regression results from Feder (1983), Ram (1986) and Rao (1989)

(a) Feder (1983): semi-industrialized countries, 1964–73

|     | Constant | $\dot{L}/L$ | $I/Q$ | $(\dot{X}/X)(X/Q)$ | $\dot{X}/X$ | $\overline{R}^2$ | $n$ |
|-----|----------|-------------|-------|--------------------|-------------|------------------|-----|
| (a) | –0.010   | 0.739       | 0.284 | –                  | –           | 0.370            | 31  |
|     | (0.55)   | (1.99)      | (4.31)|                    |             |                  |     |
| (b) | 0.002    | 0.747       | 0.178 | 0.422              | –           | 0.689            | 31  |
|     | (0.18)   | (2.86)      | (3.54)| (5.45)             |             |                  |     |
| (c) | 0.006    | 0.696       | 0.124 | 0.305              | 0.131       | 0.809            | 31  |
|     | (0.60)   | (3.40)      | (3.01)| (4.57)             | (4.24)      |                  |     |

(b) Ram (1986): all LDCs and ACs, 1960–70; Rao (1989): LDCs and ACs separately, 1960–70

|     | Constant | $\dot{L}/L$ | $I/Q$ | $(\dot{G}/G)(G/Q)$ | $\dot{G}/G$ | $\overline{R}^2$ | $n$ |
|-----|----------|-------------|-------|--------------------|-------------|------------------|-----|
| *Ram (1986)* |  |        |       |                    |             |                  |     |
| (d) | n.a.     | 0.517       | 0.118 | 1.286              | –           | 0.33             | 115 |
|     |          | (2.49)      | (4.96)| (4.63)             |             |                  |     |
| (e) | n.a.     | 0.551       | 0.114 | –                  | 0.226       | 0.34             | 115 |
|     |          | (2.69)      | (4.79)|                    | (4.77)      |                  |     |
| (f) | n.a.     | 0.504       | 0.114 | 0.672              | 0.139       | 0.35             | 115 |
|     |          | (2.45)      | (4.81)| (1.59)             | (1.92)      |                  |     |
| *Rao (1989)* |  |        |       |                    |             |                  |     |
| (g) (LDCs) | n.a. | 0.398     | 0.127 | 1.284              | –           | 0.368            | 94  |
|     |          | (1.63)      | (4.35)| (4.31)             |             |                  |     |
| (h) (ACs)  | n.a. | –0.110    | 0.213 | –0.489             | –           | 0.199            | 21  |
|     |          | (–0.14)     | (1.99)| (–0.20)            |             |                  |     |

*Note*:
Figures in parentheses denote *t*-statistics.

Equation (a) in Table 10.1 (where $Q_2 = X$, that is, exports) reports the results of what Feder terms the conventional (one-sector) neoclassical model. The coefficient of $I/Q$ is statistically significant, although somewhat higher than would be expected from the results of other production function studies. The output elasticity with respect to labour is about three-quarters, which is in accord with other studies (and approximately equal to labour's share, although the standard error is rather large).

Feder considers that the results of equation (b) 'lend strong support to the hypothesis that marginal factor productivities in the export sector are higher than in the non-export sector, as the coefficient of $(\dot{X}/X)\cdot(X/Q)$ is positive and significantly different from zero'. Equation (c) shows that the externality parameter (the coefficient of $\dot{X}/X$) is statistically significant and the estimate of $\delta$ (the productivity differential) is approximately equal to 0.75, 'implying that there is a substantial productivity differential between exports and non-exports in addition to the differential due to externalities' (Feder, 1983). (Feder also reports the results of a limited sample, but the results using these countries are broadly similar to the full sample.)

Ram (1986) likewise considers that his regression results provide support for the importance of government expenditure as a stimulus to overall economic growth. He provides results for 1960–70 and 1970–80, using statistics from a well-known Summers and Heston (1984) data set for over a hundred countries. For reasons of space, we only report results for 1960–70 (which do not differ greatly from those of the later period). It may be seen from Table 10.1, equations (d) and (e), that the coefficients of both $(\dot{G}/G)(G/Q)$ and $\dot{G}/G$ are statistically significant when included separately in the regressions. However, when both regressors are included simultaneously (equation (f)), both are statistically insignificant at the 5 per cent confidence level although the coefficient of $G/G$ is significant at the 10 per cent confidence level. The insignificance of the coefficient on $(\dot{G}/G)(G/Q)$ leads Ram to consider that $\delta/(1 + \delta)$ equals $\gamma$, and to prefer equation (e) in Table 10.1, although as Rao (1989) points out this result is almost certainly due to strong multicollinearity between the two variables. Rao also shows that while Ram reports results for the LDCs and advanced countries (ACs) pooled as well as for the LDCs only, he omits results for the ACs considered separately. Rao replicates this study, finding that the regression results for the latter are considerably poorer than those for the LDCs. For example, for equation (h) in Table 10.1, the conventional $F$-test diagnostic (not reported here) is not statistically significant even at the 10 per cent confidence level. Ram's (1989) rejoinder to this criticism is simply that the 'estimates for the ACs have no relevance to the main issue' which, may, of course, lead us to wonder why he included them in the first place.

On the basis of both cross-sectional and time-series regression results for individual countries, Ram concludes that the results generally provide strong support for the contention that the growth of government expenditure has a positive effect on the growth of output. Moreover, he considers that this procedure uses a 'reasonably defensible theoretical framework'. We now address this highly questionable assertion.

## THE PRODUCTION FUNCTION AND THE ACCOUNTING IDENTITY

Ram's view is highly questionable because there are two identities underlying the various specifications given by equations (10.11) to (10.13) which preclude giving the regression results any economic or behavioural interpretation along the lines of Feder and Ram. The specifications are merely hybrids of two underlying identities, subject to omitted variable bias. (For this reason, the various misspecification and causality tests, together with the other usual statistical diagnostics that Ram and Rao report, are not discussed in this chapter.)

The first problem is posed by the accounting identity that underlies the production function, namely:

$$Q_t \equiv w_t L_t + r_t K_t \tag{10.14}$$

where $w$ and $r$ are the real wage rate and the rate of profit.[5] Equation (10.14) is compatible with *any* production function, or indeed the absence of any well-behaved aggregate production function. Let us assume for some reason (the Kaldorian theory of distribution or a constant mark-up on unit labour costs) that factor shares are constant. Let us also assume that both the growth of wages and the rate of profit are roughly constant (the latter is often zero). Equation (10.14) may be expressed in terms of exponential growth rates as:

$$\dot{Q}/Q \equiv [a\dot{w}/w + (1-a)\dot{r}/r] + a\dot{L}/L + (1-a)\dot{K}/K \tag{10.15}$$

where $a$ and $(1-a)$ are labour's and capital's incomes shares.

Remembering that equation (10.15) is simply an identity with no behavioural counterpart (with the exception of the assumption about the growth of wages and profits), it may be integrated to give:

$$Q = A_0 e^{\varphi t} L^a K^{(1-a)} \tag{10.16}$$

where $\varphi = a\dot{w}/w + (1-a)\dot{r}/r$.

This is none other than the Cobb–Douglas 'production function', namely:

$$Q = A_0 e^{\lambda t} L^\alpha K^{(1-\alpha)}$$

where $\lambda$ is the (constant) rate of technical progress. We can see that definitionally $\lambda$ must equal $a\dot{w}/w + (1-a)\dot{r}/r$ and that $a \equiv \alpha$.

The implications of this are far-reaching. It means that the estimation of a Cobb–Douglas can provide no independent test of whether a well-behaved production function exists or whether the 'true' aggregate elasticity of substitution (if indeed this is a meaningful concept) is unity. It explains the results of Fisher's (1971) famous simulation experiments where he found that *if* factor shares were constant, the data would give a good fit to the Cobb–Douglas, even though the conditions for successful aggregation were (deliberately) violated. Thus, if factor shares are constant, we should always expect the data to give a good fit to a Cobb–Douglas production function with the output elasticities equalling the factor shares. The fact that this is often found empirically to be the case cannot be taken as confirming the assumptions of perfect competition and the marginal productivity theory of factor pricing. Thus, there is no justification for Feder (1983) to argue that 'the parameter $[b_1]$, related to labour growth, should also be significantly more than zero if labour surplus was not the prevalent situation in sample countries during the period covered'.

To see this, let us assume that there is a well-defined underlying production function for, say, agriculture and that surplus labour exists, and so the true marginal product of labour of an LDC is zero. This is shown in Figure 10.1, where employment is $L^*$ and the marginal product of labour ($MPL$) is zero. Furthermore, let us assume that agriculture is undertaken by the extended family and a certain fraction of the gross output is used for investment and the rest distributed to the workers. Let us call this latter share $a$. Because of the cooperative nature of the agricultural economy, each worker is consequently paid the average net product. The net product is total output less that used for investment purposes (viz. $aQ$). This is shown in Figure 10.1, where *abfe* is the value of total output, which equals the average product of labour (APL) times the numbers employed. The area *abcd* is devoted to investment and is equal to $(1 - a)Q$. If this is a relatively stable proportion of total output, then estimating a Cobb–Douglas will give a good fit to the data because factor shares are constant. As noted above, the imputed marginal product will be $aQ/L$ (which is actually the average net product of labour). Thus, the misleading inference will be drawn that production is not occurring in the 'uneconomic region' of input space (see Ferguson, 1971, p. 66). The data will suggest that the production function is a Cobb–Douglas no matter what is the true production function. In other words, the data cannot differentiate between the case described above and the Cobb–Douglas production function, depicted in Figure 10.2, where total output and labour's and capital's shares are the same as in Figure 10.1.

Returning to the identity, this may be written as:

$$\dot{Q}/Q \equiv [a\dot{w}/w + (1 - a)\dot{r}/r] + a\dot{L}/L + r\dot{K}/Q \tag{10.18}$$

with the usual notation, and where, as we have noted, the net accumulation of capital, $\dot{K}$, is proxied in empirical work by $I$. It should be noted, however, that

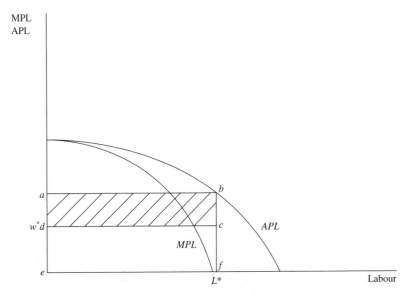

*Figure 10.1* Labour productivities given constant factor shares with surplus labour

$a\dot{w}/w + (1 - a)\dot{r}/r$, the weighted sum of the growth of real wages and the rate of the profit, is likely to vary across countries and so the intercept obtained by estimating the Cobb–Douglas relationship in growth rate form using cross-country data should be regarded as reflecting some average value.

## EXTERNALITIES AND THE SECTORAL OUTPUT IDENTITY

The other identity underlying the regression analysis may be written as:

$$\dot{Q}/Q \equiv \sum \omega_i \dot{Q}_i/Q_i \tag{10.19}$$

(where $\omega_i$ is the share of $Q_i$ in total output, $Q$, that is, $\omega_i = Q_i/Q$).

If we consider that, for example, both exports and government expenditure have important externality effects, the identity can be written equivalently as either:

$$\dot{Q}/Q \equiv 1.0[(R/Q)(\dot{R}/R)] + 1.0[(G/Q)(\dot{G}/G)] + 1.0[X/Q)(\dot{X}/X)] \tag{10.20}$$

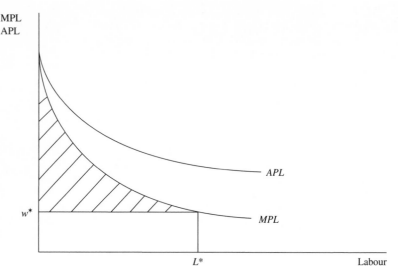

*Figure 10.2*　Labour productivities given constant factor shares with a Cobb–
Douglas production function

or:

$$\dot{Q}/Q \equiv \omega_R(\dot{R}/R) + \omega_G(\dot{G}/G) + \omega_X(\dot{X}/X) \tag{10.21}$$

where $\dot{R}/R$ is the growth of the rest of the economy.[6]

Recall equations (10.11) to (10.13) where we considered the case where there was only one sector with a supposed externality effect and/or a productivity differential compared with the rest of the economy. It can be seen from the identity given by equation (10.18), together with equations (10.19) and (10.20), that $b_1$ in equations (10.11) to (10.13) will be approximately equal to $a$ and take some value between 0.50 and 0.75; $b_2$ will be approximately equal to $r$ which is normally likely to be between 0.1 and 0.2; the coefficient of $(Q_i/Q)(\dot{Q}_i/Q)$ (that is, $b_3$), when unbiased, will approximately be equal to unity; and the coefficient of $(\dot{Q}_i/Q)$ (that is, $b_4$), when unbiased, will approximately be equal to $Q_i/Q$. We have seen that the argument can be generalized to any number of sectors.

There are two important qualifications to the preceding argument that all we are doing is estimating a hybrid of identities, none of which diminishes its importance.

The first qualification is that when the specifications are estimated using cross-country data, the individual shares $\omega_i$ are likely to vary between countries, thus reducing the goodness of fit as the estimated coefficient $b_4$ will merely reflect the (possibly biased) average share (see equation (10.21)). Consider the three-sector model where the sectors are government output, exports and the rest of the economy. In the case of a relatively homogeneous group of countries, such as the advanced countries, the degree of relative variation in the share of government expenditure is likely to be small. (See Table 10.2 for the advanced countries. The years chosen are simply the boom years near the middle of the Golden Age of economic growth, although other years present much the same picture.) However, the share of exports shows much greater intercountry variation. The problem of the variation in shares does not, of course, affect the coefficient of $(Q_i/Q)(Q_i/Q)$ in equation (10.21) which, when unbiased, will be unity for every country.

The mention of unbiasedness brings us to the second point. The rest of the economy (appropriately defined, depending upon the other regressors) in equation (10.21) does not appear in any of the specifications given by equations (10.11) to (10.13). Thus, unless the growth of the rest of the economy is

*Table 10.2*  Shares of government expenditure, exports and the rest of the economy, advanced countries

| Country | Year | Government expenditure | Exports | Rest of the economy |
|---|---|---|---|---|
| Japan | 1961 | 14.5 | 6.3 | 79.2 |
| West Germany | 1961 | 16.9 | 18.1 | 65.0 |
| Italy | 1959 | 15.3 | 9.3 | 75.4 |
| France | 1960 | 15.2 | 11.8 | 73.0 |
| Netherlands | 1960 | 15.2 | 34.8 | 50.0 |
| Denmark | 1962 | 20.3 | 23.3 | 56.4 |
| Austria | 1961 | 18.9 | 20.5 | 60.6 |
| Canada | 1966 | 18.9 | 21.2 | 60.0 |
| Norway | 1960 | 14.4 | 33.4 | 52.2 |
| Belgium | 1964 | 15.4 | 33.1 | 51.5 |
| USA | 1966 | 20.3 | 6.0 | 73.7 |
| UK | 1960 | 21.7 | 19.4 | 58.9 |
| Unweighted average | | 17.3 | 19.8 | 63.0 |

*Sources*: OECD National Accounts (various years).

orthogonal to the other regressors, the latter will suffer from omitted variable bias. (The inclusion of $\dot{L}/L$ and $I/Q$ in the regression may also affect the estimates, but we shall see below that this is not empirically important.)

Let us consider, for example, equation (10.11), where $Q_2$ is some as yet unspecified sector. We can determine the degree of bias as follows. The auxiliary regression of the weighted growth of the rest of the economy on that of $Q_2$ is given by (omitting, for expositional ease, $\dot{L}/L$ and $I/Q$):

$$(\dot{R}/R)/(R/Q) \equiv c_0 + c_1(\dot{Q}_2/Q_2)(Q_2/Q) \tag{10.22}$$

The 'biased' estimate of $b_3$ in equation (10.11) due to the omission of $(\dot{R}/Q)(R/Q)$ is $b_3 = c_1 + b_3$ where $b_3' = 1.0$. If there is no close relationship between $(\dot{R}/Q)(R/Q)$ and $(\dot{Q}_2/Q_2)(Q_2/Q)$, then we should expect a highly significant estimate of $b_3$ with a value of around unity.

Table 10.3 reports some illustrative regressions for twelve advanced countries over the period 1950–70. The period was chosen merely because it was the Golden Age of economic growth (although, strictly speaking, this ended in 1973), when there was a great deal of variation in growth rates between the advanced countries. However, since we are demonstrating a theoretical argument, the exact time period (and choice of countries) does not greatly matter.

Let us first consider the specification:

$$\dot{Q}/Q = b_0 + b_1\dot{L}/L + b_2I/Q + b_5(\dot{R}/R)(R/Q) + b_6(\dot{G}/G)(G/Q)$$
$$+ b_7(\dot{X}/X)(X/Q) \tag{10.23}$$

where one of the last three regressors is omitted (normally $(\dot{R}/R)(R/Q)$).

Equation (i) in Table 10.3(a) shows that, not surprisingly, the estimates of the 'production function' are reasonably close to what would be expected *a priori* from the accounting identity, although the fit is not particularly good. When the two combined identities are estimated (equation (j)), the coefficients of the 'production function' do not prove robust, but the coefficients of the three sectors take their expected values of unity. When either $(\dot{G}/G)(G/Q)$ or $(\dot{X}/X)(X/Q)$ is omitted, the coefficients on the remaining sectors remain statistically significant with values often not significantly different from unity. However, it is interesting to note that when $(\dot{R}/R)(R/Q)$ is omitted, the coefficients of both $(\dot{G}/G)(G/Q)$ and $(\dot{X}/X)(X/Q)$ become statistically insignificant (equation (m)). This is because there is substantial omitted variable bias as evidenced by the 'auxiliary' regression, equation (n), although it is difficult to given an economic explanation for this relationship. It is best regarded as a statistical artefact.[7] Certainly, equation (m) cannot be taken as a refutation of the hypothesis of

*Table 10.3* Regression results for advanced countries, pooled data, 1950–70

| (a) | Dependent variable $\dot{Q}/Q$ | | | | | |
|---|---|---|---|---|---|---|
| | *(i)* | *(j)* | *(k)* | *(l)* | *(m)* | *(n)*[†] |
| Constant | −0.282 | 0.026 | 0.282 | −0.298 | −0.204 | −0.230 |
| | (−0.22) | (1.03) | (0.49) | (−1.20) | (−0.15) | (−0.17) |
| $\dot{L}/L$ | 0.871 | −0.001 | 0.077 | 0.172 | 0.838 | 0.838 |
| | (3.25) | (−0.14) | (0.53) | (3.02) | (2.79) | (2.78) |
| $I/Q$ | 0.174 | −0.002 | 0.079 | 0.038 | 0.198 | 0.200 |
| | (3.70) | (−1.72) | (3.09) | (3.48) | (3.47) | (3.50) |
| $(\dot{R}/R)(R/Q)$ | – | 1.001 | 0.746 | 0.957 | – | – |
| | | (313.60) | (12.76) | (30.93) | | |
| $(\dot{G}/G)(G/Q)$ | – | 1.002 | 0.846 | – | −0.335 | −1.238 |
| | | (137.00) | (2.18) | | (−1.09) | (−1.43) |
| $(\dot{X}/X)(X/Q)$ | – | 1.040 | – | 0.966 | −0.198 | −1.336 |
| | | (60.26) | | (13.31) | (−0.23) | (−4.36) |
| $\overline{R}^2$ | 0.317 | 1.000 | 0.867 | 0.974 | 0.304 | 0.433 |
| SER | 1.544 | 0.030 | 0.681 | 0.301 | 1.559 | 1.557 |

| (b) | | | | | | |
|---|---|---|---|---|---|---|
| | *(o)* | *(p)* | *(q)* | *(r)* | *(s)* | *(t)*[‡] |
| Constant | – | −0.501 | −0.086 | −1.022 | −0.807 | −0.621 |
| | | (−1.17) | (−0.14) | (−2.10) | (−0.76) | (−0.31) |
| $\dot{L}/L$ | – | 0.050 | 0.034 | 0.204 | 0.636 | 1.188 |
| | | (0.50) | (0.23) | (1.82) | (2.79) | (2.79) |
| $I/Q$ | – | 0.048 | 0.079 | 0.097 | 0.083 | 0.071 |
| | | (2.42) | (2.72) | (5.24) | (1.69) | (0.78) |
| $\dot{R}/R$ | 0.504 | 0.493 | 0.580 | 0.483 | – | – |
| | (14.90) | (13.91) | (11.99) | (11.44) | | |
| $\dot{G}/G$ | 0.300 | 0.202 | 0.174 | – | 0.156 | −0.094 |
| | (8.55) | (4.09) | (2.40) | | (1.27) | (−0.41) |
| $\dot{X}/X$ | 0.205 | 0.168 | – | 0.159 | 0.300 | 0.266 |
| | (9.82) | (6.64) | | (5.28) | (5.11) | (2.44) |
| $\overline{R}^2$ | 0.991 | 0.932 | 0.932 | 0.904 | 0.581 | 0.246 |
| SER | 0.517 | 0.486 | 0.486 | 0.580 | 1.210 | 2.254 |

*Notes:*
[†] Dependent variable is $(\dot{R}/R)(R/Q)$.

[‡] Dependent variable is $\dot{R}/R$.

Figures in parentheses are the *t*-statistics. Constant is per cent per annum
The countries are Austria, Belgium, Canada, Denmark, France, Germany, Italy, Japan, Netherlands, Norway, the USA and the UK.
*Sources:* OECD National Accounts (various years).

the importance of these sectors in economic growth, any more than statistically significant coefficients can be taken as providing support.

Next consider equation (10.13), that is, $\dot{Q}/Q = b_0 + b_1\dot{L}/L + b_2 I/Q + b_4(\dot{Q}_2/Q_2)$.[8] The share of output of $R$, it will be recalled, is denoted by $\omega_R$ and that of $Q_2$ is $\omega_2(= 1 - \omega_R)$. If the auxiliary regression between the growth of the rest of the economy and that of the sector under consideration is given by:

$$\dot{R}/R = d_0 + d_1\dot{Q}_2/Q_2 \tag{10.24}$$

the biased estimate of the share of $Q_2$ in GDP will be given by $b_4 = (\omega_R d_1 + b_4')$, where $b_4'$ is the true value, which will approximately equal $\omega_2$.

We can gain some idea of the likely degree of bias. Consider, for example, the land-based and resource-based industries, namely, agriculture and mining. For the advanced countries, it is likely that the growth of these is largely independent of the growth of GDP. Hence, the relationship between their growth rates and the growth of the rest of the economy is likely to be orthogonal. If this is the case, the estimated coefficients ($b_4$) are likely to take the average of their sectoral shares (10 per cent and 2 per cent respectively for the advanced countries).

On the other hand, consider a sector like commerce. It is likely that in this case the growth rate will be highly correlated with the growth of the rest of the economy. In other words, a fast-growing economy is likely to have a fast-growing demand for commercial services, while the converse is also likely to be true. If, for example, the growth of commerce is the same rate as the growth of the rest of the economy for our sample of countries, then the coefficient ($b_4$) will be equal to unity.

Under the Feder/Ram interpretation, this would indicate a substantial externality/productivity differential effect. The irony is that as we add more and more sectors to the model, we know *a priori* that the value of the estimated coefficients will converge to the values of their sectoral shares. This is because the share of the rest of the economy becomes progressively smaller, the more sectors we add. In other words, the more sectors that are included, the smaller $\omega_R$ will be and, *ceteris paribus*, the less the degree of omitted variable bias resulting from not including $\dot{R}/R$ in the identity. Indeed, the more sectors that are included, the more the coefficients will approximate the (positive) value of the sectoral shares and the greater the temptation, following Feder and Ram, to ascribe this to a positive externality effect.

The auxiliary regressions, equations (10.22) and (10.23), do convey some additional information, apart from that already known from the identity, namely, the relationship between the weighted or unweighted growth rates of the two separate components of GDP. But this may be merely coincidental or may be due to differences in the growth of demand (through differing income elasticities). It does not necessarily have anything to do with differences in sectoral productivities or externalities, *pace* Feder and Ram.

An extended model based on equation (10.13) is given by:

$$\dot{Q}/Q = b_0 + b_1\dot{L}/L + b_2I/Q + b_8(\dot{R}/R) + b_9(\dot{G}/G) + b_{10}(\dot{X}/X) \quad (10.25)$$

with $\dot{R}/R$ normally omitted.

Notwithstanding the variation in export shares, it may be seen from Table 10.3(b) equation (o) that the regression of the identity $\dot{Q}/Q \equiv \omega_R\dot{R}/R + \omega_G\dot{G}/G + \omega_X\dot{X}/X$ gives a good fit, although the estimate of the average share of the rest of the economy is on the low side of 50 per cent, whereas that of government expenditure is somewhat high at 30 per cent. The reason for these discrepancies is likely to be the incidence of multicollinearity and it is noteworthy that the sum of the three coefficients is 1.09, which is not significantly different from unity.

Estimating the two identities combined (equation (p)) shows that while the coefficients of the 'production function' are again not robust, those of the three sectors are reasonably so. Equations (q), (r) and (s) report the results when one of the sectors is omitted. It can be seen that although $\dot{R}/R$, $\dot{G}/G$, and $\dot{X}/X$ are not quite orthogonal, when one variable is dropped from the regression, the coefficients of the remaining two variables are not far removed from their average sector shares, and are therefore positive and statistically significant (with the exception of $\dot{G}/G$ in equation (s)). Consequently, if we were unaware of the underlying identities, there would be a temptation to assume for any pair of sectors that they exerted a positive externality (with the exception noted above). But, of course, this argument would hold for *all* combinations of pairs of sectors because of the underlying identity. Table 10.3 clearly illustrates that all that is being captured are the sector shares, although subjected to omitted variable bias.

The specification given by equation (10.13) complicates the story somewhat since it includes both $(\dot{Q}_i/Q)$ and $(\dot{Q}_i/Q)(Q_i/Q)$, and we will not pursue this case for reasons of space (see also note 8). Nevertheless, it can easily be seen that the identities still preclude any unambiguous economic interpretation of the regression results.

As we have noted, some of these arguments were first broached by Sheehey (1990), who finds that the growth rates, over the period 1960–70, of GDP and the following sectors for 36 countries have a significant Spearman rank correlation coefficient: exports (0.482); government consumption (0.328); private consumption (0.724); investment (0.374); agriculture (0.502); manufacturing (0.616); construction (0.407); electricity, gas and water (0.456); and services (0.447). Consequently, the strong empirical link between GDP growth and export or government expenditure growth is also found between GDP growth and that of other sectors. Sheehey also casts doubt on the neoclassical interpretation of the regression results, although he overlooks the existence of

*Table 10.4*  Regressions with two sectors, advanced countries, 1950–70
Estimating equation: $\dot{Q}/Q = b_0 + b_1 \dot{L}/L + b_2 I/Q + b_4 \dot{Q}_i/Q_i$

| Sector I | $\hat{b}_4$ | (t-value) | $\overline{R}^2$ | Av. share |
|----------|-------------|-----------|------------------|-----------|
| Agriculture | 0.129 | (1.43) | 0.239 | 0.09 |
| Mining | 0.058 | (0.20) | 0.224 | 0.02 |
| Manufacturing | 0.536 | (14.62) | 0.889 | 0.33 |
| Construction | 0.267 | (5.65) | 0.544 | 0.07 |
| Public utilities | 0.078 | (1.43) | 0.239 | 0.02 |
| Transportation | 0.352 | (3.09) | 0.370 | 0.08 |
| Commerce | 0.511 | (6.95) | 0.661 | 0.13 |
| Other services | 0.605 | (3.01) | 0.604 | 0.23 |

*Note*:
The estimates of $b_0, b_1$ and $b_2$ are omitted for reasons of space.
Av. share is the average share for the 12 advanced countries of the sector in GDP.
*Source*: Cripps and Tarling (1973).

the accounting identity, as he still refers to the Feder model as consisting of 'production function regressions'.

Table 10.4 reports a similar exercise using data for the twelve advanced countries. It can be seen that all of the estimated coefficients are positive (although agriculture, mining and public utilities are statistically insignificant, they do not differ greatly from their share values). Manufacturing, construction, transportation, commerce and other services greatly exceed their share values. The reason for this is not hard to find. We are using cross-country data and so there is likely to be a strong positive correlation between the rest of the economy and the sector under consideration, to the extent that the fast-growing countries (such as Japan) tend to have fast growth in all their sectors whereas the laggards (such as the UK) tend to grow slowly across the board. Thus, omitting $\dot{R}/R$ will bias upwards the estimated coefficient of the remaining sector. However, as we have noted above, the statistically significant and large regression coefficients cannot be taken as independent evidence of the existence of externalities and/or differences in marginal productivities.

## CONCLUSIONS

To conclude, we have examined a methodology that has sought to determine statistically the importance of certain key sectors (especially exports and government services) for the growth of the whole economy. But because of the underlying identities, it has been shown that it is not possible to substantiate the inferences that Feder and Ram have drawn. The estimates would have been the same even if all the sectors had the same marginal productivities and there were no externality effects at all. It has been argued by Kaldor (1966), Cornwall (1977), and McCombie and Thirlwall (1994), *inter alios*, that a rapid growth of manufacturing will induce fast growth in the rest of the economy. If we were to repeat the above approach using manufacturing in conjunction with, or instead of, government expenditure and exports, we would find significant coefficients that support this hypothesis – but the exercise would be meaningless. Of course, it should be emphasized that the preceding critique does not mean that exports, government expenditures or manufacturing are not of great importance in the growth process. The point is simply that the Feder approach can shed no light on the issue. Work by Cornwall and Cornwall (1994a) and McCombie (1980, 1991) has shown that differences in sectoral productivities can, in fact, be a very important factor in explaining why the growth rates of the advanced countries differ.

**Notes**

1.  Of course, the importance of Wendy Cornwall's collaboration with John in a number of important papers goes without saying. For recent examples see Cornwall and Cornwall (1994a, 1994b).
2.  Landau (1983), for example, found that the larger the share of government expenditure in GDP, the lower the growth rate of GDP per capita. Thus, an *increase* in the share of government expenditure *reduces* the rate of growth of GDP. As we shall see, the reason for these different statistical results is that Landau uses the ratio of government expenditure to output as a regression whereas Ram uses some function of the growth of government expenditure. Consequently, the conclusion drawn depends crucially upon whether shares or growth rates are used. We shall show below why this is the case.
3.  This is similar to a number of models where exports are hypothesized to exert an externality effect directly on *total* output. In other words, the aggregate production function takes the form $Q = f(L, K, X)$, rather than $Q_1 = F(L_1, K_1, X)$ where $X$ denotes exports (see, for example, Sheehey, 1991, p. 112, and the references that he cites). There is a problem of equifinality here as it is not possible to distinguish between the two models (see also Ram, 1986, p. 193, footnote 5).
4.  Scott (1989) argues that depreciation of capital equipment is largely due to obsolescence, rather than physical wear and tear. This obsolescence is a price effect due to the increase in the relative price of labour over time. However, since the effect of the latter is not taken into account through an allowance for the corresponding appreciation in human capital, obsolescence should *not* be deducted from the capital measure. If this procedure is followed and gross

investment is used, Scott argues that the residual in economic growth disappears.

5.  This critique, which has been almost totally ignored in the literature (the fact that Herbert Simon (1977) thought it of sufficient importance to mention in his Nobel Prize acceptance speech, notwithstanding), has a long pedigree. It was discussed with reference to cross-industry Cobb–Douglas production functions by Phelps Brown (1957) and the argument was formalized by Simon and Levy (1963). It was extended to time-series data by Shaikh (1974, 1980) and Simon (1979), and further elaborated by McCombie (1987), McCombie and Dixon (1991), McCombie (1998a) and Felipe and McCombie (1997). The reasons as to why the critique has generally been ignored in the literature are discussed in McCombie (1998b). Carr (1989) briefly considers a similar argument with respect to government services, but does not push the reasoning to its logical conclusion.

6.  The expenditure identity is $Q \equiv C + G + I + X - M$ where $C$ is private consumption and $M$ is imports. Thus, the rest of the economy is defined as $Q - G - X$.

7.  This result is not robust and the exclusion of, for example, Japan (with a small export share but fast growth rates of exports and the remainder of the economy) significantly affects the regression estimates.

8.  The more general specification of Feder's model is given by equation (10.12) and here we have, in effect, a combination of three underlying identities. If this is generalized to three or more sectors, we get additional terms such as $(\dot{Q}_2/Q_2)(R/Q)$ (see Alexander, 1994). This does not materially alter the argument and, in practice, the estimates are plagued by serious multicollinearity. A discussion of this complication is not pursued here.

## References

Alexander, W.R.J. (1990) 'The impact of defence spending on economic growth', *Defence Economics*, 2, 39–55

Alexander, W.R.J. (1994) 'The government sector, the export sector and growth', *De Economist*, 142, 211–20

Biswas, B. and R. Ram (1985) 'Military expenditures and economic growth in less developing countries: an augmented model and further evidence', *Economic Development and Cultural Change*, 34, 361–72

Carr, J. (1989) 'Government size and economic growth: a new framework and some evidence from cross-section and time-series data: comment', *American Economic Review*, 79, 267–71

Cornwall, J. (1977) *Modern Capitalism: Its Growth and Transformation*, London, Martin Robertson

Cornwall, J. and W. Cornwall (1994a) 'Structural change and productivity in the OECD', in P. Davidson and J.A. Kregel (eds) *Employment, Growth and Finance: Economic Reality and Economic Growth*, Aldershot, Edward Elgar

Cornwall, J. and W. Cornwall (1994b) 'Growth theory and economic structure', *Economica*, 61, 237–51

Cripps, T.F. and R.J. Tarling (1973) *Growth in Advanced Capitalist Economies: 1950–1970*, Cambridge, Cambridge University Press

Feder, G. (1983) 'On exports and economic growth', *Journal of Development Economics*, 12, 59–73

Felipe, J. and J.S.L. McCombie (1997) 'Methodological problems with some recent analyses of the East Asian miracle', mimeo, Asian Development Bank

Ferguson, C.E. (1971) *The Neoclassical Theory of Production and Distribution*, Cambridge, Cambridge University Press

Fisher, F.M. (1971) 'Aggregate production functions and the explanation of wages: a simulation experiment', *Review of Economics and Statistics*, 53, 305–25

Grossman, P.J. (1988) 'Growth in government and economic growth: the Australian experience', *Australian Economic Papers*, 27, 33–43

Grossman, P.J. (1990) 'Government and growth: cross-sectional evidence', *Public Choice*, 65, 217–27

Kaldor, N. (1966) *The Causes of the Slow Rate of Economic Growth in the United Kingdom: An Inaugural Lecture*, Cambridge, Cambridge University Press

Kohli, I. and N. Singh (1989) 'Exports and growth: critical minimum effort and diminishing returns', *Journal of Development Economics*, 30, 391–400

Landau, D. (1983) 'Government expenditure and economic growth: a cross-country study', *Southern Economic Journal*, 49, 783–92

McCombie, J.S.L. (1980) 'On the quantitative importance of Kaldor's laws', *Bulletin of Economic Research*, 32, 103–22

McCombie, J.S.L. (1987) 'Does the aggregate production function imply anything about the laws of production? A note on the Simon and Shaikh critiques', *Applied Economics*, 19, 1121–36

McCombie, J.S.L. (1991) 'The postwar productivity slowdown and the intersectoral reallocation of labour', *Australian Economic Papers,* 31, 70–81

McCombie, J.S.L. (1998a) '"Are there laws of production?" An assessment of the early criticisms of the Cobb–Douglas production function', *Review of Political Economy*, 10, 141–73

McCombie, J.S.L. (1998b) 'Rhetoric, paradigms and the relevance of the aggregate production function', in P. Arestis (ed.) *Method, Theory and Policy in Keynes: Essays in Honour of Paul Davidson, Volume 3*, Aldershot, Edward Elgar

McCombie, J.S.L. and R. Dixon (1991) 'Estimating technical change in aggregate production functions: a critique', *International Review of Applied Economics*, 5, 24–46

McCombie, J.S.L. and A.P. Thirlwall (1994) *Economic Growth and the Balance-of-Payments Constraint*, London, Macmillan

Phelps Brown, E.H. (1957) 'The meaning of the fitted Cobb–Douglas function', *Quarterly Journal of Economics*, 71, 546–60

Ram, R. (1986) 'Government size and economic growth: a new framework and some evidence from cross-section and time-series data', *American Economic Review*, 76, 191–203

Ram, R. (1987) 'Exports and economic growth in developing countries: evidence from time-series and cross-section data', *Economic Development and Cultural Change*, 36, 51–72

Ram, R. (1989) 'Government size and economic growth: a new framework and some evidence from cross-section and time-series data: reply', *American Economic Review*, 79, 281–4

Rao, V.V.B. (1989) 'Government size and economic growth: a new framework and some evidence from cross-section and time-series data: comment', *American Economic Review*, 79, 272–80

Scott, M.F. (1989) *A New View of Economic Growth*, Oxford, Clarendon Press

Shaikh, A. (1974) 'Laws of production and laws of algebra: the humbug production function', *Review of Economics and Statistics*, 56, 115–20

Shaikh, A. (1980) 'Laws of production and laws of algebra: humbug II', in E.J. Nell (ed.) *Growth, Profits and Property*, Cambridge, Cambridge University Press

Sheehey, E.J. (1991) 'Exports and growth: a flawed framework', *Journal of Development Studies*, 27, 111–14

Simon, H.A. (1977) 'Rational decision-making in business organizations', Nobel Memorial lecture, 8 December, 1977 (published in *American Economic Review*, 69, 493–513)

Simon, H.A. (1979) 'On parsimonious explanations of production relations', *Scandinavian Journal of Economics*, 89, 459–74

Simon, H.A. and F.K. Levy (1963) 'A note on the Cobb–Douglas function', *Review of Economics and Statistics*, 39, 93–4

Summers, R. and A. Heston (1984) 'Improved international comparisons of real product and its composition: 1950–80', *Review of Income and Wealth*, 30, 207–62

# 11 Integration and Convergence in the European Union

Pascal Petit

## DOES REGIONAL INTEGRATION FAVOUR REGIONAL CONVERGENCE?

The development of the Common Market has undergone a number of different phases since the Rome Treaty of 1960. The successes of the original member countries in the 1960s initially helped to attract new members. Doubts followed in the late 1970s, however, when these economies experienced renewed cyclical disturbances and stagnation. Further integration (especially in the monetary sector) was perceived as a means of protection against external hazards brought on by entry into a world of flexible exchange rates. After the long recession and massive unemployment of the early 1980s, the 1986 Single Market Act was aimed at reinvigorating economic growth by extending European economic integration. Whether trade conditions had changed or whether European integration had begun to experience diminishing returns, the effects of this initiative petered out in the early 1990s, with the process of convergence slowing down (see Figures 11.1 and 11.2).[1]

This chapter addresses the question of the links between integration and convergence. It focuses on the conditions under which further integration would lead to greater convergence between European countries. This issue is crucial for the future of the European Union, even if it is not a sufficient condition for the latter's success. The question of the net growth effect of European integration is, of course, a different matter, as this also depends on the external context of the region.

To begin, we need clear definitions of the concepts of integration and convergence. In Machlup's (1977) survey, trade is the quintessence of economic integration and the division of labour its underlying principle. Accordingly, integration could be defined in terms of the relative intensity of trade relations, although it might now be appropriate to extend this definition to cover all transactions, in order to include, for example, direct investment (which increased markedly in the mid-1980s, both in Europe and elsewhere), and even non-monetary transactions, as exemplified by various acts of

149

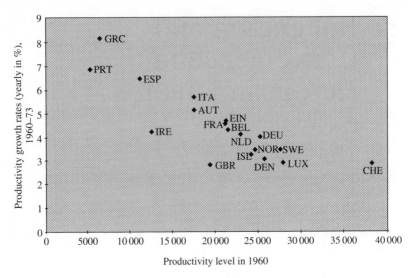

*Figure 11.1*   Convergence/divergence in Europe, 1960–73
*Source*: OECD National Accounts.

BEL – Belgium; CHE – Confederation Helvetique, i.e., Switzerland; DEN – Denmark; DEU – Germany; ESP – Spain;
FIN – Finland; FRA – France; GBR – Great Britain; GRC – Greece; IRE – Ireland; ISL – Iceland; ITA – Italy;
LUX – Luxembourg; NLD – Netherlands; NOR – Norway; SWE – Sweden; PRT – Portugal; AUT – Austria.

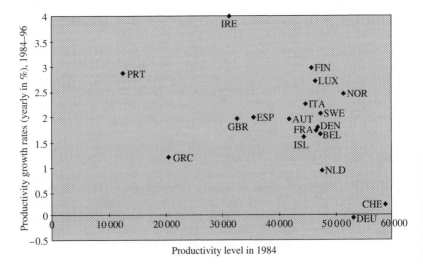

*Figure 11.2*   Convergence/divergence in Europe, 1984–96
*Source*: OECD National Accounts.

cooperation and exchanges of intangibles. This ultimately leads us to a conception of integration couched in terms of relative transaction costs: to what extent are the average costs of transactions lowered within the subset of countries constituting the region under review, as compared to transaction costs between the region and other countries?

Convergence refers to a narrowing of disparities in the levels of development of the countries in a region. It is a multidimensional process which may involve changes in welfare, productive efficiency and/or social structures. We shall focus on changes in the distribution of levels of welfare, as measured by GDP per head. This is an appropriate indicator of convergence, especially if greater equality in welfare levels is necessary for successful European economic integration (Cecchini, 1988).

While there exist some fairly reliable indicators of convergence, the measurement of integration is more contentious. A reduction in transaction costs – even if manifested only in a reduction in trade barriers – can affect transactions in very different ways, by creating or diverting trade flows, increasing intra-industry trade,[2] and modifying national institutions. This chapter will not, therefore, attempt to quantify the magnitude of different integration initiatives. It will assume that regionalization is a uniform process of integration, the speed of which can be varied by political arrangements and political will. More precisely, integration will be seen as a series of exogenous steps taken in order to facilitate transactions among countries (at one point, it will be treated as equivalent to changes in the terms of trade). On this basis, we will examine, for each successive period of European integration, a model consistent with the chief stylized facts concerning the growth of medium-sized, industrialized, open economies.

Precisely how integration affects convergence will depend on external conditions (such as the growth of external demand) and internal conditions that influence the structure and efficiency of the various economies under review. Initially, our analysis will focus on the growth pattern prevalent in the period of sustained expansion in Europe during the 1950s and 1960s. We will first investigate the direct effects of integration on convergence, and then its indirect effects operating through the formation of wages and profits. In a similar fashion, we will then assess the trade and growth pattern during the 1980s and 1990s, a period marked by a considerable slowdown in economic growth and convergence. We will show that the new growth pattern, which arose from structural changes partly induced by the previous phase of growth and which is characterized by increasing internationalization and tertiarization, seems to fuel divergence. We then give brief accounts of the new forms of competitiveness responsible for this divergence and their effect on convergence in Europe.

## A COMMON PATTERN OF CUMULATIVE GROWTH IN OPEN ECONOMIES WITH COST-BASED COMPETITIVENESS

The set of European countries that we are considering displayed rather similar patterns of export-led growth during the 1960s and early 1970s. Schemes of cumulative causation, whereby economic growth fuels productivity gains which in turn favour internal demand and exports, have been shown to give a consistent account of the medium-run features of economic growth. Following Kaldor (1966, 1970), contributions by Cripps and Tarling (1973), Cornwall (1977), Parikh (1978), and Boyer and Petit (1981) have successfully estimated more or less comprehensive forms of such cumulative causation schemes for European countries in the 1960s.[3]

To simplify our analysis, we begin with a model of cumulative causation in which the determination of exports is fully specified, while the expressions for total demand and productivity gains are stated as very reduced forms. Let us first describe the demand regime, that is, our characterization of the various influences on demand.[4] In export-led growth models (such as Dixon and Thirlwall, 1975) exports are the key stimulant of expansion since they are the only autonomous component of demand. All other components (investment, imports and consumption) are endogenous to the level of GDP. It follows that total demand is directly proportionate to the volume of exports: $Q_i = C_{i1} \cdot X_i$ where $Q_i$ and $X_i$ represent, respectively, total demand and exports in country $i$.

Demand for exports depends on the relative level of domestic and external prices, and the level of external demand: $X_i = C_{i2}(P_e/P_i)^\delta Z^\epsilon$, where $P_e$ and $P_i$ stand for the external and internal prices and $Z$ for external demand. Export success is thus chiefly determined through cost-based competition.

Domestic prices are determined by a mark-up over variable costs of production, which are, in this simplified formulation, reduced to labour costs: $P_i = C_{i3}(W_i/R_i)T_i$, where $W_i$ is the wage, $R_i$ the level of productivity, and $T_i$ the gross mark-up rate (including taxes).

The dynamics on the production side (the productivity regime) are summarized by the Verdoorn relationship between labour productivity and total output: $R_i = C_{i4} \cdot Q_i^\lambda \cdot e^{rot}$, where total output is equal to total demand, $Q_i$, and where the coefficients $C_{i4}$ and $\lambda$ capture the existence of dynamic returns to scale, as suggested by Kaldor (1966), following Young (1928). The term $e^{rot}$ represents a trend rate of technological change, where $t$ denotes time. This trend rate of technological change may, in fact, be negatively correlated with the level of productivity if steady imitation and the diffusion of best-practice techniques are typical in less productive countries (that is, if there exists a catching-up process within the productivity regime) and accordingly, we shall assign a country index to this trend, writing it as $e^{roit}$. Increasing returns, meanwhile, are induced by increases in the division of labour within an economy. The mode of internationalization is, at this stage, restricted to trade flows; the internationalization of production processes resulting from capital mobility is overlooked. The four relations described above can be expressed in terms of growth rates as follows, where lower-case variables denote proportional rates of change:

$$q_i = x_i \tag{11.1}$$

$$x_i = \delta(p_e - p_i) + \epsilon z \tag{11.2}$$

$$p_i = w_i - r_i + \tau_i \tag{11.3}$$

$$r_i = \lambda \cdot q_i + r_{0i} \tag{11.4}$$

We thus have a system of four equations with three fixed coefficients ($\delta, \epsilon, \lambda \geq 0$), one country-specific parameter (the technological trend $r_{0i}$) and four unknown variables ($x_i, p_i, r_i, q_i$) – a system that can be solved in terms of the exogenous variables $p_e, z, w_i$ and $\tau_i$. Only two of these exogenous variables, namely the rates of growth of wages and gross profit margins, are country-specific. The three coefficients are identical across countries. This is a strong assumption with regard to the productivity regime, although it is consistent with the fact that the same techniques of production and equipment were shared by the countries under review between 1960 and 1973.

Solving our system of equations, the growth rate of GDP per head (or more precisely, per person employed) can be written as:

$$r_i = \frac{1}{(1 - \lambda\delta)}[\delta\lambda(p_e - w_i - \tau_i) + \epsilon\lambda z + r_{0i}] \tag{11.5}$$

Equation (11.5) implies that cross-country differences in the rates of growth of GDP per head are mainly determined by different rates of growth of wages and gross profit margins on one hand, and different technological trends on the other. Equation (11.5) thus decomposes the convergence process into factors associated with differences in demand regimes and factors associated with differences in productivity regimes. In other words, any negative correlation between $r_i$ and initial levels of GDP per head, $R_{i0}$, must arise from relationships between $r_i, R_{i0}$, and the wage and mark-up variables $w_i$ and $\tau_i$ on one hand, and/ or between $r_i, R_{i0}$, and the trend rate of technological change on the other.

## The direct effects of integration

When Myrdal (1957) coined the term 'cumulative causation', he intended to describe a process of divergence between countries at different levels of development. However, only under certain conditions will the Kaldorian model of cumulative causation developed above result in divergence. Hence in the case where all countries have the same initial conditions, but where the effects of integration are not uniformly distributed among countries (as assumed by Dixon and Thirlwall, 1975), then growth paths will obviously diverge. However, if integration is a discrete time process which can be thought of as being equivalent to uniform (across countries) increases in the value of foreign prices $p_e$, then integration increases all growth rates by the same amount and will not affect any initial tendencies towards convergence or divergence (see equation (11.5)).[5]

In the framework above, then, regional integration has no direct effect on convergence as long as its impact is evenly distributed among countries. Is this assumption realistic? One may well imagine that improvements in transactions costs, in terms of reductions in non-tariff barriers, for instance, have a greater impact on countries at an earlier stage of industrial development, in which case integration would spur convergence (or slow down divergence, depending on which was the initial trend). This assumes a catching-up effect directly linked to the process of integration, however, and it is not obvious that this assumption is appropriate. Furthermore, the model of integration developed above is not truly apt to capture this possibility, which demands that we consider not general shifts in relative prices, but changes in the country-specific cost structures described in equations (11.3) and (11.4). We now turn to consider these mechanisms in more detail.


## THE INDIRECT EFFECTS OF INTEGRATION ON CONVERGENCE

We have assumed that demand and productivity regimes are country-specific, as a result of different wage and gross mark-up growth rates, and different exogenous technological trends. It is reasonable to think that the integration process might influence these specificities and therefore indirectly affect convergence.

Any catching-up process can stem from the convergence of either demand or productivity regimes. Demand-side catching up might occur if higher profits, brought about by lower wages, favour (under certain market conditions) greater investment and growth. This may, in turn, induce subsequent wage increases. Alternatively, differences in technological achievement, which create opportunities for imitation, are a basic channel for technological catching up, which in our terminology would result in the convergence of productivity regimes. Our questions, therefore, are first, whether there exists a process of convergence between demand or productivity regimes, and second, whether such a process is influenced by economic integration. The answer to the first question is 'yes', and convergence occurs largely through changes in the demand regimes. Dowrick and N'Guyen (1989) have shown that convergence in demand conditions is an important factor explaining catch-up by the developed economies in recent decades, supporting the similar, longer-term assessment of Abramovitz (1986). Conversely, convergence does not seem to be strongly related to differences in technological trends, as these do not seem to be (negatively) correlated with the productivity levels (see Figures 11.3 and 11.4 overleaf).

The answer to the second question, as to whether or not integration affects the dynamics of convergence, is less clear-cut. Focusing solely on the demand regime, which plays the major role in convergence, increased integration may affect relative profit margins in low-wage countries, but may also lead to some catching up in wage conditions. A simple formalization will help to clarify the issues at stake here. Let $W_{ir}$ and $T_{ir}$ represent, respectively, the wage and mark-up rates in country $i$ relative to the average wage and mark-up rates in the set of countries under review. Let $v$ be an indicator of the level of integration at time $t$. The catching-up process in wages is straightforward: wages are prone to grow more rapidly when their initial levels are low relative to those in other countries and increased integration will accelerate this process. This is expressed in equation (11.6) (with the signs of derivatives in parentheses):

$$w_i = h(W_{ir}, \ v \ ) \qquad (11.6)$$
$$(-) \ (+)$$

The catching-up process in mark-up rates is more complicated. While we assume that wage rates rise with the level of development, we shall argue that mark-up rates decline with development, as economies become more competitive and skilled in using their capital stocks efficiently.[6] Increased integration, $v$, accelerates this process, eroding rents derived from protection. This is captured in equations (11.7) and (11.8):

$$\tau_i = -g(T_{ir}, \ v \ ) \qquad (11.7)$$
$$(+) \ (+)$$

$$T_{ir} = f(R_{ir}) \qquad (11.8)$$
$$(-)$$

Equation (11.8) is based on the assumption that, *ceteris paribus*, mark-up rates are higher in less developed economies (as roughly shown in Figures 11.5 and 11.6). In the formalization above, the level of integration ($v$) tends to amplify both the higher wage rates and lower mark-up rates associated with higher levels of development.

Substituting (11.6), (11.7) and (11.8) into equation (11.5) and treating the relative wage level $W_{ir}$ as a proxy for relative welfare $R_{ir}$, we can see that, taking technological trends as given, the growth process can lead to convergence or divergence accordingly (see equation (11.9)). In effect, if the impact of the level of development on the wage rate $w_i$ (the function $h()$ in (11.9)) outweighs its impact on the mark-up rate (the function $g()$ in (11.9)), then productivity

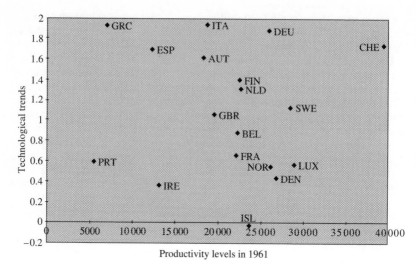

*Figure 11.3* Technological trends and productivity levels, 1961–73
*Source*: OECD National Accounts.

BEL – Belgium; CHE – Confederation Helvetique, i.e., Switzerland; DEN – Denmark; DEU – Germany; ESP – Spain; FIN – Finland; FRA – France; GBR – Great Britain; GRC – Greece; IRE – Ireland; ISL – Iceland; ITA – Italy; LUX – Luxembourg; NLD – Netherlands; NOR – Norway; SWE – Sweden; PRT – Portugal; AUT – Austria.

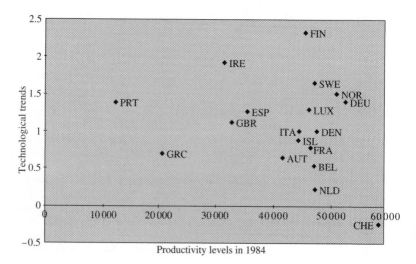

*Figure 11.4* Technological trends and productivity levels, 1984–96
*Source*: OECD National Accounts.

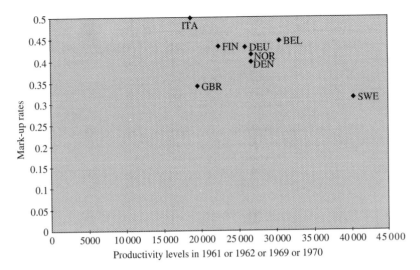

*Figure 11.5* Mark-up rates and productivity levels, 1961–73
*Source*: OECD National Accounts.

BEL – Belgium; CHE – Confederation Helvetique, i.e., Switzerland; DEN – Denmark; DEU – Germany; ESP – Spain; FIN – Finland; FRA – France; GBR – Great Britain; GRC – Greece; IRE – Ireland; ISL – Iceland; ITA – Italy; LUX – Luxembourg; NLD – Netherlands; NOR – Norway; SWE – Sweden; PRT – Portugal; AUT – Austria.

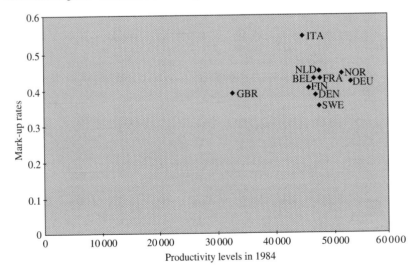

*Figure 11.6* Mark-up rates and productivity levels, 1984–94
*Source*: OECD National Accounts.

rates diverge (growth is a positive function of the productivity level $R_{ir}$). Conversely, if the effect of the mark-up, $\tau_i$, dominates, then productivity growth rates are negatively related to productivity levels and convergence occurs:

$$r_i = \frac{1}{(1 - \lambda\delta)}[\delta\lambda(p_e - h(R_{ir}, v) + g(f(R_{ir}), v) + \epsilon\lambda z + r_{0i}] \qquad (11.9)$$

A rise in the integration variable ($v$) gives more weight to both functions, $h(.)$ and $g(.)$, but as they are of opposite signs, this may either boost or slow down any initial tendency towards convergence – all the more so because integration may have different effects upon wage and profit formation.

Our contention is that during the period of sustained economic growth from 1960 to 1973, European integration led to greater equalization of profit margins than wage rates. Recall that the process of integration at that time was mainly oriented towards reducing tariff barriers and increasing direct investment. Integration did not involve measures designed to harmonize wages or labour conditions, or measures to increase labour mobility, although it did increase capital mobility. It follows that European integration in the period 1960–73 enhanced the equalization of profit margins rather than wage rates, thus encouraging convergence (see equation (11.9)).

In sum, our model suggests that integration has no direct effect on convergence if the former is simply equivalent to a change in the exchange rate. Integration may have an indirect impact on convergence, however, by enhancing the tendency towards the equalization of profit rates among countries without encouraging the equalization of labour costs (which in our formalization can be expressed as a strengthening of the impact on growth of the function $g(.)$ relative to the function $h(.)$). The process of European integration before 1973 appears, therefore, to have been favourable to convergence, adding to whatever convergence would otherwise have been achieved as a result of trade liberalization within the GATT and technological transfers.

## INTEGRATION AND CONVERGENCE WITHIN A NEW GROWTH PATTERN

Since the early 1980s, a new growth pattern has emerged with significant implications for European convergence. In the first place, the process of internationalization has changed. While the spread of foreign direct investment encouraged the equalization of profit rates during the first phase of EU growth, the recent integration of financial markets has completed this process. It follows that the equalization of profit rates among nations has not played the same role in the second phase of growth as it did in the first.

Second, the expansion of foreign trade at a rate faster than GDP has led to greater interdependency between trading partners, whether members of the EU or not. This greater dependence on external demand has increased uncertainty, affecting, in turn, investment and consumption expenditures. This has tended to dampen the demand regime of the old export-led growth model.[7]

Third, the three-layer internationalization process among developed economies (involving trade, foreign direct investment and financial markets) has modified the domain of increasing returns. With the expansion of the international organization of production, dynamic returns to scale are increasingly likely to be realized at an international level (Ethier, 1979).

These changes, all induced to a greater or lesser extent by the earlier growth dynamic, have altered the pattern of EU growth. The growth regime is now less responsive to productivity changes, thus depressing growth rates, although stagnation is not universal and some countries are clearly doing better than others. Moreover, the determinants of competitiveness seem to have shifted away from being overwhelmingly cost-based. This shift in the form of competition demands that we modify our approach to analysing the effects of integration on convergence.

Evidence of changes in the form of competition arises from the recently observed divergence of indicators of cost competitiveness and market shares (Asensio and Mazier, 1991; Magnier and Toujas-Bernate, 1992; OECD, 1992). To account for enhanced non-price competition, the current literature refers either to unexplained changes in product quality, or to general organizational changes in production and distribution. The first type of argument has mainly been developed in a Chamberlinian framework, tying imperfect competition to product differentiation (Dixit and Stiglitz, 1977; Krugman, 1980, 1981). The importance of intra-industry trade, which has been well-established at least since Balassa (1986) and Grubel and Lloyd (1975), provides the empirical grounds for this approach. Such trade, which amounts to some 75 per cent of total trade in the major European economies,[8] has not increased significantly since 1970, however. We shall therefore assume that product differentiation, although important, has not been the major factor in the trend towards greater non-price competition in the EU.

The second type of argument draws on the work on technological competitiveness associated with Fagerberg (1988), Dosi, Pavitt and Soete (1990) and Verspagen (1992), which largely concerns innovation and organizational issues. Thus competitiveness is fostered by the ability to keep innovation in close touch with markets. It involves the organization of distribution, maintenance and after-sales follow-up, keeping in touch with customers' changing tastes, and easing access to finance and communications networks. All this can be organized 'in-house' by big firms, by means of interfirm organizations (in which business services play an important role), or by developing stable user–producer relationships (Lundvall, 1988). This 'technological competitiveness' approach tends to combine two lines of argument. On the one hand, competitiveness is seen as the result of experience acquired over time, arising from a producer's involvement in the domestic market, for instance. On the other hand, advantages derive from cooperation and joint ventures among partners in the international economy. This latter potential is rather different from the old catch-up process, in which countries are highly segmented into leaders and followers. Instead, classes of countries share knowledge, techniques and ventures through the intermediation of multinational companies operating within technological clubs (see Delapierre and Mytelka, 1998). As the internationalization of production through product flows, capital mobility and the financial environment has raised new organizational issues, then, so the solutions to these issues have fostered a shift away from price competition (Landesmann and Petit, 1995). Both dimensions of the new 'technological competition' – country-specific experience and multilateral ventures – are complementary. Non-price competitiveness thus appears as 'a process of learning-innovation, imitation and organizational change – which have both sector and country specificities' (Dosi, Pavitt and Soete, 1990).

The shift towards technological competitiveness transforms the relationship between integration and convergence. Non-price competition has always been a significant factor explaining trade flows and the model used earlier does allow for this, acting through the value of the income elasticity of world demand for a country's exports. The empirical findings mentioned above suggest, however, that the importance of non-price competition has increased and that it is country-specific.[9] To adequately account for technological competitiveness, then, we must modify both the demand and productivity regimes in the model developed earlier. On the demand side, we can simply add to the export equation (equation (11.2)) a variable representing 'technological competitiveness', to capture the notion that the know-how and ability to cooperate of some countries increase their share of world demand (all of which is consistent with empirical findings on the importance of non-price competitiveness). How we should modify the productivity regime is, however, less clear. The debate regarding the post-1973 productivity slowdown draws attention to the seemingly paradoxical reduction in productivity growth rates in all sectors and in most developed economies that has accompanied the diffusion of new information technologies. These technologies are both pervasive (due to the constant miniaturization of chips) and possess a global reach (arising from their links to telecommunications networks). As such, they constitute a basic support for the new technological competition. Their effect (or lack thereof) on productivity gains raises both measurement and organizational issues. Regarding the former, it seems that quality improvements resulting from changes in the provision of goods and services are poorly accounted for (a point extensively debated by the Boskin Commission (Boskin, 1996) and its critics (Moulton and Moses, 1997)). With regard to organizational issues, most papers on the productivity paradox tend to consider organizational blockages and delays in organizational learning as major causes of the productivity slowdown.

All this suggests that we retain our initial specification of the productivity regime, expecting that parameter estimation would reveal a reduced elasticity of productivity with respect to output and a slightly larger autonomous trend rate of technological change. The latter, given the acknowledged exhaustion of basic imitation effects (which Abramovitz (1991) and Fagerberg (1991) consider a significant cause of the productivity slowdown), is now likely to be positively related to the level of development (rather than inversely related, as during the initial growth phase). Meanwhile, the variable that we are adding to the export equation to capture the two different but complementary dynamics of technological competition (the internal dynamic of cumulative learning by doing and the external dynamic of cooperation and exchange) is, in light of the nature of these dynamics, likely to be positively related to the level of development.[10] We are therefore adding to the expression for the rate of growth of GDP per head in (11.5) a variable that will foster divergence. Let $b(R_{ir})$ denote the rate of growth of the technological capabilities that largely determine the demand for exports under technological competition. The growth rate of GDP per head is now given by:

$$r_i = \frac{1}{(1 - \lambda\delta)} [\delta\lambda(p_e + b(R_{ir}) - w_i - \tau_i) + \epsilon\lambda z + r_{0i}] \tag{11.10}$$

As (11.10) shows, the changes in demand and productivity regimes discussed above promote divergence, allowing more developed countries to grow faster and to correspondingly increase their relative income advantage. Much still depends on the evolution of wages and profits, however. The growth-promoting tendencies of $b(R_{ir})$ in the more developed countries could be entirely offset by changes in wages and profits affecting the more price-sensitive components of demand. In fact, the period since the mid-1980s has been marked by a widespread moderation in wage rises and a relative rise in profits, especially in the financial sector. This may have reduced the advantage that highly developed countries have derived from the new competition, particularly during the early 1990s when interest rates were at their highest.

What, then, is the effect of further economic integration in this context? The impact of integration on growth that operates via tariff reduction is essentially unaltered: convergence is not directly affected, although the indirect effect of tariff reduction on profit equalization is considerably reduced in the new international context. The question is more open with regard to the effects of the dismantling of non-tariff barriers, however. Will this enhance the old catching-up process or reinforce differences in creative capabilities, making for convergence or divergence accordingly?

The reason that increased divergence is more likely is straightforward: integration now mainly involves the removal of invisible, non-tariff barriers (public procurements, intellectual property rights, deregulation of public services, opening of large network services, access to information and subsidies, and so forth) and countries with substantial organizational capabilities, captured through large firms or public organizations, can take greater advantage of this environment. Only government policies aimed at fostering creative capabilities in relatively less developed economies could offset this tendency, but the prospect of such policies is limited from the start by the importance of technological clubs and selective networks. Furthermore, devising the steps necessary in order to fill an 'institutional gap' and boost the creative capability of a country is a difficult task (Lundvall, 1992). Such policies might be easier to implement at the regional level, not least because the benefits of knowledge-sharing and cooperation have strong sectoral dimensions. Catching-up and innovation are done on a sectoral basis (Dollar and Wolff, 1988), by combining branch-specific imitation with innovative capabilities influenced by country-specific characteristics (recalling the notion of a national system of innovation). But even then, the design and implementation of a regional programme of scientific cooperation are daunting tasks. Furthermore, this would likely be of most benefit – at least initially – to the very countries that are the most advanced, the first goal of the EU being to compete with highly developed countries outside Europe (namely the USA and Japan), rather than the bridging of a widening technological gap within Europe.

Finally, note that EU incomes policies will not likely exacerbate the divergent growth pattern described above. No effort will be made to reduce the spread of wage rates that the EU presently experiences, while the harmonization of capital taxes will not be quickly achieved. Hence wage-cost advantages, or the financial rents that they bestow upon some less developed countries, may at least help these countries to avoid an abrupt 'U-turn' of the catching-up process.

## CONCLUSION

Our analysis of the complex issues of integration and convergence in Europe has necessarily been limited. In the first place, we chose to look at European integration as a discrete process (of exogenously imposed steps) concerning a subset of European economies at similar levels of development. We have disregarded problems posed by entry into the EU of much less developed countries in order to focus on the properties of growth in the more advanced member nations.[11] Our objectives have been to assess the conditions under which the 'common' growth regime of this set of countries favours either convergence or divergence and to analyse in this context the likely effects of increased integration.

We can conclude that during the first phase of sustained general growth in the EU, integration indirectly enhanced convergence by encouraging the equalization of profit rates and hence price differentials, thus reinforcing standard catching-up effects. During the second phase of slower growth, during which the nature of internationalization was transformed, the effects of integration have been less clear-cut. However, it would seem that the shift from cost-based to technological competition coupled with a strictly market-oriented integration process has meant that, in the absence of appropriate policies, integration has not fostered the sort of coordination of innovative systems necessary to encourage further convergence.

### Notes

1. See also the report on convergence issued in *European Economy*, 41, July 1989.
2. Increases in intra-industry trade are not a necessary result of integration, as suggested by the relative stability between 1970 and 1987 of the share of intra-industry trade in the overall trade of Germany, the UK and Italy (see *European Economy*, special issue on 'L'impact sectoriel du marche interieur sur l'industrie; les enjoux pour les Etats membres', 1990, p. 43).
3. Wider applications and general discussions of Kaldor's laws can be found in a special issue of the *Journal of Post Keynesian Economics* (March 1983). Application of the cumulative causation scheme to the issue of convergence among a broad set of developed and developing countries can also be found in Fagerberg (1991), Verspagen (1992) and Amable (1993).
4. In a cumulative causation scheme, we define the demand regime as the combination of components involved in the formation of demand. The productivity regime refers to those elements linking the dynamics of markets to the expansion of productivity (see Boyer and Petit, 1991).
5. Nor will it derail the cumulative growth process, which corresponds to steady growth patterns as long as the demand regime does not over-respond to productivity changes (Boyer and Petit, 1991).
6. This does not imply that profits are lower. Furthermore, it does not account for the effect of changes in the sectoral structure activities, whereby developing economies may turn towards activities that are of a more capital-intensive nature. This restricts the argument to the subset of European countries that are similar in terms of their sectoral structures.
7. Changes in expectations by firms constitute a shift in the demand regime, as illustrated in Skott (1990), who stresses the path-dependent nature of growth patterns.
8. According to the branch divisions used in *European Economy*, 1990, *op. cit.*
9. The model developed earlier assumes identical levels of non-price competitiveness and identical productivity regimes in all countries.

10.    The literature on learning by doing suggests that it is positively correlated with (cumulative) levels of production. Estimates of the impact of this learning by doing effect (as measured by cumulative production levels) on the exports of Japan and Italy can be found in Amable (1992).

11.    This restriction obviously avoids questions related to the possibility and desirability of catch-up amongst the new Mediterranean member nations of the EU.

## References

Abramovitz, M. (1986) 'Catching up, forging ahead and falling behind', *Journal of Economic History*, 66, 385–406

Abramovitz, M. (1991) 'The postwar productivity spurt and slowdown: factors of potential and realisation', in *Technology and Productivity*, Paris, OECD

Amable, B. (1992) 'Effets d'apprentissage, compétitivité hors-prix et croissance cumulative', *Economie Appliquée*, 45, 5–31

Amable, B. (1993) 'Catch-up and convergence: a model of cumulative growth', *International Review of Applied Economics*, 7, 1–25

Asensio, A. and J. Mazier (1991) 'Compétitivité, avantages coûts et hors-coûts et spécialisation', *Revue d'Economie Industrielle*, 55, 84–117

Balassa, B. (1986) 'The determinants of intra-industry specialization in the United States', *Oxford Economic Papers*, 38, 220–33

Boskin, M. (ed.) (1996) *Towards a More Accurate Measure of the Cost of Living*, Final Report to the Senate Finance Committee, December

Boyer, R. and P. Petit (1981) 'Progrès technique, croissance et emploi: un modèle d'inspiration kaldorienne pour six industries européennes', *Revue Economique*, 32, 1113–53

Boyer, R. and P. Petit (1991) 'Technical change, cumulative causation and growth: accounting for the productivity puzzle with some post Keynesian theories', in *Technology and Productivity: the Challenge for Economic Policy*, Paris, OECD

Cecchini, P. (1988) *1992 Le Défi: nouvelles données économiques de l'Europe sans frontières*, Paris, Flammarion

Cornwall, J. (1977) *Modern Capitalism: Its Growth and Transformation*, New York, St Martin's Press

Cripps, F. and R. Tarling (1973) *Growth in Advanced Capitalist Economies, 1950–1970*, Cambridge, Cambridge University Press

Delapierre, M. and L.K. Mytelka (1998) 'Blurring boundaries: new inter-firm relationships and the emergence of networked, knowledge-based oligopolies', in M. Colombo (ed.) *The Changing Boundaries of the firm*, London, Routledge

Dixit, A. and J. Stiglitz (1977) 'Monopolistic competition and optimum product diversity', *American Economic Review*, 67, 297–308

Dixon, R.J. and A.P. Thirlwall (1975) 'A model of regional growth-rate differences on Kaldorian lines', *Oxford Economic Papers*, 11, 201–14

Dollar, D. and E.N. Wolff (1988) 'Convergence of industry labour productivity among advanced economies, 1963–1982', *Review of Economics and Statistics*, 70, 549–58

Dosi, G., K. Pavitt and L. Soete (1990) *The Economics of Technical Change and International Trade*, London, Harvester Wheatsheaf

Dowrick, S. and D.T. N'Guyen (1989) 'OECD comparative economic growth, 1950–1985: catch-up and convergence', *American Economic Review*, 79, 1010–30

Ethier, W. (1979) 'Internationally decreasing costs and world trade', *Journal of International Economics*, 9, 1–24

Fagerberg, J. (1988) 'International competitiveness', *Economic Journal*, 98, 355–74

Fagerberg, J. (1991) 'Innovation, catching-up and growth', in *Technology and Productivity*, Paris, OECD

Grubel, H.G. and P.J. Lloyd (1975) *Intra-Industry Trade*, London, Macmillan

Kaldor, N. (1966) *Causes of the Slow Rate of Economic Growth in the United Kingdom*, Cambridge, Cambridge University Press

Kaldor, N. (1970) 'The case for regional policies', *Scottish Journal of Political Economy*, 17, 337–48

Krugman, P. (1980) 'Scale economies, product differentiation and the pattern of trade', *American Economic Review*, 70, 950–9

Krugman, P. (1981) 'Intraindustry specialization and the gains from trade', *Journal of Political Economy*, 89, 959–73

Landesmann, M. and P. Petit (1995) 'Trade in producer services, international specialization and European integration', *Service Industries Journal*, Spring

Lundvall, B.A. (1988) 'Innovation as an interactive process: from user–producer interaction to national systems of innovation', in G. Dosi *et al.* (eds) *Technical Change and Economic Theory*, London, Pinter

Lundvall, B.A. (ed.) (1992) *National Systems of Innovations: An Analytical Framework*, London, Pinter

Machlup, F. (1977) *A History of Thought on Economic Integration*, London, Macmillan

Magnier, A. and J. Toujas-Bernate (1992) 'Technology and trade: empirical evidence for the major five industrialised countries', Working Paper No. 9207, Direction des Etudes et Synthèses Economiques, INSEE, Paris

Moulton, B. and K. Moses (1997) 'Addressing the quality change issue in the consumer price index', *Brookings Paper on Economic Activity*, 1, 305–66

Myrdal, G. (1957) *Economic Theory and Underdeveloped Regions*, London, Duckworth

OECD (1992) 'Indicators of international trade and competitiveness', Working Paper No. 120, Department of Economics, OECD, Paris

Parihk, A. (1978) 'Differences in growth rates and Kaldor's Laws', *Economica*, 45, 83–9

Skott, P. (1990) 'Vicious circles and cumulative causation', in P. Arestis and Y. Kitromilides (eds) *Theory and Policy in Political Economy*, Aldershot, Edward Elgar

Verspagen, B. (1992) 'Uneven growth between interdependent countries: an evolutionary view on technology gaps, trade and growth', unpublished PhD thesis, MERIT, Maastricht

Young, A. (1928) 'Increasing returns and economic progress', *Economic Journal*, 38, 527–42

# 12 Kaldor's Growth Laws and the Principle of Cumulative Causation

Peter Skott

## INTRODUCTION

Kaldor's one-sector models from the 1950s and early 1960s aimed to resolve a puzzle in Keynesian economics: the 'stylized facts' seemed to show continued growth at near full employment in most advanced capitalist countries, and a coherent Keynesian explanation of this observation was lacking. By the mid-1960s, however, Kaldor had come to believe that the one-sector models gave a misleading picture. In reality, he argued, few, if any, economies were subject to binding labour supply constraints. He now emphasized sectoral differences, arguing that the manufacturing sector plays a key role in the growth process. This framework lends itself to the analysis of spatial problems of uneven development. 'North–South' models essentially identify the North with the secondary sector and the South with primary production, and the interaction between the two sectors thus has regional implications. The present chapter, however, is mainly concerned with uneven development across different industrial regions.

Neoclassical models of growth and international trade suggest a gradual equalization of factor incomes across regions and countries. The empirical evidence, Kaldor argued, does not confirm this prediction, and the recent literature on convergence tends to support Kaldor's position. There is strong evidence against 'unconditional convergence'. Instead, it is suggested by this literature, we may observe 'conditional convergence'. Each country may converge towards a steady growth path, but the steady growth path itself depends on a range of parameters and exogenous variables. Thus, even in a simple Solow model the steady growth path depends on, *inter alia*, the saving rate.[1]

It is logically possible that the lack of unconditional convergence may be due to international differences in the parameters of an augmented Solow model or, alternatively, to the presence of non-economic factors which have offset the economic forces making for convergence. But, influenced by Young (1928) and Myrdal (1957), Kaldor's explanation of non-convergence was different. His

166

theory contained two main elements. He argued, first, that there are sectoral differences in the degree of returns to scale. While diminishing returns prevail in the land-based activities of the primary sector, manufacturing industry is subject to increasing returns in a broad sense. Some activities in the tertiary sector may exhibit increasing returns but the scale economies are likely to be less widespread and more modest than in industry. The use of industrial products as capital goods in other sectors, furthermore, means that product innovation caused by scale economies in industry may enhance the rate of technical progress in other sectors. Although increases in industrial production primarily improve productivity in industry itself, there may therefore be derived productivity gains in other sectors.

The second element is the proposition that even advanced economies show some of the dual characteristics usually associated with underdeveloped regions: the marginal contribution of labour to output in the primary sector as well as in parts of the tertiary sector is low, and factor remunerations – in particular wage rates – differ systematically between sectors, industry having relatively high wages. The extent to which sectoral wage rates differ may not be the same for all regions and countries: for 'mature' economies the sectoral differences will be slight whereas in 'immature' economies there are large differences. But taking into account the possibility of interregional migration, Kaldor argued, one may assume that the supply of labour to industry is (almost) perfectly elastic at the ruling wage rates.[2] Apart from its role as the supplier of essential raw materials, the primary sector (and parts of the service sector) thus acts as a repository of hidden unemployment.

Kaldor never presented a definitive, formal version of the theory and most of the attention has focused on the empirical regularities commonly known as 'Kaldor's growth laws'. The next section describes the growth laws and argues that the connection with the underlying theory is tenuous. This argument is fleshed out in the following two sections, the former using the Dixon–Thirlwall formalization of Kaldor's theory and the latter an alternative, more radical formalization. The final section contains a few concluding remarks.

## THE GROWTH LAWS

In his inaugural lecture, Kaldor (1966) presented a set of econometric regressions which, he argued, shows the presence of increasing returns in manufacturing industry and the importance of cumulative causation. These regressions embody 'Kaldor's growth laws'.

The *first law* relates the growth rate of total output, $g$, to the rate of growth in manufacturing industry, $g_m$:

$$g = \alpha + \beta g_m \tag{12.1}$$

and it stipulates that $\alpha > 0$ and that $\beta \approx \frac{1}{2}$. Both scale economies in manufacturing and the existence of dual characteristics could explain the law.

According to the *second law*, Verdoorn's Law, productivity growth in manufacturing, $q_{man}$, is positively associated with the growth of manufacturing production:

$$q_{man} = \gamma + \delta g_{man} \tag{12.2}$$

where $\gamma > 0$ and $\delta \approx \frac{1}{2}$.

Finally, the *third law* states that overall productivity growth, $q$, is related positively to employment growth in manufacturing, $e_m$, and negatively to employment growth outside manufacturing, $e_{nm}$:

$$q = \rho + \mu e_m - v e_{nm} \tag{12.3}$$

The third law made its first appearance in Kaldor's (1968) reply to Wolfe's (1968) criticisms of the inaugural lecture. Both the dual characteristics and sectoral differences in scale economies may contribute to the third law.

Kaldor's original evidence covered growth rates over the period 1953–54 to 1963–64 for a cross-section of twelve industrial countries. Other writers have subsequently estimated similar regressions using a larger (or different) set of countries and/or longer (or different) time periods. Regional data for both the USA and the UK have been examined, time-series as well as cross-section analyses have been performed, and variations in the specification of the equations have also been tried.[3] The results of these studies have been mixed but for present purposes the main point is that the specification of the growth laws involves an important implicit assumption: it is assumed that the demand for manufacturing output is an exogenous variable determining productivity growth. The reverse causal chain from productivity to demand is implicitly excluded.

The problems with this exogeneity assumption were highlighted in an exchange between Rowthorn (1975a, 1975b) and Kaldor (1975b) in the *Economic Journal*. In his reply to Rowthorn, Kaldor argues that there are two fundamental differences between the neoclassical school of thought and his own Keynesian views:

> I would now regard the existence of surplus labour, and the critical role of profits and profit expectations in capital accumulation as the more basic cause of the difference of view between the neo-classical and Keynesian (or post-Keynesian) schools of thought: the question, that is, whether one regards economic growth as the resultant of demand (i.e. the growth of markets) or of (exogenously given) changes in resource-endowment. (Kaldor, 1975b, p. 895)

Profitability and surplus labour are important to the Kaldorian view because they are the motivational and permissive factors underlying the operation of cumulative causation. The existence of surplus labour ensures an elastic labour supply and implies that productivity increases will lead to a fall in unit labour costs, and because production and investment are guided by profits and profit expectations, this induces an expansion in output and employment. The presence of dynamic increasing returns implies that productivity growth depends on output growth, and surplus labour in combination with profit-driven accumulation supplies the feedback from productivity growth to output growth. The absence of the feedback from productivity to competitiveness would undermine both the critical role of profits and the principle of cumulative causation.

In a footnote, Kaldor accepts that industrial production will not be strictly exogenous and that without the two-way relationship between demand growth and productivity growth there is no cumulative causation:

> The growth of industrial output for any region is governed in part by the growth in productivity which itself influences demand through the change in competitiveness which is induced by it. It is this reverse link which accounts for the cumulative and circular nature of growth processes. There is a two-way relationship from demand growth to productivity growth and from productivity growth to demand growth; but the second relationship is, in my view, far less regular and systematic than the first. (Kaldor, 1975b, p. 895 n. 1)

The less systematic and less regular reverse link justifies, Kaldor suggested, the simplification involved in treating industrial demand as exogenous.[4] In fact, he 'would now place more, rather than less, emphasis on the exogenous components of demand, and in particular on the role of exports' (p. 896); poor UK performance, for instance, he now regarded as being due to a 'lack of international competitiveness' rather than to labour constraints as originally suggested in the inaugural lecture.[5]

Like Rowthorn, I find Kaldor's argument puzzling. Exports may, as argued by Kaldor, be the primary determinant of demand for relatively small and open economies, but the price and quality of domestically produced goods *vis-à-vis* foreign goods (the price and non-price competitiveness of the economy) must influence both export demand and import propensities.[6] There may be lags (due, for instance, to contractual commitments, informational constraints or the need for exporters to build up distribution networks) between changes in competitiveness and consequent changes in export performance, but Kaldor's evidence consists of a cross-section analysis of growth *trends*. If productivity changes affect the price or quality of output then exports should therefore be influenced by productivity growth.

There seems to be only one endogenous channel that could sever the link from productivity to demand: induced changes in wages. If nominal wage rates vary in proportion to changes in productivity and non-price competitiveness then there will be no feedback from productivity changes to demand.

Under conditions of full (or near full) employment it is easy to see how increases in productivity and non-price competitiveness may get translated into higher real wage rates. In fact, both neoclassical and Keynesian/Kaldorian models would predict this result. But it is difficult to see how the existence of surplus labour can be reconciled with the assumption that wage rates adjust in proportion to the level of industrial productivity. Workers (unions) in industry may have some direct bargaining power, even when there is surplus labour, but their bargaining power will be related to the level of real wages. The higher are real wages in industry relative to earnings in other sectors of the economy, the greater will be the loss by workers who lose their jobs, and the higher will be the potential gains to firms from breaking closed-shop agreements, firing workers with job experience and hiring new and inexperienced workers at a lower wage rate.

One cannot have it both ways. There may be surplus labour and a perfectly elastic labour supply to industry at the given sectoral wage and earnings structure, or it may be the case that wage adjustments in industry neutralize all changes in productivity, but it is difficult to reconcile the two; if there is surplus labour then productivity changes should influence competitiveness. Kaldor's position thus seems paradoxical. Cumulative causation is only important when there is a strong feedback from productivity to demand, and a weak feedback is needed in order to justify single equation methods.

## THE DIXON–THIRLWALL MODEL

In order to examine more rigorously the connection between the growth laws and the underlying theoretical argument, it is useful to formalize the theory, and in this section I shall adopt Dixon and Thirlwall's interpretation of the principle of cumulative causation. Dixon and Thirlwall (1975) set up a partial model of a small open economy facing exogenous foreign prices and foreign income levels. Algebraically, a slightly simplified version of their model looks as follows:

$$x = -\eta p_d + \delta p_f + \varepsilon z \tag{12.4}$$

$$p_d = w - q \tag{12.5}$$

$$q = \lambda_0 + \lambda g \tag{12.6}$$

$$g = \gamma x \tag{12.7}$$

where $x$ is the rate of growth of exports, $p_d$ and $p_f$ are the rates of growth of the prices of domestic and foreign output (in common currency), $z$ is the growth rate of foreign incomes, $w$ the growth rate of nominal wages in the domestic economy, $q$ the rate of growth of domestic labour productivity, $g$ the rate of growth of domestic output, and $\eta$, $\delta$, $\epsilon$, $\lambda_0$, $\lambda$, $\gamma$ are positive constants.

Equation (12.4) is derived from a standard multiplicative export demand function,

$$X = AP_d^{-\eta}P_f^{\delta}Z^{\varepsilon} \tag{12.8}$$

where capital letters are used to denote levels of a variable, lower-case letters giving the corresponding logarithmic derivatives. Equation (12.6) is based on the assumption that the mark-up on wage costs is constant, and equation (12.6) is the Verdoorn relation between productivity growth and output growth. Equation (12.7), finally, which relates output growth to the growth of exports, embodies the assumption that the income elasticity of imports, $\{1/\gamma\}$ is constant and that total output is determined by the Harrod multiplier, that is, by the requirement of balanced foreign trade.

Dixon and Thirlwall leave the rate of growth of wages, $w$, as an exogenous variable, but this assumption must be abandoned if we want to examine the implications of a *weak* connection between productivity growth and increases in competitiveness. In order to weaken the link between productivity and competitiveness, the rate of growth of wages must be influenced, directly or indirectly, by productivity growth. For simplicity, let

$$w = \mu_0 + \mu q \tag{12.9}$$

where $\mu_0 \geq 0$ and $0 < \mu < 1$, and where the restrictions on $\mu$ reflect the assumption that the feedback from productivity to competitiveness is positive but weak; $\mu = 1$ would imply the absence of a feedback from productivity to competitiveness.

Assuming, for simplicity, that equations (12.4), (12.5) and (12.7) are non-stochastic, but that (12.6) and (12.9) are stochastic with disturbance terms $u$ and $v$ respectively (where $u$ and $v$ are independent and normally distributed with mean zero and variance $\sigma_u^2$ and $\sigma_v^2$), it is readily seen that:

$$q = \lambda_0 + \lambda g + u \tag{12.10}$$

$$g = -\gamma\eta\mu_0 + \gamma\delta p_f + \gamma\varepsilon z + \gamma\eta(1-\mu)q + \gamma\eta v \tag{12.11}$$

If equations (12.10) and (12.11) adequately describe the economy, the estimation of (12.10) using single equation methods will yield inconsistent parameter estimates.[7] More precisely, if $(\hat{\lambda}_0, \hat{\lambda})$ are the OLS estimates and $(\lambda_0, \lambda)$ the true parameter values then:

$$plim(\hat{\lambda}_0, \hat{\lambda}) - (\lambda_0, \lambda) = \frac{\gamma\eta(1-\mu)\sigma_u^2}{1 - \lambda\gamma\eta(1-\mu)}(-\bar{g}, 1)\frac{1}{\overline{\overline{g}} - \bar{g}^2} \tag{12.12}$$

where:

$$(\bar{g}, \bar{\bar{g}}) = plim\left( \frac{1}{T}\sum g_t, \frac{1}{T}\sum g_t^2 \right)$$

According to Dixon and Thirlwall, 'it is the Verdoorn relation which makes the model circular and cumulative' (p. 205) because it is the positive parameter $\lambda$ which serves to amplify the effect of stochastic shocks (or of changes in exogenous variables or in other parameters) on the rate of growth of the domestic economy. From equations (12.10) and (12.11), the rate of economic growth is:

$$g = (-\gamma\eta\mu_0 + \gamma\delta p_f + \gamma\varepsilon z + \gamma\eta(1-\mu)(\lambda_0 + u) - \gamma\eta v)\frac{1}{1 - \gamma\eta(1-\mu)\lambda} \quad (12.13)$$

and the second term on the right-hand side of (12.13) (outside the parentheses) becomes a measure of the strength and importance of cumulative causation: this multiplicative term expresses the amplifying effects caused by the interaction between $q$ and $g$.

Comparing (12.12) and (12.13) it is readily seen that the importance of cumulative causation and the asymptotic bias of the parameter estimates are directly related and that they both depend inversely on the feedback parameter $\mu$. For given values of $\sigma_v^2$ and $\sigma_u^2$, parameters which make cumulative causation important will aggravate the inconsistency of single equation estimates. The inconsistency is reduced if $\sigma_u^2$ is 'small' (that is, if the Verdoorn relation gives a very close fit). Furthermore, the value of $\bar{\bar{g}}$ is increasing in $\sigma_v^2$, $\sigma_u^2$ and $\gamma\eta(1-\mu)$, and (if $\gamma\eta(1-\mu) > 0$) in $\lambda$ while $\bar{g}$ depends exclusively on the exogenous variables and the parameters attached to them. The variance $\sigma_v^2$ can be seen as a measure of the 'irregularity' of the link between productivity and competitiveness, and increasing irregularity will thus reduce the asymptotic discrepancy between $\hat{\lambda}$ and $\lambda$. In this sense, irregularity (but not weakness) of the reverse link from productivity to demand may indeed alleviate the problems of single equation estimation. To avoid inconsistency, however, $\sigma_v^2$ would have to tend towards infinity (or $\sigma_u^2$ would need to tend towards zero).

It should be noted, finally, that using the Dixon and Thirlwall specification of cumulative causation, empirical work could proceed by way of estimating long-term relations using simultaneous equations methods. In contrast, the model in the next section suggests that any analysis based on trends and averages will be inadequate, even if simultaneous equations methods are used.

## A KALDORIAN MODEL OF UNEVEN DEVELOPMENT

Unlike the Dixon–Thirlwall model, the model in this section explicitly includes sectoral differences. For simplicity, however, it leaves out the tertiary sector and assumes that the economy is divided into two main sectors, A and M.[8] The M sector may be thought of as a 'modern', capitalistic, industrial sector (producing 'machines') and sector A as a 'backward', agricultural sector (producing 'corn'). The A sector supplies consumption goods to workers in the M sector and raw material inputs to the M sector and, in addition, serves as a source of labour for the M sector: employment in the M sector is determined by the demand for labour in that sector leaving employment in sector A as the residual. There may be no overt unemployment, but the marginal contribution of labour to output in sector A is zero.

It is assumed that the production of machines takes place at two industrial centres which are, as it were, isolated M-sector islands in a sea of agricultural production. Output from the two centres is indistinguishable and, since there are no costs of transportation, will be sold at the same price, $p_m$. The capital–output ratio is the same in the two centres and constant over time, and both centres have an infinitely elastic supply of labour (from the surrounding A sector) at the ruling wage rates, $w_1$ and $w_2$ respectively.[9]

The production of machines is subject to dynamic increasing returns to scale. The rate of growth of labour productivity in each centre is positively related to the rate of capital accumulation in that centre and, ignoring production lags and variations in the utilization rate of capital, the rate of accumulation is equal to the rate of growth of production. Algebraically, this is expressed as:

$$\hat{q}_i = f(\hat{M}_i) \tag{12.14}$$

where $\hat{q}$ and $\hat{M}_i$ denote the proportionate rates of growth of labour productivity and output in centre $i$, $i = 1, 2$.

The rates of growth of production, in turn, are determined by profitability conditions:

$$\hat{M}_i = g(\pi_i, \pi_j), \quad g_1 > 0, \ g_2 < 0, \ j \neq i \tag{12.15}$$

$$\pi_i = 1 - \lambda \frac{p_a}{p_m} - \frac{w_i}{p_m q_i} \tag{12.16}$$

where $\pi_i$ is the profit share in centre $i$, and $\lambda$ is the agricultural raw material input per unit of industrial output.

Equations (12.15) and (12.16) suggest that the desired rate of growth of production in each centre depends positively on the absolute level of profitability in the centre itself and inversely on profitability in the rival centre: that is, there is some degree of capital mobility and firms are induced to invest in the centre offering the highest prospective return, current profitability acting as an indicator of future prospects.[10]

Substituting (12.15) and (12.16) into (12.14), one gets:

$$\hat{q}_i = f(g(\pi_i, \pi_j)) = h\left(1 - \lambda\frac{p_a}{p_m}, \frac{w_i}{p_m q_i}, \frac{w_j}{p_m q_j}\right), j \neq i \tag{12.17}$$

where $h_2 < 0$, $h_3 > 0$.

If it is assumed that efficiency wages in the two industrial centres are equal initially and that nominal wages grow at the same proportional rate in the two centres, it is readily seen that the two centres will have identical profit shares and hence the same rates of growth of output and labour productivity. It is also easy to see, however, that if for some reason firms in, say, centre 1 take a pessimistic view of future prospects and therefore initially expand production in centre 1 less than indicated by equation (12.15) then this pessimistic view will be vindicated by actual events: a slower rate of expansion will lead to slower rates of productivity growth, profitability in centre 1 will suffer relative to profitability in centre 2 and even if 'animal spirits' revive and expansion starts following equation (12.15), the rates of growth of output and productivity in the two centres will diverge. A similar process of divergence would result if, say, 'false trading' in the initial period led to machines from centre 2 fetching on average a higher price than centre 1 machines. The existence of increasing returns implies that the balanced growth equilibrium becomes unstable.[11]

The instability of the model has important implications. The growth laws are formulated in terms of long-run relations between trends and averages. If, however, the correct model has an unstable steady growth path, and if (as seems likely) the divergence away from steady growth is bounded because of non-linearities, short-run relations – valid at any point in time – cannot be aggregated into simple relations between the trends and averages of the same variables: the detailed time paths of the variables will be important. If, say, the specification in equation (12.4) is valid at each moment but $f$ and/or $g$ are non-linear, the average growth rate of productivity over some period will not be given as a simple function of the average profit share over the same period.

Non-linearities of the $f$- and $g$-functions are not the main problem, however. Although the model implies the existence of inherent tendencies to divergence between regions, the prediction of the long-run winners in the growth game is hazardous if the regions experience similar rates of profit and growth initially: a small shock may turn what looked like a winner into a loser. One such shock could be a reduction of money wages in the slow-growing region. The model implies that this reduction improves profitability and boosts the rate of growth of output and productivity in the region. If the cut in money wages is sufficiently large – and if money wages in the fast-growing centre are unaffected by changes in the slow-growing centre – then profitability in the initially slow-growing centre will come to exceed profitability in the initially fast-growing centre and the relative ranking of the centres in terms of growth will be reversed. Even if the money wage change is insufficient to reverse the growth ranking it will still lead to an improvement in the relative growth performance of the slow-growing centre. The growth rate of the slow-growing region will be enhanced and the growth performance of the fast-growing centre will deteriorate.

Should one expect changes in relative wages? By assumption, the two centres share a common pool of agricultural surplus labour, and there are no obvious reasons why money wages in the slow-growing region should fall relative to money wages in the fast-growing region. These labour supply assumptions are extreme, of course, and in reality the increasing 'maturity' of an economy may at some point affect wages in a fast-growing region and raise the relative profitability of production in the slow-growing region.[12] But the slow-growing region may not want to await any such endogenous response. Economic divergence may induce changes in the economic 'rules of the game'. The appearance and persistence of large disparities in economic growth rates can provoke direct political intervention. A first reaction of a slow-growing country may be to stimulate domestic demand. If this causes balance of payments problems then pressures for import controls may follow or, alternatively, a policy of devaluation (or of sectoral and/or regional subsidies) could be used to influence relative profitabilities. The model suggests that the latter policy could be highly effective (assuming that other regions and countries accept a change in the exchange rates).[13] If, however, differences in performance persist and lead to significant shifts in relative economic power between countries, major political and institutional changes can be expected. The breakdown of the Bretton Woods agreement may illustrate the argument, but the general point is simply that unstable growth paths and divergent growth rates are likely to cause political intervention and institutional change. Changes or shifts of this kind imply that *the parameters of the economic model (or even the structure of the model) may become unstable over time.*[14] An empirical analysis that focuses on long-term trends and averages thereby becomes difficult to interpret. In order to understand the growth process one needs – using Cornwall's (1994) terminology – an institutional–analytical approach in which economic outcomes interact with both policy and institutional factors.

## CONCLUDING COMMENTS

In his approach to uneven development, Kaldor focused on the social and technological differences between sectors. He emphasized, in particular, the centrifugal forces caused by the existence of (dynamic) increasing returns to scale in the secondary sector. Unfortunately, however, he never presented a precise theoretical model which includes these sectoral and spatial aspects, and the subsequent debate on Kaldor's theory has focused largely on the econometric regressions known as Kaldor's growth laws.

This chapter has outlined two simple formalizations of Kaldor's theory, and I have argued that the identification of the theory with the growth laws has been unfortunate. Kaldor's verbal argument and the notion of cumulative causation require a link between productivity growth and the growth of output, and this link has been excluded in most econometric work on the growth laws.[15] To justify exclusion, it has been suggested that the link is weak and irregular, but this argument is unconvincing. Furthermore, if the argument were true, the theory of cumulative causation would be undermined: the theory depends as much on the causal link from productivity to output as on the Verdoorn relation from output to productivity. One cannot simultaneously uphold the importance of the circular and cumulative nature of the growth process and maintain the weakness of the reverse link in the process.

These endogeneity problems arise with both the Dixon–Thirlwall formalization and the alternative specification in the previous section. But which of the two specifications is to be preferred? The assumption in the previous section of perfect substitutability between industrial goods from different centres is clearly extreme, but Dixon and Thirlwall's specification of multiplicative export and import demand functions also seems questionable. It suggests that goods produced in different regions are qualitatively different and have distinct and exogenously given price and income elasticities. The Swiss, however, did not have a natural monopoly in the manufacture of watches, and Swiss watches do not benefit from price and income elasticities that are permanently different from those of, say, Japanese watches. It is implausible to assume that induced technical progress – the Verdoorn Law – should leave the quality characteristics of goods unaffected and influence only the cost of producing goods of unchanged specification. Yet this seems to be the implicit assumption in Dixon and Thirlwall's model: income and price elasticities are (presumably) related to the quality characteristics of the goods, and induced quality changes would then imply a direct effect of output growth on the elasticities of demand and hence on demand growth (in addition to the effect via cost reductions and changes in the relative prices of goods from different regions). In view of these problems, a 'long-run demand function' with perfect substitutability between domestic and foreign industrial goods may be preferable to the Dixon and Thirlwall specification. Lack of information, consumer loyalties, existing service and retail networks, lock-in effects and so on imply that the elasticity of substitution is less than perfect in the short-run, but the larger the difference in (quality adjusted) price, the faster will be the shift towards the more competitive producer.

The precise specification of the structural model, however, does not affect the conclusion that the growth laws and the empirical techniques used by Kaldor are inconsistent with the underlying theoretical ideas: if cumulative causation is important, then single equation techniques will be inconsistent. Furthermore, the formalization in the previous section brings into question the specification of stable relations between long-term trends and averages.

This conclusion clearly implies that even if the validity of the growth laws as empirical regularities had been beyond doubt, this would not in itself have established strong support for the underlying theoretical ideas. But, conversely, in itself a lack of solid empirical support for the growth laws need not discredit the basic theoretical argument.

## Notes

1. See, for example, Barro and Sala-i-Martin (1995) and the Symposium in the July 1996 issue of the *Economic Journal*.
2. Kaldor (1966) suggested that the UK forms an exception but, in the light of additional evidence, Kaldor subsequently withdrew this hypothesis. See, for example, Kaldor (1975a).
3. See, for instance, Cripps and Tarling (1973), Cornwall (1976, 1977), Rowthorn (1975a), McCombie (1981, 1983), Thirlwall (1983), McCombie and de Ridder (1983) and Hildreth (1988–89).
4. Similar arguments have been used repeatedly in the subsequent literature. See, for example, Michl (1985, pp. 478–9).
5. Cornwall (1977), while agreeing with Kaldor's emphasis on sectoral differences and the surplus labour, reaches somewhat different conclusions with respect to the importance of exports. He concludes that 'whether growth is export-led or homespun is a somewhat secondary, peripheral matter' (p. 175) since 'the factors that lead to imaginative and successful export drives are the same factors that spur growth in the whole economy' (p. 193). If anything, however, low costs of information feedback between producers and domestic consumers may imply that homespun growth becomes more important than export-led growth (p. 193).
6. The inadequacy of price variables alone as indicators of competitiveness is emphasized by Cornwall (1977).
7. Whereas equation (12.10) is identified (in fact, overidentified), equation (12.11) is not. But for present purposes the problems involved in the consistent estimation of the complete system need not concern us.
8. The formalization is discussed in greater detail in Skott (1985).
9. Since by assumption the two sectors draw on the same pool of agricultural labour one might impose the condition $w_1 = w_2$. It is useful, however, to leave open the possibility of different wage rates.
10. A rigorous justification for the link between growth and profitability is given in Skott (1989).
11. The long-run implications of the specification in (12.17) depends on functional forms as well as on the evolution of prices and nominal wages. The difference in productivity growth $\hat{q}_2 - \hat{q}_1$ may, but need not, be increasing over time; it may even go to zero asymptotically as $t$ goes to infinity.

12.    See Skott and Larudee (1998) for a Kaldorian model with a local labour market and endogenous wage determination.
13.    It is therefore not surprising that in the 1960s and early 1970s, Kaldor advocated devaluations and wage subsidies as the main policy instruments in slow-growing countries and regions (Kaldor, 1970). Subsequently, he became more pessimistic with respect to the effects of changes in relative prices and stressed the importance of non-price competitiveness (Kaldor, 1978, 1986). This change of emphasis, whether right or wrong, influences the choice of policy instruments. It does not, however, invalidate the tendency to uneven development: a positive feedback from output growth to changes in non-price competitiveness will also tend to produce divergent growth rates.
14.    See Skott and Auerbach (1995) and Skott (1998) for further discussion of this point.
15.    Parikh (1978) is a rare attempt to estimate Kaldor's laws in a simultaneous equation framework. Parikh's procedure, however, is open to criticism; see McCombie (1983).

## References

Barro, R.J. and X. Sala-i-Martin (1995) *Economic Growth*, New York, McGraw-Hill

Cornwall, J. (1976) 'Diffusion, convergence and Kaldor's laws', *Economic Journal*, 86, 307–14

Cornwall, J. (1977) *Modern Capitalism: Its Growth and Transformation*, London, Martin Robertson

Cornwall, J. (1994) *Economic Breakdown and Recovery: Theory and Policy*, Armonk, NY, M.E. Sharpe

Cripps, T.F. and R.J. Tarling (1973) *Growth in Advanced Capitalist Economies 1950–1970*, Cambridge, Cambridge University Press

Dixon, R. and A.P. Thirlwall (1975) 'A model of regional growth rate differences on Kaldorian lines', *Oxford Economic Papers*, 27, 201–14

Hildreth, A. (1988–89) 'The ambiguity of Verdoorn's Law: a case study of the British regions', *Journal of Post Keynesian Economics*, 11, 279–94

Kaldor, N. (1966) *Causes of the Slow Rate of Economic Growth of the UK*, Cambridge, Cambridge University Press

Kaldor, N. (1968) 'Productivity and growth in manufacturing industry: a reply', *Economica*, 35, 385–91

Kaldor, N. (1970) 'The case for regional policies', *Scottish Journal of Political Economy*, 18, 337–48

Kaldor, N. (1975a) 'What is wrong with economic theory?', *Quarterly Journal of Economics*, 89, 347–57

Kaldor, N. (1975b) 'Economic growth and the Verdoorn Law – a comment on Mr. Rowthorn's article', *Economic Journal*, 85, 891–6

Kaldor, N. (1978) 'The effect of devaluations on trade in manufactures', in *Further Essays on Applied Economics*, London, Duckworth

Kaldor, N. (1986) 'Recollections of an economist', *Banca Nationale del Lavoro Quarterly Review*, 156, 1–26

McCombie, J.S.L. (1981) 'What still remains of Kaldor's laws?', *Economic Journal*, 91, 106–16

McCombie, J.S.L. (1983) 'Kaldor's laws in retrospect', *Journal of Post Keynesian Economics*, 5, 414–29

McCombie, J.S.L. and J.R. de Ridder (1983) 'Increasing returns, productivity and output growth: the case of the United States', *Journal of Post Keynesian Economics*, 5, 373–87

Michl, T.R. (1985) 'International comparisons of productivity growth: Verdoorn's Law revisited', *Journal of Post Keynesian Economics*, 7, 474–92

Myrdal, G. (1957) *Economic Theory and Underdeveloped Regions*, London, Duckworth

Parikh, A. (1978) 'Differences in growth rates and Kaldor's laws', *Economica*, 45, 83–91

Rowthorn, R.E. (1975a) 'What remains of Kaldor's laws?', *Economic Journal*, 85, 10–19

Rowthorn, R.E. (1975b) 'A reply to Lord Kaldor's comment', *Economic Journal*, 85, 897–901

Skott, P. (1985) 'Vicious circles and cumulative causation', *Thames Papers in Political Economy*, Summer. Reprinted in P. Arestis and Y. Kitromilides (eds) (1989) *Theories and Policy in Political Economy*, Aldershot, Edward Elgar

Skott, P. (1989) *Conflict and Effective Demand in Economic Growth*, Cambridge, Cambridge University Press

Skott, P. (1998) 'Economic divergence and institutional change: some observations on the convergence literature', *Journal of Economic Behavior and Organization*, forthcoming

Skott, P. and P. Auerbach (1995) 'Cumulative causation and the "new" theories of economic growth', *Journal of Post Keynesian Economics*, 17, 381–402

Skott, P. and M. Larudee (1998) 'Uneven development and the liberalization of trade and capital flows: the case of Mexico', *Cambridge Journal of Economics*, 22, 277–95

Thirlwall, A.P. (1983) 'A plain man's guide to Kaldor's growth laws', *Journal of Post Keynesian Economics*, 7, 345–5

Wolfe, J.N. (1968) 'Productivity and growth in manufacturing industry: some reflections on Professor Kaldor's Inaugural Lecture', *Economica*, 35, 117–26

Young, A.A. (1928) 'Increasing returns and economic progress', *Economic Journal*, 38, 527–42

# 13 Social Capital and the Economy

## Shaun Hargreaves Heap

### INTRODUCTION

John Cornwall has consistently argued that investment holds the key to economic growth. With the development of the so-called endogenous theories of growth, this has become a fashionable view and many governments are freshly concerned with how to encourage investment. In this chapter, I am concerned with how governments might encourage investment in a particular kind of what I call social capital: the beliefs that tie a group of people together. These beliefs are what anthropologists refer to as a group's 'culture' (see Douglas, 1978) and I explain in the next section why and when it makes sense to refer to these beliefs as a type of social capital. In particular I argue that these beliefs, like plant and equipment, can contribute to production, but they can only do so when they are jointly owned – hence the designation 'social capital'.[1] In the following section, I consider the origins of these beliefs. Unlike the recent 'communitarian' discussion of the contribution that the family and parenting make to the production of social capital (see Etzioni, 1995), I focus on the part played by people's shared experiences of consuming the products of the cultural industries: the *mélange* of sporting, arts and media goods like film and television which comprise modern entertainment. This analysis suggests that contrary to the current trend towards deregulation of these (and other) industries, a concern with the social capital of a common culture provides powerful reasons for regulating the market in these goods. The final section concludes.

### THE PRODUCTIVITY OF SHARED BELIEFS

To understand how shared beliefs can contribute to production, it helps to begin with a sketch of norm-guided or expressive action because this provides the link between these beliefs and the actions of the members of the group. The key to such a model is the simple observation that individuals often reflect on what they do and these reflections give rise to a sense of self-worth or sometimes the reverse as when feelings of embarrassment, shame or guilt are

180

experienced. Plausibly, people sometimes take action to promote the sense of self-worth (and avoid the embarrassment and shame) that comes from these reflections. Equally plausibly, the power of such reflection to influence behaviour often depends on whether the beliefs are shared by a group or not. When the beliefs are shared the standard takes on not only a public but also a more objective character. In these circumstances action acquires symbolic properties because the people sharing the belief will share the reflection that the action seems 'good', 'right', 'honourable' or some such. Hence, such action is often said to be expressive because it expresses publicly an attribute of the agent's character (their 'goodness', 'honour' or whatever is the case). Likewise such action is often referred to as norm-like because others in the group who share the beliefs can be expected to act in a similar way when faced with similar circumstances as they will reflect similarly on how their self-worth is promoted in that situation.

It is a matter of philosophical concern whether the reflections that generate self-worth must always have a public character, but this is not the occasion for a foray into the private language debate. The point here is that people *sometimes* act in a particular way when they belong to a group with shared beliefs because the shared beliefs of a group endow the action with symbolic properties that make the action seem publicly to be the 'honourable', or the 'right', or the 'just', or the 'good' thing to do. I am not concerned with whether such judgements must always be public. It is enough, to put this the other way round, that no one is immune from the odd feeling of guilt, shame or embarrassment.

The precise influence that these shared beliefs have upon action will depend on the character of those beliefs. I am interested in those cases where the beliefs supply non-instrumental reasons for action: that is, where they point to action that is different to the one supplied by an instrumental calculation of what will best satisfy an individual's own preferences. For example, in a prisoners' dilemma game, a reflection on what 'honour' or some shared sense of acting 'justly' demands might point the person towards cooperative play when a strict instrumental logic points to defection. Two observations are worth making here. First, this way of expressing what interests me about the character of these beliefs (that is, that they qualify instrumental calculations) begs a deeper question. It implicitly assumes self-worth *cannot* be treated as another kind of preference. If self-worth were just another kind of preference, then the return from acting 'honourably' in the game could be factored into the pay-offs and so preserve the instrumental account of action. The influence of honour would simply tilt the instrumental scales towards cooperation. This is not the place to discuss the relative merits of these two ways of capturing the influence of shared beliefs regarding honour and the like on action. As a matter of fact, I believe there are good reasons for preferring to qualify the instrumental model of action rather than try to change the pay-offs in that model (see Hargreaves Heap, 1997) and hence my choice of expression. But the argument in this chapter does not turn on this way of putting it. The point is that even if self-worth is treated as a kind of preference, it is significantly different from the kind of preference that ordinarily motivates an instrumentally rational agent because it depends on the judgements of others. This in turn creates a new source of influence over an individual's actions to that found in the standard economists' model of action. In short, for the purposes of this chapter, how one chooses to describe that influence is less important than the fact that there is one.

Second, the shared beliefs need not always have such a non-instrumental character. For instance, they might value something like wealth maximization with the result that expressive action in support of self-worth yields actions that are in most cases indistinguishable from what would be expected from a simple instrumental calculation regarding how best to satisfy one's own preferences. My reason for focusing on shared beliefs that supply an additional non-instrumental reasons for action is that these beliefs have the potential for making a productive contribution in societies (like those of North America and Europe) where economic decisions tend otherwise to be dominated by instrumental calculation. Consider, for instance, two types of economic interaction in the absence of such non-instrumental shared beliefs that have respectively the form of a prisoners' dilemma and a battle of the sexes game. These are two types of interaction that lie at the heart of many economic exchanges and both have the potential for generating Pareto inferior outcomes when exclusively instrumentally motivated agents play them.

The prisoners' dilemma can be found in the simplest of exchanges, like the one depicted in Figure 13.1 where the buyer has a choice between a high and a low price and the seller has a choice between expending high and low effort on producing a commodity of high or low durability. Both may prefer the (high price, high durability) combination to the (low, low) equivalent and yet the dominant strategy for each is to play 'low' in the absence of mutual trust in the keeping of agreements or the ability to write and enforce contracts. The result is the (low, low) inferior outcome.

The contrast with the situation where such interactions occur between people who belong to a group that share non-instrumental beliefs can be sharp.

| | | Player A | |
|---|---|---|---|
| | | *High price* | *Low price* |
| **Player B** | *High durability* | 2,2 | 0,3 |
| | *Low durability* | 3,0 | 1,1 |

*Figure 13.1*  The prisoners' dilemma

| | | Player A | |
|---|---|---|---|
| | | *Cinema* | *Walk* |
| **Player B** | *Cinema* | 2,3 | 0,1 |
| | *Walk* | 1,0 | 3,2 |

*Figure 13.2*   The battle of the sexes

The presence of such beliefs could enable each agent in the prisoners' dilemma to trust each other to play the (high, high) pair as each might recognize that this is the 'honourable' thing to do in the circumstances (for a version of this argument applying to corporate cultures and trust within a corporation, see Aoki (1990), Casson (1991) and Fukuyama (1995). Of course, whether this is the case or not will depend on the character of the shared beliefs. The point is that the potential for such action exists once there are such beliefs.

The battle of the sexes game depicted in Figure 13.2 captures the basic element of any bargaining situation where both stand to benefit from agreement, but there is a range of possible agreements that advantage each agent rather differently. In this instance, there are two Nash equilibria in pure strategies: they could both go for a walk or they could both go to the cinema. These are the potential points of agreement and each Pareto dominates the non-Nash outcomes. The problem is that, with two Nash equilibria and in the absence of some way for the agents to coordinate on one rather than the other, it is possible that the agents will fail to coordinate and play a non-Nash pair of strategies.[2] Again the contrast with what could happen when there are norms that influence behaviour is clear. The contribution will depend on the character of the norms, but it is easy to see how a norm of justice could be helpful in such circumstances as it could supply a reason for preferring one distribution of the benefits over the other. In short, it could act as a coordinating device that selects one of the Nash equilibria in pure strategies and so avoids a Pareto inferior outcome.

Three things are worth noting about the character of a group's shared beliefs in circumstances where they do affect outcomes in these ways. First, these beliefs must appear to both players to be rooted in some set of values or standards that are independent of any individual's narrow self-interests, otherwise they will not work their productive magic. In other words, even though the beliefs actually serve the self-interests of each player by guiding action to a Pareto superior outcome, they cannot be held for this reason. To see this consider the prisoners' dilemma. Suppose A believes that the only reason that the B believes playing 'high' is the 'honourable' thing to do is because this action serves B's self-interest, then A will also appreciate that the best outcome for B is to play 'low' (whatever A does) and so A will expect B, on mature reflection of what serves B's interests, to play 'low'. 'Honour' here cannot be a device that simply serves B's self-interest or B will find that the best action is to play 'low'. This is the logic of pure self-interest and the only way to escape this logic is if there is some criterion other than self-interest by which 'honour' is judged. The same applies to the battle of the sexes game. If A's sense of justice selects the outcome that favours A just because it favours A's interest, then it is difficult to see why B would subscribe to A's sense of justice since if one's sense of justice simply depends on how it contributes to one's own self-interest, then B will find that justice demands the outcome favouring him or her. (In effect this kind of argument explains in part the earlier decision to refer to this aspect of beliefs in terms of their licensing of non-instrumental reasons for action.)

Second, it is plain that while the shared beliefs in my illustrations have the unintended effect of promoting economic activity, there may be cases where they have the reverse effect. This seems a simple consequence of the fact that the beliefs modify the relation between action and narrow self-interest. In some settings, like the specific prisoners' dilemma illustration, this modification may actually promote self-interest, but there will be other settings where this may not be the case (see Olson, 1982).

Third, it is worth pointing out what is perhaps obvious: namely, the beliefs must be shared if they are to work this magic. It is no good in the prisoners' dilemma interaction if only one player finds 'high' is the 'honourable' course of action because (high, low) will result. Similarly the beliefs about justice must be shared in the battle of the sexes game, otherwise there is no guarantee that one person's sense of what is 'just' will coincide with that of the other. Since the beliefs in these examples contribute to output and since they have to be shared to do this, they warrant being called a type of social capital.

Granted that cultures which value non-instrumental reasons for action can be productive in the ways that I have sketched, it is natural to wonder whether there is enough of such cultures; and, if not, how investment in them might be encouraged.

On the first point, it is not difficult to find prima-facie evidence that the Anglo-American economies have a cultural deficit in this sense. For instance, Putnam (1995) argues on the basis of evidence regarding membership of voluntary associations that social capital has declined since the 1960s in the USA. More specifically, it is well-known that Japanese contracts are far less detailed than their North American counterparts and the simplest explanation of this difference is that the Japanese rely on trust in the relationship to lubricate economic exchanges rather than legal force. And generally the high use of legal services in the USA suggests a relative inability to resolve disputes informally. Likewise, the relatively high incidence of strike activity in the Anglo-American economies points to difficulties in selecting equilibria in bargaining games. As a final piece of evidence, notice that even politicians in Anglo-American economies appear to recognize this deficit as it has become a rare matter of agreement in political debate that there has been an unfortunate decline in the sense of community. Thus, it seems there is reason to be interested in how a non-instrumental culture is generated.

## THE ORIGIN OF CULTURE

There are two general types of explanation of the origin of a group's culture. Either they arise as a matter of intention, through explicit discussion, persuasion and agreement within the group or they arise as the unintended consequence of actions taken for other reasons (such as the pursuit of self-interest). The clearest recent statement in the latter tradition of 'spontaneous order' comes from Sugden (1986). Here he follows Schotter (1981) by arguing that repeated interactions between people in an evolutionary setting can give rise to conventions. For instance, consider an interaction at a crossroads which is akin to the battle of the sexes game. There are two motorists driving towards the same intersection on different roads and each has a choice between speeding up and slowing down. The pay-offs are captured in Figure 13.3. It is easy to see that each will benefit by a convention that enables each to decide who should 'speed up' and who should 'slow down'. Furthermore any basis of distinguishing between the two motorists will do the trick and, once one distinction starts to be used, each has an incentive to follow it.[3] At motoring crossroads one thinks of rules like 'give way to the right' or 'priority to the major road' and so on, but in the crossroads of life, it is just as likely that the basis could be age or sex as in 'give way to old' or 'priority to men'.

Sugden then draws on Hume to argue that beliefs like the 'artificial virtue' of justice get attached to these conventions. The simplest modern explanation of this process would draw on cognitive dissonance theory by arguing that people like to rationalize their actions and when they find they are doing something like giving priority to men with no apparent instrumental reason to explain the action, they begin to adjust their beliefs in such a way as to make the action

| | Player A | | |
|---|---|---|---|
| | | *Speed up* | *Slow down* |
| **Player B** | *Speed up* | 0,0 | 2,1 |
| | *Slow down* | 1,2 | 0,0 |

*Figure 13.3*  Interaction at a crossroads

seem justified on other grounds (Festinger, 1957). Hence one might conjecture that, for instance, a patriarchal gendered view of the world could develop as people try to make sense of the male priority convention which has emerged in the evolutionary play of these games; and in this way the convention of giving priority to men acquires the normative properties of seeming the 'right', 'natural', 'proper' (or whatever) thing to do.

The explicit discussion of beliefs and their adoption through persuasion is not inconsistent with the Humean version of spontaneous order since the attribution of 'artificial virtues' like justice to types of behaviour is liable to occur in some conscious manner through discussion with others. Of course, it might be argued that the beliefs could be purely private on the Humean account. But this is implausible because while divergent beliefs might permit coordination in one type of interaction, this would be a matter of luck and so would not be generally helpful in a range of interactions. To apply the same beliefs to a *range* of interactions and achieve coordination with others it matters that the beliefs are shared and this sharing will only come through some form of discussion. The difference in this respect between the two accounts of how cultures emerge concerns whether the beliefs develop autonomously to influence behaviour or arise as part of a process of rationalizing behaviours that have already been established. This is an interesting difference, but I want to focus on the matter of agreement: people need to discuss their beliefs in order to come to share them. A key question follows: how is it that people hold these discussions?

This is not something that is typically considered by the 'spontaneous order' tradition, perhaps because the extension of the argument is self-evident. The natural extension is that discussions also arise spontaneously in the course of these repeated interactions. However, if this is the kind of explanation offered, it actually seems implausible. Recall the earlier observation that these beliefs must have a non-instrumental character to work. This makes the construction of beliefs difficult around the actual interaction that they will serve. To see this, imagine trying to justify the convention that 'men get priority' at the actual crossroads of life. The conventional character of such a rule is only too apparent if the crossroads is where the discussion takes place and an argument by any man for a convention favouring men in these circumstances will simply seem exactly what it is, that is self-serving. Or to take up Hume's way of putting it, the 'justice' of the arrangement is 'artificial' and holding a discussion about the justice of any arrangement at the actual crossroads seems bound to bring out the artifice. The implication, then, is that societies need dedicated institutions for discussion, they cannot just piggy-back on the interaction that they may serve. This is an important concession to the view that discussions occur autonomously.[4] In practice, the autonomous institutions of discussion are unmysterious.

Such discussions are sometimes formally organized in the political institutions of a group and this sometimes results in legislation that encodes explicitly the group's beliefs. Discussions also take place informally in groups over lunch, in the pub, on the street and across the garden fence. This may not be obvious at first sight, but gossip about friends quite naturally involves comment on and evaluation of other people's behaviour and the same is often the case with the other central topic of discussion: what was seen the night before on TV or at the movies or in the sporting arena. It is in the discussion of behaviour in a 'soap' on TV or of a character in a film or a person on the sports field that people engage, albeit often implicitly, in a discussion of ideas. I state this as a matter of fact, but it can hardly be a matter of theoretical surprise as abstract principles often require a concrete setting before they can be properly appreciated. In the remainder of this chapter I shall focus on the informal discussions that are a source of common culture largely because the scope for formal discussion within political institutions seems to have been undermined by the growing perception that politics is no more than the pursuit of self-interest by other means. The rise of the Public Choice school is testament to this and it has had precisely the same corrosive effect on the potential for discussion that I have argued is likely when discussions are located at the point of exchange where the economic interests manifestly collide.

This concentration on informal discussion is also in marked contrast with much of the recent literature on declining social capital. This literature has often focused on the contribution of the family in this respect and the so-called 'parenting deficit' (see, for example, Etzioni, 1995). Etzioni may be right when he argues that the source of, in his terms, a moral sensitivity is the experience of a familial unconditional relationship, but this leaves open the question of how different families come to share not just a moral capacity but specific views regarding what justice or morality might require in any setting. This requires something more than good parenting. It requires agreement between people outside of their families and this explains why I concentrate on informal discussion outside the family.[5]

Consider two propositions concerning the potential for informal discussions to generate a common culture. First, there is only scope for discussion when people within a group share the same experience. There is, after all, only so much that can be said on the basis of a review of the movie or last night's episode of a soap or a newspaper report on last night's match as compared with the actual thing. Second, since the shared experience is a resource for such discussion, the character of shared beliefs that emerge from such discussion will depend on the material found in the shared experience. Of course, the outcome of discussions will depend on much else, but these seem simple inferences from the general idea that the output of any process depends on the inputs.

If these propositions are accepted, then it seems unwise in the current condition to rely on the free play of market forces in the organization and regulation of the sporting and cultural events that form the common material for informal discussions. Take the first proposition. Since the ability to participate in activities is often based on income one can expect discussions to develop most easily between people within a group who enjoy similar income levels. Indeed there seems to be no obvious reason for worrying about the development of norms within subgroups of this kind. Conversely, the scope for discussions that are open to the whole group will depend under a market arrangement on the degree of income inequality and there are obvious reasons to worry about the potential for generating a common culture under a market arrangement when income inequality is extreme. Indeed, it is this fact, I suspect, that helps to make sense of the growing concern among politicians over the decline in 'community'. It seems that what politicians must be worried about is not some general decline in community, since casual empirical evidence suggests that most people belong to a variety of communities in OECD countries. What is more plausibly lacking is the particular sense of community that encompasses both the rich and the poor in these societies and in the USA and the UK this seems to be unavoidably connected to the growth in income inequality.

At first glance, it may seem that there is a clear exception to this argument in the experience of television, where the device of advertising finance has allowed markets to throw up services which are 'free' to all. But, actually the experience of television illustrates precisely the problem with leaving the generation of a common culture to the free play of the market. Until now the television market has been highly regulated and TV viewing has been both a potential and actual shared experience of the kind that I have associated with the building of a common culture across income groups (see, for example, Garnham, 1994). However, the government restriction on the operation of markets in this industry was underpinned until relatively recently by the restricted radio frequency spectrum which curtailed the number of broad-casters and the lack of decoding devices to enable consumers to be charged for viewing a programme. It was these restrictions and the regulatory response that helped throw up the universal advertising-based TV channel. These conditions, though, no longer exist and the regulatory framework in most OECD countries is being relaxed. In these new circumstances many commentators doubt that the 'free' advertising-based channels will survive in the long run as the advent and gradual market penetration of the decoding technology enables pay-to-view television (see, for example, Veljanovski, 1989). The reason is simple: the marginal revenue (including advertising revenue) in all imaginable cases is negative when the price of a TV programme is zero and so raising the price above zero is bound to be attractive.

The conventional analysis of this change holds that there is a clear advantage as consumer choice will expand (basically because the price mechanism enables the intensity of minority tastes to be signalled in a way that the currency of an advertising system, that is, the numbers of viewers, does not. See

Spence and Owen (1977)). This is, of course, correct so long as there are no external effects associated with the exercise of these consumer choices. But on my account there are. The development of a more highly varied set of TV programmes that caters better to the variety of individual tastes also undermines the mass viewing market which had hitherto been a building-block in a common culture. In so far as a common culture is valued, then this is an important external effect which can create a free-rider problem in the provision of a common culture. To see this in more detail, notice that any individual's defection from the mass market to his or her niche programme market has no perceptible effect on the size of the mass market and the potential for it to generate a common culture. So it will seem in the individual's interest to switch to his or her preferred programme niche, but when all individuals do this the mass market has been destroyed and with it the contribution that TV had made to the generation of a common culture. If a common culture is sufficiently highly valued, this is a classic free-rider problem where the unrestrained pursuit of individual interest produces a collectively self-defeating outcome. The great virtue of markets is that they give rein to the pursuit of individual interest, but when the pursuit of individual interest involves a free-rider problem then markets will fail and there is a strong case for some kind of regulation. This is my argument in a nutshell.

In fact, I suspect that with respect to some programmes, something approaching a mass TV viewing market will survive the general adoption of pay-to-view TV. In other words, the free-rider problem is not as acute as I have just suggested. My reason for supposing this is simply that the impulse to watch the same programme as others because it forms a topic of conversation over lunch with one's immediate group is sufficiently strong in some cases to encourage people to forgo what might otherwise be their preferred and idiosyncratic choice of programme. In addition, there are coordinating devices like national newspaper comments on programmes and old habits from a world where the programme diet was restricted that tend to link one small group with another in these choices and this helps build a mass market. However, in so far as this is the case, I still have doubts about the efficacy of the market system. In this instance, the problems relate to the second proposition above: that the scope for exploring and developing a common culture through informal discussion depends in part on the nature of the material that is being discussed. The point here is that there seem to be good reasons for supposing that market provision of TV programmes, movies and sports events tends to undermine the non-instrumental content of these activities (and hence their direct contribution to a non-instrumental common culture).

This is perhaps clearest in the case of sporting events where the exposure to market forces increases the incentives towards winning and this drives out the non-instrumental 'sporting values' of the activity. This is not just a matter of sportsmanship vanishing. It is also the artistry of the activity. When winning becomes the only point of playing sport, then there is no internal restraint on the foul (and external restraints are imperfect substitutes as they only catch the grosser examples, like Tyson's second bite of Holyfield's ear).

Every sports fan will appreciate this worry, but it is perhaps less obvious that a similar point might apply to the extension of market relations into television, the movies and other products of the cultural industries. There are nevertheless some reasons for supposing the worry is more general. For instance, it would seem difficult to argue that competition for readers among newspapers has unambiguously promoted the cause of 'truth' in that part of the industry. Furthermore, in television there is scope for a similar effect, particularly when the demand for a programme depends on the number of other people who are watching it. In such cases what gets watched is largely a matter of how a coordination game is solved. There are many offerings and only some succeed. It is a kind of hit/flop market which is rather like a sporting event where the winner takes all (Frank and Cook, 1995). As in most coordination games there is no guarantee that people will actually coordinate on the best offering.

In fact, in media markets there are rather strong reasons for supposing that poor programmes will drive out the good ones. Bandwagons roll and what starts them is an early success and an early success is usually associated with something that captures the eye. Fortunately, this is sometimes the reputation of the performers or the directors or the writers. But unfortunately, it is also programmes that are violent, sensational and have simple messages (Boorstein, 1961). Programmes that are complicated in content do not immediately catch the eye. The precise connection between these attributes and the prospects for the generation of a non-instrumental common culture are more complicated than the sporting example. But there is enough to see the worry. Violence is a mark of the unrestrained pursuit of self-interest and in so far as frequent portrayals of violence have a legitimizing effect, then it will be plain that this bias in programming is not helpful for the development of a non-instrumental common culture.

## CONCLUSION

This chapter turns on what is, in many respects, a rather old-fashioned argument. Put simply, the only economies that are rich are those that have the capacity to know that they are rich; being well-off is not enough (or, as this has more famously been put, to know the price of something is *not* to know its value). We need values that explain why at the very least the pursuit of self-interest is right and more generally why this pursuit should be modified in a variety of ways. The simple pursuit of individual interest is not enough. But where do such values come from?

In this chapter, I have focused on the values that are embodied in a *common* non-instrumental culture. I have argued that they constitute a kind of social capital and that they are nurtured in part by the shared experiences that are the topics of informal discussions over lunch and across the garden fence. These shared experiences often come from what are called the cultural industries (the media and sporting industries which provide so much of what is modern entertainment) and the chapter presents some reasons for doubting that the free market organization of these industries will serve a common culture well. Some kind of public regulation is required; and this is especially important now because there is terrific pressure towards deregulation in some of these industries: notably the television industry where technical change has undermined the traditional rationale for government regulation and where its deregulation is having profound knock-on effects on the sporting part of the cultural industries.

## Notes

1. The use of the term social capital in this context is common among non-economists. See Coleman (1988), Fukuyama (1995) and Putnam (1995).

2. It is sometimes argued that in the absence of a coordinating device, the unique Nash equilibrium in mixed strategies should commend itself to players of the battle of the sexes game. In these circumstances, the same worry surfaces as the play of the mixed-strategy Nash equilibrium generates a high probability of a Pareto inferior outcome.

3. One might expect for this reason that a convention will emerge to select one of the Nash equilibria and so avoid one of the Pareto inferior outcomes. However, it is worth remarking that in pure coordination games where the Nash equilibria are Pareto rankable, there is no similar expectation. Although a convention seems likely to emerge for similar reasons in these settings to select a Nash equilibrium, there is no reason to suppose that it will select the Pareto superior one. In this respect, 'spontaneous order' may be a poor substitute for intentional discussion.

4. In effect, this line of argument supplies an evolutionary rationale for the emergence of institutions that explicitly help guide evolution, thus dissolving the opposition between these two kinds of account.

5. Likewise when Putnam (1995) points to the way that TV has reduced face-to-face contact during leisure time, this may help explain a fall in some generalized willingness to trust other people that is generated unconsciously through face-to-face contact, but it will not explain why people might no longer associate having a trusting disposition with their self-worth.

## References

Aoki, M. (1990) 'Toward an economic model of the Japanese firm', *Journal of Economic Literature*, 28, 1–27

Boorstein, D. (1961) *The Image: A Guide to Pseudo-Events in America*, New York, Harper & Row

Casson, M. (1991) *The Economics of Business Culture*, Oxford, Clarendon Press

Coleman, J. (1988) 'Social capital in the creation of human capital', *American Journal of Sociology*, 94, S95–120

Douglas, M. (1978) *Cultural Bias*, London, Royal Anthropological Society

Etzioni, A. (1995) *The Spirit of Community*, London, Fontana Press

Festinger, L. (1957) *A Theory of Cognitive Dissonance*, Stanford, CA, Stanford University Press

Frank, R. and P. Cook (1995) *The Winner-Take-All Society*, New York, Free Press

Fukuyama, F. (1995) *Trust*, London, Fontana

Garnham, N. (1994) 'The broadcasting market and the future of the BBC', *Political Quarterly*, 65, 11–20

Hargreaves Heap, S. (1997) 'Expressive reason', in U. Maki (ed.) *The Economic Realm*, Cambridge, Cambridge University Press

Olson, M. (1982) *The Rise and Decline of Nations*, New Haven, CT, Yale University Press

Putnam, R. (1995) 'Bowling alone: America's declining social capital', *Journal of Democracy*, 6, 65–78

Schotter, A. (1981) *Economic Theory of Social Institutions*, Cambridge, Cambridge University Press

Spence, M. and B. Owen (1977) 'Television programming, monopolistic competition and welfare,' *Quarterly Journal of Economics*, 92, 103–26

Sugden, R. (1986) *The Economics of Rights Cooperation and Welfare*, Oxford, Basil Blackwell

Veljanovski, C. (1989) *Freedom in Broadcasting*, London, Institute of Economic Affairs

# Part III
# The Political Economy of Unemployment and Inflation

# 14 The Rise of Unemployment and Working Poverty: An Evolutionary Macroeconomic Perspective

John Foster

## INTRODUCTION

Over the past twenty years, we have witnessed a steady increase in the underlying rate of unemployment in OECD countries. At the same time, there has been a parallel increase in the numbers of working poor. Gottschalk (1997) has reported that, in the United States, those in the lower half of the earnings distribution were significantly worse off in an absolute sense in 1994, compared to 1973. Over the same period, the poverty rate rose by 31 per cent even though US mean real per capita income increased by 27 per cent. In other words, the poverty-reducing effect of economic growth was more than offset by increasing inequality. Only those in the top 20 per cent of the earnings distribution were better off in 1994 compared to 1973. Similar tendencies exist in other OECD countries, although the unemployment/working poverty mix varies, depending on the particular institutional and regulatory arrangements in different countries.

Rising unemployment and inequality present the most serious socio-economic problems that we face at the conclusion of the twentieth century. They cause personal anguish for countless millions of people, eroding the social fabric of our societies and fuelling a rise in political extremism, predominantly of the right-wing variety. However, it is difficult to discern a clear explanation of why these problems have arisen if we confine ourselves to mainstream economic analysis. Furthermore, even well-intentioned governments have had great difficulty in formulating a set of satisfactory economic policies to address these problems. Many government representatives still hold the simplistic view that a high rate of economic growth is the answer. However, budget deficits and fast monetary growth are now viewed so negatively in the international financial system that it is no longer possible for governments to pursue expansion aggressively. Even in the USA, where fiscal policy remained expansionary in the 1980s and economic growth was above average for the OECD, no solution was found to the rising inequality problem. The reverse of 'trickle down' occurred.

In the decade following the Second World War, there emerged a Keynesian consensus as to what caused unemployment and how to cure it. We had the rise of macroeconomics as a policy-driven specialism, while microeconomics remained the province of neoclassical economic theory. Today, over sixty years on from the Great Depression, macroeconomics has all but lost its early postwar direction. The causes of unemployment are now discussed in terms of microeconomic theory. Thus, unemployment and inequality are seen predominantly as the outcome of individual optimizing decisions with regard to work–leisure choices and the acquisition of human capital. For example, to explain rising inequality, both Johnson (1997) and Topel (1997) argue that skill-based technological change has led to a rise in demand for labour with significant schooling and a fall in the demand for unskilled labour. However, there is no convincing explanation as to why such technological change has occurred or why there has not been a shift back towards technologies using less-skilled labour as it has become cheaper. The size of the market imperfection involved seems to fly in the face of the neoclassical economics which underpins the analyses of both of these distinguished economists.

In this chapter, I would like to revive the idea that macroeconomics can still provide an analytical framework in which we can better understand the rising unemployment and inequality problems which we currently face in the OECD. In achieving this objective, I shall be following the lead of John Cornwall's contributions (and in particular Cornwall, 1990) by setting macroeconomics in a political economy context and acknowledging that the aggregates with which we deal overlay evolutionary processes continually at work in the economic system. However, what I have to offer is conjectural and only intended to provide a research agenda for empirical inquiries well beyond the scope of this short essay.

## THE RETREAT FROM KEYNES: A MATTER OF TIME

Macroeconomics deals with aggregates and those engaged in research in the field attempt to provide an understanding of variables which are of concern to government, such as unemployment, inflation and the growth of aggregate output. In the immediate postwar era, macroeconomics was discussed in some form of Keynesian framework and unemployment was the primary focus of macroeconomic policy. However, by the 1970s, the emerging inflation problem resulted in the ascendancy of an IS–LM variant of Keynesianism which could be expressed in terms of general equilibrium and was amenable to integration with neoclassical microeconomics. By the 1980s, a full retreat to the 'classical' AS–AD framework, in a stochastic rather than a deterministic setting, had occurred. As the analysis of single-agent economies became acceptable, macroeconomics became, in effect, a branch of microeconomics. 'New Keynesians', who continued to argue for stabilization policy, accepted this neoclassical counter-revolution and relied upon information asymmetries, market failures and competitive imperfections to generate arguments for government intervention. Generally, some logical consistency was sacrificed in exchange for an enhanced ability to generate theoretical outcomes that could be related to the stylized facts of historical experience (see Mankiw, 1989). The result has been a disjointed set of special cases, far removed from the economics of Keynes, supported by casual empiricism (that is, story-telling).

Keynes offered us a tantalizing mix of Marshallian neoclassical theory and historical analysis upon which to construct and develop macroeconomics. However, for over fifty years, the historical dimension has been gradually whittled away in mainstream macroeconomic analysis and, with it, the ability of macroeconomists to relate meaningfully to real world experience. Mainstream economic theorists came to understand the devastating impact of mixing long-run equilibrium theory with even a small amount of history. Setterfield (1993) shows this powerfully in the context of the literature concerning natural rate of unemployment theories augmented by the 'hysteresis' analogy.

Keynes, like Alfred Marshall, understood the power of history, but it was a standpoint which became largely confined to the marginalized Post-Keynesian and institutionalist schools of thought in the postwar era. However, even as late as the 1970s, the institutionalist, John Kenneth Galbraith, could still oppose the 'neoclassical synthesis' strongly enough to be selected as the representative of 'fiscal Keynesians' in televised debates with Milton Friedman, the 'monetary Keynesian' (or monetarist). However, the dramatic failure of prices and incomes policies, strongly advocated by Galbraith, had, by the mid-1970s, led to a decisive victory for neoclassical general equilibrium thinking in macroeconomic theory, suitably amended with an expectational perspective. By the 1980s, this shift was so complete that even Milton Friedman came to protest against the anti-interventionist New classical economics which had grown from his eclectic monetarist ideas.

What macroeconomists lost in basing their analysis upon ahistorical long-run general equilibrium theorizing was any real ability to deal with the impact of ongoing structural change in the economic system, in the form of technical, organizational and institutional change. The favoured models depicted macroeconomic dynamics as the outcome of exogenous shocks upon flows through a fixed economic structure. Thus, dynamics were conceived of as disequilibrium processes between old and new stable equilibrium positions and due to 'frictions', such as adjustment lags and/or expectational lags. These processes were seen as lying outside the timeless economic theory preferred to deal with stable equilibrium outcome states. Such atheoretical processes allowed the translation of timeless hypotheses into dynamic forms which had a time dimension. However, such specifications were not historical because the disequilibrium dynamics specified constituted fully reversible processes, subject only to some persistence.

For both Marshall and Keynes, actual economic processes in historical time contained irreversibilities which precluded the use of neoclassical long-run equilibrium thinking to understand their behaviour over long periods. Irreversibility gives rise to structural adaptations which themselves give rise to new structural configurations that also have irreversible properties. In such circumstances, fundamental uncertainty is present. Thus, both Marshall and Keynes concluded that the long period has to be viewed as predominantly historical in character and, therefore, unanalysable using 'mechanical' equilibrium models which are only appropriate as short-period approximations. Neither provided any formal analysis of this 'evolutionary' aspect of economic systems, but they did acknowledge it in the manner in which they delimited the application of the mechanical modes of reasoning which they both used (see Foster, 1989, 1993).

Unsurprisingly, economic forecasters, using predominantly linear models built from neoclassical general equilibrium theorizing, have had a poor record, being unable to embrace the structural change which has been ever present in the historical periods over which their time series span. Somewhat limply, they have tended to include, *ex post*, dummy variables to capture, for example, regulatory changes. Also, unrestricted by the dictates of economic theory, they rely upon increasingly complex lag structures to find a dynamic recipe which can proxy the impact of ongoing structural change. Thus, models can be propped up statistically until the next predictive failure comes along. Even a cursory examination of such models shows that lag structures play such a dominant role that they are, essentially, historical models in which attempts are made to include 'theoretical' cross-restrictions which rarely stay the same for very long.

The gradual rejection by 'Keynesians' of Keynes's attempts to set macroeconomic analysis in historical time is well-known, but the parallel rejection of Marshall's attempts to impose severe limits on the applicability of neoclassical microeconomics has been less obvious. In many respects, the demise of macroeconomics owes more to the latter than the former: the modern conversion of macroeconomics to aggregated microeconomics could not have occurred without the radical shift from the economics of Marshall to that of Walras, involving the removal of any consideration of the role of history.

The retreat from Keynes has been essentially a retreat from confronting vital features of history in economic analysis. The 'generalization of the *General*

*Theory'*, which Joan Robinson (1952) saw as the postwar challenge for macroeconomics, never occurred. Instead, an ideological conflict broke out which involved competing visions of the equilibrium structure of the economy. Are markets imperfect or competitive? Is macroeconomic equilibrium the outcome of a market mechanism involving individuals or a distributional mechanism involving groups? Is the logic of neoclassical production theory valid? Thus, vital scientific questions concerning the dichotomy of history versus equilibrium in macroeconomics were neglected except for a few Post-Keynesians with Austrian leanings, such as Shackle (1974) and, following his conversion to Post-Keynesianism in the 1970s, Hicks (1974).

## BEYOND KEYNES: THE SCHUMPETERIAN ECONOMY

Is it possible to provide a new approach to macroeconomics which can allow, in an abstract way, for the processes of structural change which we observe in history? In many respects, a new approach has been in the making for some time. For example, many of the points that have been made above have already been made powerfully by John Cornwall throughout his academic career and they lead to a theoretical and empirical approach which attempts to cater for the structural change that occurs in history. By offering an understanding of how the focus of equilibrium continually changes because of structural change, Cornwall has been able to provide explanations of macroeconomic history which isolate the main tendencies of structural change while retaining some useful aspects of conventional economic analysis. From such a basis, his anticipations of future macroeconomic conditions in capitalist economies, at different points in his career, have been remarkably accurate. Unfortunately, the success of Cornwall's approach to macroeconomics has not been widely acknowledged in the mainstream, even by people who label themselves 'Keynesian'. Many economists have demonstrated great difficulty in relating to research which does not begin in the theoretical framework that is ingrained in their thought processes.

In *Evolutionary Macroeconomics* (Foster, 1987), I attempted to take a more abstract approach to that of Cornwall in order to provide an alternative analytical framework for macroeconomic analysis which would allow, explicitly and *ex ante*, for the existence of structural change, emanating from the creative, cooperative and competitive behaviour of individuals and groups. I stressed the philosophical and psychological perspectives taken by Keynes, concerning the economic behaviour of individuals. I also stressed the revolutionary nature of his principle of effective demand, as a powerful systemic abstraction of a process set in historical time, depending upon the existence of money in valuation and exchange, unlike the imagined moneyless 'circular flow' in a timeless Walrasian general equilibrium model. However, Keynes's macroeconomic model is, necessarily, a limited one: it deals with the circular flow of income and expenditure as an equilibrating process where there is no automatic requirement that equilibrium should be at any particular level of aggregate output, such as that consistent with some definition of full employment. Why the circular flow grows in the long term is not explained – Keynes explicitly excludes long-period analysis of the path of output. The economy will evolve, and the circular flow equilibration process must go on as a necessity of history and the continued existence of economic institutions.

Joseph Schumpeter also thought in terms of the circular flow and effective demand, but in a more dynamic way. He pointed out that any insufficiency of aggregate demand can prevent not only the utilization of existing capacity but also the formation of new capacity. Since he viewed cyclical fluctuations as the form that growth takes, he was less interested in government intervention in recessions and depressions and more concerned with the capacity of the financial system to make the investment component of aggregate demand effective by advancing an adequate amount of credit. Like Keynes, he was concerned with private sector inadequacies of a systemic nature, but in the context of the promotion of innovation and growth.

Both Keynes and Schumpeter saw psychological factors as crucial in inducing fluctuations in economic activity. The former referred to 'animal spirits' (the will to action in preference to inaction) and the latter to the entrepreneur, who was the embodiment of such a cognitive condition. Thus, in a world where irreversibilities proscribed much of the flexibility presupposed by neoclassical economists, some economic agents were viewed as having a psychological predisposition which enabled them to engage in acts of creativity in the presence of fundamental uncertainty. However, in 1936, Keynes was not very interested in the expansion of the capital stock and the embodiment of technical change, but in its contraction and the associated impact upon employment.

As irreversibilities led to the cumulative destruction of productive and human capacity, it was pessimism which dominated the climate of confidence. Since the equilibrium of the circular flow is conditioned by irreversible features emanating from the history of the economic system, loss of structure results in lower and lower flow equilibrium positions. The price system, which mediates flows of supply and demand through a given structure, cannot deal effectively with situations of structural disintegration and the associated complex non-linear feedback mechanisms which come into play. For example, the factories of bankrupt firms will be sold for a tiny fraction of the value that would have prevailed when they were all going concerns, with repercussions on creditor financial institutions and their other customers. In the uncertainty of structural collapse, the price mechanism cannot operate effectively. Behind Keynes's shrinking circular flows lies not rigidities in wages and/or prices, as New Keynesians would have us believe, but rather the destruction of productive structure and the deterioration of human skills.

Keynes focused upon the income/expenditure flows running through the vast dynamic complexity of the economy, simply because he believed that it was deficiencies in aggregate expenditure which were the central problem and that these could be reversed by the overseer of the economy, namely government, which had the power to vary tax and expenditure flows by edict. The private sector was seen as being handicapped in its ability to reverse decline in such circumstances because the extreme uncertainty associated with structural disintegration led to a strong unwillingness to lend. Essentially, Keynes depicted the Great Depression as a crisis in confidence which could be reversed by the demonstrable confidence of a spending government. Despite the mechanical character of the circular flow model, it overlays a complex psychological story.

However, Keynes was quite aware of the fact that recessions were not solely due to short-term crises in confidence and that long historical waves of growth and decline, of the type identified by Kondratiev and analysed by Schumpeter, existed. As has been pointed out, Schumpeter's explanation of the endogenous dimension of such waves also depended upon confidence, particularly that of entrepreneurs in driving the developmental process of innovation and imitation on from preexisting inventions. Keynes was aware that the Great Depression was part of a long downswing, in some sense, and that the proliferation of unused economic resources would provide the basis for the emergence of a new upswing driven by entrepreneurial behaviour. However, he believed that government could and should intervene when the problem of collapsing confidence was particularly acute, generating very high unemployment and underutilized capacity as well as threatening the social fabric and national security.

Keynes did not advocate stabilization policy as 'fine-tuning' but, rather, as a strategy for disaster prevention. The Great Depression was not a mere recession and Keynes's prescriptions were not intended for continuous application to remove the latter condition. However, even in the limited context of the Great Depression, Friedrich Hayek warned Keynes that, once fiscal stabilization, backed by monetary permissiveness, became an accepted interventionist principle, it would itself assume some troublesome irreversible properties. Being largely outside the price mechanism, Hayek argued that the public sector would be vulnerable to rent-seeking behaviour, and political considerations, such as winning elections, would lead to excessive spending. As it turned out, Hayek's pessimism was only partially vindicated. The monetary and fiscal expansion that characterized the postwar period provided credit conditions which facilitated the new developmental upswing – there was no shortage of effective demand in the Schumpeterian sense. It was only in the 1970s, at the top of the Kondratiev cycle, that the Hayekian problem became apparent.

By introducing a Schumpeterian perspective, we can see that Keynes's macroeconomic analysis was necessarily limited and overzealous acceptance of his policy recommendations led to the evolution of an economy that he had not envisaged. In other words, the economy altered its structure because of a key organizational innovation: a new kind of government involvement, releasing scale economies and the consolidation of a new form of industrial structure. Can we adapt macroeconomic analysis to allow for such evolutionary change in a way that can help us understand the emergence of unemployment and poverty in the OECD?

## AN EVOLUTIONARY MACROECONOMIC PERSPECTIVE

In his macroeconomics, Keynes disaggregated income/expenditure flows only minimally. To make his point in a closed economy, it was enough to split expenditure into that of consumers, investors and government. They were chosen because their aggregate behaviour was presumed to differ in important ways. The key problem was that investment in capital involves a commitment to stock which displays a high degree of irreversibility. Therefore, investors are nervous and capricious in their behaviour, anxiously looking at the actions of other investors when deciding what to do. Collective decisions to cut back investment because of anticipated slackening of consumer demand generate a feedback, whereby anticipations are vindicated. Thus, dynamics become endogenous and this encouraged the development of multiplier/accelerator models of the business cycle by Samuelson (1939) and Hicks (1950). Keynes had not attempted to formalize such a process since he clearly did not believe that an accelerator coefficient would be stable across history and he was largely vindicated by the failure of econometric research concerning the business cycle after his death. Indeed the accelerator made few people happy. For the equilibrium theorist, it was an atheoretical construction and for close followers of Keynes is was a matter of misplaced concreteness.

The problem in extending Keynes's approach is that he focused primarily upon economic breakdown and the introduction of a stabilizing government to avert depressions. Necessarily, Keynes's circular flow model is fixed structurally, in the sense that the marginal propensity to consume is related to income in a mathematical manner, otherwise the multiplier could not be discussed as a stable magnitude. Such an abstraction does not deal with underlying economic complexity and the manner in which this complexity changes but, rather, the income–expenditure flows that facilitate the maintenance and development of that complexity – Keynes was dealing, not with the coordinating role not of the market but, more generally, of money flows. Thus, his model reflects the organization of the economic system as one of monetary exchange and contracting. It is limited in its scope because of the way that business investment is dealt with. The effects of fluctuations in business confidence on the circular flow, and thus unemployment, are captured but there is no evolutionary dimension to the model which can help us address the emergence of underlying structural unemployment and associated working poverty.

It is straightforward to disaggregate investment expenditure in a manner which reflects the dynamics of a Schumpeterian economy:

1. Strategic investment, which involves expenditure on items which help defend market share, such as marketing and sales promotion, product differentiation and the erection of entry barriers and a range of other rent-seeking activities.
2. Investment in expenditure which is necessary to keep production going. This includes the provision of stocks of inventories throughout the production process and maintenance and repair expenditures.
3. Investment in cost-cutting methods, such as organizational improvement and labour saving technologies
4. Investment in research leading to inventions and the innovation of new products and new production techniques.

Schumpeter addressed all four of these investment categories, indicating that the most important for economic evolution is (4). Category (3) was also regarded as involving innovation, but only of the incremental, Marshallian, type. Keynes, in effect, focused upon (2) in his model – buffer stocks are critical to the working of the multiplier process. Investment in the capacity to seek rents in (1) was for Keynes, as it was for Marshall, a matter of ethics. Category (3) was accepted, in the sense that he allowed for 'economizing' investment behaviour which is sensitive to the cost of capital. Category (4) was designated as entirely psychological and subject to the ebb and flow of confidence. Keynes appreciated fully that Categories (3) and (4) are fundamental in determining the position of any short-run macroeconomic equilibrium. As has been noted, he shared with Marshall the view that the equilibrium construct could provide insights in appropriate temporal contexts.

At any level of aggregation in the economy, the flow of investment expenditure will contain all four components. However, an emphasis on each has different implications for economic evolution. Let us, then, examine them in turn.

*Category (1)* is, in essence, political and a strong emphasis on this type of investment will be at the expense of other categories, particularly category (4). At the level of the economy, it leads to the predominance of economic structures which are organized along authoritarian lines. A shift towards category (1) investment at any level may well increase employment, as was the case in the 1930s in Nazi Germany. The political imposition of strong hierarchical order, in societies which were previously in disorder, can yield employment pay-offs. Spillover into category (2) and (3) investment can lead to further employment gains and, for a while, productivity gains. However, since category (4) investment in the private sector is the fountain of economic evolution, such systems tend towards inertia, productivity decline and ultimate collapse. Such societies are not characterized by unemployment but rather by the ever increasing immiserization of the working poor. In societies emphasizing category (1) investment, we do, indeed, have Hayek's 'road to serfdom'.

*Category (2)* investment is necessary to keep structures going. However, overemphasis on (2) at the expense of (3) and (4) results in inertia and ever escalating costs because of the presence of entropy processes and analogous tendencies towards disorder in all structures. There is a rising tendency for labour to be absorbed for the purposes of maintaining an increasingly inert system. The Soviet system before its demise tended to emphasize category (2) investment patterns with little category (3) 'economizing' or category (4) enterprise. However, slowly dying economic systems do not generate unemployment, only slowly falling productivity and wages.

*Category (3)* investment often occurs when capital equipment has depreciated to the point where it needs to be replaced. Cost-cutting strategies, which normally involve capital/labour substitution, are adopted. When the task to be performed is relatively well-defined, it is possible to apply conventional investment appraisal techniques. Investment in organizational rearrangement can also occur. The outcome of this type of investment is generally labour-saving. In orthodox economics this is the primary way of looking at investment. Overemphasis on this type of investment, at the expense of category (4), can lead to rising unemployment simply because insufficient new jobs and associated training programmes are generated in emergent industries. However, the linkage between categories (3) and (4) is a complex one – Joseph Schumpeter suggested that this kind of investment can sometimes lead to the unintended consequence that a firm enters a new, category (4) niche. For example, the purchase of a replacement machine tool with much more accurate tolerances may lead to the possibility of producing novel, high precision products.

*Category (4)* investment is difficult because it creates novelty and opportunity in the future and the benefits are not easily quantified *ex ante*. Category (3) can involve profit maximization but (4) is limited to profit-seeking. The profits might well be expropriated by someone else in the uncertainty which prevails. Nonetheless, managers know that, without entrepreneurial activity of this type, the organization will struggle to survive in the longer term. Generally, through the creation of novelty, such investment is employment-enhancing. Entrepreneurs who have been successful in category (4) investment, earning above normal profits, may begin to switch to category (1) defensive investment if their market niche is limited and, thus, the Schumpeterian circle of creative destruction is closed.

*Table 14.1*  Possible long-term impacts of different categories of investment

| Category | Unemployment | Inequality | Productivity |
|----------|--------------|------------|--------------|
| 1 | Lower | Raise | Lower |
| 2 | Lower | Lower | Lower |
| 3 | Raise | Raise | Raise |
| 4 | Lower | Lower | Raise |

Once we categorize investment in this way, we can see that shifts in the component structure of investment can raise or lower net employment and earnings inequality. The hypothesized effects are summarized in Table 14.1.

The degree of openness of the system that we are considering is also important. For example, if category (3) investment involves the importation of capital goods, then labour-saving is not compensated by increased demands for labour in domestic producer goods industries. This will be aggravated by the attendant leakage of expenditure overseas. However, if it is category (4) investment, such as the importation of novel ideas, then there should be an employment creation effect plus a productivity effect to offset the leakage effect.

Thus, without an understanding of the composition of investment and how it has changed over time, we cannot understand the impact of investment upon unemployment and poverty. Clearly, this suggests a research programme which would involve the categorization of both public and private sector investment. With such knowledge, it would then be possible to model, for example, skilled and unskilled employment and corresponding productivity and wage levels. Thus, we could understand the macroeconomic (or systemic) implications of ongoing structural change. Furthermore, by examining the magnitude of investment and its changing composition, we could make a judgement concerning the likely stability of the economic system under investigation.

## THE EMERGENCE OF UNEMPLOYMENT AND POVERTY: SOME CONJECTURES

It is possible to offer some conjectures for future examination through theoretical and empirical research. In this short essay no more than a sketch of possibilities can be offered. I shall present these in the form of a narrative, rather than in any formal way.

From a Schumpeterian perspective, the phase of innovative activity and associated economic growth in the postwar period, up to the early 1970s, was unparalleled in human history. Berry (1991) has shown that the long upswing of the postwar era is quite distinct from others in that it manifests significantly greater average rates of inflation, starting earlier and lingering longer. Accelerating inflation at the end of long upswings has been identified with rent-seeking struggle. Thus, it would appear that this was much more intense than in previous cases. Furthermore, the long downswing has been much more gradual with unemployment rising much more slowly over a longer period.

There is no doubt that Hayek was correct in arguing that stabilization policy would not be used sparingly and neutrally only to deal with extreme macroeconomic conditions. However, in the mixed economy setting, 'serfdom' did not eventuate, but rather a different developmental path was followed. The role and functions of government changed fundamentally, as its representatives sought an explicit economic role as a stabilizer and provider of public goods. The provision of infrastructure, public education, public health and a higher degree of economic stability did not enslave but, rather, provided new kinds of opportunities for economic development in the private sector.

In retrospect, it seems that greater public involvement in the economy may have altered the structure of the private sector towards greater industrial concentration. Cohen and Klepper (1996) have provided evidence in support of Schumpeter's contention (Schumpeter, 1942) that large firms have been able to implement R&D strategies that encourage concentration, even in the United States where there has been strong anti-trust legislation. It can be argued that the activities of big government encouraged the growth of big firms, taking advantage of economies of scale. These could be enjoyed because of, for example, the public provision of transportation and telecommunications infrastructure, allowing extensive geographic marketing and distribution. The provision of public education could provide labour with the organizational and technological skills to manage such firms as well as the appropriate ideological, cultural and social attitudes that were compatible with a mass consumption society. A commitment to stabilization policy allowed large firms to expand with more confidence and a loose monetary policy meant that borrowing was inexpensive. Unemployment and social security arrangements enabled many of the private costs of disposing of unwanted labour to be passed on to government.

Galbraith (1972) subscribed to this view and perceived the political implications of such evolutionary developments. He viewed the rise in US trade union membership in the 1960s as the emergence of 'countervailing power' against powerful corporate interests. Postwar governments struggled to curb the rent-seeking activities of tight oligopolies. In turn, representatives of the latter influenced the political and economic agendas of governments. Whereas Schumpeter's entrepreneur is driven into an uncertain future on a wave of optimism, the managers of mega-corporations manipulate the future with cynicism: consumers are conditioned, politicians are influenced and the rise of radical 'paradigm-shifting' innovations is suppressed through the construction of effective barriers to entry. Marcuse (1964) offered a sociological perspective on this process with predictions concerning the emergence of an underclass which were to prove remarkably accurate.

In the Schumpeterian depiction of the long wave, the peak is characterized by firms, empowered by the profits of innovation, resorting to rent-seeking activities to survive. However, in his early writings, Schumpeter (1912) argued that such firms would succumb to the competitive process of creative destruction. In his later writings, Schumpeter (1942), in recognition of the fact that large firms had come to engage in significant research and development activities, became less certain that this would occur and argued that it might be necessary for governments to 'socialize' such firms, encouraging their innovative tendencies and discouraging rent-seeking activities.

His doubts about the future reliability of the process of creative destruction seem to have been well-founded. The existence of extensive government intervention seems to have allowed firms to enjoy economies of scale, conferring monopolistic power on large, growing corporations throughout the postwar long-wave upswing. Economies of scale resulted in high rates of productivity growth and associated high rates of economic growth, consistent with the political aspirations of governments. However, such a process could not go on without limit. By the late 1960s, the possibilities of further expansion of profits through mergers, acquisitions and other scale-enhancing manoeuvres became limited by the countervailing power of strong labour unions and the impact of emerging budgetary problems upon government investment spending. By the end of the 1960s, labour-saving strategies had become widespread in the private sector and the programme of closures in labour-intensive industries in the public sector began to gather speed.

Thus, the accelerating inflation of the late 1960s and the 1970s can be viewed as indicative of a power struggle between corporate and union power (Cornwall, 1990), conditioned by the willingness of governments to accommodate wage inflation by monetary expansion. Rising unemployment, as firms began to adopt labour-saving strategies, did not mitigate this inflationary process significantly because the superfluous labour 'shaken out' was not much in demand and, therefore, not central to the wage inflation process to begin with. Thus, we had the emergence of the phenomenon of stagflation which was also a (less pronounced) feature of the end of earlier long-wave upswings.

In the 1970s, real rates of interest fell to record levels because of a combination of high inflation and monetary policies designed to hold down nominal interest rates. These represented adverse conditions for the financial system and this gave rise to a political movement which was symbolized in the rise to power of the Joseph/Thatcher group in the British Conservative Party. By the 1980s, financial interests had reversed the situation and, in so doing, blunted the ability of governments to target unemployment. As large firms continued to introduce labour-saving capital, investment became increasingly focused on category (3) rather than (4). Furthermore, the marginal cut-off for an investment project became very high, as real interest rates rose to record levels. Tougher industrial relations laws meant that trade unions could do little about redundancy and the resultant decline in membership allowed employers to dominate in wage disputes.

By the mid-1980s, real rates of return had reached unprecedented high levels, as did the real cost of capital for those wishing to engage in innovative activity. In a world where investment depends critically on the availability of retained earnings and on a capacity to markup the cost of capital into prices, path-breaking innovation becomes difficult. Thus, investment became dominated by large firms investing in techniques to make their productive processes more efficient and to protect their markets from potential entrants. Thus, the net effect of category (3) dominance was a steady upward trend in unemployment and/or poverty. New innovations did not diffuse at a fast enough rate to create enough new jobs. Released labour either ended up in the low-wage/low-productivity service sector or unemployed.

The unprecedented power vested in big business in the era of the mixed economy appears to have resulted in what I have referred to as an 'invisible plateau' (Foster, 1987) after the long-wave peak in the 1970s. The rent-seeking successes of concentrated industries reduced the turmoil of a long-wave downswing and delayed the emergence of a fundamentally new innovation diffusion process. The implementation of monetarist and balanced budget policies did not damage large firms as much as small firms thus, enhancing the relative strength of the former and repressing the sector from which fundamental innovative change is likely to come. Clearly, this is quite a different problem to that considered by Keynes in the Great Depression. Instead of the emergence of mass unemployment for a relatively short period, as in the 1930s, the rise of unemployment and poverty has been spread over two decades as the homogenization of goods and services, capital investment and the utilization of low-cost labour in the Third World has allowed continual downsizing to occur.

## CONCLUDING REMARKS

Should these conjectures have any validity, what are the policy implications? Cornwall (1990) argues that the key is to introduce institutional arrangements that will ensure that inflation will not rise again, then governments will be free to stimulate aggregate demand in their economies and reduce unemployment.

However, it is becoming more apparent, eight years after John Cornwall completed his book, that globalization and the power of the financial system have reduced the extent to which governments can stimulate their own economies by increasing expenditure. This has been no more in evidence than in his own country, Canada, which has been spun into economic and political turmoil because of both in the 1990s. Furthermore, if unemployment is more of a structural, rather than an expenditure deficiency, problem, as has been suggested here, then it is possible that new rounds of stimulative spending will further reinforce the existing industrial power structure and further delay the much needed transition phase towards a new Schumpeterian innovation swarm, emanating from the implementation of new ideas by entrepreneurs.

It would be unwise to speculate unduly on policy on the basis of mere conjectures, but, in the future, government spending will have to flow through very well-developed industrial policies to promote genuine innovation processes if it is to be effective in reducing unemployment. It may make sense to spend on digging holes and filling them up again in a depression, but spending has to be much more carefully targeted in a world where unemployment has emerged because innovation has been repressed. Updated regulatory frameworks will have to be developed to curb the rent-seeking behaviour of tight oligopolies and to tilt the balance towards small enterprises. It is not clear that the unilateral reduction of protection which has been so strongly favoured in some countries, such as Australia and New Zealand, is the best policy to promote Schumpeterian competition. Trade liberalization favours large multinational firms which can take advantage of global economies of scale, enabling them to erect entry barriers against small innovative indigenous enterprises.

A great deal has been made in the 'New Growth Theory' literature of the advantages in investing in education. However, the Schumpeterian (and Austrian) perspective stresses the importance of variety and diversity in the knowledge stock. Blanket public spending on post-school education can lead to homogeneity and an emphasis upon obsolete forms of vocational learning, much of which contributes little to innovation. Higher education often seems as if it is, predominantly, a wasteful and discriminatory way of screening people into high-earning occupations. Above all, the view which still prevails today in many government circles, that reducing real wages is the route to prosperity, needs to be banished to the static and illusory world where such thinking belongs.

## References

Berry, B.J.L. (1991) *Long-Wave Rhythms in Economic Development and Political Behaviour*, Baltimore, MD, Johns Hopkins University Press

Cohen, W.M. and S. Klepper (1996) 'A reprise of size and R&D', *Economic Journal*, 106, 925–51

Cornwall, J. (1977) *Modern Capitalism: Its Growth and Transformation*, London, Martin Robertson

Cornwall, J. (1990) *The Theory of Economic Breakdown: An Institutional-Analytical Approach*, Cambridge, MA, Blackwell

Foster, J. (1987) *Evolutionary Macroeconomics*, London, Unwin Hyman

Foster, J. (1989) 'The macroeconomics of Keynes: an evolutionary perspective', in J. Pheby (ed.) *New Directions in Post-Keynesian Economics*, Aldershot, Edward Elgar

Foster, J. (1993) 'Economics and the self-organization approach: Alfred Marshall revisited?', *Economic Journal*, 103, 975–91

Galbraith, J.K. (1972) *The New Industrial State*, 2nd edn, Boston, MA, Houghton Mifflin

Gottschalk, P. (1997) 'Inequality, income growth and mobility: the basic facts', *Journal of Economic Perspectives*, 11, 21–40

Hicks, J.R. (1950) *A Contribution to the Theory of the Trade Cycle*, Oxford, Oxford University Press

Hicks, J.R. (1974) *The Crisis in Keynesian Economics*, Oxford, Basil Blackwell

Johnson, G.E. (1997) 'Changes in earning inequality: the role of demand shifts', *Journal of Economic Perspectives*, 11, 41–54

Keynes, J.M. (1936) *The General Theory of Employment, Interest and Money*, London, Macmillan

Mankiw, N.G. (1989) 'Real business cycles: a new Keynesian perspective', *Journal of Economic Perspectives*, 3, 79–90

Marcuse, H. (1964) *One-Dimensional Man*, London, Routledge & Kegan Paul

Robinson, J. (1952) *The Generalization of the General Theory and Other Essays*, London, Macmillan

Samuelson, P.A. (1939) 'Interactions between the multiplier analysis and the principle of acceleration', *Review of Economics and Statistics*, 21, 75–8

Schumpeter, J. (1912) *The Theory of Economic Development*, Cambridge, Cambridge University Press

Schumpeter, J. (1942) *Capitalism, Socialism and Democracy*, New York, Harper

Setterfield, M.A. (1993) 'Towards a long-run theory of effective demand: modelling macroeconomic systems with hysteresis', *Journal of Post-Keynesian Economics*, 15, 347–64

Shackle, G.L.S. (1974) *Keynesian Kaleidics*, Edinburgh, Edinburgh University Press

Topel, R.H. (1997) 'Factor proportions and relative wages: the supply side determinants of wage inequality', *Journal of Economic Perspectives*, 11, 55–74

# 15 A Post-Walrasian Explanation of Wage and Price Inflexibility and a Keynesian Unemployment Equilibrium System

David Colander

The issue of wage- and price-level flexibility has been at the heart of macroeconomic debates over the past fifty years, and it continues to be central to modern theoretical macro debates. As the in-vogue macro models have shifted from assumptions of instantaneous flexibility of prices to assumptions of fixed prices and wages, and back again, so too have the younger economists' general acceptance of different macro models. The early Keynesian models were built on a foundation, and acceptance, of relatively fixed wages and prices, and within that foundation the Keynesian models found general support among then young economists, with older economists for the most part sticking with their earlier Classical views. Then, when economists tried to develop micro foundations for that wage- and price-level flexibility, and did not find reasonably good explanations for it, the young economists abandoned those Keynesian models and switched to more Classical models. Keynesian economists, who in the interim had become old economists, dismissed the Classical models as irrelevant game-playing.

The failure to reach a resolution on this issue, and the failure of one group to convince the other group, suggests that the problems involved here go deeper than simple logic. The argument presented in this chapter is that the difference between the two views is more fundamental than merely believing or not believing in menu cost, or efficiency wage explanations of wage and price fixity. The argument is that the differences are a matter of vision: the two alternative assumptions represent fundamentally different visions of how markets work in the economy. I have elsewhere called these different visions the Post-Walrasian vision and the Walrasian vision (Colander, 1996).

In a Post-Walrasian vision, wage and price inflexibilities require no partial equilibrium microfoundations. Instead, they have what I call a systemic microfoundation – by which I mean that its explanation for wage and price flexibility lies in the theory of institutions underlying the markets, not in the decisions of individuals given otherwise perfectly competitive markets. Accepting this systemic microfoundation gives one a fundamentally different view of the macroeconomic problem than does the Walrasian vision. Specifically, it puts Keynesian economics on as firm a microfoundation as New Classical economics. They just assume different institutional structures. Deciding between these two microfoundations makes the choice of which model to use *an empirical issue*, unresolvable by analytic debate.

The Post-Walrasian vision is not new; it has been around for a long time, maintained by a diverse group of economists, one of whom is John Cornwall. John has been steadfast in maintaining this vision, both in his writing and in the legacy of understanding he has passed on to his students. Thus, it is a privilege to contribute this Post-Walrasian essay to a volume in his honour.


THE POST-WALRASIAN VISION

The Walrasian framework has, at its core, a general equilibrium theory which pictures abstract markets coordinating economic activity through changes in relative prices. Markets somehow exist, and coordinate costlessly. This vision is well-known and I will not discuss it here. The Post-Walrasian framework is based on a fundamentally different vision of the economy than is the Walrasian framework. The Post-Walrasian vision is of a functionally complex economy, by which I mean an economy with complex dynamics and multiple equilibria.

In a functionally complex economy, coordination mechanisms, such as an institutionally specified market, are necessary; some unspecified 'market' cannot be assumed to coordinate individuals' actions. How is this institutionally specified coordination accomplished? In the Post Walrasian vision the coordination is accomplished via institutions that place constraints on individuals. These institutions limit individuals' range of choice, thereby reducing the set of achievable equilibria. Given institutions, there may be a unique equilibrium, but *that equilibrium can only be understood in reference to the institutions that play a central role in determining it.* In order to have a full analytic model within the Post-Walrasian vision, one must (1) model the institutions within which individuals interact; (2) explain how those institutions are compatible with the assumptions of individual rationality that one has made; and (3) explain how those institutions play a role in the determining the equilibrium of the economy.

In modelling those institutions, I have argued that a sequential modelling approach is necessary. All questions cannot be addressed simultaneously, and, at any moment in time, most individuals simply accept large numbers of institutions, and the constraints those institutions place on them, in order to reduce the complexity of decision-making to a manageable level.

In the absence of sequentially determined decision-making, and acceptance by individuals of social conventions and institutions, the complexity of interactions would lead one to expect that aggregate results would fluctuate wildly. That does not happen to anywhere near the degree that the complexity of the interactions would lead one to predict. Walrasians interpret that lack of fluctuation as an indication that their unique equilibrium approach is the correct one. Post-Walrasians interpret that lack of fluctuation differently; they see it as an indication of the central role of institutions limiting the interactions in the economy to manageable proportions for individuals, and thereby creating a surface stability over a core of chaos.

Thus, the Post-Walrasian view is that the economy processes information in a quite different way than is assumed in the Walrasian view. In Post-Walrasian economics much of the information-processing is built into existing institutions, and is not fully understood by the participants. Specialists may understand parts of it and they may be working on changing institutions to take advantage of that understanding, but the complexity of the economy precludes a full understanding and complete reliance on the results of their analysis. Post-Walrasian rationality has local, institutionally based, characteristics; it is bounded, not global, rationality.

## INSTITUTIONS AS OPERATING SYSTEMS

An analogy to a computer may shed some light on this Post-Walrasian view of the role of institutions. A computer has a general design, an operating system, software built around that operating system, and sub-software built around that software. In using the computer most individuals take the existing software for granted, much as they take institutions for granted. They operate within the limitations of that software, and their rationality is defined by that software. Thus, when someone asks, 'Why hit Control Z when the computer isn't responding?', the answer is, 'That's what one does.' Implicit in this response is the acceptance of a DOS environment. In a MAC environment, hitting Control Z is meaningless. Other aspects of rationality carry over between the two environments – double-clicking with a mouse, for example, to open a file.

The same thing happens with institutions: individuals accept the constraints imposed by institutions on their actions as necessary constraints to operate in a complex environment. When asked why one drives on the right-hand side of the street, one responds, 'That's what one does.' Similarly when asked why one displays the degree of honesty that one does, a real person does not respond, 'I have analysed the situation and determined that, given the costs and benefits, that is the optimal degree of honesty to reflect', as a Walrasian *Homo Oeconomicus* would. Instead, a Post Walrasian individual would say, 'It's what is right.' Now this does not mean that Post-Walrasian *Homo Oeconomicus* is honest, or that he or she does not take the costs and benefits of being honest into account. Instead it simply means that there is a large non-linear cost to determining optimal actions, and in many areas, the rational decision is to learn what is, and is not, institutionally acceptable, and generally follow those institutional rules.[1] Post-Walrasians follow what Herbert Simon calls process rationality.

This sequential choice view of how the economy operates also dictates the modelling strategy used. To have a full model one must have a set of multiple nested systems – one explaining why institutions and sub-institutions are adopted. Most models will not concern such grand theories; instead they will accept existing institutions as given, and incorporate the constraints – like knowing about double-clicking or Control Z – of those institutions into the analysis. One of the most important considerations for individuals will be limiting the nature of the decision they are making – efficiently reducing the amount of information-processing they can do. Thus, the macro constraints on micro behaviour will be a central part of any but the grandest of models. They certainly play a central role in all short-run analysis; they place constraints on the type of behaviour that can reasonably be assumed.

This computer analogy also sheds light on the multiple equilibria aspect of Post-Walrasian macroeconomics, how it pictures institutions leading people to choose among those equilibria, and the approach to policy it suggests. In the grandest of models there are many operating systems, and the choice of one of them will exclude others. Most policy issues are addressed – given an operating system – and hence it is difficult to make any global statements about optimality from models derived from observations grounded in existing institutions. The results garnered from such models will be at best suggestive about policy.

## THE POST-WALRASIAN PRODUCTION FUNCTION

In terms of textbook modelling of the macro economy, the difference between the two visions can be conveyed pedagogically in the specification of the aggregate production function. In the Walrasian vision, that production function is generally seen as an individual firm production function writ large – you have a big capital, and a big labour, variable, rather than a small capital and small labour variable, otherwise the issues are the same.

In the Post-Walrasian vision, that jump from individual to aggregate is unacceptable. The problem of production for the economy as a whole is quite different from the problem of production for one individual. In a real world economy, complex trades have to take place to make the aggregation meaningful and those complex trades require a specified institutional structure. Thus, when one aggregates one must simultaneously adjust the model of aggregate production to correspond to the institutional structure that allows the economy to trade. *In a complex economy production for the economy requires trading institutions, conventions, and social mores that make that trading possible.* Complicated game-theoretic interactions must be resolved, and conventions developed that provide an acceptable level of stability for the economy. Market structures that reflect the complexity of that process, and which play a role in making coordination in a complex system possible, incorporate institutional solutions to those game-theoretic problems. What this means is that in the Post-Walrasian vision, *market structure is not exogenous to the system, but endogenous to the core of the system.* Market structure is part of the economy's operating system.

The formal analysis of endogenous market structures with sequentially determined equilibria is an enormously complicated issue. My interest in this chapter is not in that formal specification, which is an emerging research programme, but in finding a pedagogical way of conveying these ideas to students. With the standard aggregate production function doing so is impossible. Coordination issues are implicitly embodied in the specification of the aggregate production function, and are not considered. The standard analysis jumps from the individual firm to the aggregate without any discussion of the coordination problems among firms that are required to be solved before one can logically make such a jump.

To capture the aggregate coordinating problems that exist in the aggregate, but do not exist in the individual production functions, the aggregate production function must be modified to allow for the potential coordinating problems that can develop. The modification I have proposed (Colander, 1995) is to include a coordination variable in the aggregate production function. The change means that, instead of being specified as a direct relationship between inputs and outputs, as it is in the standard Walrasian production function, the aggregate Post-Walrasian production function is specified with an explicit coordination variable in it:

$$q = f(K, L, C)$$

Coordination is achieved by the institutional structure, of which markets are a part; that coordination will involve discretionary action by various actors in the economy. It is, itself, a produced good, requiring capital and labour; thus it has its own production function:

$$C = f(K, L)$$

What is important about this coordination when thinking about wage and price flexibility is that the market structures that society chooses to coordinate will impose certain constraints on the market coordination. These constraints create market coordination problems when viewed in relation to perfectly competitive markets, but they are necessary constraints. Without them the economy would be worse off. It is that insight – that institutional constraints are inevitable to make a functioning market – that is central to the Post-Walrasian microfoundations of macro analysis.

While adding a coordination variable to the production function may look like a small change, it has enormous implications. It requires that the choice of institutions be integrated with the analysis of market coordination within institutions. This modification also changes the role of economists in the economy. Using the standard Walrasian production function, economists are placed outside the system. In this coordination-augmented aggregate production function, economists have an explicit role: they are the economy's investment in analysing and improving coordination. Their job is a technical one – to help the economy find the optimal method of coordination. Thus, economists are not outside the economy, but are, instead, system engineers who study how different institutions coordinate, who help advise how to design new institutions, and who give advice on how to coordinate activities given existing institutions.

This respecification blurs the distinction between market and non-market institutions. It removes the implicit presumption (that there is in the standard Walrasian approach) that a perfectly competitive economy will operate efficiently. Given different degrees of coordination, the same inputs can bring about different outputs. There is no assumption of a unique equilibrium, and both real and nominal output can be expected to fluctuate independently of relative price changes as strategic decision-making results in different outcomes.

With this modified production function, one must ask how wage- and price-level flexibility affects coordination – a question that from a Walrasian framework is a non-question. In the Walrasian interpretation, it is a tautology that if there is wage- and price-level flexibility, the economy will be better off than if there is not. There is an assumed long-run anchor – the equilibrium arrived at if perfect wage- and price-level flexibility exists – that can serve as a reference point by which one can judge short-run positions. In the Post-Walrasian view, that anchor does not exist; thus there is nothing necessarily wonderful about wage- and price-level flexibility. In that Post-Walrasian view, the degree of wage- and price-level flexibility is built into the market institutions, and cannot be separated from the workings of the market.

## THE INTERPLAY BETWEEN VARIOUS DIMENSIONS OF COORDINATION

In my thinking about the macroeconomic coordination accomplished by the market, I find it useful to distinguish three interdependent dimensions of coordination. One is the institutional coordination accomplished by the system coordinating institutions; a second is the coordination accomplished by discretionary actions by players in the market given those institutions, and a third is the coordination accomplished by discretionary government actions given the chosen institutions. While both the second and third types of coordination involve discretion, it is discretion that is built into the institutional structure. This division leaves two interactive areas of coordination – market coordination and government policy coordination. But it is important to remember that these two types of coordination reflect choices made in the systemic institutional structure coordination.[2]

Why might the optimal institutional design involve less than instantaneous price and wage flexibility? One answer is that in order to handle the complex trades our economy requires, a monetary system with a unit of account is chosen. This decision to use a monetary unit of account imposes significant constraints upon the allowable degree of price-level flexibility in the system. Once one defines contracts in nominal terms, any significant fall in the price level would create tremendous redistribution of wealth, driving many firms and individuals bankrupt. As they go bankrupt, other firms they owed money to would go bankrupt and soon the whole economy would likely be in shambles. True, one could redo all contracts so that they were indexed, but that indexation would be extraordinarily costly and would undermine many of the advantages of the monetary unit of account system. Indexing contracts would involve systemic change, and could not be accomplished in any short-run period. In my view many of the social conventions that current markets have, such as relatively fixed nominal wages and prices, play a role in this extra-market systemic coordination function. Individuals know that when they go to a store the prices they will face are roughly the same as they were the last time they were at that store. That knowledge is necessary for our current market system to operate.

The choice of a 'less than instantaneous flexible price' market structure means that coordination problems will exist that discretionary action by market players will not resolve. One of those coordination problems will involve coordination of suppliers' expectations of demand. These are important, given our existing market structure, because the amount firms supply depends on the expected demand for their product, and thus, expected demand becomes a determinant of the quantity suppliers choose to supply. If the institutional coordination factor allows such fluctuations in expected aggregate demand, aggregate supply will fluctuate, and, as it does, actual aggregate demand will also fluctuate.

What I am arguing is that the degree of an economy's wage and price flexibility is most sensibly thought about as a systemic constraint. Any equilibrium that the economy arrives at because of that constraint – even ones involving large amounts of unemployment and underutilized resources – can reasonably be considered an (institutionally-constrained) equilibrium, even though, viewed from an unconstrained system, it might be seen as a disequilibrium.

The above discussion does not deny the near tautology that unemployment can only exist if the wage is, in some sense, inflexible. This is true whether or not you have a Walrasian or Post Walrasian system. *If you have perfectly flexible wages, you cannot have unemployment.*[3] But would the people in a system necessarily want perfectly flexible prices and wages? That is a more complicated question.

In a Walrasian system in which full employment is synonymous with optimal output, it is relatively easy to give a yes answer: if you can have perfectly flexible wages, you would want them. It is also not beyond reason that even if one cannot have perfectly flexible wages, one would want to have as flexible wages as possible, that is, the more flexible wages one has, the closer to optimal output the economy will reach. That proposition is the essence of the Walrasian vision and use of a full-employment equilibrium as the long run.

## HOW WAGE AND PRICE FLEXIBILITY CAN UNDERMINE INSTITUTIONAL COORDINATION

In a Post-Walrasian system, wage flexibility can undermine the coordinating functions of existing markets, and can be associated with a much lower level of overall output. Once one has chosen an operating system with relatively fixed nominal wages and prices, significant changes in those wages and prices involve giving up the current operating system, significantly lowering the achievable potential output. So, while unemployment can be eliminated by flexible wages and prices, doing so will not necessarily improve social welfare. To see this, consider Table 15.1.

*Table 15.1*  Macroeconomic operating systems and their effects on aggregate output

|   | Potential output and (actual output) | Operating system's degree of wage and price flexibility | Unemployment (%) |
|---|---|---|---|
| A | 100 (80) | Relatively fixed | 10 |
| B | 50 (50) | Perfectly flexible | 0 |

Picture state A as a short-run disequilibrium of our current economy in which the economy has fallen into an expectational conundrum causing actual output to be 20 per cent below potential output and unemployment to be 10 per cent. The reason for that unemployment is inflexible wages. But the relatively fixed wages and prices are inherent in the operating system. If one institutes a policy to achieve perfectly flexible wages and prices, and hence achieve a full employment equilibrium, one would have to give up the current operating system. Doing so leads one to state B. It is an equilibrium system that does not depend on the current operating system. It is a full employment state, but it is highly unproductive. It involves production in an economy in which the social stability imposed by relatively fixed wages – stability that was necessary to make full use of modern technology – is absent.

In a Post-Walrasian system, it is not at all clear (interpret: almost impossible) that the system would want perfectly flexible wages. Specifically, if wage-level flexibility reduces the degree of institutional coordination in the economy, it can reduce the potential output equilibrium that the economy has arrived at sufficiently to make the full employment equilibrium less desirable than the unemployment disequilibrium. Which of these two composite choices would society make? If some method exists of transferring income from employed individuals to unemployed individuals, it is quite obvious that there would be a strong argument for state A.

So that I can be clear, in Figure 15.1 I put the argument geometrically in terms of the coordination augmented production functions and labour market analysis. Let us assume that the economy starts fully coordinated both structurally and expectationally within the existing institutional structure. The production function is $F^*(C^*)$, the asterisk standing for the optimal institutional structure and the optimal expectations coordination given that institutional structure. The marginal product of labour, given perfectly coordinated expectations, is given by the $D_L^*(C^*)$ curve. The supply of labour is assumed perfectly inelastic at $L^*$. Given this situation the economy is at a full employment equilibrium with output level $Q^*$ and full employment of labour $L^*$.

Now assume that an expectational demand shock hits the system that makes suppliers believe that other suppliers are going to reduce output. Expectational coordination falls from $C^*$ to $C'$ and the existing production function shifts down to $F^*(C')$. This fall causes the demand for labour curve to shift down to $D_L^*(C')$, and, since the existing system involves fixed wages and prices, that shift embodies a decrease in labour demand from $L^*$ to $L'$. The constrained labour market equilibrium is at point A. The reduction in workers hired brings the worker's marginal product back to where it initially was equal to the real wage. The system is in an under-full employment equilibrium due to the fixed wages, but it is at a lower output level, $Q'$, because of the suppliers' demand expectations coordination problem.[4]

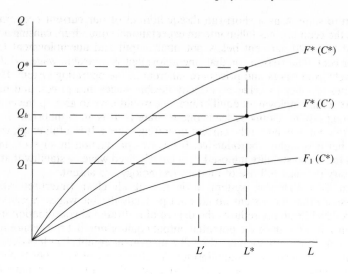

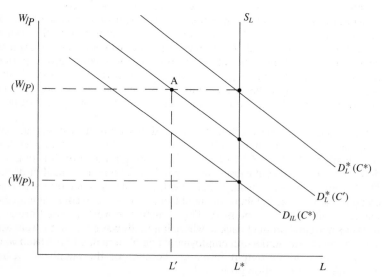

*Figure 15.1* The coordination-augmented production function and labour market

That under-full employment equilibrium, however, may be the best that the economy can do under existing coordinating institutions. To see this, let us now consider what would happen if perfectly flexible wages and prices were imposed on the system. That would change the institutional coordination of the system, and it might shift the production function down further, say to $F_1(C^*)$, and the demand for labour curve to $D_{1L}(C^*)$. The production function falls because we have removed the coordinating function that the market structure connected to fixed wages and prices was providing.[5] Given that production function, $F_1$, the economy would be at full employment but it would be at a lower level of output, $Q_1$, than it would be at if it maintained an inflexible wage- and price-level operating system. Thus, *wage flexibility* would bring about full employment, but would *reduce output* by $Q$-$Q_1$. The loss in structural coordination exceeds the market coordination gained by instituting the wage- and price-level flexibility.

The above simple example captures the central idea of the Post-Walrasian explanation of the role of wage- and price-level flexibility.[6] Too much wage- and price-level flexibility may be bad for the economy. In economics we have a habit of arguing that if slightly tweaking an equilibrium improves the situation, then continuing in that direction will do even more good. Post-Walrasians argue that this extension does not necessarily follow. To ask whether, given an inflexible wage level system, slightly modifying the degree of wage flexibility will improve the efficiency of the system, is quite different to asking whether a movement to a perfectly flexible wage system will improve the efficiency of the system. According to the Post-Walrasian approach much of the debate about wage-level flexibility has confused the two questions.

## IS THE POST-WALRASIAN EXPLANATION THE KEYNESIAN EXPLANATION?

While I would not say that Keynes, or even all Keynesians, had this Post-Walrasian explanation of wage- and price-level stability in mind when they discussed wage and price flexibility, I would say that, at least some of the time, they had it in the back of their minds, and it was one of the explanations they used to justify their assumptions. They fully understood that while a flexible aggregate price level might theoretically 'save' the economy from having any unemployment, practically it would not. Consider the following statements:

*Keynes on a flexible wage policy*

While a flexible wage policy and a flexible money policy come, analytically, to the same thing, inasmuch as they are alternative means of changing the quantity of money in terms of wage-units, in other respects there is, of course, a world of difference between them.

Having regard to human nature, it can only be a foolish person who would prefer a flexible wage policy to a flexible money policy... (Keynes, 1936, p. 268)

### Abba Lerner on the role of wage flexibility

The [Keynesian/neoclassical synthesis] with its assumptions as spelled out by Keynes, shows how flexibility of wages leads to full employment. Only an inflexibility would prevent the automatic mechanism from bringing about full employment. Why then did Keynes repeatedly insist that inflexibility downward of wages (and consequently of prices) was not the issue and would make depressions worse rather than better?

The answer to the puzzle is to be found in distinguishing between two different meanings of 'flexibility.' The flexibility required for the Neo-Classical model is an *ideal* flexibility that Keynes considered of no relevance for any problem of the real world. The spelling out of the implicit assumptions was undertaken by Keynes only in order to show up the ideal and impractical nature of the implied flexibility, and all the more effectively to *reject* the assumptions and to dismiss any reliance on that kind of flexibility. Indeed he did not even find it possible to take it seriously. (Lerner, 1978, p. 63)

### Paul Samuelson on the role of wage and price flexibility

We always assumed that the Keynesian underemployment equilibrium floated on a substructure of administered prices and imperfect competition. I stopped thinking about what was meant by rigid wages and whether you could get the real wage down; I knew it was a good working principle, a good hypothesis to explain that the real wage does not move down indefinitely so long as there is still some unemployment. Thus I assumed a disequilibrium system, in which people could not get on the supply-of-labour curve...

I guess I should emphasize this: [during the Depression] I spent four summers of my college career on the beach at Lake Michigan. I did not have a wealthy family and they could have used the income that I would have produced if I had worked, but it was pointless to look for work. I didn't even have to test the market because I had friends who would go to 350 potential employers and not be able to get any job at all. I was very conscious that the unemployed had no way of going to General Motors and offering to work for less than those who were already working there, no way of displacing already-employed workers. Moreover, the question would be: Why didn't little firms take over the automobile industry, or the steel industry, by starting up in Tennessee with low wages? And the answer to that was we thought of the Fortune 500 companies as requiring a tremendous amount of capital. Free entry was not a feasible thing and there was over-capacity in all lines. This goes back to the system being floated on imperfect competition and increasing returns technologies. (Samuelson in Colander and Landreth, 1995, p. 161)

*Samuelson on the nature of equilibrium in a model*

[When I didn't worry about microfoundations] I also probably had in mind, if you want to know why my conscience wasn't worse, the lectures I had in mathematical economics from Old Edwin Bidwell Wilson. He started life as a mathematician and mathematical physicist and was Willard Gibbs' last protege. He would describe equilibrium like this: You leave your car in the MIT parking lot overnight. The rubber tire is a membrane which separates the inside of the tire from the atmosphere, and because of this stiff wall there's an equilibrium difference in pressure. Wilson would say, 'Come back a thousand years later, and that tire will be flat.' That was not strict equilibrium. It's just a very slowly adjusting disequilibrium. The time period was involved. (Samuelson in Colander and Landreth, 1995, p. 163)

## CONCLUSION

The above argument will, I suspect, provoke four types of reactions in readers who do not share the Post-Walrasian vision. Keynesians will react in two ways.

Some will say that it is obvious, and hardly worth saying. My answer to this group is that what is obvious to one group often is not obvious to others; seemingly unresolvable debates occur when something obvious is not explained, and that obvious explanation incorporated in the argument. As Keynesian ideas were formalized, this obvious explanation for wage- and price-level flexibility was implicitly ruled out by the Walrasian unique equilibrium simultaneous equation framework within which the formalization was done. Had the Keynesian model explicitly stated the need for an institutional framework that incorporated fixed, or slowly adjusting, wages and prices as a systemic constraint, not as an imperfection, many of the latter debates could have been avoided.

Other Keynesians will say that it is not what Keynes or the Keynesians had in mind at all, and they will be able to point to other quotations where Keynes and the Keynesians supported a quite different view. My answer to this group is that they are right. Keynes, and Keynesians, said many things, many of them inconsistent. My argument for this Post-Walrasian systemic explanation of wage- and price-level stability is formulated for economists of the 1990s who are trained in a different fashion, and in a different tradition than earlier economists. Arguments are part of a framework of discussion, and it is unlikely that arguments made fifty years ago would have the same structure as arguments made today. My only historical point is that this view is consistent with some aspects of earlier Keynesian thinking, such as that which John Cornwall has consistently expounded. Clearly, if it had been consistent with all aspects, they would have said it explicitly rather than simply mentioning it in places.

Similarly, New Classicals will respond in two ways. Some will argue that the systemic constraint argument is too easy – it misses the point that markets adjust, and while, yes, the market may experience systemic constraints in the short run, in the long run wage and price flexibility will reign, and that coordinating through the market price adjustment is the best policy. My answer to this group is that nothing in the argument presented precludes the possibility that long-run wage and price flexibility may be the best policy. But that is an argument that must be made, and current Classical models do not make it. They simply assume it. Once one accepts that wage- and price-level flexibility imposes a systemic constraint on the system, the effect of that systemic constraint on that equilibrium must be incorporated into the dynamics of one's explanation. If one accepts this view, then the nature of the macro models and forms of argumentation in macro will change. Specifically, searching for a microfoundation independent of the structure of the economy will no longer be a meaningful search.

Others will respond, 'So that is what is meant by Keynesian economics; had I known it I never would have become a New Classical, and I would have followed a quite different research agenda.' (This would only be said in their heads, and would be quickly forgotten via cognitive dissonance.) 'But since I have already established too much specific human capital in my current research agenda, I will simply continue in my current path, and ignore any such Post-Walrasian arguments.'

To this last group, I have little to say other than that their answer itself shows the importance of systemic constraints, and shows how a profession can get moving toward an undesirable equilibrium and remain there, even though almost all individuals know a preferable equilibrium exists.

## Notes

1.  By including a psychic cost of being dishonest one can make the cost/benefit approach tautological, but that simply translates institutions into something that affects the individual's taste and hence part of the analysis since tastes can no longer be assumed exogenous.

2.    This overall framework of viewing coordination encompasses the Walrasian view as an extreme case of institutional choice – one assigning all discretionary coordination to the market, and none to government policy.

3.    It is possible by assuming no equilibria to require qualifications to this statement, but even discussing those qualifications only makes sense in a Walrasian framework; in a Post-Walrasian framework it is a silly debating point irrelevant to the central debate.

4.    It is possible for analytic purposes to divide the cause of the unemployment up into two components. The fall from $Q^*$ to $Q_h$ (the output derived from $F^*(C')$ with employment $L^*$) is due to expectational coordination problems; the fall from $Q_h$ to $Q'$ is due to the fixed real wages that is necessary for the $F^*$ production function to exist.

5.    That fixity provided sociological coordination – getting people to accept the existing relativities without objecting to the current system, or having a breakdown of existing social norms.

6.    The central ideas carry through to the real world even though the example presents the choice far too starkly. The issue is seldom so clear. Operating systems can be changed and tweaked, and each operating system may be associated with different degrees of wage-level flexibility. One might be able to modify the system so it had more wage-level flexibility, but no price-level flexibility. The analysis of doing so is, however, an institutional analysis, and must be analysed within a larger context than is generally done.

## References

Colander, D. (1995) 'The stories we tell: a reconsideration of AS/AD analysis', *Journal of Economic Perspectives*, 9, 169–88

Colander, D. (ed.) (1996) *Beyond Micro Foundations: Post Walrasian Macroeconomics*, Cambridge, Cambridge University Press

Colander, D. and H. Landreth (eds) (1995) *The Coming of Keynesianism to America*, Aldershot, Edward Elgar

Keynes, J.M. (1936) *The General Theory of Employment, Interest and Money*, New York, Harcourt Brace

Lerner, A. (1978) 'Keynesianism: alive, if not so well, at forty', in J. Buchanan and R. Wagner (eds) *Fiscal Responsibility in a Constitutional Democracy*, Boston, MA, Martinus Nijhoff

# 16 Unemployment and Post-Keynesian Monetary Theory

Steven Pressman[1]

Unemployment once again plagues the world economy. Since the beginning of the 1990s, unemployment rates in Europe have averaged close to 10 per cent. Things have become so bad that even Sweden, once proudly boasting unemployment rates consistently below 2 per cent, has watched helplessly while 13 per cent of its labour force cannot find work.

Things are not much better in the rest of the developed world. Canadian unemployment appears stuck at double-digit levels; Japanese unemployment, while still low by European standards, continues to rise and remains at thirty-year highs. Only the United States has come anywhere close to approaching full employment levels during the 1990s. But economic expansion cannot go on for ever. At some point the peak of the 1990s business cycle will be reached, a downturn will begin, and the US economy will cease to be an economic anomaly.

High and rising unemployment throughout the world naturally raises the question: 'What is causing this problem?' As the world has come to expect from a group of economists, many different answers to this question have been proposed. (For contemporary mainstream views see Federal Reserve Bank of Kansas City (1995); for non-mainstream views see the *Review of Political Economy* (1995).)

One of the major themes in the work of John Cornwall has been the necessity of Keynesian demand management policies to remedy the problem of unemployment. In fact, a large part of his work has argued that such policies have worked in the past to reduce unemployment. Cornwall has also argued that one obstacle to employing Keynesian demand management policies has been the fear of inflation. As a practical matter, therefore, anti-inflationary policies must accompany demand management policies in the real world. For this reason Cornwall (1983, 1990, 1993, 1994; Cornwall and Cornwall, 1996) has argued vehemently and cogently for an incomes policy to deal with inflation so that traditional macroeconomic policies can focus on reducing unemployment.

But there is a second obstacle standing in the way of using demand management policies. This is a theoretical dispute among economists regarding the nature of unemployment itself. Mainstream, neoclassical macroeconomists usually argue that unemployment is due either to people searching for new and better jobs (Hall, 1970), or else that it is due to imperfections in the labour market (Friedman, 1968). The policy solutions stemming from this analysis are, respectively, to do nothing and to remove labour market imperfections (like unions and minimum wage laws) so that wages adjust to their equilibrium level and clear the labour market.

Non-mainstream economists reject these propositions. In particular, Post-Keynesians deny that economies will adjust to full employment, and argue that labour market equilibrium can be reached at less than full employment. A fundamental tenet of Post-Keynesian economics is the belief that involuntary unemployment stems from some of the essential characteristics of a monetary production economy (see Dillard, 1948; Davidson, 1972, 1982, 1994; Minsky, 1975, 1986; Moore, 1978; Wray, 1990). Economies with credit money can experience unemployment; in contrast, barter economies (those without money) are worlds in which Say's Law holds and where unemployment cannot exist. Similarly, according to the Post-Keynesians, models that incorporate credit money into their universe can explain the existence of unemployment, while economic models that fail to include credit money cannot explain the presence of unemployment. Because of their sharp focus on money as a cause of unemployment, Post-Keynesians have drawn boundaries between themselves and other heterodox schools of economic thought, such as Sraffians and Marxists, who tend to see unemployment as stemming primarily from the nature of the production relationship.

The remainder of this chapter examines the Post-Keynesian argument about money and unemployment in greater detail. The first section presents the Post-Keynesian view that money causes unemployment in a developed capitalist economy. The second section looks at three different economies where people are self-employed – one economy that relies on barter, one that relies on commodity money, and one that relies on credit money. It argues that unemployment is unlikely to arise in any economy where most people are self-employed. This is true regardless of whether the economy is a barter economy, a commodity money economy, or a credit money economy. The third section then examines three different economies where people are not self-employed, but must offer their labour services to others in order to survive. This section argues that unemployment can exist in such economies, whether trade takes place through barter or with the help of credit money. The final section concludes by pulling together the key points of the previous two sections, and by arguing that it is the production relationship that leads to involuntary unemployment. However, this conclusion needs to be qualified in two important respects. Post-Keynesians are correct that introducing money makes unemployment more likely in a production economy. And somewhat paradoxically, although the Post-Keynesian explanation of unemployment is incorrect, their policy prescriptions remain valid and important.

## THE POST-KEYNESIAN VIEW OF THE CAUSES OF UNEMPLOYMENT

The standard Post-Keynesian view is that unemployment stems from a monetary production economy, with the emphasis placed on the adjective (money) rather than the noun (production). In what follows the focus will be primarily on the work of Paul Davidson. This is justifiable since Davidson has been at the forefront of Post-Keynesian monetary theory for several decades, as well as being editor of the *Journal of Post Keynesian Economics*. He has written several books stressing the fact that it is money, and the nature of money, that is responsible for unemployment. Without doubt he is the most prominent Post-Keynesian monetary theorist. However, this section does not depend entirely on the work of Paul Davidson; similar remarks from other Post-Keynesians, and from Keynes himself, will show that the themes emphasized by Davidson are indeed major themes of the Post-Keynesians.

These themes are quite simple and straightforward. Davidson and other Post-Keynesian monetary theorists have argued that unemployment results from characteristics of the real world that involve money and monetary relationships. Unemployment exists because of the nature of money, and because transactions take place in real world economies that use bank or credit money.

In addition, Davidson contends that the essential features of money are not captured in general equilibrium models, or in Sraffian models, or in any other production-oriented models, where money plays no role. This latter argument has become an important source of friction between American Post-Keynesians and the Sraffian or neo-Ricardian school. In fact, the two schools have become sharply and deeply divided on this issue. The Post-Keynesians have castigated the Sraffians for failing to allow money in their model, and therefore for failing to allow for unemployment through the lack of demand in a monetary economy. On the other hand, the Sraffians have criticized the Post-Keynesians for making logical errors or violating key economic assumptions when they put money into their economic models and then attempt to explain unemployment based on the characteristics of money. Eatwell and Milgate (1983, p. 161n) find this objectionable and claim that it is important to 'smoke out the imperfectionist interpretations of Keynes's theory of output and employment'. The Post-Keynesian school, which introduces inefficiencies into the real economy via money and the monetary economy, is the main imperfectionist interpretation of Keynes that is 'smoked out' (and then treated quite harshly – see, for example, the essay by Magnani in Eatwell and Milgate (1983)).

Davidson (1994, p. 17) argues that money matters in the real world in both the long run and the short run, that unemployment is the normal outcome of an entrepreneurial money-using economy, and that several essential characteristics of money lead to unemployment. Similarly, Dillard (1948, pp. 201ff.) argues that unemployment results from sticky interest rates. It is the downward inflexibility of interest rates that is the cause of unemployment; and it is money, or at least the nature of credit money in a developed capitalist economy, that leads to unemployment. And Minsky (1975, 1986) contends that unemployment results because at times, both lenders and borrowers face great uncertainty. Lenders are unsure that the money they lend out will be repaid, and thus demand high interest rates; while borrowers expect lower returns and thus are less likely to want to borrow money. Davidson, Dillard and Minsky all follow Keynes (1964, ch. 17) in arguing that money is at root responsible for unemployment, since it is money that affects interest rates, which in turn affects the level of employment.

Money, according to Davidson (1994, p. 18; 1972, pp. 145f.) has two essential characteristics that lead to unemployment in a world with an unpredictable and unknowable future. Money plays an important role in creating unemployment because it has a zero elasticity of production and because there are no substitutes for money. The former characteristic refers to the fact people do not produce money. In an economy where most money is bank money, greater demand for money does not create employment the way that a greater demand for goods and services creates jobs. The second characteristic of money refers to the fact that there are no substitutes for money as a store of value. Only money will be able to fulfil future contractual obligations, and only money can be used in the future to purchase goods and services. Because the future is uncertain, there is no substitute for holding money to take care of future obligations or to meet future needs. Individuals will need money in order to pay for things in the future, and businesses will require money to meet their contractual obligations, such as payrolls and interest payments on past borrowing. Thus, money has an elasticity of substitution that is near zero: 'as the exchange value of money rises there is no tendency to substitute some other factor for it' (Keynes, 1964, p. 231).

Following along the lines of Davidson and Keynes, Dillard sees the low elasticities of production and substitution as leading to a situation where the demand for money does not result in a corresponding demand for labour. He also adds a third characteristic that is important for creating unemployment in a monetary economy. For Dillard (1948, ch. 8), in a world of uncertainty there will always be a high demand for money as a store of value. Thus, the linkage is made between money, interest and employment, and this connection explains the title of Keynes's famous book. It is the characteristics of money that keep interest rates from fluctuating in a manner that would generate the full employment of labour resources.

We can now pull together the Post-Keynesian argument regarding unemployment. If people wish to hold money, and do not want to spend money, there will be too little demand for goods and services. Businesses will cut back production and lay off workers. Those laid off will not be able to move into the money-producing sectors of the economy (that is, banks and the Federal Reserve Banks) because greater demand for money does not require many additional workers to meet this demand. Workers who get laid off will become unemployed and will remain unemployed, barring any economic policies to increase aggregate expenditures.

Likewise, the shift in demand towards money and away from goods and services will not increase the value of money relative to other goods, and thereby increase the demand for other goods, because there is no substitute for money as a means of payment in the future. Interest rates do not fall and do not create additional purchasing power. Anyone wishing to buy something in the future must hold money. And since the future is uncertain people will want to hold money and will need to hold money.

In fact, unemployment has the potential to increase uncertainty and thereby increase the demand for money to meet future obligations. Workers who read newspaper articles about lay-offs at one corporation after another, and who see friends lose their jobs, will naturally worry that they might be next. These workers will likely increase their demand for money, saving more and buying less, so that in the event that they become unemployed, they will have a bigger cushion to weather the hard times without a job or steady income.

Moreover, banks will be worried about the ability of borrowers to repay their loans in an economy with high unemployment and inadequate demand. They will either stop lending entirely, or they will have to raise interest rates on loans to compensate for the fact that loans are unlikely to be repaid. This, too, will tend to keep unemployment from adjusting to the full employment level (Minsky, 1986; Wray, 1990).

To summarize, it is money and the monetary economy that creates and perpetuates unemployment according to the Post-Keynesian school. Abstract models of the economy that dispense with money cannot explain how unemployment arises. These models are thus impotent to devise economic policies to deal with the problem of unemployment. Or, as Davidson (1994, p. 27) writes: 'In sum, Keynes's principle of effective demand demonstrates that, in a non-ergodic world, it is the existence of nonreproducible assets that are held for liquidity purposes and for which the products of industry are not gross substitutes that is the fundamental cause of involuntary unemployment.'

## THE POST-KEYNESIAN ARGUMENT IN A SELF-EMPLOYMENT ECONOMY

Unfortunately, demonstrating that unemployment exists in a monetary economy and that it results from people holding money does not clinch the argument that unemployment is *necessarily* the result of credit money or a monetary production economy. It may be the case that unemployment can arise in any sort of economy. If this is true, then the Post-Keynesian story would be a special case of the more general principle that all economies can experience unemployment. Alternatively, it may be that unemployment only arises in certain types of economies, and that monetary economies are just one of many different situations in which unemployment can exist. Unless Post-Keynesians demonstrate that unemployment cannot and does not exist in other situations, they cannot claim that money is the root cause of unemployment and that unemployment exists only because of money.

Real world economies are characterized both by the use of credit money and the need to offer one's labour services in order to receive the goods and services necessary for continued survival. Post-Keynesians, by failing to distinguish between money and employment relations as a cause of unemployment, have ignored this other potential cause of unemployment. Because money and wage labour go together in the real world, it is easy to conflate and confuse them, and to focus on only one of these two potential causes of unemployment. Our goal will be to separate the monetary and the labour-related causes of unemployment, and to show that the latter factor is also important.

Our procedure in the rest of this section is as follows. We examine three simple, hypothetical economies where everyone is self-employed. First, we examine an economy that employs barter rather than money. A second economy employs commodity money, but not credit money. Finally, we look at an economy where money is created when banks or financial institutions make loans. In the next section we repeat the procedure, but we examine three situations in which individuals typically offer their labour services to employers.

We begin with a simple agrarian economy where everyone is self-employed. So that we do not exclude the possibility of unemployment by definition for any self-employed economy, we define unemployment here as a condition whereby individuals who work or seek work in order to meet their material needs are unable to find work that will provide for these needs. We do not assume anything about wages or about the extent to which employment fully provides for all the things one desires. These are important issues; however, they are not germane to the question of unemployment. Unemployment is an important economic problem not because people are unable to earn everything they want, but rather because people are unable to earn enough to survive.

To begin, suppose that in our simple agrarian economy everyone produces most of the goods that they themselves consume. In this case, unemployment is, indeed, impossible. Individuals work for themselves, their work provides for their material needs, and their own demand for goods determines how much they work.

We have a slightly more interesting situation when individuals specialize in producing certain goods, and then barter with others for the goods that they do not produce themselves. According to standard and sacred economic principles regarding the benefits of specialization and trade, such practices should improve everyone's standard of living. More goods can be produced with specialization, and trade allows for greater consumption of the additional output.

However, such specialization and trade should not lead to unemployment in our simple, agrarian economy. If having more goods leads to a greater demand for leisure, people will cut back on their work time; but they remain employed because they are still producing goods that meet most of their material needs (remember the definition of 'unemployment' we have adopted and our reason for adopting it). Some individuals may want to increase their standard of living and use the productivity gains from specialization to consume more goods. The problem these people face is that those individuals who demand more leisure have reduced their demand for goods. Some of the individuals who desire more goods may be able to trade with one another and thereby succeed in improving their living standard. Alternatively, they may be able to produce some of the goods they desire but cannot obtain through trade. Finally, they may have to reduce production because they cannot find anyone willing to trade for the additional output they might produce. Even in this last case, these people are not unemployed; they do have a job and do provide for their own subsistence needs.

It is only in the following situation that we even come close to the possibility of unemployment in a self-employed, barter economy. If someone produces goods that are not in demand at all, this person is not earning his livelihood and is not providing for his physical needs – although he is producing something. While in one sense self-employed (because this person is working at producing something), this individual is really unemployed, since employment provides no income and fails to provide for subsistence. Hence, we have unemployment here in the short run. However, if this person is able to shift production towards goods that are in greater demand, or towards those goods that he needs and would like to consume (food for humans rather than hay for horses), he will be producing his own subsistence needs and should not be counted as unemployed. Thus in our self-employed barter economy, employment is assured in the long run if individuals are flexible in what they produce and can produce sufficient output to meet their own subsistence needs.

We now introduce commodity money or fiat money into the economy. Following Moore (1988) fiat money is taken to be an asset (like gold, silver, or government paper) that, unlike credit money created by banks, generates no corresponding liabilities. With the introduction of commodity money, individuals attempt to sell goods for some commodity which serves as the means of exchange, rather than bartering for goods that are needed but not produced at home. For simplicity we assume that gold and silver serve this function, and examine the effect of the existence of commodity money in the form of gold and silver on unemployment.

Again, it is necessary to consider what happens to the individual producing some commodity for which there is little demand because few people want to turn over gold or silver to obtain that good. Initially, this individual is not earning enough to survive. With insufficient gold or silver, he cannot demand other goods and services. But the situation here is not really all that different from the barter case. With little demand for his output, the individual faces a choice. He must either decide to enjoy more leisure time and a lower material standard of living, or he must change the goods he produces so that others want them. Switching the type of output produced will yield more commodity money and a greater ability to use that commodity money to purchase other things. Again, there is no unemployment as long as people can be flexible and produce more of the things that they want and/or more of the things that other people are willing to give up commodity money for. Of course, there is a greater possibility that demand shortfalls will arise due to the fact that commodity money is more likely to be hoarded than goods. But on the other hand, when a demand for goods does not exist, people can 'find employment' by staking a claim and producing commodity money. If a sufficient number of 'free' (that is, unowned) mines exist, unemployment is not a possibility.

With credit or bank money things do not change very much. One important difference is that money can no longer be mined or produced. Rather money gets created by the banking or financial system when loans are made. To simplify, we assume that most money takes the form of bank deposits, and money gets created when banks make loans.

It should be noted here that the two essential characteristics of money identified by the Post-Keynesians hold in this sort of economy. Unlike the commodity money economy, in a credit money economy, whenever there is little demand for goods and great demand for money, there is no possibility of producing money. Money is produced and created by banks. If loans are not demanded, money is not created. And even when money is created by banks, this is not a very labour-intensive activity. Moreover, there is no substitute for bank money when dealing with an uncertain future in a bank-money economy – bank deposits are needed to deal with future obligations and needs. Thus, the standard Post-Keynesian characteristics of money are present in this case.

Yet, like the commodity money case, there should be no unemployment here. As long as people can switch production, and produce more of those goods in greater demand (either by themselves or others), they can still work and produce and earn their livelihoods. Moreover, in a credit money economy there are greater possibilities for borrowing money to produce goods when demand is low. In a commodity money economy, borrowing is constrained by the supply of gold and silver coins in existence and the willingness of people hoarding these coins to lend them at a certain interest rate. In a credit money economy, with fractional bank reserves, the lending that can take place will exceed the amount of money that is originally deposited into the financial institution. Thus, lack of demand by others in a credit money economy provides a smaller constraint on achieving full employment than lack of demand in a commodity money economy or in a pure barter economy.

If the analysis of this section is correct, then Post-Keynesian arguments about money being the one and only cause of unemployment cannot be correct. For when we introduce credit money into an economy where everyone is self-employed, unemployment fails to rear its ugly head. As long as individuals can produce things that meet their own material needs they can not be considered unemployed.

Unemployment certainly can arise in a self-employed economy. Moreover, one does not need to be an economist to recognize such a possibility. In *The Grapes of Wrath*, John Steinbeck described how the farmland in the Midwest became a dustbowl. Farmers whose land could not grow crops any more found themselves unemployed and unable to provide for their own material needs. The weather and the Great Depression destroyed a large part of the self-employed farm economy.

However, it is not clear that this unemployment has anything to do with money or the characteristics of a monetary economy. Rather, Steinbeck's 'Okies' became unemployed because of changes that occurred in the self-employed economy. This economy was no longer viable. The land, which previously could sustain families, was no longer able to do so; families could no longer support themselves with home production and were forced to find jobs elsewhere. Following the path taken by the Joads in Steinbeck's classic novel, we now move from the self-employment economy to the wage–labour economy.

## THE POST-KEYNESIAN ARGUMENT IN A WAGE–LABOUR ECONOMY

In this section, we consider three cases where few individuals are self-employed and self-sufficient. Instead, most people offer their labour services in order to earn incomes and provide for their sustenance.

As in the previous section, we begin with the barter case. Workers offer their services to employers in exchange for a fraction of the goods and services they produce during the course of the day; workers then seek to barter these goods for the other goods and services that they might want. This case clearly brings out the fact that workers do not receive all the output that they produce during the day. Business owners or entrepreneurs extract some output in the form of a surplus.

Can involuntary unemployment exist under such conditions? The Post-Keynesian response must be 'no', for there is no money and no credit money here; but I think the correct answer to this question is 'yes'. Somewhat ironically, the possibility of unemployment in a barter economy that contains wage–labour relationships comes from Keynes himself – specifically, from the famous banana parable from the *Treatise on Money* (Keynes, 1958–60, pp. 176ff.). It is well-known that numerous problems plague this parable. For example, it is a one-sector, one-commodity world, which precludes the possibility that changes in relative prices can eliminate temporary bouts of unemployment. Hayek (1931) criticized the banana parable, arguing that if the model were extended to include another good, such as machinery, lack of demand for bananas would lower the price of bananas and raise the price of machinery. This change in relative prices would then assure full employment as workers laid off from the banana-producing sector would find jobs in the sector that is producing new machines. When Keynes (1973, p. 233) briefly allowed investment goods into his model (banana-cutters), he ruled out by assumption the possibility that higher prices for these machines could increase their output (and thus increase employment). Robinson (1933) criticized the banana parable because, while it implied that equilibrium output could be at any level, the *Treatise* lacked a theory of output. Generating even further confusion, the banana parable explains lay-offs and unemployment by means of a falling price of bananas, which leads to losses by businesses and thus reduced production and hiring. Left unexplained by Keynes is how the relative price of bananas could possibly fall when bananas are the only commodity produced.

Yet the banana parable is less important for its logical flaws and more important for its vision. The parable demonstrates what Keynes was thinking about regarding the possibility of unemployment and the potential causes of unemployment (see Dimand, 1988; Skidelsky, 1992). It shows that for Keynes in general, and for the banana economy in particular, a lack of demand for goods leads to reduced production. This, in turn, leads to lay-offs and unemployment. In what follows, this case is made using a two-sector, two-good model. The two goods will be bananas and huts, and the two sectors will be an agricultural sector that produces bananas and a manufacturing sector that produces huts.

Suppose that in this economy people desire to hoard the existing stock of goods they possess, or become averse to bartering. One explanation for such behaviour, which is consistent with the usual rationality assumptions made by economists, is that many people believe that the particular goods they hold will increase most in value over the next several months. These beliefs cannot all hold true in a two-good world, since one of the two goods must increase in value by more than the other good. However, within a group of rational individuals, everyone can simultaneously *believe* that they are holding the good that will increase most in value. In a world with an uncertain future, everyone can have different beliefs about the best goods to hold, or which goods will appreciate most. In all likelihood, some people will be wrong in their beliefs; but being wrong does not make these people irrational.

A more complicated explanation for the desire to hoard goods would focus on the costs of bartering relative to the gains to be made from bartering. If people think the costs of bartering exceed the gains, they will keep the current set of goods that they hold and not even attempt to barter them for other goods that might be more desired.

Making the usual Post-Keynesian assumptions, we suppose that only capitalists or entrepreneurs in the two producing sectors will hoard goods. Workers, in contrast, consume all the goods they receive in exchange for their labour services, or barter these goods for some other goods that they then consume.

Entrepreneurs in both the banana-producing sector and the hut-producing sector will want to hoard some goods, for this is the only way that they can save. But entrepreneurs will want to hoard goods only up to some limit. Unlike credit money, there are storage costs from hoarding commodities and there is also the possibility of spoilage. Thus, as hoards of bananas and huts rise, the marginal benefit of additional hoards will decline while the marginal cost of additional hoards will increase. At some point entrepreneurs in both sectors will find that the marginal benefit of accumulating more goods is less than the marginal cost of accumulating hoards of goods. At this point entrepreneurs have reached the maximum amount of goods they desire to hoard. There is no more demand for hoards. Furthermore, even before this point is reached, some entrepreneurs will face a situation whereby the benefits from extra hoards of bananas or huts will be less than the benefits of producing and storing additional output. When this point is reached, production should cease.

This saturation point may be reached when all workers are employed producing goods. Alternatively, it may be reached before all workers offering their labour services get hired. In this case, some workers will be unable to find work. They will be unable to earn enough to meet their subsistence needs, and they will be unemployed according to our definition. Under such circumstances, these workers cannot solve their unemployment problem by offering to work for lower wages. Since wages are paid in the form of goods, lower wages paid out to workers will increase the surplus output of entrepreneurs, which is already at or beyond the maximum desired level.

Workers, as a whole, could solve the unemployment problem by increasing their demand for goods and buying some of the surplus hoards that entrepreneurs do not want. The problem they face, however, is that they do not have the goods to do this. Earning subsistence wages or less, they already consume all that they earn, and they have no past savings to use as a means of increasing demand and saving their jobs. Moreover, they have no ability to borrow and consume more today than they earn, another means of increasing demand and maintaining levels of full employment.

In addition, changing relative prices, or shifting production from one sector to another, will not help solve the unemployment problem that exists in the banana-and-hut economy. Both bananas and huts are being hoarded to the maximum level desired by entrepreneurs; entrepreneurs in both sectors do not want to produce any more goods since such goods will only add to the stock of undesired hoards.

By similar reasoning, anyone who is laid off will not be able to convince other employers to make them a job offer. Other employers also face a lack of demand for their output, and have problems bartering away all the goods that they produce and do not want to keep. Hence other employers are unlikely to expand production and employment.

If teamwork and morale problems are not an issue, if experience is irrelevant, and if efficiency wage theory turns out to be wrong, a firm may think about replacing its existing work force with those people recently laid off from other firms, who now offer their labour services for less. But this action will not solve the aggregate unemployment problem. At best it merely shuffles the problem from one group of workers to another. Even worse, because of interrelationships between distribution and demand (see Pressman, 1997), lower wage rates will reduce overall spending (or the desire to barter) and thus lead to even greater unemployment. And perhaps worst of all, if unemployed workers receive less output, the employer surplus increases, causing a further decline in production.

In this non-monetary production economy, Say's Law fails to hold – the supply of goods does not necessarily result in a demand for those goods and a supply of workers does not lead to a demand for those workers. Firms may produce goods and not be able to barter them to other firms or individuals. Under such circumstances, there will be a shortfall of demand. Firms will lay off workers; and workers will be unemployed as long as there is not enough demand for the goods they produce.

Notice again that there is no money in this economy. As in the banana parable, unemployment results quite simply from the desire to hoard goods. Consequently, unemployment cannot be the result of introducing money into a modern production economy. Introducing bank money into the story does make matters worse, however, as we shall see below.

But first consider the introduction of commodity money. Since money is not perishable (it is a good store of value) and has only minor holding costs (two important qualities of money identified by Keynes (1964)), people will desire to hoard more money than they would hoard automobiles, clothing, food or shelter. This makes the lack-of-demand problem much worse in a monetary economy than it is in a banana-and-hut economy.

Another consequence of introducing commodity money is that laid-off workers may now be able to meet their survival needs by producing money. The existence of mines containing these precious metals becomes a potential outlet for unemployed workers. When gold and silver are demanded rather than goods, production shifts from making goods to making fiat money. As long as such possibilities exist, workers cannot be unemployed. Such possibilities will exist if anyone can lay claim to their own mine, or if the entrepreneurs who own gold and silver mines have an infinite demand for labour because they have an infinite demand for hoards of commodity money.

Finally, let us consider the full-blown monetary production economy, where workers are hired by businesses and where exchange takes place with credit money created by banks. The introduction of credit money has one important result – money can no longer be mined. Therefore, a greater demand for money cannot be met by expanding the production of money.

As a result, we face unemployment for the same reasons discussed in the wage–labour barter economy – there is insufficient demand for goods and services. Businesses cannot solve the problem of too few sales by shifting production to those goods that are in greater demand; they can only lay off workers. Workers, similarly, cannot solve the problem of insufficient demand by offering to work for less; they can only solve the problem by buying more. But buying more entails their having money to purchase goods, or else convincing employers that they will purchase more goods if they are hired. Since workers for hire lack the money to buy goods without a job, and since they cannot be held accountable for promises to buy goods that were made when they were hired, insufficient demand continues and insufficient demand will remain a major problem. Workers must be laid off. Here, unemployment exists for all the reasons cited by the Post-Keynesians – people want to hoard money and production of bank money requires few workers.

Finally, we come up against the major difference between the self-employed economy and the wage–labour economy. In the self-employed economy, workers remain employed so long as they have the ability to contribute towards their own subsistence. They are employed because they are essentially their own employer and they have the ability to produce goods that will prevent them from starving. In the wage–labour economy, workers are unable to produce such goods because they lack adequate land and adequate capital. The only way they can earn a living and avoid starvation is by selling their labour services. Absent sufficient demand for these services, workers become unemployed. Thus the essential prerequisite for unemployment is not money, but an economy in which workers do not have the means to support themselves, and must survive by offering their labour services to others. Nonetheless, the essential Post-Keynesian vision holds true – the existence of credit money in a production economy means that greater demand for money reduces demand for goods, which in turn reduces the demand for labour and generates additional unemployment.

## SUMMARY AND POLICY CONCLUSIONS

We have seen above that unemployment cannot exist in a simple economy where individuals are able to produce goods for their own subsistence. This is true regardless of whether or not the economy relies on money to facilitate trade. On the other hand, in a wage–labour production economy, unemployment is likely to arise regardless of whether or not money is used. Here, the lack of demand due to hoarding limits (or ceilings) will lead to a lack of demand for labour. Since workers are not self-sufficient and since employers will not hire additional workers, even at lower wages, workers cannot meet their subsistence needs. These workers can only be classified as unemployed. Consequently, it is not money that creates unemployment. Rather, unemployment arises because of the nature of the production relationship – the fact that some people must offer their labour services for hire, and cannot support themselves by producing on their own. However, money does matter since money and the essential characteristics of money make the unemployment problem more severe.

Because money matters in this latter sense, Post-Keynesian policy prescriptions for achieving full employment continue to hold. A focus on increasing and stabilizing effective demand is the simplest and most direct means of mitigating unemployment, especially since, as we have seen, the unemployment problem initially arises from a lack of demand for goods. In addition, it is easier to expand demand than it is to change employment relationships. Stimulative fiscal and monetary policy, stable exchange rates to facilitate international trade, redistributive policies, and policies to encourage production and consumption rather than speculation all become pragmatic solutions to the unemployment problem. In contrast, attempts to change production relationships will involve great disruption of the capitalist system, will face great political opposition, and will likely incur great transitional costs.

**Note**

1.  Earlier versions of this chapter were presented at the Eastern Economic Association Meetings and at the New School for Social Research Post Keynesian Workshop. The author thanks the participants at these sessions, especially Ahmed Al-Hassan, Paul Davidson, Thomas Michl and Roy Rotheim, for their helpful comments.

**References**

Cornwall, J. (1983) *The Conditions for Economic Recovery: A Post-Keynesian Analysis*, White Plains, NY, M.E. Sharpe

Cornwall, J. (1990) *The Theory of Economic Breakdown: An Institutional-Analytical Approach*, Cambridge, MA, Basil Blackwell

Cornwall, J. (1993) 'Full employment in the 1990s', *Challenge*, 36 (November/December), 4–11

Cornwall, J. (1994) *Economic Breakdown and Recovery: Theory and Policy*, Armonk, NY, M.E. Sharpe

Cornwall, J. and W. Cornwall (1996) 'A Keynesian framework for studying institutional change and evolutionary processes', in S. Pressman (ed.) *Interactions in Political Economy: Malvern After Ten Years*, London, Routledge

Davidson, P. (1972) *Money and the Real World*, London, Macmillan

Davidson, P. (1982) *International Money and the Real World*, London, Macmillan

Davidson, P. (1994) *Post Keynesian Macroeconomic Theory*, Aldershot, Edward Elgar

Dillard, D. (1948) *The Economics of J.M. Keynes: The Theory of Monetary Policy*, New York, Prentice-Hall

Dimand, R. (1988) *The Origins of the Keynesian Revolution: The Development of Keynes's Theory of Employment and Output*, Stanford, CA, Stanford University Press

Eatwell, J. and M. Milgate (eds) (1983) *Keynes's Economics and the Theory of Value and Distribution*, New York, Oxford University Press

Federal Reserve Bank of Kansas City (1995) *Reducing Unemployment: Current Issues and Policy Options*, Federal Reserve Bank of Kansas City

Friedman, M. (1968) 'The role of monetary policy', *American Economic Review*, 63, 1–17

Hall, R.E. (1970) 'Why is the unemployment rate so high at full employment?', *Brookings Papers on Economic Activity*, 3, 369–402

Hayek, F.A. (1931) 'Reflections on the pure theory of money of Mr. J.M. Keynes', *Economica*, 11, 270–95

Keynes, J.M. (1958–60) *A Treatise on Money*, 2 vols, London, Macmillan

Keynes, J.M. (1964) *The General Theory of Employment, Interest and Money*, New York, Harcourt Brace

Keynes, J.M. (1973) *The Collected Writings of John Maynard Keynes, Vol. XIII: The General Theory and After*, London, Macmillan

Minsky, H. (1975) *John Maynard Keynes*, New York, Columbia University Press

Minsky, H. (1986) *Stabilizing an Unstable Economy*, New Haven, CT, Yale University Press

Moore, B. (1978) 'Monetary factors', in A.S. Eichner (ed.) *A Guide to Post Keynesian Economics*, Armonk, NY, M.E. Sharpe

Moore, B. (1988) *Horizontalists and Verticalists*, Cambridge, Cambridge University Press

Pressman, S. (1997) 'Keynes, taxation and income distribution', *Journal of Income Distribution*, 7, 29–44

*Review of Political Economy* (1995) 7, 2 (special issue on high unemployment in the world economy)

Robinson, J. (1933) 'The theory of money and the analysis of output', *Review of Economic Studies*, 1, 22–6

Skidelsky, R. (1992) *John Maynard Keynes: The Economist as Saviour*, London, Penguin

Wray, L.R. (1990) *Money and Credit in Capitalist Economies*, Aldershot, Edward Elgar

# 17 Wage Determination, Capital Shortage and Unemployment: A Comparison between Germany and the UK

Philip Arestis and
Iris Biefang-Frisancho Mariscal

## INTRODUCTION

This chapter relates to John Cornwall's work in two major ways. First, we develop a conflict model of inflation which is similar in spirit to Cornwall's (1990) claim that there exists an inflationary bias in capitalism unless decentralized wage- and price-setting behaviour is coordinated by means of an incomes policy. Second, Cornwall has long proclaimed the importance of investment spending for maintaining full employment (see, for example, Cornwall, 1979), a thesis that is very much in tune with one of our main propositions regarding the importance of capital shortages in creating unemployment.

In the 1980s, unemployment received comparatively little attention in the UK and Germany. Traditionally, German politicians, frequently on the recommendation of the Bundesbank, have been mainly concerned with price stability. Also, during the Conservative government in the UK, low inflation rates became a prime economic target. In both countries, unemployment was ignored. Since the mid-1990s, however, renewed interest in unemployment has emerged. The European Commission issued a major publication in 1995 entitled *Employment in Europe*, and the *OECD Jobs Study* (1994) is another important work on this problem and a clear indication of change.

Although there are now numerous publications concerned with explanations of and solutions to the European unemployment problem, we are still a long way from a consensus. Most orthodox studies (OECD (1994), Layard, Nickell and Jackman (1991), Franz and Gordon (1993) are representative examples) suggest that the solution to the unemployment problem is to be found in the labour market. Conventional views include the ideas that real wages are too high (or, more precisely, wage costs are too high), the unemployment insurance system is too generous, workers are not sufficiently skilled to satisfy firms' needs, and insiders dictate a real wage that is above the market clearing level. As a consequence, during the past fifteen years or so, the UK has implemented policies designed to reduce labour market rigidities by, for example, reducing benefits for the unemployed and abolishing some fundamental union rights. These measures may have reduced union militancy and increased the incentive to work, but they have been utterly unsuccessful in reducing unemployment significantly and persistently.

More recently, the German government has also become very keen with the idea of dismantling the *Sozialstaat*. Sick pay has been reduced from 100 per cent to 80 per cent of wages, and proposals for work on Saturdays, and a greater facility for small firms to dismiss workers, have been introduced (*The Economist*, May 1996).

The model we suggest here does not reject the idea that there are rigidities in the labour market and that aggressive unions or high levels of unemployment benefits put upward pressure on wage demands which may cause unemployment. These ideas are incorporated in our model. However, we go one step further to suggest that supply-side factors are not the only ones that affect the level of unemployment; there is, additionally and importantly, the effect that investment has on employment. We even argue that the malfunctioning of the labour market might have been promulgated by capital shortage, in which case supply-side policies would have to be complemented by demand policies if unemployment is to be reduced. The theoretical model is discussed in the next section.

In the third section we report empirical evidence which supports the capital shortage hypothesis for Germany and the UK.[1] The data utilized are annual and most variables cover the period from 1966 until 1994. Data for Germany refer to the united Germany from 1991 onwards (unless otherwise stated), which means that some of our conclusions should be treated with caution given the break in the data for Germany.

THE THEORETICAL MODEL

Before we turn to the capital shortage hypothesis, we first present the model of wage determination in which this hypothesis is embedded, albeit in an informal manner.[2] The basic idea of the model is that conflict arises at the workplace over labour productivity and the real wage (Shapiro and Stiglitz, 1984). After firms have hired workers, they have to ensure that the work is actually done, since workers regard work as generally unpleasant and try to provide as little effort as possible. Firms, however, are interested in a high degree of work effort and a low real wage, as high work effort and low wages reduce unit labour costs and ultimately increase firms' profits. The device which firms have to discipline workers is the threat of dismissal. Whether this threat is effective depends on a number of factors. Some of the factors that affect workers' effort are the level of the real wage they receive, the economic opportunities outside the firm, customs and pay norms, the ideological climate, and their feeling of being fairly treated. Taking each of these in turn, we assume that workers' effort or labour productivity increases with the real wage that the firm offers. If opportunities outside the firm are favourable, workers are less concerned about losing their jobs if they are dismissed. Opportunities outside the firm depend upon the real wage which workers receive in alternative employment, the probability of actually getting alternative employment and, in case they remain unemployed, the level of unemployment benefits.

Workers compare their own wage with that of other groups of workers and over time, a structure of wage relativities has developed (Keynes, 1936; Hicks, 1975). Workers are concerned to preserve or to improve their position in this wage hierarchy and they resist any wage that violates their position.

The notions of receiving a fair wage for a fair day's work and the ideological climate are related to the conflict between employers and employees over income distribution (Rowthorn, 1977, 1995). Wages are negotiated in a decentralized bargaining process and, if productivity remains constant, the wage settlement provides workers with a negotiated wage share. After the claims of the government and foreign sectors are satisfied, firms receive a negotiated profit share, which is the residuum from the bargaining process. After the wage bargain, firms set prices so as to achieve their target profit share. Since wage and price setting are not centrally coordinated, there is no mechanism that ensures that the conflicting claims of the private sector are reconciled. Generally, there will be a gap between the target profit share, which is determined by firms' pricing decisions, and the negotiated profit share, which is the result of the bargaining process. If the aspiration gap is greater than zero, workers' real wage is lower than was negotiated and conflict in the labour market arises. This conflict may result in a fall in labour productivity, or, more dramatically, in industrial action. Only if the aspiration gap is zero may we derive an equilibrium unemployment rate (where the aspiration gap is a function of aggregate demand).

The behaviour of wage setters depends on demand conditions in the labour market, where a higher level of employment tends to increase the negotiated wage share. Shifts in the resulting wage curve may come about through changes in the ideological climate, real unemployment benefits, taxation, or import prices. Prices are determined by the target profit share (mark-up) and normal unit costs, where the former depends on demand conditions in the product market. Demand conditions in the product market may be proxied by capacity utilization. If economic activity is high and firms produce at 'full' capacity

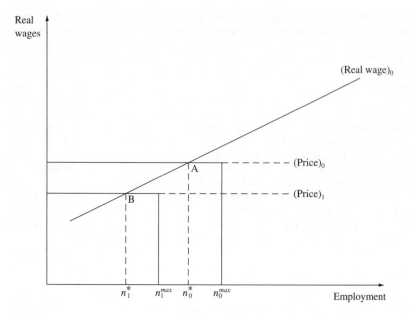

*Figure 17.1* Pricing, real wages and the determination of equilibrium employment

levels, they may raise prices without fear of losing market share, as their competitors are in a similar position. On the other hand, if firms produce below 'normal' capacity, an increase in price may be accompanied by a loss in sales and profits. It is generally accepted that prices are set by imperfectly competitive firms as a constant mark-up over normal unit labour costs. The resulting price curve is rather flat at average output levels as depicted in Figure 17.1. Capacity utilization is explained by the level of the capital stock and the level of economic activity, here proxied by the level of employment. As Figure 17.1 shows, we may have different levels of equilibrium employment which are compatible with varying capital stocks.

For a given capital stock, there is a maximum employment level $n_0^{max}$, which can only be expanded moderately in the short run due to the production technology employed.[3] The intersection of the price and wage curves represents an equilibrium situation in the sense that the aspiration gap is zero. In Figure 17.1, the 'equilibrium' employment level is $n_0^*$. Assume that the economy is shocked as during 1973/4 and 1978/9, where oil prices rose dramatically and increased firms' costs. During these episodes, firms raised prices to preserve their profit shares, shifting the price curve downwards, reducing the bargained real wage and thus increasing conflict in the labour market. In order to stop a price–wage spiral, policies that curbed demand were implemented.[4] The fall in demand reduced inflation and capacity utilization. In response, capital was scrapped to the level $n_1^{max}$ and actual equilibrium employment settled at $n_1^*$. After oil prices fell and restrictive demand policies were abandoned, employment rose, but could not, in the short run, reach previous levels because of the limit $n_1^{max}$. Only if scrapped capital had been replenished would previous levels of employment have been possible. There is thus a fundamental asymmetry in the dynamics of employment in response to severe shocks, as unemployment can develop rapidly, but may take a long time to subsequently fall. Indeed, capital-scrapping may give rise to hysteresis effects, thus severely reducing employment opportunities. This might happen if the restoration of initial conditions (in terms of demand, profitability and so on) does not entice firms to rebuild scrapped capacity, even though initial conditions would have been sufficient to entice them to retain existing capacity prior to the demand shock/capital-scrapping episode. This sort of asymmetry turns on the existence of start-up costs unique to new entrants that are not relevant in the profit calculations of incumbent firms.

Critics of the capital shortage hypothesis argue that there is nothing problematic here (Blanchard, 1988; Lindbeck, 1993). Investment responds to changes in profitability and the cost of investment, and this process can simply take a long time. Following the oil price shocks, the recovery in demand, higher-capacity utilization and the fall in oil prices should have increased profits and profit expectations and encouraged firms to expand capacity. This would not occur, however, if increases in labour demand were absorbed by wage rises. It is further argued that although capital accumulation takes time, curing problems on the supply side of the labour market (insider power, long-term unemployment and so on) will take a long time and until these problems are solved, capacity is not a constraint.

In the following section, we provide evidence that responses to capital-scrapping are not as smooth as critics of the capital-scrapping hypothesis suggest.

## PRELIMINARY EMPIRICAL RESULTS

The major question we want to address is whether or not there is any evidence that a slowdown in capital accumulation has adverse effects on employment and if so, what policy implications follow.

First, we want to see whether capital-scrapping or a slowdown in investment actually took place in Germany and the UK in response to the oil price shocks and whether, as a result, the economies became locked into smaller capital stocks, normal capacity utilization rates and high unemployment. Second, we

*Table 17.1* Unemployment, investment and capacity utilization rates in Germany and the UK, 1966–94

| Period | $u_{UK}\%$ | $\Delta k_{UK}\%^1$ | $\Phi_{UK}\%$ | $u_G\%$ | $\Delta k_G\%^2$ | $\Phi_G\%^3$ |
|--------|-----------|--------------------|---------------|---------|-----------------|--------------|
| 1966–73 | 2.1 | 3.5 | 89.0 | 1.1 | 5.1 | 97.8 |
| 1974–78 | 3.8 | −0.3 | 84.0 | 3.7 | 3.3 | 95.4 |
| 1979–81 | 6.3 | −4.8 | 81.5 | 3.9 | 3.4 | 96.8 |
| 1982–94 | 10.5 | 3.3 | 88.2 | 7.6 | 3.5 | 95.5 |
| 1966–73 | 2.1 | 3.5 | 89.0 | 1.1 | 5.1 | 97.8 |
| 1974–94 | 8.3 | 1.4 | 86.2 | 6.0 | 3.4 | 95.6 |

*Notes*:
1. Data refers to the manufacturing sector.
2. Data was only available until 1993 (NIESR).
3. Data was not available before 1970 (Sachverständigenrat, 1994/5).

want to examine whether or not the adjustment mechanism proposed by critics of the capital shortage hypothesis was thwarted by excessive wage claims. If so, then this would indicate a deficiency in the labour market that could only be remedied by supply-side policies.

We now turn to the first point. Table 17.1 illustrates the situation in the UK and Germany over the period 1966 until 1994.[5] The time periods are as follows: the pre-first oil price shock period (1966–73), the period after the first oil price shock (1974–8), the period of the second oil price shock (1979–81), and the period after the second oil price shock (1982–94).[6]

We have adopted the following notation: $u$ is the unemployment rate, $\Delta k$ is the rate of growth of the capital stock, and $\Phi$ denotes the capacity utilization rate. The subscripts *UK* and *G* stand for the United Kingdom and Germany respectively, and data from 1991 onwards refer to East and West Germany.

We discuss the UK first. After the first oil price shock, unemployment almost doubled from 2.1 per cent to 3.8 per cent, while the rate of growth of the capital stock fell from 3.5 per cent to −0.3 per cent. At the same time, capacity utilization fell by about 5 percentage points. The effects of the second oil price shock were even more dramatic, in that the unemployment rate tripled in comparison to the pre-oil price shock average, capacity utilization fell by about 8 percentage points and the rate of growth of capacity dropped to −4.8 per cent. After the second shock, the unemployment rate rose to an average of about 10 per cent, while at the same time capacity utilization and the growth of the capital stock recovered to rates somewhat less than their pre-shock levels.

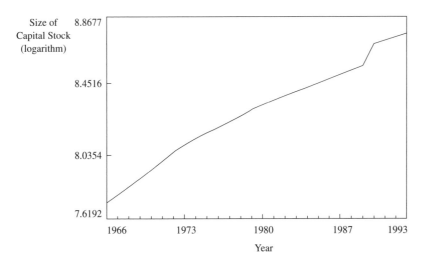

*Figure 17.2* The expansion of the German capital stock, 1966–93

A comparison between the pre- and post-shock periods summarizes and enforces the findings: in the latter periods, the unemployment rate is 4 times higher, capital growth is 2.5 times less than during the pre-shock period and capacity utilization is just below its pre-shock rate. Although the average rate of growth of capital during the last thirteen years of our sample is commensurate with the pre-shock rate, the economy would have needed a much higher growth rate in order to make up for the capital-scrapping between 1974 and 1981. It is remarkable that only after this period did the unemployment rate reach its peak.

Turning to Germany and to Figure 17.2, the picture is not very different with respect to the underlying developments during each of the periods, although the German performance is rather better than that of the UK. In contrast to the UK, the rate of growth of the capital stock suffered a major reduction immediately after the first oil price shock and never subsequently returned to its pre-shock heights. We should note, moreover, that following the inclusion of East Germany in the data after 1990, there is a significant break in the series which makes the rate of growth of the capital stock appear higher than it actually was.

The behaviour of the German unemployment rate is very similar to that of the UK, as Figure 17.3 reveals. Meanwhile, from 1966 to 1973, capacity

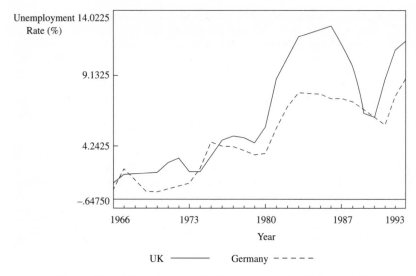

*Figure 17.3* Unemployment in Germany and the UK, 1966–93

utilization averaged about 98 per cent, similar to its rate during the last thirteen years. We may therefore conclude that in Germany as in the UK, capacity utilization returned to its previous rate, unemployment rose substantially and the rate of growth of the capital stock fell substantially in the wake of the oil shocks.

We now turn to the second question, namely, whether or not wage claims were excessive in the sense that after the oil shocks, the recovery in demand was absorbed by high wages which increased unit labour costs and prevented unemployment from falling. One way to investigate this hypothesis is to look at the development of real product wages and labour productivity. If wage growth exceeds productivity growth over time, this may indicate, *ceteris paribus*, that the income distribution favours wage-earners and that the profit rate has fallen. As investment depends on (expected) profits, the shortage in capital may be due to the malfunctioning of the labour market, assuming a 'stagnationist' investment function. The following data shed light on the change in labour's share, calculated on the basis of the real product wage. From 1970 to 1973, German labour share grew on average by 1.4 per cent, compared to an average growth rate of about 0.1 per cent between 1961 and 1969.[7] After that, it fell continuously. From 1974 until 1990, labour's share fell at an average rate of −0.5 per cent. In the UK, meanwhile, the real wage share fell at an average rate of −0.4 per cent between 1961 and 1969. This compares with an average rate of increase of 0.4 per cent between 1970 and 1973. Since 1974, the wage share in the UK has remained virtually unchanged.

On the whole, the data suggest that any gains in labour's income share were offset by subsequent losses (or else previous losses were made up for in later periods). There is no evidence that during the recovery (that is, after the fall in oil prices), higher profitability was absorbed by excessive wage costs which then increased unemployment dramatically. Instead, the evidence suggests that since the first oil shock, labour's income share has fallen continuously in Germany, while in the UK it has remained approximately constant.

In summary, both the UK and Germany seem to have been locked into the same pattern of high unemployment, low capacity growth and about normal capacity utilization over the past twenty years. Furthermore, there does not seem to be any evidence that the fall in investment is due to excessive wage claims, particularly after the oil price shock periods.

An interesting and important question that remains to be addressed is why capacity growth remained low and unemployment remained high *after* the shocks, when oil prices fell? Our hypothesis is that in response to the rise in oil prices, domestic firms increased prices so as to preserve their profit share. As a consequence, the actual real wage was lower than the bargained wage and workers resisted the resulting fall in income by demanding higher wages in order to anticipate price inflation. Governments interrupted the price–wage spiral by introducing restrictive demand policies. The hypothesis is that although these policies may have been necessary at the time, they persisted for far too long, and after oil prices fell, governments did not act to stimulate investment.

First, we look at interest rates and the budget deficit. Interest rates are costs of borrowing and affect investment directly, in that high interest rates (and low profit expectations, which are typical for a recession) deter investors. Fiscal policy is an important means of stimulating economic activity and the budget deficit is an indicator of how expansionary or contractionary fiscal policy is. Turning first to the monetary indicator, we consider real long-term interest rates on bonds (of a minimum three years' duration) for both countries, as long-term interest rates are likely to have more impact on investment decisions than short-term rates. Real interest rates in the UK were very volatile between 1966 and 1994. Between 1974 and 1981, average real interest rates were negative. However, from 1982 onwards, real interest rates rose sharply to an average of 4.9 per cent. This compares with an average rate of 2.6 per cent between 1966 and 1973. Although real long-term interest rates in Germany were not as volatile as in the UK, they also rose sharply after 1979. Between 1966 and 1973, they averaged 2.8 per cent, between 1979 and 1981 they increased by a factor of 1.8 and have remained at an average of about 4.4 per cent since 1982. In both countries, then, there was a marked rise in real interest rates after the second oil price shock and this has surely affected investment adversely.

Turning to real budget deficits as a fraction of real GDP for both countries, the picture looks similar in both cases (see Figures 17.4 and 17.5). In the early 1970s, the budget deficit increased significantly and was then consolidated from 1975 onwards. The dramatic increase in the early 1970s was due to the sudden fall in income tax revenues as a consequence of the decline in profits and rise in unemployment. Both governments reacted by reducing expenditures.

Although the list of indicators discussed here is incomplete,[8] we may nevertheless draw some cautious conclusions. The German government did not prevent the dramatic increase in real capital costs during and after the oil shock periods. This likely deterred investment. Furthermore, it consolidated its budget deficit at a time when domestic demand was depressed due to high transfers to oil-producing economies. This may have contributed to the disappointment of profit expectations and consequently reduced investment. Once a fall in the rate of growth of capacity occurs, policies that encourage investment are necessary. The history of the budget deficit does not indicate that this happened in Germany.

The real cost of capital was negative during the shock period in the UK, which might lead us to expect that investment flourished during this time. However, no such result materialized. Moreover, subsequent monetary and fiscal policies in the UK were similar to those pursued in Germany. The criticisms of German policies outlined above therefore apply equally well to those pursued in the UK.

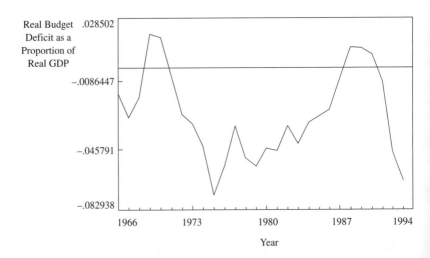

*Figure 17.4*  UK real budget deficit as a proportion of real GDP, 1966–94

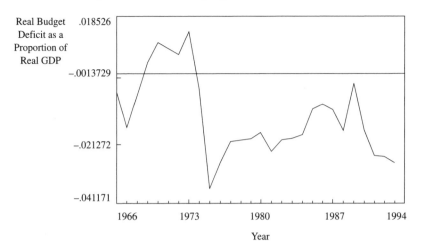

*Figure 17.5*   German real budget deficit as a proportion of real GDP, 1966–94

CONCLUSION

We have presented a model of wage and unemployment determination emphasizing the importance of capital accumulation for employment. We have shown that there is evidence to suggest that our hypothesis, that recent high unemployment rates resulted from a slowdown in the rate of capital formation, is valid for the UK and Germany. Furthermore, we have seen that unemployment in these countries is apparently not the result of excessive wage demands.

We are aware that this analysis is descriptive and that our results and conclusions should therefore be interpreted cautiously. However, we have rigourously and successfully tested our hypothesis for the UK elsewhere (Arestis and Biefang-Frisancho Mariscal, 1997). In light of this, the similarities between UK and German experience noted above provide further evidence that our hypothesis should be taken seriously.

In sum, we find that in both the UK and Germany, there exists a capital shortage that is partly responsible for the persistent high levels of unemployment in these countries. In the UK, capital-scrapping took place in both shock periods and during no subsequent period did capacity grow so as to make up for this loss. In Germany, capacity grew at a much lower rate than before the shocks. Once investment has fallen, it appears to take a long time to recover and create noticeable employment effects. The consequences include long-term unemployment, which is accompanied by a loss of skills – something that supply-side policies are addressing. Perhaps some of the problems currently accredited to the malfunctioning of the labour market could have been avoided if active demand-side policies had been implemented during and after the oil shocks. Perhaps contemporary policy-makers should take greater account of the demand side, paying particular attention to the need for a tax policy that provides incentives for investment, low real interest rates and stability of the financial system.

## Notes

1.  We have estimated and tested a wage model for the UK and we have found a significant effect of capital stock on employment (Arestis and Biefang-Frisancho Mariscal, 1997).
2.  For a more formal discussion see Arestis and Biefang-Frisancho Mariscal (1997).
3.  Output may be increased by overtime work and higher-than-normal capacity utilization. These measures are, however, costly.
4.  Bean (1989) uses the same diagram and discusses an upward shift in the wage curve.
5.  Our use of annual data is due entirely to their ease of availability.
6.  There is no exact way to distinguish between these periods and unfortunately our results are sensitive to the way the periods are defined. The last two rows in the table compare the immediate pre-shock period and the post-shock periods.
7.  The data for Germany are calculated from Franz and Gordon (1993).
8.  For example, investment is crucially dependent on profit expectations, which we have not discussed.

## References

Arestis, P. and I. Biefang-Frisancho Mariscal (1997) 'Conflict, effort and capital stock in UK wage determination', *Empirica*, 24, 179–93
Bean, C.R. (1989) 'Capital shortage and persistent unemployment', *Economic Policy*, 8, 12–53
Blanchard, O.J. (1988) 'Comment on Nickell: the supply side and macroeconomic modelling', in R.C. Bryant, D.W. Henderson, G. Holtham, P. Cooper and S. Symonsky (eds) *Empirical Macroeconomics for Interdependent Economies*, Washington, DC, Brookings Institute.
Blanchard, O.J. and L. Summers (1986) 'Hysteresis and the European unemployment problem', *NBER Macroeconomics Annual*, Cambridge, MA, MIT Press
Cornwall, J. (1979) 'Macrodynamics', in A. Eichner (ed.) *A Guide to Post-Keynesian Economics*, White Plains, NY, M.E. Sharpe

Cornwall, J. (1990) *The Theory of Economic Breakdown: An Institutional–Analytical Approach*, Oxford, Basil Blackwell

European Commission (1995) *Employment in Europe*

Franz, W. and R.J. Gordon (1993) 'German and American wage and price dynamics', *European Economic Review*, 37, 719–62

Hicks, J. (1975) *The Crisis in Keynesian Economics*, Oxford, Basil Blackwell

Keynes, J.M. (1936) *The General Theory of Employment, Interest and Money*, London, Macmillan

Layard, R., S. Nickell and R. Jackman (1991) *Unemployment*, Oxford, Oxford University Press

Lindbeck, A. (1993) *Unemployment and Macroeconomics*, Cambridge, MA, MIT Press

OECD (1994) *The OECD Jobs Study, Part 1*, Paris, OECD

Rowthorn, R.E. (1977) 'Conflict, inflation and money', *Cambridge Journal of Economics*, 1, 215–39

Rowthorn, R.E. (1995) 'Capital formation and unemployment', *Oxford Review of Economic Policy*, 11, 26–39

Shapiro, C. and J.E. Stiglitz (1984) 'Equilibrium unemployment as a worker discipline device', *American Economic Review*, 74, 433–44

*The Economist* (1996) 'Germany: is the model broken?', 4–10 May, 21–3

# 18 The Institutional Determinants of Unemployment

Wendy Cornwall[1]

## INTRODUCTION

This chapter investigates the links between unemployment rates in a group of OECD economies and their institutions, for the period 1960–89. Institutions govern behaviour, and so are among the most fundamental determinants of how, and how well, an economy functions. By governing economic behaviour, they shape economic mechanisms, and through them influence the effectiveness of economic policy, placing constraints on the policy choices available to governments. Institutions also reflect the social preferences which influence the goals that governments pursue. The focus here is on the extent to which institutional differences can explain differences in unemployment rates, both over time and among countries.

Earlier studies have concentrated on institutions of the industrial relations system; others have emphasized political institutions and policy. Here, elements of each are used in a simple optimization framework, in which observed unemployment rates are the outcome of governments' efforts to optimize their political preferences subject to the prevailing Phillips curve; both preferences and the Phillips curve depend upon institutions; political preferences also depend on power. The resulting model develops earlier ideas that have emphasized the political economy aspects of the unemployment–inflation issue (see, for example, Cornwall, 1994; Hibbs, 1987).

The approach stands in contrast to the current mainstream propensity to rely on variations of vertical Phillips curve analysis, and on microeconomic variables such as work–leisure choices to explain differences in unemployment. Studies of unemployment within this school of thought often include institutional variables to explain the position of the vertical Phillips curve and differences in unemployment among countries or over time. In this chapter institutional variables are expected to be among the determinants of both the position and the slope of the Phillips curve. The assumption is that there are trade-offs between unemployment and inflation, and the costs of low unemployment depend, at least in part, on institutional variables. While the

254

Phillips curve imposes the supply-side constraints, the existence of trade-offs reveals the Keynesian roots of this work. There is a role for aggregate demand policy, and it is to stabilize the economy at the preferred point on the Phillips curve. This is a political decision, and depends not only on the ideological preferences of governments, but also on their response to the preferences of the electorate and the power of interest groups. These in turn depend on the history, traditions and institutions of the country. The objective here is to probe beneath the details of specific labour market characteristics and particularly of specific macroeconomic policies in order to explore the more fundamental institutional basis that influences, via the choice of policies and of labour market structures, the level of unemployment.

Pooled cross-section and time-series data are used to estimate a reduced form equation derived from the political preference function and the Phillips curve. Under reasonable assumptions, these two structural equations will yield complex non-linearities in the reduced form, so that a linear approximation is estimated. The results support the hypothesis that institutions and political preferences are significant among the determinants of the unemployment rate. The next section presents the analytical framework, followed by a discussion of the model and data used for estimation. The remaining two sections provide an analysis of the regression results and the conclusion.

## THE ANALYTICAL FRAMEWORK

The model consists of a political preference function which determines the disutility of pairs of values of the unemployment and inflation rates, which is to be minimized subject to the existing Phillips curve.[2] It provides a useful starting point for this study, because the characteristics of both the government's preference function and the Phillips curve constraint are heavily influenced by prevailing institutions. However, it is clearly based on the assumption that the Phillips curve is downward-sloping, so that there are trade-offs between unemployment and inflation that governments can exploit. The reader should note that the model is used as a expository device, and overstates the precision with which governments act; multiple policy goals, lack of information and policy mistakes make such precision highly unlikely. Fortunately, all that is needed in practice is the assumption that political preferences differ enough to produce consistent differences in unemployment outcomes as governments attempt to optimize.

### The Phillips curve

Almost all economists agree that the Phillips curve is downward-sloping in the short run, but many argue that it is vertical in the long run. Essential to the vertical Phillips curve is the assumption that wage bargaining is always in real terms. Whether the resulting long-run equilibrium unemployment rate is called the *natural rate* or the *NAIRU*, its value is exogenously determined by 'supply side' variables; discretionary aggregate demand policies have no lasting effect on unemployment, only on inflation. The natural-rate hypothesis assumes that labour markets clear, so that there is no involuntary unemployment (Friedman, 1968). The secular rise in unemployment since the mid-1970s and the persistence of high rates have provided data to support the view that this increase is largely attributable to a rise in involuntary unemployment.[3] The most common response was to replace the concept of the natural rate by the NAIRU. While retaining the assumption that wage claims and settlements are always in real terms, this concept allows involuntary unemployment to exist in equilibrium, that is, at the NAIRU. This leads to an internal inconsistency in the model, since by definition the involuntarily unemployed are willing to work for a real wage equal to *or less than* the current real wage. This inconsistency is either ignored,[4] or it is alleged that involuntary unemployment is caused by the real wage being too high. But this does not solve the problem. As Keynes noted, labour bargains for money wages, and real wages are set in the product market as firms decide what is to be the mark-up over costs.[5] The theoretical difficulties are resolved if the assumption of real wage bargaining is dropped; but of course then the Phillips curve is no longer vertical.

The assumption here is that the Phillips curve is downward-sloping in the relevant range, that is, that there is a long-run trade-off between unemployment and inflation that governments can exploit. The curve may be very steep or even vertical at very low rates of unemployment, but there is evidence that it is relatively flat at high unemployment rates.[6] The Phillips curve can be written as:

$$\dot{p} = f(U; V_1)$$

where $\dot{p}$ and $U$ represent the inflation and unemployment rates, and $V_1$ is a vector of variables that influence its slope and position. These can be regarded as belonging to two classes. First, there are economic variables such as productivity growth, an import price index, and, to introduce external demand conditions, unemployment in the trading partner countries. Second, there are institutional variables. These are included to capture the effects of different and changing industrial relations systems. Other explanations of differences in the position of Phillips curves among countries have included such regulatory measures as payroll taxes and various dimensions of the welfare state, particularly the ratio of unemployment benefits to wages, with mixed results.[7] Rather than isolating individual regulations, which are relatively easily (and sometimes frequently) changed, the emphasis here is on institutions that have a broader and more persistent influence on labour market behaviour.

**The political preference function**

The political preference function measures the disutility ($M$) of pairs of unemployment and inflation rates. It is assumed to be strictly convex, ensuring that it yields strictly concave indifference curves. In addition to being a non-linear function of inflation and unemployment rates, its parameters are determined by political and institutional variables. It can be written as:

$$M = M(\dot{p}, U; V_2) \qquad M_p, M_u > 0$$

where $V_2$ is a vector of political and institutional variables. The parameters of the preference function vary with the political party in power, and it is expected that left-leaning governments will attach a relatively greater weight to unemployment than will right-of-centre governments, yielding steeper indifference curves. Put simply, the left-leaning government will accept a larger increase in inflation to achieve a given reduction in unemployment than the right-wing government. Preferences are also influenced by custom and tradition, leading to different weights, and so different slopes, even among countries with similarly left- or right-wing governments. For example, if a country has a historically strong aversion to inflation, such as Germany, this is likely to increase the relative weight attached to inflation by any government it may elect.

**Optimization**

Any observed unemployment outcome can be interpreted as the result of the government acting to optimize its preference function subject to the existing Phillips curve. The preference function measures disutility, so that the indifference curve closest to the origin is preferred. In Figure 18.1, this is shown at point A, the point of tangency between the Phillips curve (PC1) and the indifference curve (IC1). Should the Phillips curve shift to PC2, there is greater disutility at the optimum point B. The effect of alternative preference functions is shown in Figure 18.2, where the steeper indifference curve (ICL) depicts the effect of a more left-wing government than curve ICR. Given the prevailing Phillips curve, optimization occurs at point A, with lower unemployment and higher inflation than at point B, which would be the choice of a right-wing government.

Since the parameters of both preference function and Phillips curve are dependent upon institutional variables (as well as the more familiar economic variables), each observed (optimal) unemployment rate can be represented by a reduced form equation:

$$U = U(V_1, V_2)$$

where the vectors $V_1$ and $V_2$ contain the institutional and other exogenous or predetermined variables.[8] Estimation of this reduced form will provide

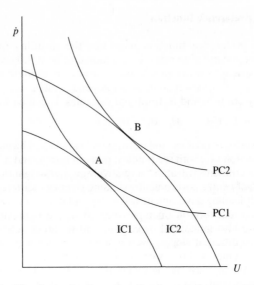

*Figure 18.1*    The determination of optimal unemployment and inflation

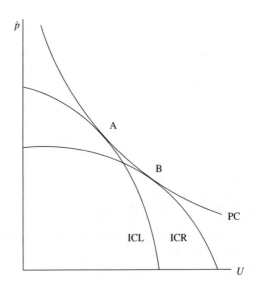

*Figure 18.2*    The effect of different preferences on optimal unemployment and inflation

information about the importance of institutional variables in explaining the differences in unemployment rates both among countries and over time.

## DATA AND MODEL ESTIMATION

Given the properties of the political preference function and the Phillips curves, and the assumption that institutional variables determine their parameters, even the simplest specifications lead to complex non-linearities in the reduced form. In addition, measures of institutional characteristics are inevitably imprecise and, in the case of indices, frequently include a significant subjective element. Given these problems, a simple specification seemed appropriate. Initial efforts to test for some simple non-linearities in the reduced form, such as interactions among the explanatory variables, did not yield useful results, and, as in similar studies, a linear approximation is adopted here. This, and some of the variables included, has the advantage of allowing closer comparison with other work.

The sample includes eighteen OECD countries, and covers four sub-periods: 1960–7, 1968–73, 1974–9 and 1980–9.[9] For the *ith* country in period *t*, the initial specification was:

$$U_{it} = a_0 + a_1 LV_{it} + a_2 CBI_{it} + a_3 EMS_{it} + a_4 STR_{it} + a_5 WU_{it} + a_6 LINF_{it}$$
$$+ a_7 IMP_{it} + a_8 PROD_{it} + \epsilon_{it}$$

where the variables are defined as follows:

| | |
|---|---|
| $U$ | average unemployment rate |
| $LV$ | proportion of left-of-centre votes |
| $CBI$ | index of central bank independence |
| $EMS$ | dummy variable for membership in the European monetary system |
| $STR$ | logarithm of the average strike volume, lagged one period |
| $WU$ | weighted average unemployment rate of the other seventeen countries in the sample scaled by the country's own exports to GDP ratio |
| $LINF$ | average inflation rate, lagged one period |
| $IMP$ | average rate of import price inflation, scaled by the imports to GDP ratio |
| $PROD$ | average productivity growth rate |

As suggested above, the left-of-centre votes variable is a measure of political preferences for inflation and unemployment. Party control theory of government economic policy argues that preferences are ideologically based, and uses such variables as the distribution of cabinet posts and parliamentary seats among political parties to explain policy choices in terms of the relative power of political movements (see, for example, Cameron, 1984; Tufte, 1978; Hibbs, 1977, 1987). It also emphasizes the role of organized interest groups in determining this relative power. Countries with strong centralized labour movements are therefore more likely to elect leftist governments, which have a strong preference for low unemployment.[10] However, in democratic systems governments have to get elected and reelected, so that the assumption here is that their *effective* political preferences reflect the general political coloration of the electorate. The proportion of left-of-centre votes can be interpreted as a measure of the extent to which any government must modify its ideological preferences. Whether 'delivered' by a well-organized labour movement or simply representative of broad-based public preferences, a high proportion of left-of-centre votes will force right-wing governments to move towards the centre, and will provide leftist governments with the power base to resist the claims of organized business and financial interests. The use of left votes may circumvent some of the problems with multi-party states which often have coalition governments. It also helps to differentiate Japan and Switzerland, which have low unemployment, from high unemployment countries like the USA and Canada; while they all consistently elect right-wing governments, the percentage of left votes, averaged over the period, is 38 per cent for Japan and 26 per cent for Switzerland, compared to zero for the USA and around 15 per cent for Canada.[11]

Political preferences also depend on institutional and historical factors that temper the effect of voting patterns, leading to differences over time, and especially among countries. One example is the level of aversion to inflation, which is proxied here by an index of central bank independence.[12] Of the several indices available, the Cukierman, Webb and Neyapti (1992) aggregate legal central bank independence index was chosen, in part because of its coverage of all the countries included in this study. It also covers the entire period used here, and allows for variation over the period. Moreover, it examines more of the statutory dimensions of independence than other indices. Interpreted as an indicator of social preferences, it may partially explain, for example, why two equally 'left-wing' countries experience different unemployment outcomes. The country with the more independent central bank is expected to have flatter indifference curves, showing its relatively greater willingness to accept higher unemployment to keep inflation low.

Since membership in the European Monetary System is voluntary, it too reflects political preferences; a dummy variable is included to capture its effects. It has been shown that the monetary policy of EMS members is affected by the coordination of their exchange rate policies, and that inflation rates are lowered (Cukierman, 1992; Jenkins, 1996). In the model used here, this preference for low inflation would reduce the slope of the indifference curves.

As a measure of conflict in industrial relations, the strike volume is among the determinants of the position of the Phillips curve. It is the number of man-days lost per thousand workers, and is lagged one period, primarily to allow time for any changes in industrial relations to become sufficiently established to demonstrate their longer-term effects.[13] Cooperation and trust between labour and management at the firm level reduces conflict in general, but most relevant here, in wage negotiations. For example, in these negotiations it is management that provides information regarding the financial condition of the firm and its productivity performance. Low productivity growth or a weak financial position will persuade labour to moderate its wage demands, provided that it has confidence in the assessment. Then, conflict is reduced, and strikes are less likely.[14] Higher levels of strike activity are expected to act via wage bargaining to worsen the inflation–unemployment trade-off.

Given the wide differences in openness among the economies in the sample, as well as the rapid expansion of trade in the earlier years covered, there is considerable variability in exposure to the international economic environment. Since the bulk of their trade is within the OECD, the average unemployment rate for the other economies in the sample is included for each as an indicator of the external demand conditions it faces; scaling it by the export to GDP ratio allows for different levels of openness, both among countries and over time. Clearly, this 'world unemployment' variable is centred upon trade, and does not explicitly consider other dimensions of globalization, such as increased capital mobility. However, the effect on unemployment of all aspects of increasing globalization is included in the rates used to compute the variable.

Lagged inflation is also among the frequently used determinants of the position of the Phillips curve, but here it is the average rate for the previous sub-period so that it requires careful interpretation. Because of the relatively long time lag, it cannot be regarded as a simple inflationary expectations variable. It is a measure of the cumulative effects of past inflation on the position of the Phillips curve, an influence attributable to behavioural and institutional changes in the postwar era. Important among these changes was the increasing power of labour. Labour's pursuit of 'fair wages' led employers to accept the protection of real and relative wages as a legitimate objective of wage settlements.[15] Past inflation also affects the Phillips curve via the restrictive policies it elicits, generating hysteretic effects.[16] Moreover, its role extends beyond the Phillips curve, since a country's historical inflation experience is likely to influence political preferences. In this context, while it is possible that a country might become increasingly tolerant of inflation, the widespread use of restrictive policies over the past two decades suggests that the reverse is true, and that lagged inflation is positively related to unemployment.

Both import price inflation and the productivity growth rate influence the position of Phillips curves by affecting production costs. The import price variable was weighted by the share of imports to GDP to capture changing vulnerability to movements in international commodity prices over a period of rapidly increasing international interdependence. The productivity growth rate is customarily used as a determinant of the position of Phillips curves derived from a wage inflation equation in a system with mark-up pricing.

In addition to the variables listed above, a measure of corporatism was also tested. Corporatism indices quantify some of the key features of industrial relations systems, in order to focus more directly on the institutions that govern wage setting and influence the inflation cost of low unemployment.[17] Although the aim here is to investigate the underlying institutions, rather than specific labour market structures, the inclusion of a corporatism index provides a simple test of the power of the other institutional variables to capture these labour market characteristics. If they are adequate to the task, the coefficient of the corporatism index would not be significantly different from zero. The widely used Crouch index includes the broadest group of countries,[18] which it ranks according to the degree of social consensus; there is one value for each country, so that it does not record any changes which may have occurred over the period. In addition, its construction gives heavy weight to the centralization of unions and of collective bargaining itself. This leads to understatement of the degree of consensus for some economies, particularly for Switzerland and Japan.[19] Lastly, the index alone cannot adequately differentiate among those countries with low consensus. However, in spite of these shortcomings, it appears to be useful when used in conjunction with a strike volume variable (see, for example, McCallum, 1986).

The results of the estimation are to be found in Table 18.1, and are discussed in the next section. In interpreting the roles of the institutional variables used for the estimation, it must be noted that some of them are likely to have overlapping effects, at least for some countries. For example the strike variable captures the level of industrial 'harmony', which is quite often achieved by removing contentious matters to the political arena; the left votes variable is intended to capture the general preferences of governments toward the competing claims of capital and labour. Since left-wing governments, well-developed welfare systems and social consensus are often found together, for some countries we could expect a strong negative correlation between the strikes and the proportion of left votes. However the simple correlation for the entire sample ($-0.19$) is not significant at the 5 per cent level.

ESTIMATION RESULTS

In Table 18.1, equation (1) reports the results for the initial specification. The estimated coefficients of the import price inflation variable, the productivity growth rate and the corporatism index are not significantly different from zero at any acceptable level of significance. For the remaining variables, the

*Table 18.1* Regression results for the reduced form unemployment equation

| | Equation (1) | Equation (2) | Equation (3) | Equation (4) | Equation (5) |
|---|---|---|---|---|---|
| Left-of-centre votes | −4.034 (2.83) | −4.050 (2.89) | −4.877 (4.20) | −4.535 (3.77) | − |
| Central bank independence | 3.403 (2.74) | 3.438 (2.87) | 3.036 (2.64) | 2.810 (2.45) | 4.949 (4.35) |
| Membership in the EMS | 2.926 (4.16) | 2.967 (4.53) | 3.016 (4.60) | 3.149 (4.87) | 2.754 (4.01) |
| Strikes | 0.946 (6.47) | 0.936 (6.79) | 1.005 (8.05) | 1.001 (8.17) | 0.966 (6.66) |
| 'World' unemployment | 1.034 (3.76) | 1.015 (4.21) | 0.944 (4.04) | 0.794 (3.27) | 1.218 (5.01) |
| Lagged inflation | 0.186 (3.10) | 0.187 (3.27) | 0.195 (3.43) | −0.037 (0.28) | 0.155 (2.62) |
| Import price inflation | −0.023 (0.21) | − | − | − | − |
| Productivity growth rate | −0.012 (0.12) | − | − | − | − |
| 1974–89 dummy $x$ lagged inflation | − | − | − | 0.198 (1.88) | − |
| Crouch index of corporatism | −0.161 (1.13) | −0.163 (1.17) | − | − | −0.366 (2.88) |
| Constant | 3.911 (4.00) | 3.828 (4.72) | 4.210 (5.65) | 4.851 (6.01) | 2.109 (3.61) |
| Adjusted $R^2$ | 0.8177 | 0.8232 | 0.8222 | 0.8289 | 0.8031 |
| Hocking test critical value | − | 2.0492 | 2.0656 | − | 2.0656 |
| Hocking Sp | − | 0.0273 | 0.4625 | − | 2.7239 |

*Notes*:
The figures in parenthesis are the absolute values of the *t*-statistics. The eighteen countries included are: United States, Japan, Germany, France, Italy, United Kingdom, Canada, Australia, Austria, Belgium, Denmark, Finland, Ireland, The Netherlands, New Zealand, Norway, Sweden and Switzerland. There were four observations for each, for the years 1960–7, 1968–73, 1974–9, 1980–9.
*Sources*: Voting data, Mackie and Rose (1991); central bank index, Cukierman *et al.* (1992); strike data, *ILO Yearbook of Labour Statistics*, various issues; corporatism index, McCallum (1986). OECD data are used for the remaining variables. Further details will be provided on request.

coefficients have the expected signs, and all are significantly different from zero at the 5 per cent level. Following Hendry's specification method, import price inflation and productivity growth were dropped from the equation. The Crouch corporatism index was retained at this stage; estimation of equation (2) confirmed its lack of explanatory power in the presence of the remaining variables. It was therefore dropped to yield equation (3), a procedure verified by Hocking's test statistic for model selection (Sp).[20]

Equation (3) was tested for structural change, using dummy variables for both intercept and slopes. Equation (4) reports the sole example for which the hypothesis of no structural change could be rejected on the basis of a one-tailed test at the 5 per cent level of significance. This implies that there was a shift in the coefficient of lagged inflation between 1973 and 1974, and is consistent with a change in attitude towards less tolerance of inflation. However, in the sample lagged inflation before 1974 shows relatively little variability so that it cannot explain much for the 1960–73 period. Consequently, this finding may be the result of the sample used for the estimation, rather than evidence of a true parametric shift.

The negative coefficient of the left-of-centre votes variable confirms earlier results, as does the positive coefficient of the strike variable (see, for example, Cornwall, 1994, p. 140). Neither is sensitive to changes in the specification, and both are always significantly different from zero.

In all of the specifications tested, the central bank independence index demonstrates a strong partial correlation with higher unemployment. Although studies of central bank independence have concentrated almost exclusively on its relation to inflation, Alesina and Summers (1993) claim that independence of the central bank is a 'free lunch' since it is uncorrelated with real variables, including unemployment. These claims are based on simple correlations alone, and in spite of their wide acceptance have met with serious criticism.[21] The results reported here strongly suggest that when the effects of other relevant variables are accounted for, there is no free lunch. However, interpretation of the index must be undertaken with caution. As stated above, it is used here as an indicator of social preferences, in particular as a measure of aversion to inflation, which is expected to show itself as a greater willingness to accept higher unemployment to achieve inflation targets. This view implies that it is the aversion to inflation (however quantified) that is correlated with unemployment and also with the level of independence of the central bank.[22]

The positive coefficient for the European Monetary System dummy variable indicates a high unemployment cost associated with membership, *ceteris paribus*. The cost is attributable to the required coordination of monetary policy to maintain the exchange rate target.[23]

In all of the equations, the coefficient of the 'world unemployment' variable is significant, with a value of about one. This is as expected, given the extent of trade among them, and sufficient time within each period covered to allow the transmission of changes to occur. An example serves to clarify interpretation of this variable: for an economy with an export to GDP ratio of 0.4, if unemployment in the other countries rises by an average of one percentage point, its own unemployment rate will rise by about 0.4 percentage points.

Further investigation of the Crouch corporatism index showed that its coefficient was never significantly different from zero, as long as the left votes variable was included. When left votes are omitted, as in equation (5), the equation is misspecified according to the Hocking test.[24] These results suggest that the left votes variable is picking up preferences that in some countries have led to the establishment of corporatism in various forms. This may be because it captures concern with unemployment on a more fundamental level than the corporatism index, by representing a political constituency whether or not it has the formal voice provided by institutions of corporatism. Unlike the Crouch index, it allows for change over time so that it can reflect changes in support for low unemployment.

These results support the contention that unemployment outcomes can be linked to some of the fundamental institutional characteristics of countries. While the usual caveats obtain regarding the values of the coefficients, their signs are as expected and the *t*-statistics and adjusted *R*-squares are highly significant. Experiments using the corporatism variable also suggest that these underlying institutional characteristics have explanatory power comparable to the more commonly used measures of labour market structure.

## CONCLUSION

The aim of this chapter has been to provide information about some of the fundamental determinants of unemployment outcomes in advanced industrial economies. Some institutional structures foster cooperation between labour and employers, allowing wages to be determined without compromising inflation or balance of payments targets. When cooperation is absent, restrictive policies and high unemployment are needed to meet these targets. What has been attempted in this chapter is to shed light on the basic institutions and preferences that result in some countries developing a cooperative wage-setting system of whatever type, while others do not. The type of industrial relations system will affect the policy options open to government, but as long as the Phillips curve is downward-sloping, there is still a choice to be made. These same fundamental institutions and preferences influence this choice.

To provide a context for this work, consider two other studies of unemployment in the OECD: one stresses labour market characteristics, the other includes both labour market and policy variables. In the context of a long-run vertical Phillips curve model, Layard *et al.* (1991, pp. 433–4) use measures of coordination in wage setting, benefits to the unemployed and several dimensions of labour contract rigidity to explain unemployment. Changes in the rate of growth of the M1 money stock enter interactively with the contract rigidity variables. There is no explicit measure of fiscal policy. Thus labour supply plays the dominant role in explaining unemployment. In contrast, McCallum (1986) uses measures of the strength of both fiscal and monetary policies, as well as the Crouch corporatism index and a strike variable, and concludes that aggregate demand policies explain a large part of unemployment differences among the OECD economies.

The conclusion that aggregate demand policies are important is entirely in keeping with the Keynesian basis of this chapter. But here the search for deeper causes goes beyond both particular characteristics of the labour market and particular policies. The key question is *why* certain aggregate demand policies are chosen, and the answer depends upon the same underlying institutions and preferences that determine the structure of wage bargaining and the labour market, as well as upon the distribution of power. It is these that are linked to unemployment outcomes in this study.

These fundamental institutions determine labour market behaviour and whether or not it is harmonious, what type of wage determination will arise, and what configuration of rules and regulations will govern treatment of the unemployed. They also determine the constraints on what aggregate demand policies can be used, and how well these policies work to stabilize the economy – for example, social bargains to solve inflation and payments problems permit lower unemployment. The claim here is that acting through these channels, institutions are among the more important determinants of unemployment rates.

### Notes

1.  I wish to thank the Mount Saint Vincent University Research and Development Fund for the financial support provided for this work.
2.  This model was originally used by Lipsey (1965) and later by Trevithick (1976) to provide a definition of full employment that is consistent with other objectives of economic policy. It is implicit in partisan control theory (see, for example, Hibbs, 1987).
3.  The characteristics of the unemployed and of unemployment are documented in Clark and Summers (1979), Main (1981) and Hasan and de Brouker (1982). The continuation of restrictive policies in the intervening years ensures that these characteristics still persist. For Canada, see Fortin (1996), who attributes the greater bulk of unemployment in Canada to restrictive policy.
4.  Some recent empirical work clearly demonstrates the arbitrariness of main-stream unemployment theory. Estimates of the equilibrium unemployment rate are defined as the 'average rate of unemployment around which the economy

fluctuates' (Mankiw, 1994, p. 118 and Fig. 5.1) or by fitting a trend to actual unemployment rates (*Unemployment: Choices for Europe*, Centre for Economic Policy Research, London, 1995, ch. 3).

5. Dow (1990) provides a thorough discussion of the wage rigidity argument. For a more detailed analysis of the theoretical weakness of these views, see Cornwall and Cornwall (1997).

6. McCallum (1986) provides empirical support for such a non-linear Phillips curve, and discusses other similar findings. More recently, Fortin (1996) provides similar evidence for Canada.

7. The variables are used to measure real wage rigidities, which are then used to explain unemployment (see, for example, Layard *et al.*, 1991). However, others claim that labour market rigidities fail to explain differences in unemployment (McCallum, 1986; Freeman, 1995).

8. Similarly, there is a reduced form equation for inflation, $\dot{p} = P(V_1, V_2)$. It should also be noted that the vectors $V_1$ and $V_2$ may have some elements in common.

9. The data for the more recent period, in addition to being preliminary, does not cover a complete business cycle; it is further complicated by the unification of Germany.

10. A useful discussion of party control theory is found in Cornwall (1994, ch. 4).

11. An intriguing question is whether the apparent shift to the right over the past fifteen years or so represents a change in preferences, such as greater concern with deficits, debt and inflation, or whether this phenomenon is explained by changing constraints (such as globalization). The variables described in this section, while not chosen to answer this question, nevertheless yield estimates that suggest that both preferences and constraints have changed, and that these changes explain changes in unemployment outcomes.

12. Debelle and Fischer (1994) show that countries with a greater aversion to inflation will tend to have more independent central banks. Posen (1995) attributes central bank independence to the level of effective opposition to inflation by financial interest groups. He shows an index of this opposition to be strongly correlated directly with the degree of central bank independence and negatively correlated with inflation.

13. Since strike activity is likely to depend partially on contemporaneous unemployment rates, this may reduce a possible simultaneity problem.

14. McCallum (1983) and Paldam (1980) provide further discussion of these points. For example, McCallum cites Hicks's argument that with social consensus management is accorded greater credibility by labour, and strikes are avoided (p. 785).

15. Perry (1975) uses lagged inflation as a measure of this legitimacy; Hicks (1974) also emphasized the role of fairness in wage determination.

16. See, for example, Blanchard and Summers (1987).

17. Hall (1994) stresses the coordination of wage bargaining and central bank independence as joint determinants of lower inflation without high unemployment costs.

18. Developed but not published by Crouch, the index is used by McCallum (1986), where it appears in Table 4.

19. For a discussion of different models of consensus, see Cornwall (1994, ch. 5) and Soskice (1990).

20.   Unlike other specification test statistics, this one assumes the regressors to be stochastic.
21.   Similar claims have been made for a number of indices. Jenkins (1996) tests several, including the Cukierman *et al.* index used here. He, as well as Cargill (1995), provides convincing evidence that these claims are vastly overstated.
22.   See note 11. The clear inference here is that in these economies central bank independence *per se* has little or no effect on either unemployment or inflation. This is consistent with the Cukierman *et al.* (1992) results for less developed countries.
23.   While the cost of joining the EMS or a similar exchange rate agreement would be relatively small for countries whose existing exchange rate policies required only minor adjustment, the unemployment cost of strict adherence to exchange rate targets appears to be substantial. Nevertheless, for individual member countries it may be that the costs of not joining would be even higher, if failing to join caused loss of export markets. This is a clear possibility for smaller economies that rely heavily on trade with Germany.
24.   Because of the apparent misspecification, interpretation of equation (5) is risky. However, when compared to the other equations, the increased coefficient of the central bank independence index is consistent with the view that such independence carries high unemployment costs for countries without institutions of corporatism.

## References

Alesina, A. and L. Summers (1993) 'Central bank independence and macroeconomic performance: some comparative evidence', *Journal of Money, Credit and Banking*, 25, 151–62

Blanchard, O. and L. Summers (1987) 'Hysteresis in unemployment', *European Economic Review*, 31, 288–95

Cameron, D. (1984) 'Social democracy, corporatism, labor quiescence, and the representation of economic interest in advanced capitalist society', in J. Goldthorpe (ed.) *Order and Conflict in Contemporary Capitalism*, New York, Oxford University Press

Cargill, T.F. (1995) 'The statistical association between central bank independence and inflation', *Banca Nazionale del Lavoro Quarterly Review*, 48, 159–72

Centre for Economic Policy Research (1995) *Unemployment: Choices for Europe*, London, CEPR

Clark, K. and L. Summers (1979) 'Labour market dynamics and unemployment: a reconsideration', *Brookings Papers on Economic Activity*, 1, 423–31

Cornwall, J. (1994) *Economic Breakdown and Recovery: Theory and Policy*, Armonk, NY, M.E. Sharpe

Cornwall, J. and W. Cornwall (1997) 'The unemployment problem and the legacy of Keynes', *Journal of Post Keynesian Economics*, 19, 525–42

Cukierman, A. (1992) *Central Bank Strategy, Credibility, and Independence: Theory and Evidence*, Cambridge, MA, MIT Press

Cukierman, A., S.B. Webb and B. Neyapti (1992) 'Measuring the independence of central banks and its effect on policy outcomes', *World Bank Economic Review*, 6, 353–98

Debelle, G. and S. Fischer (1994) 'How independent should a central bank be?', in *Goals, Guidelines, and Constraints Facing Monetary Policymakers*, Federal Reserve Bank of Boston Conference Series No. 38

Dow, J.C.R. (1990) 'How can real wages ever get excessive?', National Institute of Economic and Social Research, Discussion Paper No. 196

Fortin, P. (1996) 'The great Canadian slump', *Canadian Journal of Economics*, 29, 761–87

Freeman, R. (1995) 'The limits of wage flexibility to curing unemployment', *Oxford Review of Economic Policy*, 11, 63–72

Friedman, M. (1968) 'The role of monetary policy', *American Economic Review*, 58, 1–17

Hall, P. (1994) 'Central bank independence and coordinated wage bargaining: their interaction in Germany and Europe', *German Politics and Society*, 31, 1–23

Hasan, H. and P. de Brouker (1982) 'Duration and concentration of unemployment', *Canadian Journal of Economics*, 15, 735–56

Hibbs, D. (1977) 'Political parties and macroeconomic policy', *American Political Science Review*, 71, 1467–87

Hibbs, D. (1987) *The Political Economy of Industrial Democracies*, Cambridge, MA, Harvard University Press

Hicks, J. (1974) *The Crisis in Keynesian Economics*, New York, Basic Books

Jenkins, M. (1996) 'Central bank independence and inflation performance: panacea or placebo?', *Banca Nazionale del Lavoro Quarterly Review*, 49, 241–70

Layard, R., S. Nickell and R. Jackman (1991) *Unemployment: Macroeconomic Performance and the Labour Market*, Oxford, Oxford University Press

Lipsey, R.G. (1965) 'Structural and demand deficient unemployment reconsidered', in A.M. Ross (ed.) *Employment Policy and the Labor Market*, Berkeley, University of California Press

McCallum, J. (1983) 'Inflation and social consensus in the seventies', *Economic Journal*, 93, 784–805

McCallum, J. (1986) 'Unemployment in OECD countries in the 1980s', *Economic Journal*, 96, 942–60

Mackie, T. and R. Rose (1991) *The International Almanac of Electoral History*, London, Macmillan

Main, B. (1981) 'The length of employment and unemployment in Great Britain', *Scottish Journal of Political Economy*, 28, 146–64

Mankiw, G. (1994) *Macroeconomics*, 2nd edn, New York, Worth

Paldam, M. (1980) 'Industrial conflict and the Phillips curve: an international perspective', Memo 80-4/5, Institute of Economics, Aarhus University

Perry, G. (1975) 'Determinants of wage inflation around the world', *Brookings Papers on Economic Activity*, 2, 403–47

Posen, A.S. (1995) 'Declarations are not enough: financial sector sources of central bank independence', in B. Bernanke and J. Rotemberg (eds) *NBER Macroeconomics Annual 1995*, Cambridge, MA, MIT Press

Soskice, D. (1990) 'Wage determination: the changing role of institutions in advanced industrialized countries', *Oxford Review of Economic Policy*, 6, 36–61

Trevithick, J.A. (1976) 'Inflation, the natural unemployment rate and the theory of economic policy', *Scottish Journal of Political Economy*, 23, 37–53

Tufte, E. (1978) *Political Control of the Economy*, Princeton, NJ, Princeton University Press

# Works by John Cornwall

## Books

*Growth and Stability in a Mature Economy*, London, Martin Robertson, and New York, John Wiley & Sons, 1972

*Modern Capitalism: Its Growth and Transformation*, London, Martin Robertson, 1977, and New York, St Martin's Press, 1978

*The Conditions for Economic Recovery: A Post-Keynesian Analysis*, London, Martin Robertson, and White Plains, NY, M.E. Sharpe, 1983; Etaslibri, Milano, 1985

(With Wendy Maclean) *Economic Recovery for Canada: A Policy Framework*, Toronto, Lorimer, 1984

*The Theory of Economic Breakdown: An Institutional–Analytical Approach*, Oxford, Basil Blackwell, 1990

*Economic Breakdown and Recovery: Theory and Policy*, Armonk, NY, M.E. Sharpe, 1994

## Edited volumes

*After Stagflation: Alternatives to Economic Decline*, Oxford, Basil Blackwell, and Armonk, NY, M.E. Sharpe, 1984; and Etaslibri, Milano, 1985

*The Capitalist Economies: Prospects for the 1990s*, Aldershot, Edward Elgar, 1991

## Articles and chapters in books

'Economic implications of the Klein–Goldberger model', *Review of Economics and Statistics*, 41 (May 1959) 154–61

(With W.H. Locke Anderson) 'Problems of growth policy', *Review of Economics and Statistics*, 43 (May 1961) 163–74

'The lagging United States growth rate: discussion', *American Economic Review*, 52 (May 1962) 87–93

'Three paths to full employment growth', *Quarterly Journal of Economics*, 77 (February 1963) 1–25

'The structure of fiscal models', *Quarterly Journal of Economics*, 79 (November 1965) 608–22

'Postwar growth in Western Europe: a re-evaluation', *Review of Economics and Statistics*, 50 (August 1968) 361–8

'The role of demand and investment in long term growth', *Quarterly Journal of Economics*, 84 (February 1970) 48–69

'Some comments on the role of demand and investment in long term growth: a reply', *Quarterly Journal of Economics*, 85 (May 1971) 344–8

'The "ceiling" and the "Domar effect" as stabilizers', *Kyklos*, 27 (1974) 99–123

'A reformation of Thalberg's non-linear theory of the cycle', *Swedish Journal of Economics*, 77 (1975) 179–92

272 *Works by John Cornwall*

'Diffusion, convergence and Kaldor's laws', *Economic Journal*, 86 (June 1976) 307–14. Reprinted in J.E. King (ed.) *Economic Growth in Theory and Practice: A Kaldorian Perspective*, Aldershot, Edward Elgar, 1994

'The relevance of dual models for analyzing developed capitalist economies', *Kyklos*, 30 (1977) 51–73

'A Post-Keynesian view of macrodynamics', *Challenge*, 21 (May/June 1978) 11–17. Reprinted in A. Eichner (ed.) *A Guide to Post-Keynesian Economics*, White Plains, NY, M.E. Sharpe, 1979

'Towards full employment and price stability: a review article', *Kyklos*, 31 (1978) 662–78

'Economic growth: two paradigms', *Journal of Post Keynesian Economics*, 1 (Spring 1979) 69–90

'Modern capitalism and the trend towards de-industrialization', *Journal of Economic Issues*, 14 (June 1980) 275–89

'Unemployment and inflation: institutionalist and structuralist views: a review article', *Journal of Economic Issues*, 15 (March 1981) 113–27

'Do we need separate theories of unemployment and inflation?', *Canadian Public Policy*, 7 (April 1981) 165–78

'Some implications of an inflationary bias', in J. Cornwall (ed.) *After Stagflation*, 1984

'Inflation and modern capitalism', in R. Parboni (ed.) *L'Europa Nela Crisi Economica Mondiale*, Milano, Franco Angeli, 1984

(With Wendy Maclean) 'In place of fear', *Policy Options* (January/February 1984) 47–52. Reprinted in E. Kierans (ed.) *More Jobs, Better Security*, Halifax, Institute for Public Policy, 1987 (with Wendy Cornwall)

'The causes of unemployment', in *The Unemployment Problem: Policy Options and Implications*, Ottawa, The Conference Board, 1986

'Economic recovery: the relevance of Keynes' (in German), *Wirtschaft und Gesellschaft*, 12 (1986) 309–21

(With Wendy Cornwall) 'The political economy of stagnation', *Journal of Economic Issues*, 21 (June 1987) 785–93

'Structural change and economic breakdown', *Économie Appliquée*, 40 (1987) 655–80

'Inflation as a cause of economic stagnation: a dual model', in J.A. Kregel (ed.) *Inflation and Income Distribution in Capitalist Crisis: Essays in Memory of Sidney Weintraub*, London, Macmillan, 1988

'The welfare state in a programme of economic recovery', in P. Davidson and J.A. Kregel (eds) *Macroeconomic Problems and Policies of Income Distribution*, London, Edward Elgar, 1989

'Markets are not enough' (in Chinese), in D. Ziji (ed.) *Macroeconomic Control and Macroeconomic Policy in China*, Proceedings of the Xiamen International Conference on Macro Control and Macro Policy, Xiamen, China, 1989

'Prospects for unemployment in the 1990s with hysteresis', in J. Cornwall (ed.) *The Capitalist Economies*, 1991

(With Wendy Cornwall) 'Export-led growth: a new interpretation', in W. Milberg (ed.) *The Megacorp and Macrodynamics: Essays in Memory of Alfred Eichner*, Armonk, NY, M.E. Sharpe, 1992

'Stabilization of mature economies: what did we learn from the collapse of the 1930s?', in K. Villupillai (ed.) *Nonlinearities, Disequilibria and Simulation: Quantitative Methods in the Social Sciences*, London, Macmillan, 1992

'Economic malfunction and the role of the state', in A.P. Thirlwall (ed.) *Keynes and the State*, London, Macmillan, 1993

'Full employment in the 1990s', *Challenge*, 36 (November/December 1993) 4–11

(With Wendy Cornwall) 'Structural change and productivity in the OECD', in P. Davidson and J.A. Kregel (eds) *Employment, Growth and Finance: Economic Reality and Economic Growth*, Aldershot, Edward Elgar, 1994

(With Wendy Cornwall) 'Growth theory and economic structure', *Economica*, 61 (May 1994) 237–51

'Notes on the trade cycle and social philosophy in a Post-Keynesian world', in G.C. Harcourt and P.A. Riach (eds) *A 'Second Edition' of The General Theory*, Volume 1, London, Routledge, 1997

(With Wendy Cornwall) 'A Keynesian framework for studying institutional change and evolutionary processes', in S. Pressman (ed.) *Interactions in Political Economy: Malvern After Ten Years*, London, Routledge, 1996

(With Wendy Cornwall) 'Two views of macroeconomic malfunction: the "Great Inflation" and its aftermath', in P. Arestis and M. Sawyer (eds) *Employment, Economic Growth and the Tyranny of the Market*, Aldershot, Edward Elgar, 1996

(With Wendy Cornwall) 'Unemployment prospects of modern capitalism', in P. Arestis and M. Sawyer (eds) *Economic Theory and Economic Policy*, London, Routledge, 1996

(With Wendy Cornwall) 'The unemployment problem and the legacy of Keynes', *Journal of Post Keynesian Economics*, 19 (Summer 1997) 525–42

(With Wendy Cornwall) 'Unemployment costs of inflation targeting', in P. Arestis and M. Sawyer (eds) *The Political Economy of Central Banking*, Aldershot, Edward Elgar, 1998

## Entries in reference volumes

'Economic growth', *Encyclopaedia Britannica*, 1973 (revised 1991)

'Capitalism', *Encyclopedia of Economics*, New York, McGraw-Hill, 1981 (revised 1992)

'Industrialization and de-industrialization' and 'Economic growth', *The Social Science Encyclopedia*, London, Routledge & Kegan Paul, 1984

'Long cycles', 'Inflation and growth', 'Stagflation' and 'Total factor productivity', *The New Palgrave: A Dictionary of Economics*, London, Macmillan, 1987

'Stagflation', *The New Palgrave Dictionary of Money and Finance*, London, Macmillan, 1991

'John Cornwall', in P. Arestis and M. Sawyer (eds) *A Biographical Dictionary of Dissenting Economists*, Aldershot, Edward Elgar, 1992

'What remains of Keynes?', in T. Cate *et al.* (eds) *The Encyclopedia of Keynesian Economics*, Aldershot, Edward Elgar, 1997

## Forthcoming

(With Wendy Cornwall) *Modelling Capitalist Development*, Cambridge, Cambridge University Press

'An alternative view of the slump', in V. Chick (ed.) *Keynes and the Post Keynesians*, London, Macmillan

'John Cornwall', in P. Arestis and M. Sawyer (eds) *A Biographical Dictionary of Dissenting Economists, Revised Edition*, Aldershot, Edward Elgar
(With Mark Setterfield) *Modern Capitalism: from the Golden Age to the Age of Decline*, Aldershot, Edward Elgar

# Index